THE
LORDSHIP
OF ENGLAND

THE LORDSHIP OF ENGLAND

Royal Wardships
and Marriages in
English Society and Politics

1217 – 1327

SCOTT L. WAUGH

PRINCETON UNIVERSITY PRESS
PRINCETON, NEW JERSEY

Library of Congress Cataloging-in-Publication Data

Waugh, Scott L., 1948-
The lordship of England : royal wardships and marriages in English society
and politics, 1217-1327 / Scott L. Waugh.
p. cm. Bibliography: p. Includes index.
ISBN 0-691-05509-2 (alk. paper)
1. Great Britain—Politics and government—1154-1399.
2. Monarchy—Great Britain—History. 3. Feudalism—England.
4. Guardian and ward—Great Britain. 5. Marriage—Great Britain.
6. England—Social life and customs—Medieval period, 1066-1485.
I. Title.   DA225.W38 1988   942.03′4—dc19   88-1134   CIP

CONTENTS

v

TABLES

FIGURES

PREFACE

The origins of this book lie in two sources, one general, the other more specific. My interest in the feudal nature of royal power was initially fired, when I was an undergraduate, by J.E.A. Jolliffe's assertion (in his *Constitutional History*, p. 173) that "history cannot afford to ignore the habit of thought bred in the private life of the honours, and, far more than the tenets of schoolmen, with which it often conflicts, it is the governing thought behind political action." I do not know what history can or cannot do, but the statement offered interesting advice for historians. The phrase resonated in my mind long after I read it until the work of Professor S.F.C. Milsom, especially as reinterpreted by Professor Eleanor Searle, offered an approach to testing Jolliffe's assertion. This book, then, is an analysis of how the habits of action and thought of the honorial courts, as reconstructed by Milsom and Searle, survived into the thirteenth century at the level of relations between the Crown and its chief tenants.

My intellectual debts begin with the work of those three scholars and extend through a number of colleagues, friends, and institutions that have helped to keep this study moving forward. To begin with, I am particularly grateful for the careful reading given the complete manuscript by Professors James Given, Robert C. Palmer, and Michael Prestwich. They corrected foolish errors and offered excellent advice. The finished product reflects their effort in many ways, though, of course, they are not responsible for any defects that remain. I have benefited as well from the astute comments, criticisms, and conversation of Joyce Appleby, Robert Brenner, Sande Cohen, Richard Rouse, David Sabean, and Eleanor Searle. They have been challenging and generous colleagues, and their ideas have deepened my understanding of lordship, kinship, and ideology. The manuscript is also stronger for the advice of Paul Brand and David Carpenter. Their expertise has helped me enormously in particular areas of law and politics and, perhaps more important, their humor and conviviality helped me through long hours at the Public Record Office in London.

The hours would have seemed all the longer but for the generosity of the Keepers and Staff of the Public Record Office. From my first foray there as a graduate student in 1970, I have found the Staff exceptionally helpful and courteous, which has been important since most of the research for this book was carried out there. Unfortunately, I did not have reason to spend as much time at the British Library or Bodleian Library at Oxford, but each was equally generous and helpful. Finally, the Trustees and Staff at the Henry E. Huntington Library have provided assistance in research as well as an intellectually and aesthetically rich setting in which I have shaped the final versions of this manuscript. Each of these institutions has left an imprint on my research and thought. On a more material level, grants from the Henry E. Huntington Library, the American Philosophical Society, the Research Committee of the Academic Senate of the University of California, Los Angeles, and the National Endowment for the Humanities enabled me to carry out much of the research and writing and to enjoy the hospitality of these institutions.

Various individuals have generously assisted me: Timothy Keirn, Catherine Kelly, and Joseph Huffman with particular items of research; Terry Nixon with the interpretation of some Anglo-Norman letters; and Roy Hendricks, Tom Mount, and Waugh Controls Corporation with drafting the genealogical charts. I owe an equal debt to many friends whose insights, companionship, and encouragement lightened the burden of a scholastic enterprise whose clerical monotony sometimes grinds one down: the late Andrew Appleby, Robert C. Ritchie, Royston Stephens, David Shapiro, Mr. and Mrs. Anthony Solomon, and my dissertation advisor, Professor F.R.H. DuBoulay, who has always provided a model of intelligent scholarship and humane conduct.

Finally, this work is in large part about families. Anyone who studies family history is influenced, explicitly or implicitly, by his or her own family experience. I can only speculate about the extent to which my experience squares with that of the men and women I have chosen to study. I do know that for me it has been very rich. I owe an incalculable intellectual and material debt to my parents, Charles and Lorraine Waugh, who not only financed my scholastic ambitions but warmly encouraged them and stimulated my curiosity. My wife and son, Joan and Caleb, now constitute the center of my life and provide an even more stimulating environment. If our feelings and thoughts about family are sparked by living relationships, death brings deeper reflection about the meaning of those relations. The deaths of my mother Lorraine, my brother Stuart, and my son Andrew Stuart have at the very least demonstrated to me the power of family bonds. My life is richer for having known them and I dedicate this work to their memory.

A note on the tables and genealogical charts: The figures in most of the tables are given in marks—that is, two-thirds of a pound (13s. 4d.). The genealogical charts have been compiled from a variety of sources as indicated in the notes at the appropriate places in the text. All of the charts have been simplified and arranged to emphasize kinship connections. In cases where it is important to show the correct order of birth, numbers have been added in parentheses (1, 2, etc.) to indicate the individual's place in the order. The order of marriages has been indicated, where essential, by numbers before or after the equal sign which stands for marriage. If important and available, the date of the marriage has been inserted in parentheses above the equal sign. These dates are taken from Cokayne's *Complete Peerage* and usually indicate the earliest date at which the marriage appears in the records. The abbreviations *dsp* and *dvp* mean, respectively, "died without posterity" (died *sine prole*) and "died in the father's lifetime" (died *vita patris*). Family names are notoriously irregular; in most cases, I have followed Sanders, *English Baronies*, and the *Complete Peerage*.

ABBREVIATIONS

Full citations are given in the Bibliography.

BIHR	*Bulletin of the Institute of Historical Research*
BL	British Library
Bliss, *Papal Letters*	*Calendar of Entries in the Papal Registers Relating to Great Britain and Ireland: Papal Letters*
BNB	*Bracton's Notebook*
Book of Fees	*Liber Feodorum: The Book of Fees Commonly Called Testa de Nevill (1198–1293)*
Bracton	Henry de Bracton, *De Legibus et Consuetudinibus Angliae*
Byerly and Byerly, *RWH*	*Records of the Wardrobe and Household, 1285–1286*
CChR	*Calendar of the Charter Rolls, 1226–1516*
CChRV	*Calendar of Chancery Rolls, Various, 1277–1326*
CChW	*Calendar of Chancery Warrants (Privy Seals), 1244–1326*
CCR, [date]	*Calendar of the Close Rolls (1272–1485)*
CFR	*Calendar of the Fine Rolls*
CIM	*Calendar of Inquisitions Miscellaneous (Chancery), Henry III–Henry V*
CIPM	*Calendar of Inquisitions Post Mortem, Henry III– 7 Richard II*
Close Rolls	*Close Rolls of the Reign of Henry III*
CPR, [date]	*Calendar of the Patent Rolls (1232–1509)*
CRR	*Curia Regis Rolls*
DBMRR	*Documents of the Baronial Movement of Reform and Rebellion, 1258–1267*
DNB	*Dictionary of National Biography*
Dugdale, *Monasticon*	William Dugdale, *Monasticon Anglicanum*
EB	Ivor J. Sanders, *English Baronies*

EHR	*English Historical Review*
ERF	*Excerpta e Rotulis Finium*
EYC	*Early Yorkshire Charters*
Eyton, *Antiquities*	Robert W. Eyton, *Antiquities of Shropshire*
Foedera	*Foedera, Conventiones, Litterae, et Cujuscunque Generis Acta Publica etc.*
Glanvill	*The Treatise on the Laws and Customs of the Realm of England Commonly Called Glanvill*
HBC	Edmund B. Fryde and Frederick M. Powicke, eds., *Handbook of British Chronology*
HKF	William Farrer, *Honors and Knights' Fees*
HMC	Historical Manuscripts Commission
Maitland, *Memoranda de Parliamento*	*Records of the Parliament Holden at Westminster on the Twenty-eighth Day of February, in the Thirty-third Year of the Reign of King Edward the First*
Moor, *Knights*	Charles Moor, *Knights of Edward I*
Paris, *Chronica Majora*	Matthew Paris, *Chronica Majora*
Parsons, *CHEC*	John Carmi Parsons, ed., *The Court and Household of Eleanor of Castile*
Patent Rolls	*Patent Rolls of the Reign of Henry III (1216–1232)*
Pipe Roll, [regnal year]	Pipe rolls published by the Pipe Roll Society, London
PP	*Past and Present*
PRO	Public Record Office, London
RH	*Rotuli Hundredorum*
Rot. Chart.	*Rotuli Chartarum, 1199–1216*
Rot. Dom.	*Rotuli de Dominabus et Pueris et Puellis de Donatione Regis in XII Comitatibus*
Rot. Lit. Claus.	*Rotuli Litterarum Clausarum, 1204–1227*
Rot. Ob. et Fin.	*Rotuli de Oblatis et Finibus*

Rot. Orig.	*Rotulorum Originalium*
Rot. Parl.	*Rotuli Parliamentorum, ut et Petitiones, et Placita in Parliamento*
SANHS	*Somerset Archaeological and Natural History Society*
Select Cases	*Select Cases in the Court of King's Bench, Edward I–Edward III*
Select Charters	*Select Charters and Other Illustrations of English Constitutional History*
Stapleton, "Wardrobe Accounts"	Thomas Stapleton, "Brief Summary of the Wardrobe Accounts of the Tenth, Eleventh, and Fourteenth Years of King Edward the Second"
Statutes of the Realm	*Statutes of the Realm, 1101–1713*
TEAS	*Transactions of the Essex Archaeological Society*
Tout, *Chapters*	Thomas F. Tout, *Chapters in the Administrative History of Medieval England*
TRHS	*Transactions of the Royal Historical Society*
VCH	*Victoria History of the Counties of England*
Vita	*Vita Edwardi Secundi*
YAJ	*Yorkshire Archaeological Journal*

THE
LORDSHIP
OF ENGLAND

INTRODUCTION

Medieval kings of England derived power from two sources. They were sovereign monarchs—heads of a powerful administrative apparatus that enabled them to command armies, dispense justice, and fill their coffers. At the same time, however, they were suzerains—feudal overlords whose immediate tenants were the most powerful families in the kingdom. Kings exercised royal lordship, as it will be called, personally. It gave them sweeping powers over the lands, marriages, and families of the elite and opportunities to show favor through patronage. This is a study of the exercise of that power and its effect on political relations in England during the thirteenth and early fourteenth centuries.

Royal lordship was more effective in this period than at any other time. The king's determination to preserve his feudal authority in the wake of Magna Carta generated an institutionalization that made his tenants' obligations virtually inescapable. By the close of the thirteenth century, royal officials closely monitored the land transactions, deaths, and widows of those who held lands directly from the king: the tenants-in-chief. Nevertheless, the exercise of royal lordship was not necessarily harmful. The king often acted on the feudal principle of reciprocity and promoted or protected his tenants and their families. Royal lordship, moreover, provided a framework of law, institutions, and norms within which families could pursue the acquisition and preservation of property. The central argument of this study, therefore, is that royal lordship buttressed the king's honor and the institutions of royal government while simultaneously helping to integrate the Crown and landed elite into a highly cooperative polity. The relationship was not free of tension, and disagreements erupted between lord and tenants, but contestants did not challenge the basic framework within which they lived. These relations and the scope of the king's seigniorial authority will be delimited by investigation of the legal basis of royal lordship, the administration and use of his feudal resources, and the fate of widows and wards.

For at the heart of this study lies a fundamental dilemma that every society has faced: the provision for orphans and widows. The form that those provisions took for the elite of medieval England—wardship, marriage, and dower—arose out of the particular character of feudal landholding. Land was not owned by a family; it was held by an individual as a tenement in return for specific

3

services. That dependent tenure gave the landlord—in this case the king—an interest in and power over the tenement, the heirs, and the widow's marriage when a tenant died leaving only minors as heirs. From that authority, the lord derived honor and prestige as well as concrete benefits in the form of income and patronage. It was also his responsibility to protect wards, to take care of their land, and to ensure that they were suitably married. His authority overrode that of any kin, including the widowed mother. Wardship and marriage were thus bound up in three critical sets of power relations: kinship, landholding, and clientage. The exercise of feudal lordship at the highest levels of English society could only have been of profound political importance.

Historians in recent years have revised our understanding of feudal lordship, marriage, and politics in important ways. The emphasis in feudal studies has shifted away from military service alone to an examination of all of the legal, social, and political ramifications of the lord-tenant relationship. Lordship over knightly tenants in the eleventh and twelfth centuries is now seen as an interlocking set of claims and obligations growing out of the premise that a lord accepted a man as his tenant and gave him land in return for service. The lord's powers over marriage, wardship, and inheritance, his feudal incidents, were crucial in commanding land and service. The customs and ideals that sprang from this reciprocal bargain profoundly influenced social relations and the development of law at every level of English society.[1] Marriage was likewise embedded in relations of property and power. Personal consent to one's own marriage was essential, but choice of partners was narrowly circumscribed. The formation of a marriage re-

---

[1] This shift begins with Samuel Thorne's analysis of inheritance in "English Feudalism and Estates in Land," *Cambridge Law Journal* 23 (1959): 193–209, but has been taken farther by S.F.C. Milsom in *The Legal Framework of English Feudalism* (Cambridge, 1976). The work of Eleanor Searle has bridged the gap between honorable and agrarian lordship and has demonstrated a continuity in the purposes, institutions, and procedures of lordship from the highest to the lowest levels of English society (*Lordship and Community: Battle Abbey and Its Banlieu, 1066–1538* [Toronto, 1974]; and "Seigneurial Control of Women's Marriage: The Antecedents and Function of Merchet in England," *PP* 82 [1979]: 3–43). The connection among lordship, property holding, and politics has been made by James C. Holt in "Politics and Property in Early Medieval England," *PP* 57 (1972): 3–52. Recently, Robert C. Palmer has developed an ambitious synthesis of this development over the twelfth and early thirteenth centuries, "The Origins of Property in England," and "The Economic and Cultural Impact of the Origins of Property, 1180–1220," *Law and History Review* 3 (1985): 1–50, 375–396.

4

quired careful negotiation, for it involved the transfer of land and valuables, the potential for inheritance, and the hopes for the foundation of a family.[2] Historians have thus begun to delineate the important role of marriage and family relations in distributing wealth and power.[3] Finally, political relations between the king and the landholding elite are now viewed as essentially cooperative rather than conflictive. From the time of the Norman Conquest, they shared an interest in the protection of property, the defense of the realm, and the maintenance of social order.[4] They likewise shared the values, benefits, and obligations of feudal lordship, for all of the greater lords held lands of the king in addition to commanding tenants of their own. Cooperation broke down when the

[2] Michael M. Sheehan, "The Formation and Stability of Marriage in Fourteenth-Century England: Evidence of an Ely Register," *Mediaeval Studies* 33 (1971): 228–263; Richard H. Helmholz, *Marriage Litigation in Medieval England* (Cambridge, 1974); Robert C. Palmer, "Contexts of Marriage in Medieval England: Evidence from the King's Court circa 1300," *Speculum* 59 (1984): 42–67.

[3] The studies of Sidney Painter and Michael Altschul related the family to the feudal system, but their work has not been followed up for the thirteenth century (Sidney Painter, "The Family and the Feudal System in England," *Speculum* 35 [1960]: 1–16; Michael Altschul, *A Baronial Family in Medieval England: The Clares, 1217–1314* [Baltimore, 1965]). The most recent work on family has primarily related to the early Middle Ages, of which the most significant has been by Eleanor Searle, "Women and the Legitimisation of Succession at the Norman Conquest," *Proceedings of the Battle Conference on Anglo-Norman England III* (Woodbridge, 1980): 159–170, 226–229; "Family Reconstruction and the Construction of a Polity," paper presented at the California Institute of Technology–Weingart Conference (1981); "Kinship to State: Normandy in the Eleventh Century," paper presented at the California Institute of Technology–Weingart Conference (1983); "Fact and Pattern in Heroic History: Dudo of St.-Quentin," *Viator* 15 (1984): 119–137; and by James C. Holt, "Feudal Society and the Family in Early Medieval England: I. The Revolution of 1066," *TRHS*, 5th ser., 32 (1982): 193–212; 33 (1983): 193–220; "II. Notions of Patrimony," ibid., 33 (1983): 193–220; "III. Patronage and Politics," ibid., 34 (1984): 1–25; and "IV. The Heiress and the Alien," ibid., 35 (1985): 1–28. A notable exception to this emphasis on the earlier period is Joel T. Rosenthal, "Aristocratic Marriage and the English Peerage: Social Institution and Personal Bond," *Journal of Medieval History* 10 (1984): 181–194.

[4] The notion of cooperation has been explicitly stated by Michael Prestwich: "It makes more sense to see the normal pattern of political life as one of co-operation and collaboration between the two" (*The Three Edwards: War and State in England, 1272–1377* [New York, 1980], 146). This idea underlay Albert B. White's *Self Government by the King's Command* (Minneapolis, 1933), and figures prominently in the analysis of several recent historians, most notably David A. Carpenter, "King, Magnates, and Society: The Personal Rule of King Henry III, 1234–1258," *Speculum* 60 (1985): 39–70; John R. Maddicott, "Magna Carta and the Local Community, 1215–1259," *PP* 102 (1984): 25–65; and Anthony Tuck, *Crown and Nobility, 1272–1461* (London, 1985).

elite perceived royal actions as harmful to those shared interests, but conflict was the exception rather than the rule.

Royal lordship embodied each of these elements of medieval society. It affected marital choices and kinship patterns. It offered patronage and economic opportunities. And because it was so critical to the family's well-being, it led to misunderstandings and political conflict. It opens to view, therefore, the social setting of royal power and hence offers a rich field for the analysis of political relations in medieval England.

Yet, with the notable exceptions of J.M.W. Bean and Sue Sheridan Walker, historians have devoted little attention to the king's feudal rights in the thirteenth century.[5] The history of royal lordship has been divided into three distinct phases. In the first, from the Norman Conquest down to the reign of John, that lordship has been seen as arbitrary and, indeed, almost authoritarian, provoking a reaction by tenants-in-chief who imposed restrictions on it in Magna Carta.[6] In the last phase, the Tudors established the Court of Wards, which formed an important part of the government until its abolition in the seventeenth century.[7] The middle phase, from roughly 1217 to 1485, has been viewed as a period of "de-

[5] John M. W. Bean, *The Decline of English Feudalism, 1215–1540* (Manchester, 1968). Recently, Sue Sheridan Walker has explored the legal aspects of royal lordship in "Royal Wardship in Medieval England" (Ph.D. diss., University of Chicago, 1966); "Violence and the Exercise of Feudal Guardianship: The Action of 'Ejectio Custodia,' " *American Journal of Legal History* 16 (1972): 320–333; "Proof of Age of Feudal Heirs in Medieval England," *Mediaeval Studies* 35 (1973): 306–323; "The Marrying of Feudal Wards in Medieval England," *Studies in Medieval Culture and Society* 4 (1974): 209–224; "Widow and Ward: The Feudal Law of Child Custody in Medieval England," in *Women in Medieval Society*, ed. Susan M. Stuard (Philadelphia, 1976), 159–172; "The Action of Waste in the Early Common Law," in *Legal Records and the Historian*, ed. John H. Baker (London, 1978), 185–206; "Feudal Constraint and Free Consent in the Making of Marriages in Medieval England: Widows in the King's Gift," *Historical Papers* (1979): 97–110; and "Free Consent and Marriage of Feudal Wards in Medieval England," *Journal of Medieval History* 8 (1982): 123–134. There is no study of the revenues from royal lordship comparable to studies of royal taxation, nor a study of the escheator comparable to those of the sheriff or coroner, except for E. R. Stevenson, "The Escheator," in W. A. Morris and Strayer, *The English Government at Work* (Cambridge, 1947), 2: 109–167.

[6] The abuses of lordship are chronicled in an exaggerated fashion in J.E.A. Jolliffe, *Angevin Kingship* (London, 1963), while more specific information about the relationship between lordship and Magna Carta can be found in James C. Holt, *Magna Carta* (Cambridge, 1965).

[7] Henry E. Bell, *An Introduction to the History and Records of the Court of Wards and Liveries* (Cambridge, 1953); Joel Hurstfield, *The Queen's Wards: Wardship and Marriage under Elizabeth I* (London, 1958).

cline" languishing between the peak of royal lordship just prior to
Magna Carta and its revival by the Tudors.

Historians' views of the king's feudal authority in this latter period have been dominated by certain assumptions growing out of
the historiography of the English constitution. One assumption
has been that kings valued their lordship only for the profits it
provided and that otherwise it did not perform a significant function in government or politics.[8] Constitutional historians have not
found a place for it in their scheme of the development of institutional kingship, because they have often seen it as an Anglo-Norman relic useful for its revenues but not playing a prominent role
in the great constitutional conflicts after Magna Carta.[9] It has received vastly greater attention from Tudor historians writing in
that tradition precisely because, as they have argued, the Tudors
institutionalized feudal lordship and gave it a place alongside the
great central offices of government.[10] Another assumption has
been that feudal relations were inherently conflictive and that between the thirteenth and fifteenth centuries tenants-in-chief has-
tened the decline of feudal lordship by employing legal devices to
evade their obligations. That assumption has been based on the
belief that family sentiment and attitudes about marital choice
were roughly the same as they are today. Families thus chafed under a regime that irrationally deprived them of that choice by selling marriages to the highest bidder and that took lands away from
the family when the heir was a minor. In this constitutional view,
therefore, royal lordship, as an obsolete and anachronistic feudal
relic, caused dissension between the Crown and tenants-in-chief,
who steadily undermined it.

It is important, therefore, to analyze what actually happened to
families under the king's feudal lordship. The necessary starting
point is the social context of landholding and marriage during the
thirteenth and early fourteenth centuries. Although landed wealth
was the most important determinant of status and of the ability to
perform a public role in peacetime and war, it was subject to cen-

[8] Bean, *Decline*, 6; Bryce Lyon, *A Constitutional and Legal History of Medieval England* (New York, 1980), 132. For the use of feudal incidents as patronage, see Stevenson, "The Escheator," 136; and Joseph R. Strayer, introduction to W. A. Morris
and Strayer, *The English Government at Work*, 2:22.

[9] For example, J.E.A. Jolliffe, *The Constitutional History of Medieval England: From
the English Settlement to 1485* (New York, 1967), 331.

[10] Geoffrey R. Elton, *The Tudor Revolution in Government: Administrative Changes in
the Reign of Henry VIII* (Cambridge, 1966), 221–223.

trifugal forces. Women's rights to land, grants to family members, and politics pulled estates apart over time, making family status precarious. The burden of supporting relatives, moreover, grew along with the general increase in the population. The law offered property holders little help in relieving this burden. It denied them control over the descent of property after their deaths, obliging them to deduct any provisions for children or relatives from the estate during their lifetimes. Viewed from the perspective of the present, inheritance and descent appear to have occurred with a mechanical certitude. From the perspective of the actors themselves, however, procreation and survival were highly uncertain. Landholders, therefore, had to devise strategies that could provide for the contingencies of birth and death and that would enable them to support noninheriting children without jeopardizing the inheritance. They were trapped by conflicting desires. They wanted, above all, to ensure the smooth descent of land from one generation to another, but they also wanted to support all of their children.

Marriage was the most crucial of these strategies. Because marriage altered the configurations of inheritance and kinship, it had to be controlled by the family and by the social network in which the family was enmeshed. In selecting marital partners, English landholders demonstrated a preference for social endogamy, that is, marrying within a group of known families of similar status, function, and territorial interests. Marriage and kinship helped to shape the identity of groups and of the elite as a whole by giving individuals a common stake in the descent of lands. The emphasis on kinship relations and inmarrying was not unusual in premodern societies, but what was important in England was the interdependence of kinship, landholding, and status.[11] That interdependence created a matrix of interests, associations, and values that shaped the expectations of participants and therefore deeply influenced their attitudes toward their feudal landlord—in this case,

[11] Georges Duby has developed the most comprehensive model of endogamous marriage for medieval France in "Lignage, noblesse et chevalerie au XIIe siècle dans la région mâconnaise: Une révision," *Annales ESC* 27 (1972): 802–823; and in *Medieval Marriage: Two Models from Twelfth-Century France* (Baltimore, 1978). There is a massive literature in anthropology devoted to kinship and marriage, and the most influential in terms of this study have been the works of Jack Goody cited in Chapter 1; Robin Fox, *Kinship and Marriage: An Anthropological Perspective* (New York, 1983); Louis Dumont, "The Marriage Alliance," in *Kinship: Selected Readings*, ed. Jack Goody (Harmondsworth, 1971), 183–198; Pierre Bourdieu, *Outline of a Theory of Practice* (Cambridge, 1977), 1–71.

the king.[12] The development and consequences of this matrix are the subject of the first chapter.

It was at the points of marriage and inheritance, two vital aspects of family life in the Middle Ages and two crucial components of cooperation between families of the elite, that the king's feudal power and the interests of families intersected. The king demanded a recognition of his lordship in the form of homage and relief when heirs inherited their estates. He took wardship, that is, custody of children and their lands when a tenant died leaving an heir or heirs underage. With wardship, he gained the right to marry the children as he pleased. To maintain his lordship and its incidental rights, the king also controlled the alienation of lands held directly of the Crown, demanded consent to the marriages of heiresses, potential heiresses, and widows, and supervised the assignment of dowers and the partition of lands among female co-heirs. The evolution of these feudal powers before and after Magna Carta is examined in the second chapter. Furthermore, as the Crown institutionalized its authority during the thirteenth century, these feudal obligations became a constant, compulsory, and unavoidable aspect of the lives and landholding of wealthy tenants-in-chief, a process described in Chapter 3.

How the king exercised his power, therefore, became even more critical. The king of course tried to profit from lordship, as he did from every aspect of his authority, but he did not merely use his authority to tax tenants-in-chief. He personally supervised the enforcement and disposal of his rights and used them primarily as patronage, so that they became an essential strand in the fabric of power and influence around the court. The king's use of his feudal rights is a complex subject and is analyzed in detail in Chapter 4. The analysis shows, in fact, that the reciprocal ideology of feudal lordship survived into the thirteenth century and that to a great extent it conditioned royal policy. Cooperation between the king

---

[12] Holt, "Feudal Society and the Family III," 23, suggests that lordship, neighborhood, and family were discrete entities: "So the family bond seems to have been at its strongest when it was less trammeled by other ties of local association or lordship. . . . There were other ties, of lordship and neighborhood, which themselves helped to determine how families behaved." He thus weighs particular manifestations of kinship against what he suggests are *competing* associations to determine whether kinship was important. The argument here, however, is that the *totality* of kinship ties and their consequences shaped the identity and outlook of the elite and that they were interdependent on lordship and neighborhood. It is that interrelationship, especially at the highest level of English society, which characterized the polity that developed in England.

9

and the elite was maintained at several levels and, indeed, fostered cooperative relations within the elite itself.

An important theme of the book is therefore the role of feudal lordship in royal patronage. Wardships were given, sold, or leased to ministers and family members, earls, barons, knights, and other landholders. Such gifts had the effect of temporarily redistributing the wealth of tenants-in-chief through the elite, giving them a stake in royal lordship. It also reinforced a sense of mutual dependence and responsibility within the elite, for control of one another's lands and heirs was constantly circulating among them. Each family was confronted with two contrasting possibilities: on the one hand, the likelihood that its own lands and children might fall under royal lordship; on the other, the opportunity of acquiring desirable wards, lands, or widows' marriages. No tenant-in-chief could be confident that his family and estate would avoid wardship altogether. It was a sobering thought and may have restrained many guardians in exercising the rights they acquired from the king. Indeed, because of the frequency of minorities among tenants-in-chief, the arrangement of marriages by guardians occupied an important place in family strategies for alliance or descent.

The vast majority of the marriages arranged by the king or guardians were not objectionable, and in some cases they advanced the ward's interests. It is clear that wards had little opportunity to choose their own partners, but it is equally evident that guardians respected their right of consent and did not apply undue force in arranging marriages. As seen in Chapter 5, most marriages conformed to the patterns of social endogamy practiced by families, formed bonds between different groups or factions, and facilitated the descent of lands. The king was as interested as his tenants in ensuring the stability of landholding and descent, for he depended on them and their wealth for military leadership, administrative personnel, and political advice and consent. He did not tolerate abuses that seriously jeopardized their families and property.

The remarkable institutionalization of royal lordship and the consequent power of the monarchy in this respect may be surprising since in other areas, feudal authority was clearly eroding. The powers of mesne landlords had declined significantly since the twelfth century in the face of tenants' resistance to service and under the impact of royal justice. They lost the ability to discipline recalcitrant tenants, and the emphasis in feudal lordship shifted away from service to the income provided by feudal incidents.

Thus, the original rationale for the feudal system and the most important component of lordship—military service—deteriorated from the late twelfth century onward. The king tacitly recognized his inability to command sufficient knight service by instituting compulsory knighthood for all subjects who held land worth a certain amount. He shifted the criteria for knighthood from tenure alone to tenure and the value of property. Even then, there were large numbers of landholders whom he was unable to compel to become knights. Tenants-in-chief successfully reduced the service they owed the king and resisted his demands for additional or unpaid service. The king was even forced to cut back on his demands for scutage. Finally, Magna Carta imposed clear limits on the king's exercise of his feudal rights and seemed to deprive him of much of his authority.

Under these circumstances, English kings were determined to protect the feudal powers that remained to them. That determination coupled with the utility of feudal incidents to the tenants-in-chief ensured that royal lordship performed an essential role in the formation of the English polity in the thirteenth century. Mesne lords accepted that determination because during the thirteenth century they, too, vigorously protected their rights. Furthermore, because marriage was so vital in social relations and landholding, they pressed the king for valuable wardships and marriages. The Crown's drive to define, articulate, and institutionalize its feudal authority thus met with little resistance over the course of the thirteenth century. As a result of this process, by the early fourteenth century, the king exercised extensive control over the lands and families of the elite. That control brought him revenues, but it also gave him important political leverage that he could use to reward his friends.

Nevertheless, like all landlord-tenant relations, royal lordship engendered tensions that sometimes destroyed cooperation and erupted into conflict. Tenants-in-chief were wary of the way in which the king exercised his rights and protested any abuses that they perceived. The pattern of political opposition to royal lordship between 1200 and 1327, as explored in Chapter 6, is revealing because the tenants-in-chief consistently repeated certain themes. Again and again they protested the king's right of prerogative wardship that deprived them of their rights as mesne lords, waste by royal officials or guardians that diminished the value of estates, and the disposal of patronage that could deprive them of the rewards they expected from the king. "Primer seisin," or the king's right to take first possession of tenements held of him on the death of the tenant and to hold them until the heir performed homage, likewise came under attack because of the potential losses to tenants while their lands were in royal custody. Tenants-in-chief were thus extremely sensitive to the economic impact of royal lordship. At other times, they complained about the marriages arranged by the Crown or guardians, about the actions of administrators, and about other aspects of royal lordship; such as control of alienations. Yet there is no evidence of a deep-rooted hostility to feudal lordship itself. Not only did they not exploit every political crisis to assert their opposition to royal lordship, they never enunciated an alternate view of political organization. By 1327 the king had surrendered none of the essential attributes of lordship or prerogatives that he exercised in the wake of Magna Carta. He did exercise them more efficiently. Tenants-in-chief largely accepted and supported that feudal framework, though they were quick to call for administrative adjustments whenever they felt that the exercise of lordship harmed their interests.

The period from 1217 to 1327, therefore, represented a critical phase in the development of royal lordship and of political relations in general. By studying the exercise of royal lordship over such a long period, it is possible to see the underlying continuities as well as the peculiarities in royal policy. Furthermore, significant changes occurred in government during the period through increased definition and specialization in law, administration, and finance. Royal lordship was swept into that process. In terms of the family, it was a period in which the estates of tenants-in-chief were particularly subject to royal lordship. Tenants could not bequeath their lands, they could not direct the descent of property after their deaths, and they could not avoid the incidents of royal lordship. Their strategies for the descent and protection of property had to conform to the rules of feudal lordship as well as the rules of the Church. The period closes with the introduction of legal devices and techniques designed to give the tenant greater leverage over the descent and distribution of family lands: jointures, entails, and uses. These devices eventually had a significant impact on the scope of the king's authority, but in the short run, their importance was greater within the family. Finally, the period saw the last phase of the expansion of the medieval economy. This was the period of high farming in which landholders undertook the direct exploitation of their estates. They had an acute interest in agrarian income, and hence in the acquisition and preservation of demesne lands and in the enforcement of their lordship over unfree tenants. Strategies of marriage and descent were crucial to the maintenance of this seigniorial regime because they ensured the continuity of proprietorship necessary to keep the estate, in terms of both land and authority, intact. Royal lordship, therefore, reached the peak of its strength in a period in which tenants-in-chief were exceptionally active in the governance of the realm and in which they were most concerned about the impact of government on their finances, about the arrangements for marriage and descent within their families, and about the condition of their estates and their lordship over the unfree.

Several limitations of this study should be noted. It deals with royal lordship only over lay estates in England. It does not pretend to cover the king's lordship in Wales, Ireland, or Scotland, or over ecclesiastical estates. The English tenants-in-chief, moreover, were a diverse lot. They ranged from peasants with only a few acres of land to the wealthiest landholders in the kingdom. The treatment of these tenants varied according to their status. This study concentrates primarily on those at the top, on what may be called the political ranks of the tenants-in-chief. These generally ranked as knights or higher and participated in one way or another in royal government or served consistently in royal armies. Furthermore, although the institutionalization of lordship is analyzed in some detail, the book does not provide a history of the office of escheator nor an analysis of the personnel. Finally, any historical study of this length tends to be reductionist, and I should point out at the outset that I do not see royal lordship as the principle cause of political conflict, that it was not the only form of patronage available to the king, and that it was not the only framework for cooperation within the elite and between the elite and the king. It opens to view, however, in a unique way, the fundamental workings of relations between the king and the elite.

Government records form the bulk of the sources used in this study. Most of that information is derived from the enrollments of royal writs or commands on the Chancery rolls, though the Exchequer enrollments of writs and legal processes are also informative. The most significant Exchequer sources are the accounts of the escheators, and variations in those accounts over time show changes in the exercise of lordship. Letters and petitions from private sources provide some insight into the process of acquiring wardships and marriages, but it is hard to build up a complete picture of the disposal of any given wardship. Because the king ex-

ercised the power of consent over the marriages of the female relatives of tenants-in-chief, the royal sources include some
information, such as marriage contracts, that reveals the process of
forming family alliances. More can be derived from the plea rolls.
Yet, sources for family arrangements, other than the dispersal and
acquisition of property, are not nearly so abundant as those for the
exercise of royal lordship from the king's standpoint. There is little
information about two vital types of consultation: those among
family members about marriage and property, and those within
the royal council about the disposal of the king's rights. These
areas of the stage are left dark, and activities within them can only
be inferred from other sources.

· 1 ·

MARRIAGE, KINSHIP, AND PROPERTY

The acquisition, preservation, and cultivation of property absorbed the energies of families at all levels of society in medieval England. For members of the elite, this preoccupation meant devoting as much care to the marriage of children as to the management of lands and tenants. Family obligations caused economic difficulties as real as those brought on through indebtedness, bad management, forfeiture, or economic change and led to the loss of land or revenue. Thus, however great their desire to consolidate wealth in the hands of the eldest son, landholders did not hesitate to support younger sons, daughters, and widows. They also faced the prospect that if they did not leave a male heir the estate would be divided between women. To cope with these dangers and uncertainties, landholders devised various strategies for acquiring and protecting land, one of the most important of which was marriage. Marriage offered an opportunity to acquire land and the potential for future acquisition through inheritance. It fostered group cohesion by uniting families in a network of kinship and shared interest in one another's property. And it had far-reaching political consequences, because it was in this context of marriage and landholding that the king exercised his feudal incidents—rights that seriously affected marital plans.[1]

INHERITANCE AND DEMANDS ON THE ESTATE

English custom directed the bulk of an estate to the eldest male heir, but it also called for the distribution of land to other family members, a form of "diverging devolution."[2] Property seldom de-

---

[1] Much of the argument and evidence in this chapter has appeared previously in Scott L. Waugh, "Marriage, Class, and Royal Lordship in England under Henry III," *Viator* 16 (1985): 181–207. In a few instances, as noted, that material has been updated or corrected.

[2] Jack Goody has discussed the concept of "diverging devolution" in various contexts. See, inter alia, Jack Goody and S. J. Tambiah, *Bridewealth and Dowry* (Cambridge, 1973), 1–58; Jack Goody, "Inheritance, Property and Women: Some Comparative Considerations," in Goody et al., *Family and Inheritance* (Cambridge, 1976), 10–36; idem, *Production and Reproduction: A Comparative Study of the Domestic Domain* (Cambridge, 1976); and idem, *The Development of the Family and Marriage in Europe* (Cambridge, 1983).

scended intact from one individual to another. It was used instead to support the entire family. Sisters and younger brothers, theoretically left out of the inheritance under primogeniture, in fact often received a premortem share of the inheritance in the form of gifts from the holder of the estate. Widows controlled at least a third of the estate for their lives after the death of their husbands, regardless of any subsequent marriages. The ideals of diverging devolution, providing for all family members, and patrilineage, concentrating wealth in a male heir, were equally important to all landholders, though not all were equally lavish to noninheriting children.[3] For every family in every generation there was a strong possibility that some lands would devolve away from the patriline, forcing landholders to make up the loss and to prevent the estate from wasting away.[4]

This fission intensified whenever women inherited because, from the late twelfth century onward, estates were divided equally among female heirs.[5] Feudal custom preferred male heirs to female, yet because it also preferred the nearest blood relative to distant relations, women inherited in the absence of a direct male heir.[6] Daughters inherited before their father's younger brothers,

[3] For an example of one family that did not give much, see Emma Mason, "The Resources of the Earldom of Warwick in the Thirteenth Century," *Midland History* 3 (1975): 67–75.

[4] Frederick Pollock and Frederic W. Maitland, *The History of English Law before the Time of Edward I* (Cambridge, 1968), 2:15–16, 240–363, 420–428; Theodore F. T. Plucknett, *Legislation of Edward I* (Oxford, 1962), 110–135; Frederick M. Powicke, "Loretta, Countess of Leicester," in *Historical Essays in Honour of James Tait*, ed. John G. Edwards, Vivian H. Galbraith, and Ernest F. Jacob (Manchester, 1933), 252–258; Kenneth B. McFarlane, *The Nobility of Later Medieval England* (Oxford, 1973), 61–82; Emma Mason, "*Maritagium* and the Changing Law," *BIHR* 49 (1976): 286–289; J. P. Cooper, "Patterns of Inheritance and Settlement by Great Landowners from the Fifteenth to the Eighteenth Centuries," in Goody et al., *Family and Inheritance*, 198–233; Painter, "The Family and the Feudal System"; Holt, "Politics and Property"; Searle, "Seigneurial Control."

[5] S.F.C. Milsom, "Inheritance by Women in the Twelfth and Early Thirteenth Centuries," in *On the Laws and Customs of England: Essays in Honor of Samuel Thorne*, ed. Morris S. Arnold et al. (Chapel Hill, 1981), 60–89; Holt, "Feudal Society and the Family IV," 1–28. The tenurial problems of partitions are discussed in the next chapter.

[6] *Glanvill* (VII.3), 75–77; Bracton, 2:190–194. In neither case were these men the actual authors, but I have chosen to use the personification in both cases for the sake of simplicity. On this issue, see Paul Hyams, *King, Lords and Peasants in Medieval England: The Common Law of Villeinage in the Twelfth and Thirteenth Centuries* (Oxford, 1980), xx n. 1, 83 nn. 2, 3, who was writing in light of the revelations of Samuel E. Thorne in the translator's introduction to Bracton, 3:i–liii.

16

and sisters before their uncles. Property descended as a "unitary right." Yet all women of the same degree, or of the same relation to the landholder, had equal claims on the inheritance. It did not matter whether they were "of the father and the same mother [or of the mother and same father] or different ones."[7] Since the inheritance was treated as a unity, all the daughters of a given property holder, by one or more wives or husbands, who were equally close to the property holder and hence to the property, shared the inheritance equally. For example, Gilbert de Lesteneston married three times and had one daughter by each of his wives. On his death in 1246, his property descended to all three daughters.[8]

The frequency and impact of women's inheritance can be seen in the fate of English baronies between 1200 and 1327. By that time a baron had no specific legal functions or privileges, and the term did not denote a precise economic rank. At one end the group included knights, squires, and serjeants who comprised the bulk of the tenants-in-chief, while at the other it encompassed the wealthiest lay landholders in England who were the leaders of the landed elite. Here *the elite* is defined as those landholders with sufficient wealth, expertise, and inclination to participate in the important functions of the medieval state. The elite was not an undifferentiated mass but can be divided, like the ranks of the barons, into two groups according to their public importance. At the top were about a hundred magnates or *proceres*: earls, barons, wealthy knights, and ministers who served on the king's council, performed the higher functions of law and administration, led his forces in war, and whose wealth and power covered the kingdom as a whole. The second level comprised knights and wealthy gentry who served the king in local and central institutions and whose wealth was concentrated in one or two counties. The two groups were not mutually exclusive and status did not divide them with geologic fixity. No barriers of law or privilege prevented interrelationships or movement between them. The so-called peerage had not yet come into existence to demarcate clearly the difference between gentry and aristocracy.[9] Contemporaries nevertheless distin-

[7] Bracton, 2:194.

[8] *ERF*, 2:231–232; *CPR, 1247–1258*, 492; PRO, E.13/18 m. 69d. For another example, see *EB*, 74, 145; *CIPM*, 3:29 (Marmion-Kilpeck).

[9] For discussions of social rank, see Noël Denholm-Young, "Feudal Society in the Thirteenth Century: The Knights," *History* 29 (1944): 107–119; Josiah Cox Russell, "Social Status at the Court of King John," *Speculum* 12 (1937): 319–329; idem, "Attestation of Charters in the Reign of John," *Speculum* 15 (1940): 480–498; George

guished between those who wielded influence across the community of the realm as a whole and those whose authority was more localized. Although not socially homogeneous, this secular elite along with its ecclesiastical peers comprised a class distinct from the mass of peasantry who worked their lands and were subject to their legal and economic authority. The baronies offer a representative sample of the lay portion of the landholding elite and yield important data about the social and political consequences of marriage, descent, and female inheritance.[10]

The hazards of life in the Middle Ages were so great that families could not count on the unbroken descent of property through fathers and sons. The descent of the sample baronies is summarized in Table 1.1. There were 192 known and probable baronies in 1200. Down to 1327 they experienced approximately 635 generational changes, that is, points at which a barony passed on to the next generation. In 144 cases (22.7 percent of the time) the baron died childless and the property passed to a collateral line or to women. None of the original 192 baronies in this period actually escheated to the Crown due to a total failure of heirs, though a fair number came into the king's hands by sale, grant, or forfeiture. [11]

L. Haskins, "Charter Witness Lists in the Reign of King John," *Speculum* 13 (1938): 319–325; Nigel Saul, *Knights and Esquires: The Gloucestershire Gentry in the Fourteenth Century* (Oxford, 1981), 6–35; and J. Enoch Powell and Keith Wallis, *The House of Lords in the Middle Ages: A History of the English House of Lords to 1540* (London, 1968), 219–231, 303–315.

[10] The baronies are taken from *EB*. Wherever possible, this information has been supplemented with details from George E. Cokayne, *The Complete Peerage* (London, 1910–1959), and other sources as noted. For evaluations of Sanders, see Ralph H. C. Davis, "What Happened in Stephen's Reign," *History* 40 (1964): 1–12, and Ra-Gena DéAragon, "The Growth of Secure Inheritance in Anglo-Norman England," *Journal of Medieval History* 8 (1982): 381–391. I have calculated the number of baronies in 1200 as follows: Sanders lists 204 known and probable baronies. Of these, 22 had been partitioned before 1200 into 52 portions, giving a total of 234 baronies and portions. Of these, 25 had been consolidated into other baronies by inheritance or acquisition and 17 had fallen under royal control, leaving 192 separate baronies or portions. This total differs from that in "Marriage, Class, and Royal Wardship," because there, 3 portions of baronies (Aldington, Hunsingore, and West Dean) that were in the hands of heiresses who married other barons were counted as distinct baronies in 1200, whereas it seems more sensible to include them among the baronies consolidated before 1200. The nature of the barony in the thirteenth century is described in *EB*, v–viii, and in Ivor J. Sanders, *Feudal Military Service in England: A Study of the Constitutional and Military Powers of the Barones in Medieval England* (Oxford, 1956), 1–28.

[11] Sanders states that some of the baronies held by Edmund of Cornwall "escheated" on his death in 1300, but his lands seem to have passed to Edward I by

TABLE 1.1 THE DESCENT OF 192 BARONIES, 1200–1327

Descending Entirely through Male Heirs		
Father to Son	36	
Collateral Males[a]	25	
Total	61	31.8%
Inherited by Women (at least once)[b]		
Single Heiresses	43	
Two or More Coheirs	67	
Total	110	57.3%
Granted, Sold, or Forfeit		
	21	10.9%
Total	192	100.0%

[a] On the deaths of two holders of baronies that had been partitioned before 1200, the portions reverted to the collateral lines of the coheirs and have been included here.

[b] 13 baronies descended to women on more than one occasion, so that over the period as a whole, baronies were inherited by women 124 times.

Nevertheless, continuity in the male line could not be guaranteed. Some families ran through several male heirs. William Marshal, the renowned knight and royal counselor, died in 1219 leaving five sons. Yet between 1219 and 1245, each of them died childless, one after the other, eventually leaving the inheritance to their five sisters. The extinction of the male line was sufficiently remarkable to engender rumors of prophecy and a curse on the family, but the earldoms of Chester, Arundel, Huntingdon, and Winchester likewise fell to sisters when their brothers died childless in the early thirteenth century.[12] In 21 of the cases in which the tenant-in-chief died childless, the barony went to a sister, aunt, or niece. Taking all of the generational changes into consideration, men usually inherited. Yet baronial estates fell to women 19.5 percent of the

inheritance (*EB*, 10, 44, 93; *CIPM*, 3:604). For sales, etc., see *EB*, 47, 65, 90, 94, 126, 132.

[12] Paris, *Chronica Majora*, 4:492–495; Cokayne, *Complete Peerage*, 1:238–239, 10:365–377, 12:2:751–754; *EB*, 2, 61–62; Ronald Stewart-Brown, "The End of the Norman Earldom of Chester," *EHR* 35 (1920): 26–54. The number of generations is calculated from Sanders. The count begins with the succession of the heir to the first holder of the barony to die near 1200 and ends with the succession of the last holder recorded by Sanders. The count includes instances in which a barony passed by grant or other means from one person to another, even if it did not strictly represent a generational change.

time, and less than a third of the original baronies descended through males over the period as a whole.[13]

Women's inheritance, therefore, profoundly affected the distribution of wealth within the elite. Inheritance by a single woman did not disrupt estates. Through marriage her inheritance merged with her husband's property to form a new patrimony. In at least ten cases, the heirs of these unions highlighted their attachment to the property by taking their mother's or grandmother's family name, that is, the name associated with the land.[14] Inheritance by more than one woman was more significant for the distribution of wealth because it shattered estates. The biographer of Edward II thus lamented the partition of the Clare inheritance after the premature death of the earl of Gloucester in 1314. Like the Marshal partition seventy years earlier, it spawned rumors of a prophecy. This time it was Simon de Montfort who supposedly laid the curse on the family at the battle of Evesham (1265) when he denounced the earl of Gloucester for deserting Simon's cause. A generation later Edward III deplored the fact that women's inheritance had reduced the number of titles and had weakened the realm.[15] The process of fission is laid out in Table 1.2. It went even further than that. Of the 185 fragments listed in the table, 28 were subsequently partitioned, making 75 more, of which another 5 fragmented into 12 pieces. Altogether, the 67 baronies inherited by more than one woman eventually devolved into 246 particles, some of them quite small. As can be seen in the table, estates usually fell to only one or two women, though large families were not unheard of. William Marshal had ten surviving children in 1219, while at the other end of the period, Roger de Mortimer, the first earl of March, had eleven children, seven of them girls.

The greatest danger to an estate, as Bracton noted, was that it would be partitioned in successive generations, eroding it into ever

[13] Only one-eighth of the leading families of the Welsh Marches survived through the male line between 1284 and 1390 (R. Rees Davies, *Lordship and Society in the March of Wales, 1282–1400* [Oxford, 1978], 48–49). See also McFarlane, *The Nobility*, 172–176, for calculations of the rate of extinction in the fourteenth century.

[14] *EB*, 3, 5, 9, 26, 33, 56, 68, 80, 81, 100, 115, 128; and Cokayne, *Complete Peerage*, 5:126, 12:1:497–500. For an example of the use of Christian names for filiation see *The Beauchamp Cartulary Charters, 1100–1268*, ed. Emma Mason (London, 1980 for 1971–1973), xxiv.

[15] *Vita*, 73; Nicholas Trivet, *Nicolai Triveti Annalium Continuatio*, ed. Anthony Hall (Oxford, 1722), 25; Altschul, *A Baronial Family*, 165–174; *Reports from the Lords Committees Touching the Dignity of a Peer of the Realm* (London, 1822), 3:97–99 (on the effects of partitions), 5:29.

TABLE 1.2 THE IMPACT OF WOMEN'S INHERITANCE ON BARONIES

	Baronies Affected						
	Number of Heiresses[a]						
	1	2	3	4	5	6	Total
Daughters	36	18	8	5	—	—	67
Sisters, aunts, nieces, etc.	21	17	11	3	4	1	57
Total of baronies affected	57	35	19	8	4	1	124
Net total[b]	43	35	19	8	4	1	110
% of net	39.1	31.8	17.3	7.3	3.6	.9	100
Resulting fragments	—	70	57	32	20	6	185
Total number of heiresses	57	70	57	32	20	6	241

[a] Does not include those women holding baronies in 1200.

[b] 5 baronies descended to single heiresses twice, and 1 barony fell to single heiresses three times, leaving 50 baronies. Of those 50, 7 were later partitioned by coheiresses, leaving a net total of 43 affected only by inheritance by a single female heir.

smaller pieces.[16] The Marshal inheritance offers an instructive example. After the death of the last brother in 1245, five sisters partitioned the estate. Two of those sisters produced only daughters, further subdividing their portions. Eve married William de Braose and passed her fifth of the barony on to four daughters, while Sibyl and her husband, William de Ferrers, passed her fifth on to seven daughters, one of whom had four more daughters and coheirs. By the mid-thirteenth century, those seven women had contracted a total of twelve marriages, but only eight of the matches produced children and one of the women died in 1274 without surviving descendants. In fact, in 1327, when the last descendant of another of Sibyl's coheirs died without children, royal escheators could find only five male representatives of all of Sibyl's offspring.[17]

At any given time, a significant portion of the elite's wealth was in the hands of heiresses or widows. The extent of their control

[16] Bracton, 2:222. The discussion arose because of the partition of Chester; see Stewart-Brown, "Chester," 39–47.

[17] Cokayne, *Complete Peerage*, 4:197–199; 10:364 n. a; B. W. Greenfield, "Meriet of Meriet and of Hestercombe," *SANHS* 28 (1883): 178–179, 183–185; *CIPM*, 7:46; *De Antiquis Legibus Liber: Chronica Majorum et Vicecomitum Londoniarum, 1188–1274*, (London, 1846), xvii–xxiv; Moor, *Knights*, 3:163–164. A similar process occurred after the death of Ranulph de Blundeville in 1232; see Stewart-Brown, "Chester."

can be glimpsed in some lists of knights and potential knights drawn up by sheriffs to determine liability for compulsory knighthood.[18] For example, a list of landholders for Northamptonshire in 1297 shows ninety-seven knights in the county, forty-one squires (*armigerii*), and twenty women (16 percent). A list of the holders of £40 worth of land by knight service in Shropshire in 1300 records that six of the thirty-two or more lay landholders (19 percent) were women. Finally, a return from a Gloucestershire inquest in 1344 records that of more than sixty lay landholders, twenty-four were widows or heiresses, and that they held approximately 13 percent of the assessed wealth.[19] Of course, the accidents of birth, death, and inheritance that caused family wealth to devolve outward could likewise reunite fragments. The barony of Burgh by Sands, for instance, was partitioned between two daughters on the death of Hugh de Morvill in 1202, but was reconstituted seventy years later through inheritance.[20]

Demography and inheritance customs, therefore, could have serious political repercussions. As it subdivided estates over time, women's inheritance weakened the concentration of land and lordship that constituted the power of the elite and led to a redistribution of wealth. The corrosiveness of inheritance could be neutralized to some extent through marriage. All nine of the coheirs to the Marshal and Chester inheritances were married to barons at the time of the partitions, meaning that the wealth was contained within the ranks of the baronage. At the other end of the period, marriage and inheritance combined to produce a dramatic concentration of wealth in the hands of Thomas of Lancaster. True, as Edward II's biographer stressed, Thomas was of noble, even royal, kinship, but the control of such wealth gave him inordinate power. The politics of Edward's reign were distorted further when the Clare estate was partitioned after 1314, robbing the elite of any counterweight to Lancaster. Then Edward foolishly compounded these problems by marrying two of the Clare heiresses to mere courtiers rather than to other members of the established nobil-

---

[18] For the problems in using these lists, see Scott L. Waugh, "Reluctant Knights and Jurors: Respites, Exemptions, and Public Obligations in the Reign of Henry III," *Speculum* 58 (1983): 954, and the works cited there.

[19] *Parliamentary Writs and Writs of Military Summons* (London, 1827–1834), 1:288–290; PRO, C.47/1/6/22; C.47/2/52. For an analysis of the later list, see Saul, *Knights and Esquires*, 33–35.

[20] *EB*, 23–24, 58, 115. The Percy barony of Topcliff underwent a similar process; see *EYC*, 11:3–7; *EB*, 148.

ity.[21] Inheritance, especially when it thus involved women, was a dangerous point of transition, with the potential for realigning wealth and power.

Aside from inheritance, family members asserted other claims that could dissipate property or disrupt finances. Dower was the most prevalent and most seriously affected family income. A widow's right to at least a third of her deceased husband's property during her lifetime was well protected by the common law.[22] And among baronial landholders, wives often outlived their husbands, as can be seen in Table 1.3.[23] The even greater rate of survival for second wives undoubtedly reflects the advanced age of the barons when they remarried as well as the fact that they seem to have preferred younger women to widows as second wives. In such a circumstance, an heir might have to wait in vain for the death of a stepmother who was nearly his coeval in order to obtain his full inheritance.

Some widows were especially long-lived and carried the dowers they accumulated, along with any inheritance or dowry, to subsequent husbands. One glaring example was Isolda, the daughter and eventual sole heir of William Pantolf, who married five husbands in succession between about 1180 and 1223. She may have been exceptional, but widows often remarried at least once.[24] Although the dower was only a life grant, and families could recover lands that widows alienated, the loss of a third of the estate while the widow was alive nonetheless seriously depleted the heir's in-

[21] *Vita*, 28–29, 62–63, 94.

[22] Pollock and Maitland, *History of English Law*, 2:420–426; Plucknett, *Legislation*, 120–125. The economic consequences of dower rights and the position of widows has been more extensively analyzed in peasant communities than at the level of the elite. See Jan Z. Titow, "Some Differences between Manors and the Effects on the Conditions of the Peasants in the Thirteenth Century," *Agricultural History Review* 10 (1962): 1–13; and Peter Franklin, "Peasant Widows' 'Liberation' and Remarriage before the Black Death," *Economic History Review*, 2d ser., 39 (1986): 186–204.

[23] The information for marriages and remarriage has been taken from Cokayne, *Complete Peerage*, and *EB*.

[24] She married (1) Hugh Munpincun, d. 1186; (2) Walter de Tateshal, d. 1199; (3) Henry Biset, d. 1208; (4) Walter de Baskerville, d. 1213; (5) Amaury de St. Amando, d. 1241; and she died ca. 1222–1223 (Cokayne, *Complete Peerage*, 11:295–296; 12:1:648–649; *CRR*, 1:196, 214; 7:185, 193, 263, 319; 9:129–130, 324; 11:35 [no. 204]; *Pipe Roll, 10 John*, 198–199; *16 John*, 113; *Patent Rolls*, 1:131; *Rot. Ob. et Fin.*, 500, 511; *Rot. Lit. Claus.*, 1:224, 289; *Book of Fees*, 2:1337). For the examples of Christiana Ledet, Margery Darcy, Joan de Cokefield, Margery de Badlesmere, and Margaret de Say, see *EB*, 33, 43, 52–53, 67–68, 75; and Cokayne, *Complete Peerage*, 4:50–51; 9:258–261; 11:98–99; 12:2:20–22.

come. It was not unusual, moreover, for successive generations of widows to survive, thereby delaying an heir's full enjoyment of his inheritance until the deaths of his mother, grandmother, and perhaps even great-grandmother.[25]

Women also received a portion of the family property on their marriage. A dowry represented an internal rearrangement of the inheritance for the purpose of supporting a woman and her new family, if she produced one. If she or her heirs within three generations failed to have children, the land reverted to the donor's family, for neither she nor her husband or heirs performed homage for the dowry.[26] Furthermore, if it turned out that a woman who had received a marriage portion became a coheir of the property, then she had a choice in the partitioning of the property. She could put her dowry back into the pot with the rest of the inheritance and then apportion the land, or she could keep her dowry and make no further claim on the inheritance. Bracton bluntly states that "she either contributes her marriage portion or departs without any share at all . . . she has the choice of contributing it or not."[27] The possibility of choice shows how custom equated a marriage portion with a share of the inheritance.

After 1300, when marriage portions came to be paid in cash, it is possible to calculate the impact of marriage on a family's wealth with some precision, but prior to that most dowries at the upper ranks of society were made in land, and the precise economic effect of marriage portions on estates is less easily determined.[28] One inquest to determine the value of a ward's marriage noted that the dowry of the ward's grandmother was due to descend to him on her death and would make the marriage so much more valuable. Landholders were sufficiently concerned about the effects of such grants to seek legal measures to protect their right of reversion if a recipient died without an heir.[29]

Custom did not provide so much protection for the interests of younger sons and brothers as it did for those of widows and

[25] McFarlane, *The Nobility*, 65–66; George A. Holmes, *The Estates of the Higher Nobility in Fourteenth-Century England* (Cambridge, 1957), 14; Painter, "The Family and the Feudal System," 200, 213–214. Property valuations sometimes noted that lands held in dower reduced the value of a wardship (e.g., PRO, SC.1/22/193).

[26] Milsom, *Legal Framework*, 142–146; Pollock and Maitland, *History of English Law*, 2:15; Plucknett, *Legislation*, 125–129.

[27] Bracton, 2:223–224.

[28] Holmes, *Estates*, 43–44; McFarlane, *The Nobility*, 84–88; Lawrence Stone, *The Crisis of the Aristocracy* (Oxford, 1967), 288–292.

[29] *CIPM*, 1:862; Plucknett, *Legislation*, 125–135.

daughters. Glanvill reveals the mixed emotions that such provisions aroused. He warned that because fathers bore greater affection for their younger sons, they were apt to disinherit the elder. Fathers, therefore, could not grant younger sons any of the inheritance without the heir's permission. Their position was thus worse than that of a bastard, with regard to inherited lands. Glanvill also pointed out, however, that fathers displayed great generosity toward their sons.[30] By the thirteenth century, as a result of legal change, there was little that prospective heirs could do to prevent parents from alienating as much of the patrimony as they pleased.[31] It does not appear that parents often disinherited eldest sons, but they frequently gave land to younger sons and brothers. When John Lestrange of Knockin, Shropshire, granted half of his manor of Lytcham, Norfolk, to his daughter Alice toward her marriage around 1260–1261, he delivered the other half to his younger son, Robert, with the consent of their brothers, Hamo and Roger.[32]

As a consequence of grants between family members, kinship and lordship often intertwined, reaffirming the need for cooperation within families. Lord and tenant could be cousins. The heir of a tenant holding by military service came into the wardship of his lord. The lord married the boy to his own daughter and remitted the service of the fee, making it a kind of grant in free marriage.[33] Thenceforth, lord and tenant were collateral members of the same family. A grant in marriage after three generations, or a grant to a younger son, behaved in the same manner. The Yorkshire family of Paynel and the Dorsetshire family of Keynes, for example, shared the manor of Coombe Keynes, Dorset, as a result of intermarriage. Both families descended from a certain Letitia who married successively the head of each family in the early thirteenth

[30] *Glanvill* (VII.1), 70–71; Painter, "The Family and the Feudal System," 208–211; Altschul, *A Baronial Family*, 31, 193–194, 245, 260; Holt, "Feudal Society and the Family III," 8–9.

[31] *Glanvill* (VII.1), 69–74. Milsom, in *Legal Framework*, 121–132, explains the heir's loss of control over gifts, while Bracton, 2:224, 3:278–279, raises the possibility of parents' granting away all of their property and thus depriving an heir of his inheritance. For examples, see Cokayne, *Complete Peerage*, 4:118–120, 10:335–336; and Holt, "Feudal Society and the Family III," 7.

[32] Eyton, *Antiquities*, 10:274. Examples can be found in a wide range of sources, e.g., Mortimer Cartulary, BL, Harleian MS 1240, fol. 40; Mohun Cartulary, Egerton MS 3724, fols. 11, 57v; John Smyth, *The Berkeley Manuscripts*, Vol. 1: *The Lives of the Berkeleys* (Gloucester, 1883), 119–121, 147–149.

[33] *CIPM*, 3:473, at p. 366.

century. The Paynels acquired their share of the manor through Letitia and held it of their relatives or in-laws, the Keynes. Two half brothers, John Paynel and William Keynes, became brothers-in-law when each married one of the coheiresses of Adam de Per-ington.[34] The rule that a man or woman could not be both lord and heir helped to distinguish the claims of family and lordship when an individual acquired land from the family. Yet the nature of conveyancing in medieval England meant that family grants added the obligations of lordship to the responsibilities of kin-ship.[35]

Property, therefore, often changed hands during the thirteenth and early fourteenth centuries, but it did not necessarily migrate out of the family. Widows, daughters, sisters, and brothers constantly pressured the family estate for support, and this pressure generated a considerable movement of land within the family and between families. Land drifted away from the patriline, though not far, and it often remained connected through tenurial obligations.

Family demands were not the only forces causing the erosion of estates, though they were the most constant. Indebtedness, grants to religious houses, and forfeiture could also chip away at an inheritance. These factors were intermittent and inconsistent, varying from estate to estate and according to the practices of land-holders. The economic expansion from the twelfth century onward produced a rise in prices that created increased wealth for some families and hardship for others, who had to sell off portions of their estates to relieve their indebtedness. Under these circumstances, a family could easily cut back on religious donations and, by the thirteenth century certainly, the great era of religious grants had passed.[36]

[34] *EYC*, 6:11–16; *CIPM*, 2:184, 320, 433, 637. When John died in 1276, he left behind his wife, his grandmother Letitia, and a Lady Joan, all of whom held dowers.

[35] Painter, "The Family and the Feudal System," 201; Milsom, *Legal Framework*, 139–142.

[36] The impact of the inflation on small landholders has been widely debated. See Paul D. A. Harvey, "The English Inflation of 1180–1220," *PP* 61 (1973): 3–30; Edmund King, "Large and Small Landholders in Thirteenth-Century England," *PP* 47 (1970): 26–52; Peter R. Coss, "Sir Geoffrey de Langeley and the Crisis of the Knightly Class in Thirteenth-Century England," *PP* 68 (1975): 3–37; David A. Carpenter, "Was There a Crisis of the Knightly Class in the Thirteenth Century? The Oxfordshire Evidence," *EHR* 95 (1980): 721–752; Saul, *Knights and Esquires*, 205–

Political miscalculation could be more dangerous. The fate of William de Braose in the reign of John, William de Ferrers after the Barons' War, or Thomas of Lancaster and his followers under Edward II are reminders of the worst hazards of rebellion against the Crown.[37] At least twenty-one of the baronies suffered forfeiture at some point between 1200 and 1327. Land could fall in and out of family control over several generations as a result of political opposition.[38] The dangers of rebellion are most obvious at the level of baronies, because, as the political leaders of the country, magnates were most visible in political opposition and punishment. Yet the aftermath of the Barons' War, or the Contrariants' rebellion in 1321–1322, shows that landholders further down the social ranks suffered equally with their more illustrious companions.[39] English landholders were fortunate in that they were not often forced to choose between their loyalties. Political confrontation rarely escalated to outright rebellion, and major political upheavals occurred at widely spaced intervals, in the reigns of John, Henry III, and Edward II. Moreover, most families recovered forfeited lands within a generation or so.

Forfeiture, even if only temporary, offers a dramatic illustration of the vulnerability of lay estates. They were never fixed units; instead, their dimensions fluctuated according to the changing tempo of pressures from politics, religion, and economic change. These demands, moreover, accelerated the centrifugal force exerted on the patrimony by the family. They were not unimportant and at times could be the most critical factors in determining a family's wealth and status. Their effect, however, was less constant than that made generation after generation by widows, siblings,

---

253; and Rodney H. Hilton, *A Medieval Society: The West Midlands at the End of the Thirteenth Century* (London, 1966), 23–64.

[37] For Braose, see Wilfred L. Warren, *King John* (Berkeley and Los Angeles, 1978), 184–187; and *EB*, 7, 21, 108. For Ferrers, see McFarlane, *The Nobility*, 254–256. For Lancaster, see Natalie Fryde, *The Tyranny and Fall of Edward II, 1321–1326* (Cambridge, 1979), 69–86.

[38] For one example, see *EB*, 141–142; and *HKF*, 1:25–29. Fourteen of the twenty-one baronies were permanently forfeited to the Crown, but of those fourteen, eight had been under the control of foreigners, including Scots or Welsh. A number of baronies in the twelfth century had come under royal control and were used for patronage or for supporting the royal family in the thirteenth century.

[39] Clive H. Knowles, "The Resettlement of England after the Barons' War, 1264–1267," *TRHS*, 5th ser., 32 (1982): 25–41; N. Fryde, *Tyranny*, 69–86; Scott L. Waugh, "The Confiscated Lands of the Contrariants in Gloucestershire and Herefordshire, in 1322: An Economic and Social Study" (Ph.D. thesis, University of London, 1975).

and noninheriting children. The family itself posed the greatest threat to the integrity of the lay estate, and there was a real danger that it would be whittled away within a few generations.

FAMILY STRATEGIES FOR CONSOLIDATION AND ACCUMULATION

If family relations threatened the estate, they also offered a means of protecting it. Landholders wanted to acquire new land to modulate the impact of these demands and to harmonize the contradictory impulses of patrilineage and diverging devolution. In many cases, that could be done by straightforward purchase. But acquisition was more often a complex social process, achieved through and involving landholders in networks of clientage, neighborhood, and family. Gifts, inheritance, and marriage were equally important devices for replenishing estates. The relationships they created, moreover, were crucial for the maintenance of social cohesion among landholders as well as for the preservation of individual patrimonies.

A cultural framework defined by secular and canon law limited landholders' options. The principles of inheritance, a primary feature of that culture, developed during the first century of English feudalism. With the advent of a legal system based on formal written procedures, those principles hardened into legal rules. Custom lost its malleability. Whereas in the twelfth century, lords and tenants occasionally adjusted inheritance to their particular needs, such adjustment was not possible after Henry II's legal reforms.[40] Inheritance became automatic as the royal courts applied strict rules from which they tolerated little deviation. The change was not unwelcome, for it protected heirs from rapacious lords or relatives, but it did limit the ability of families to act on their own to counteract the effects of diverging devolution.

The law restricted landholders in other ways. Feudal custom as well as the Church forbade adoption in most cases.[41] A man with-

[40] Milsom, *Legal Framework*, 154–186; idem, "Inheritance by Women," 62–69; Holt, "Politics and Property," 13–19; idem, "Feudal Society and the Family I," 197–199, 204–206; Palmer, "Origins," 1–50.

[41] Goody, *Development of the Family*, 48–82. In England, Glanvill stated emphatically that "only God, not man, can make an heir (*solus Deus heredem facere potest, non homo*)" (*Glanvill* [VII.1], 71, though he was referring to an attempt by a landholder to disinherit one person in favor of another). See also Milsom, *Legal Framework*, 109. Bracton repeated Glanvill's pronouncement but went on to describe a "kind of adoption (*quasi per adoptionem de consensu et voluntate parentum*)" in which "a wife has had a child by someone other than her husband, and where, though this is in fact

out a male heir could not extend the patriline, circumvent female inheritance, or prevent an escheat by creating an heir. Indeed, English law limited a landholder's options even more than canon law. According to the Church, children born to a couple before they married were legitimized by the marriage. English barons, however, steadfastly refused to accept the Church's position and denied such children the right to inherit.[42] Furthermore, an English landholder could not bequeath land, only chattels. He had no means of directing the descent of his lands after he died. He could grant land only inter vivos.[43] Provisions that he wished to make for daughters, younger sons, or brothers thus reduced the resources available to him. Finally, once such grants had been made, English law had no right of *retrait lignagier* by which his heir could recover alienated lands.[44] He could only hope to strike a bargain with his relatives.

During much of the thirteenth century, therefore, families lacked legal devices to help them rationalize the distribution of land within the family and reduce its costs. Over that century, families and their lawyers, along with the king and judges, gradually refined the rules governing possession and inheritance. By 1300 legal instruments were available to families that gave them greater discretion over the use and descent of family lands. In the mean-

---

true, the husband has taken the child into his house, avowed him and raised him as his son, or if he has not avowed him expressly has not turned him away; he will be adjudged legitimate and his father's heir, whether the husband does not know that the child is not his or is in doubt, because he is born of the wife, [that is] provided it can be presumed that he could have fathered him" (Bracton, 2:184, 186). The barony of Chiselborough descended in this way (*EB*, 34; Bracton, 2:186–187; *CRR*, 13:4–5 [no. 24]).

[42] Richard H. Helmholz, "Bastardy Litigation in Medieval England," *American Journal of Legal History* 13 (1969): 360–383; Pollock and Maitland, *History of English Law*, 2:396–398; Searle, "Seigneurial Control," 26–27; Bracton, translator's introduction by Thorne, 1:xv–xvii.

[43] Michael M. Sheehan, *The Will in Medieval England: From the Conversion of the Anglo-Saxons to the End of the Thirteenth Century* (Toronto, 1963), 107–119, 266–281; Bean, *Decline*, 29–31; Holt, "Feudal Society and the Family I," 197–199, 204–206. The statement made here corrects the misstatement I made in "Marriage, Class, and Royal Lordship in England under Henry III," *Viator* 16 (1985): 190: "He could not grant land out of his patrimony . . ." It should read, "He could *only* grant land . . ."

[44] Pollock and Maitland, *History of English Law*, 1:344, 2:446; Cooper, "Patterns of Inheritance and Settlement," 253–254, 303; Ralph E. Giesey, "Rules of Inheritance and Strategies of Mobility in Prerevolutionary France," *American Historical Review* 82 (1977): 271–278.

time they relied on three primary strategies to consolidate and to extend their patrimonies.

Patronage was one. Families felt the power of the monarchy not only through forfeiture, but also through gifts of lands, assets, and rights. The most obvious examples of accumulation through patronage occurred within the royal family. Henry III, for example, constructed sizable patrimonies for his brother, Richard of Cornwall; for his brother-in-law, Simon de Montfort; and for his younger son, Edmund of Lancaster, out of the lands of baronies that fell into his hands for one reason or another.[45] Favorites also gained from royal generosity. Early in the thirteenth century, William de Briwerre and his family acquired three baronies from the Crown, while in a display of excessive generosity, Edward II granted Gaveston virtually the same baronies that Richard of Cornwall had held.[46] These grants were exceptional, and by the thirteenth century kings seldom raised men from the dust directly to the nobility. Most members of the elite sought royal gifts to help offset the loss of land and income. The Clare and Mortimer families offer good examples of the way in which a family could use royal patronage to help it build a sound territorial base.[47]

In the second place, families purchased or acquired land.[48] They exploited the freedom of alienation and security of title guaranteed by the royal courts after Henry II's reforms not only to obtain land from strangers but also to pressure their free tenants into giving up their tenancies. In that way they could restore land to their patrimonies that had been granted out as fees or serjeanties the century before.[49] Wealthy families steadily accumulated land through the fourteenth century, so that if they did not suffer a

---

[45] Richard obtained the baronies or portions of Beckley, Berkhampstead, Bradninch, Eye, Launceston, Trematon, and Wallingford (*EB*, 10, 14, 21, 43–44, 60, 90, 93); Montfort received Leicester and Embleton (*EB*, 42, 61); and Edmund later received Embleton, Lancaster, Leicester, Monmouth, Pontefract, and Tutbury (*EB*, 42, 61, 64, 126–127, 138, 149).

[46] Briwerre obtained Horsley, Lavendon, and Odcombe (*EB*, 122, 128, 132).

[47] Altschul, *A Baronial Family*, 17–28; R. R. Davies, *Lordship and Society*, 53–55; Holmes, *Estates*, 10–11. The Mortimer Cartulary shows the importance that the family attached to the forfeited properties it acquired from Henry III and Edward I (BL, Harleian MS 1240, fols. 35, 44–45v).

[48] For examples of baronies passing from one holder to another through purchase, see *EB*, 64, 65, 66, 67, 103–104, 110, 122, 130–131, 150.

[49] Eleanor Searle, "The Abbey of the Conquerors: Defensive Enfeoffment and Economic Development in Anglo-Norman England," in *Proceedings of the Battle Conference on Anglo-Norman England II* (Woodbridge, 1979), 162.

failure of male heirs their estates tended to grow larger. They could also become more compact and efficient.[50] Landholders, moreover, sometimes aimed their acquisition at reconstituting patrimonies fractured by diverging devolution. When Thomas de Berkeley acquired the barony of Beverstone, Gloucestershire, from Thomas ap Adam in 1330, he restored part of his own barony of Berkeley, which had been broken off a century and a half earlier to provide an inheritance for a younger son.[51]

Other families put their acquisitions to work as marriage portions or as endowments for younger sons. Such grants followed a customary distinction between patrimony and acquisition that had developed in England after the Conquest. According to Glanvill, a landholder who held both inherited and purchased land could dispose of the purchase without reference to his heir. Landholders often used acquisitions to provide gifts for their other children.[52] In the twelfth century, the use of purchased lands was complicated by restrictions on grants in substitution and the problems raised by the lord-and-heir rule. By the thirteenth century, however, the distinction had lost its legal force for landholders other than tenants-in-chief. Free land had become fully alienable under the impact of royal justice, though the lord-and-heir rule still applied.

Families nevertheless continued to use acquired land for family grants. The Mortimers, for example, obtained the manor of Much Marcle, head of the barony of Much Marcle in Herefordshire, from the Ballon family after a long, arduous campaign of economic, legal, and physical harassment that began after the Barons' War. Once they finally had possession of the manor in the early fourteenth century, Roger de Mortimer and his mother did not absorb it into the Mortimer patrimony. Instead, they granted it to one of Roger's daughters and her husband for their lives as a marriage portion. The fact is notable because of the effort expended to obtain the manor and because it consisted of 370 acres of demesne arable, 40 acres of demesne meadow, 2 water mills, and rents from free and unfree tenants, all of which was worth more

---

[50] Holmes, *Estates*, 9. McFarlane doubted that the greater nobility spent much on land purchases (*The Nobility*, 83–84). For the development of the Berkeley estate and early enclosures that doubled the value of the lands, see Smyth, *Berkeley Manuscripts*, 1:113–114, 140–142, 154–161, 189–190; and PRO, SC.12/36/11.

[51] *EB*, 13, 14; Smyth, *Berkeley Manuscripts*, 1:53–54. For another example, see *EB*, 103–104.

[52] *Glanvill* (VII.1), 70–73; Milsom, *Legal Framework*, 121, 123, 125, 151; Holt, "Politics and Property," 12–19; idem, "Feudal Society and the Family II," 213–214.

than £100 a year.[53] It would have made a valuable addition to the patrimony, though Roger calculated that it could be put to better use supporting a daughter. It is also possible that he gave it away because he felt uncertain about the title. In any case, families used acquired lands in many different ways. In the mid–thirteenth century, William de Ferrers first granted the manor of Nobottle, Northamptonshire, which his family had acquired from Henry II, to his clerk, Robert de Mercinton, for Robert's life. Second, after Robert's death, he gave a portion of the manor in free marriage to John de Vipont with his daughter Idonia. Finally, the remainder of the manor went to his widow, Margaret, as part of her dower. Margaret, with the permission of her eldest son, Robert de Ferrers, who had the right of reversion, then granted her share in the manor to her younger son, William.[54]

The desire to meet the conflicting aims of diverging devolution and patrilineage, therefore, often determined landholders' participation in the land market and the nature of the market itself to some extent. Landholders wanted to acquire lands to endow younger sons and daughters and to make up for losses incurred through earlier alienations or partitions. As a result, property often circulated within the ranks of lay landholders, not according to the dictates of the market, but rather in response to family and social needs. That circulation was vital to the economic well-being of individuals, their families, and the landholding class as a whole.

The third and most important strategy was marriage. Because diverging devolution affected a group of landholders as well as individuals, they needed to keep the wealth circulated through inheritance and family grants within a group of known families,

[53] PRO, SC.6/1145/6; C.133/9, no. 16. The Mortimer campaign can be traced through William H. Cooke, *Collections towards the History and Antiquities of the County of Hereford, in Continuation of Duncumb's History* (London, 1882), 3:4–7, 23–24; *Placitorum in Domo Capitulari Westmonasterii Asservatorum Abbreviatio* (London, 1811), 168, 175, 234; *CPR, 1258–1266*, 505; *CPR, 1266–1272*, 67; *Calendar of the Plea Rolls of the Exchequer of the Jews* (London, 1929), 3:155, 193; *Year Books of Edward II* (London, 1903), 1:43–48; BL, Lansdowne MS 905, fols. 76–77, 84–84v; Harleian MS 1240, fol. 20; PRO, KB.27/101 m. 4d, /106 m. 31d, /140 m. 42; Just.1/302 m. 12d, /303 mm. 6, 21; CP.40/78 m. 47d, /80 m. 26d, /81 m. 54; SC.8/343/16, 184. For the grant in marriage, see *CPR, 1354–1358*, 587; *Rot. Orig.*, 1:252; *CFR*, 3:26; and Cokayne, *Complete Peerage*, 6:62–63.

[54] *HKF*, 1:240–242. Another widow obtained her grandson's permission to grant dower land to her granddaughter in marriage (PRO, Just.1/1230A m. 29d). For other examples of families granting lands acquired through royal grants as marriage portions or dowers, see *RH*, 1:13, 15, 59, 65, 71, 92, etc.; Eyton, *Antiquities*, 9:18–27; and *VCH, Berkshire*, 4:532.

where that circulation could, to some extent, be predicted and controlled. And since women's rights to land created much of this movement, one of the most effective devices for channeling wealth in specific directions was marriage. It wove individuals and families throughout the landholding elite into networks of affinity, blood relations, and tenure. Those networks were not accidental. Landholders used marriage alliances to contain and to manipulate the potentially hazardous devolution of wealth brought about through family custom. This marriage strategy meant that the marriages of both boys and girls had to be rigorously supervised to prevent marriages that might disrupt the transmission of inheritance, marriage portions, and dowers among families. Women's rights to land created expectations and responsibilities that demanded cooperation between families, and the foremost example of that cooperation is marriage.

At the simplest level, marriage offered an opportunity to acquire land. One family's loss was another's gain, though donors did not give up all hope of reacquiring lands given in marriage. From the husband's standpoint, his wife's marriage portion or inheritance was an acquisition. Families often kept women's land, as it might be called, distinct from the paternal inheritance to endow daughters, younger sons, and widows. In at least two passages, Bracton implies that families routinely used women's land in this way.[55] And his statements were borne out in practice. In the twelfth century, Odard of Bamburgh, the sheriff of Northumberland, granted land to his daughter Gunhilda and her husband as a marriage portion, and they gave the same land in marriage to their daughter Emma and her husband. It then descended to Emma's

[55] The first allusion that I have found occurs in Bracton's explanation of how a dowry is treated in the partition of an inheritance among women. He asks in passing, "And what if a woman in her liege widowhood gives one of her several daughters her whole maritagium [*totum maritagium suum*]?" (Bracton, 2:224). The second is in his discussion of *cui in vita*. While explaining the distinction between grants of a woman's inheritance made by coercion and those for an honest reason, he defines an honest reason as one "where a gift is made to their son or in maritagium with a daughter" (4:31). A defendant in a writ of right in 1220 claimed, albeit unsuccessfully, that the land in question had been granted by his grandfather to an aunt in marriage and that when her descendants failed, the land reverted to his mother as his grandfather's heir. He claimed that *because* he was the youngest of four sons, his elder brothers granted him their right to the marriage portion (*CRR*, 8:213–215). See also Holt, "Politics and Property," 12; and Painter, "Family and the Feudal System," 212–213.

heir, Christina, who gave it to her younger son, Simon.[56] Other families used marriage portions to dower widows. Henry I granted the manor of Badmondisfield, Suffolk, to Sibyl de la Falaise in marriage with Baldwin de Boullers. They had a daughter, but after Sibyl died Baldwin married once again, and on his death his second wife, Margery, received Badmondisfield as her dower. She and Baldwin had a son Stephen, and Stephen's son Robert married a Hillary de Trussebut. Margery outlived her son and grandson, and when she died Badmondisfield went to Hillary as dower. Robert had died childless, so that the manor came into the possession of Sibyl's descendants only on Hillary's death.[57] Families also leased women's lands to outsiders, children, and widows to raise cash and ease economic pressures on the patrimony. Such agreements took a variety of forms and turn up in a wide range of sources, indicating how widespread the practice was.[58]

The imaginative uses that landholders devised for women's lands show the high premium they placed on temporary acquisitions, which enhanced the family's economic options and provided a means of endowing children without disturbing the patrimony. The landscape of lay estates can thus be conceptualized as a mosaic of relatively stable patrimonial centers (*caputs* in the case of baronies) between which drifted parcels of land acquired by marriage, lease, or grant. The flow of land within the interstices was deter-

[56] PRO, KB.26/129 m. 7d; *Book of Fees*, 2:1117–1120, 1122, 1128; Northumberland County Historical Committee, *A History of Northumberland* (Newcastle upon Tyne, 1893–1940), 2:11, 13:158–159. For other examples of familial grants of marriage portions, see *CIPM*, 1:304; PRO, C.132/15, no. 19; Just.1/623 m. 13; /624 m. 16; *CIPM*, 2:305; Eyton, *Antiquities*, 2:222–225; *EB*, 62, 65–66; *CPR, 1292–1301*, 599; Cokayne, *Complete Peerage*, 4:118 n. c, 5:442 n. d, 6:665 n. n; H. C. Maxwell Lyte, "Burci, Falaise and Martin," *SANHS* 65 (1920): 16–20; George T. O. Bridgeman, "Some Account of the Families of Beysin, Morehall, and Clopton, Lords of Billingsley, Co. Salop," *Transactions of the Shropshire Archaeological and Natural History Society* 1 (1878): 286, 288; *Beauchamp Cartulary*, xlv; Dugdale, *Monasticon*, 5:437 (to younger son); and two cases involving the Ferrers family in *Close Rolls*, 6:219; Stewart-Brown, "Chester," 31; *Book of Fees*, 2:969, 975; Cokayne, *Complete Peerage*, 4:196–197, 5:305–310, 340–342; *EB*, 61–62.

[57] *CRR*, 16:313–316 (no. 1611); *VCH, Essex*, 7:149; *CIPM*, 1:166, 318, 809; John Horace Round, "Gaynes in Upminster," *TEAS*, n.s. 11 (1909): 98–100; idem, "The Manor of Colne Engaine," *TEAS*, n.s. 8 (1900): 192–198.

[58] For examples, see PRO, C.132/11, no. 15; *CIPM*, 1:220; *Close Rolls*, 6:513; PRO, E.210/127; CP.25(1)/74/26/595; /193/4/207; /282/7/152, 153; E.368/44 m. 12d; E.159/49 m. 6; DL.27/56; E.13/10 mm. 2, 4; /22 m. 14d; Just.1/1202 m. 4; KB.26/140 m. 15d and /185 m. 15; *Percy Chartulary*, ed. M. T. Martin (London, 1911), 441–442 (no. MXLVI); BL, Egerton Charters, 785; *CChR*, 2:133.

mined partly by economic necessity and partly by family affection or loyalty. In some cases, the parcels were absorbed into the patrimony, but often they were set adrift once again, especially by marriage or grant to younger daughters and sons. While in the custody of the patriline, those parcels could be put to economic service through leases. Clearly, in such a scheme there was a fine balance among demography, endowments, acquisitions, and economic ruin. It cannot be said that every landholder foresaw the delicacy of the balance or acted rationally with regard to the estate. Yet it seems plausible to assert that most perceived a difference between the longevity of the patrimony and temporary acquisitions in which the latter could ideally be used to protect the former. Families were on the lookout for such opportunities. And by the end of the thirteenth century, when such lands were granted out, they could be tethered to the patrimony by conditional grants that provided for the kind of reversion traditionally contained in marriage grants.

The temptation to profit from the alienation of marriage portions and dowers was so great in the thirteenth century that it prompted legislation and royal intervention intended to protect the interests of reversioners. In midcentury, the barons complained that recipients alienated lands that had been granted in marriage, even if there was no heir, thereby depriving the donors of the right of reversion. On other occasions, the king acted to prevent widows from alienating their dowers to the disinheritance of their children.[59] These complaints and the grants that lay behind them reveal the dual interest of landholders in family grants. On the one hand, as donors they did not want to loosen restraints on the alienation of dowers and dowries in order to protect their rights of reversion. On the other, as donees they wanted as much latitude as possible over lands they acquired in marriage in order to enjoy fully the economic benefits. In either case, their actions were circumscribed by custom and law.

Marriage itself was subject to such restraints. The clearest restrictions were those of the Church, which had established definite criteria for a valid marriage by the beginning of the thirteenth century.[60] The marriage was accomplished through the exchange of

[59] PRO, E.13/17 m. 12d.

[60] Much has been written in recent years about the development of the canon law on marriage. The following works have been used for this study: Helmholz, *Marriage Litigation*; Henry Ansgar Kelly, *Love and Marriage in the Age of Chaucer* (Ithaca, 1975), 163–176; John W. Baldwin, *Masters, Princes, and Merchants: The Social Views*

MARRIAGE, KINSHIP, AND PROPERTY

words of present consent. The Church emphasized that consent must be freely given for the marriage to be valid and held as invalid any vows given under duress or deception.[61] A match could not be forced on an unwilling partner. Validity, however, depended not only on consent but also on the relationship between the two partners. The Church forbade consanguineous marriages, that is, between individuals related within four degrees. Affinity, usually arising because of marriage, likewise impeded an individual from legitimately marrying any of his or her affinal relations within four degrees.[62] The prohibition is important because it meant, theoretically, that close cousins could not marry to rejoin lands partitioned through female inheritance or to reabsorb dowries. Nor could a man who failed to have heirs by one wife, and so acquire her inheritance, marry her sister and try again. The evidence concerning the observation of these prohibitions by baronial landholders is ambiguous. Barons certainly did not treat them as absolute barriers and arranged some marriages clearly within the prohibited degrees. Such marriages, however, were not frequent, and landholders did not flout the Church's rules.[63]

In order to conform to those rules, marriage had to be exogamous at the level of the family. Women married out, and men brought in their wives. Marriage, however, did not sever all ties between the landholder and his daughters, sisters, or aunts. Tenurial obligations bound the families together for three generations at least. A landholder was thus likely to have some formal association with his in-laws throughout his life: to the husbands of his sisters, aunts, and nieces, to his sons-in-law, and to his wife's father, brothers, or uncles.[64] In this manner, tenure and kinship tended to reinforce one another.

Within this context of formal rules, the marriages of English landholders conformed to a set of less clearly enunciated but none-

---

of Peter de Chanter and His Circle (Princeton, 1970), 1:332–337; Michael M. Sheehan, "Formation and Stability of Marriage," 228–263; and idem, "Choice of Marriage Partner in the Middle Ages: Development and Mode of Application of a Theory of Marriage," *Studies in Medieval and Renaissance History*, n.s. 1 (1978): 3–33.

[61] Helmholz, *Marriage Litigation*, 90–94; Sheehan, "Choice of Marriage Partner," 8–16.

[62] Pollock and Maitland, *History of English Law*, 2:364–399, esp. 386–389; Helmholz, *Marriage Litigation*, 77–87; Goody, *Development of the Family*, 134–146.

[63] For an example of a marriage between first cousins, see George Ormerod, *The History of the County Palatine and City of Chester*, ed. Thomas Helsby, 2d ed., 3 vols. (London, 1875–1882), 2:42, 3:384–388 (Ardern-Wasteneys).

[64] See Milsom, "Inheritance by Women," 71, 83, for the tenurial scheme.

theless equally powerful preferences. To begin with, landholders generally arranged the marriages of their sons and daughters to protect and acquire land. Regional interests also weighed heavily in contracting marriages. Thus, a landholder seeking to consolidate his territorial interests might seek a wife for himself or wives and husbands for his children from families with lands near his own and use dowries or inheritance to round out his estate. Regional interests could dovetail with yet another consideration: politics. Marriages were arranged to consolidate relations among landholders who shared the administration and power in a county or region. Among the wealthiest barons, that consolidation occurred at the level of the kingdom as a whole. Another consideration was status. Although status was only crudely defined during the thirteenth and early fourteenth centuries, marriages seem to have conformed to gradations of wealth and power. Within the elite, differences in status among knights, ministers, and magnates were not insuperable, and acceptable marriage partners could be found in a number of landed families. Nevertheless, barons *tended* to marry into baronial families, knights into knightly families, and so forth. That fact, however, may be deceptive. That is, a baron may not have sought a marriage alliance with another baronial family *because* they were both barons, but because their families had intermarried before, because they had a specific reason for a marriage alliance, or because of a familiarity arising out of shared social, administrative, or economic interests. In other words, they might have identified themselves as social equals not because of a title or rank, but because of their community of interests. Alliances were formed on several levels and were solidified and renewed in different ways.

Marriages, therefore, were socially endogamous; that is, landholders tried to arrange marriages for their children within a circle of near social equals, distant cousins, or neighbors. Endogamy was intended not merely to exclude outsiders who might be socially undesirable, but more importantly to help solve the problems posed by demography and inheritance customs. Practiced over many generations, endogamy created a consanguineous group through which claims to inheritance, property, and lordship were widely diffused. Landholders created a kinship matrix within which land fragmented by diverging devolution could circulate to the mutual benefit of the families bound by marriage and kinship and without fear that it would be siphoned off to unknown or undesirable outsiders. Inmarriage, moreover, refined the perception of group interest by identifying the preservation of wealth with the social cohesion achieved through kinship and the choice of marriage partners. By its very nature, kinship allowed affiliation with different groups at different levels. A loose sense of identity thus tied wealthy barons and knights together, but within that larger network existed clusters of landholders united by kinship, clientage, and vicinity. Identity depended on which strands an individual wished to stress. Similarly, kinship suggested but did not dictate political alliances. Leaders of political opposition certainly tried to mobilize kin and clients. Yet because open defiance of the Crown could be so traumatic, individuals sometimes balked at joining despite ties of kinship or clientage connecting them to the rebel leaders. Likewise, few marriages were arranged with an eye toward high politics or opposition to the Crown. Such opposition was relatively spontaneous compared to marital arrangements that aimed at longer-range goals.[65] Taking all of these factors into consideration, it is clear that families wanted as much freedom as possible in marrying their children, for on those arrangements depended the maintenance of their wealth and power.

The role of endogamy stands out clearly in brother-sister co-marriages and cousin marriages. A co-marriage could take the form of either marriages between brothers of one family and sisters of another or marriages between the sister and brother of one family and the brother and sister of another—a "sister exchange" (Figure 1.1).[66] The latter was most ideal in terms of preparing for the accidents of inheritance. Not only did dowries balance one another, but it guaranteed that property would descend within the two families, unless both couples were childless. In 1237, for example, Henry III confirmed an agreement in which Peter de Brus, baron of Skelton, married his son Peter and his eldest daughter, Joan, to Hillary and Peter, daughter and son of Peter de Mauley and Isabel, heiress of the barony of Mulgrave.[67] Arrangements like

---

[65] Holt has warned that stressing any particular family tie over others will "convey a false impression" of political significance (James C. Holt, *The Northerners: A Study in the Reign of King John* [Oxford, 1961], 67; and see idem, "Feudal Society and the Family III"). For an excellent analysis of the difficulty in mobilizing opposition, see John R. Maddicott, *Thomas of Lancaster, 1307–1322: A Study in the Reign of Edward II* (Oxford, 1970), 259–317, esp. 276, 295–297.

[66] For "sister exchange," see Fox, *Kinship and Marriage*, 87. For examples in medieval England, see Milsom, "Inheritance by Women," 79–80; McFarlane, *The Nobility*, 86; Altschul, *A Baronial Family*, 46; and *HKF*, 1:57.

[67] *EB*, 67, 77; *CPR, 1232–1247*, 196, 398. The strategy failed because both of the Brus children died without direct heirs.

this were fairly common within the landed elite, though they did not all come about through foresight and planning.[68] Opportunism sometimes played a part. Aubrey de Vere (d. 1194) acquired the marriage of Isabel, the daughter and heir of Walter de Bolbec,

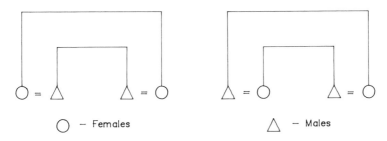

○ — Females   △ — Males

FIGURE 1.1. Brother-Sister Co-marriages

from the king and married her to his eldest son, Aubrey. Isabel, however, died without children in 1206. At that point, Aubrey's younger brother Robert quickly married Isabel's aunt Isabel who was now one of two coheirs to the barony of Whitchurch. The match turned out splendidly for Robert. He acquired half of the barony, and when Isabel's younger sister and coheir died without heirs, her half likewise went to Isabel and Robert.[69]

This last example demonstrates that effects similar to those of brother-sister marriages could be achieved through matches between siblings and cousins. These arrangements produced more complex kinship networks, as illustrated in Figure 1.2. For three generations, Mortimer men and women drew wives and husbands from a pool of cousins descended from or allied by marriage to the Marshal family. Ralph de Mortimer's two sons, Roger and Hugh, married Marshal descendants early in the thirteenth century, giving each line a claim in the Marshal patrimony. In the following generation, Edmund married his son Roger to Joan, great-granddaughter of Walter de Lacy, baron of Weobley, and his

[68] *ERF*, 1:167–168 (Dive-Mucegros); *EB*, 17 (Bolam-Cauz), 35 (Gloucester-Ulster), 47, 131 (Grelley-Longchamp); George Wrottesley, ed., "The Chetwynd Chartulary," *William Salt Society* 12 (1891): 255; Cokayne, *Complete Peerage*, 6:109–112 (Chetwynd-Grendon), 5:127 n. a, 132 (Mandeville–Fitz Walter), 6:349, 8:538 (Martin-Hastings), 12:2:299–301 (Wake-Beauchamp); *EB*, 24; *CRR*, 11:247 (no. 1223); 12:66–67, 177–179, 324–325 (nos. 360, 866, 1576) (Multon-Lucy). Before they married, Simon de Berevill and the widow of William de Huscote agreed to a marriage between their sons and daughters by their first marriages (*CRR*, 3:306).

[69] *EB*, 52, 98; Cokayne, *Complete Peerage*, 10:208–210. Aubrey Junior died without children, so Robert also inherited the barony of Hedingham.

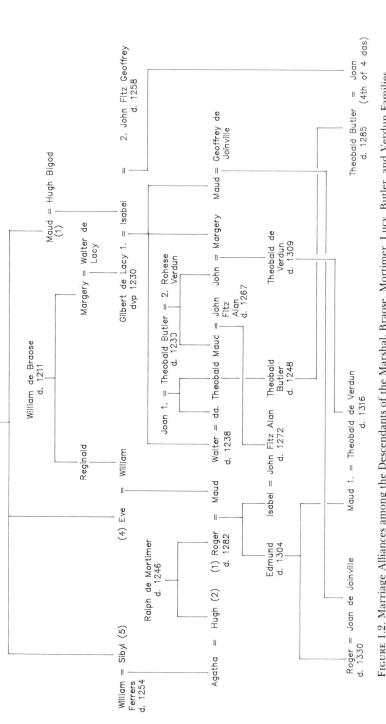

FIGURE 1.2. Marriage Alliances among the Descendants of the Marshal, Braose, Mortimer, Lucy, Butler, and Verdun Families

daughter Maud to Walter's great-great-grandson, Theobald. Theobald and Joan were descended from Walter's granddaughters and coheirs, Margery and Maud respectively. In this case, marriage gave the Mortimer patriline a stake in half of the lordship of Ludlow, which replaced Wigmore as the center of the Mortimer empire, and it laid the groundwork for the eventual reunification of the lordship through purchase from their cousins. Those matches were the product of yet another set of cousin marriages between descendants of the Marshal and Braose families earlier in the thirteenth century.[70] This kind of arrangement is schematized in Figure 1.3. Though it was several steps removed from brother-sister marriages, it reproduced the contingencies for keeping inheritances within a set of kin when property descended through two or more sisters, and it formed alliances between siblings and collateral lines of cousins.[71]

In other cases, marriage directly allied two collateral lines, as in Figures 1.4 and 1.5.[72] Alliances of this kind seem to have been rarer than those described above, but it is difficult to arrive at any statistical certainty. It is clear, however, that even when blood relations were present, they were not necessarily the determining factor in arranging marriages. When Roger de Mortimer (d. 1330) wanted to marry his daughter Catherine to Thomas, the minor son and heir of Guy de Beauchamp, he had to obtain a papal dispensation because the couple were cousins, both descended from the Roger de Mortimer who died in 1214. They were also descendants of William Marshal because both families had recently married Marshal descendants. Finally, the couple was distantly related through the Braose family. There were thus excellent reasons for the families to intermarry. The immediate aim of the match, however, was to settle a territorial dispute. Thomas de Beauchamp was

[70] Dugdale, *Monasticon*, 6:1:351; *EB*, 7–8, 95; Cokayne, *Complete Peerage*, 1:239–240, 2:448–449, 4:199, 9:274–283, 10:364 n. a, 12:2:246–250; Eyton, *Antiquities*, 3:38–41; George E. Watson, "The Families of Lacy, Geneva, Joinville and La Marche," *Genealogist*, n.s. 21 (1905): 1–16, 73–82, 163–172, 234–243.

[71] A represents the Mortimer-Braose-Ferrers marriages in Figure 1.3; B is based on the Valance-Balliol-Hastings marriages (Cokayne, *Complete Peerage*, 6:345–348, 647 n. k, 10:381 n. c; *CPR, 1266–1272*, 323; *CIPM*, 1:719; *EB*, 25, 118–119; John R. S. Phillips, *Aymer de Valence, Earl of Pembroke, 1307–1324: Baronial Politics in the Reign of Edward II* [Oxford, 1972], 2–3); C represents the Mortimer-Verdun-Joinville marriages; and D the Braose-Marshal-Lacy marriages in Figure 1.3.

[72] For the Clifford marriages and descent, see Eyton, *Antiquities*, 5:147; *EB*, 35–36, 115; Cokayne, *Complete Peerage*, 5:639 n. c, 642 n. c. The Longspee descent from Rosamond is questionable; see *DNB*, s.v. "Clifford, Rosamond."

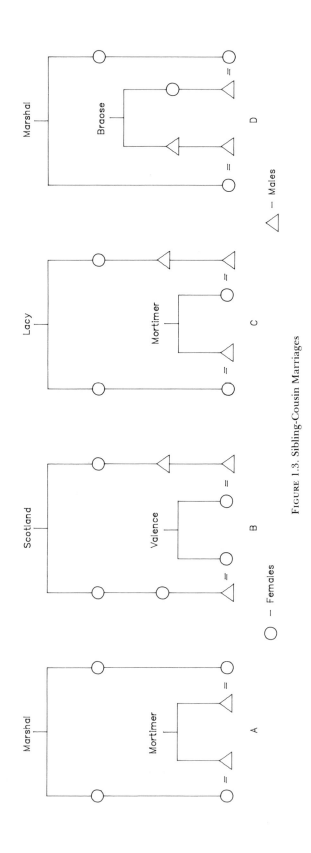

FIGURE 1.3. Sibling-Cousin Marriages

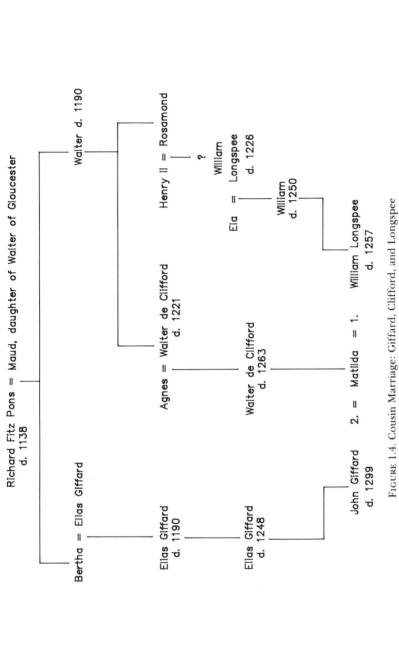

FIGURE 1.4. Cousin Marriage: Giffard, Clifford, and Longspee

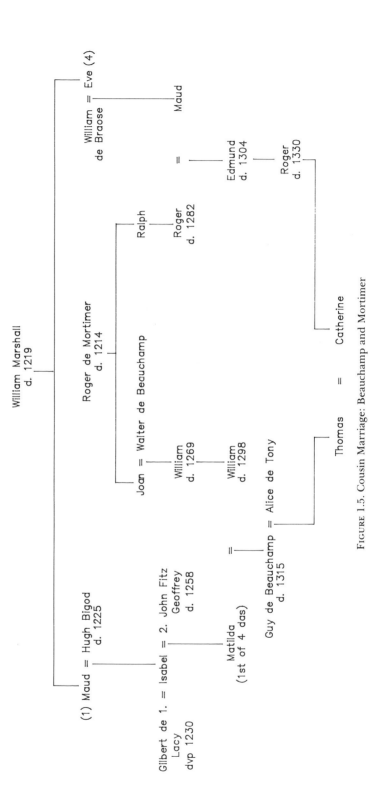

FIGURE 1.5. Cousin Marriage: Beauchamp and Mortimer

the heir to the Tony estate, and the Mortimers had been locked in a fierce struggle with the Tonys over Elfael in Wales. The dispute stretched back to the mid–thirteenth century and had its origins in the partition of the Braose patrimony. Roger de Mortimer seized the opportunity presented by Thomas's minority to marry the boy to his daughter Catherine and thereby settle the dispute by merging the family claims, as the dispensation noted.[73] The bilateral nature of descent in medieval England enhanced the importance of marriage because couples could fuse competing or complementary claims to property. Cousin marriages thus opened the door to reconstituting inheritances fragmented by marriage or women's inheritance. Furthermore, matches between cousins or between siblings and cousins offered another way of forging the multiplicity of ties to kin, neighbors, and associates that families valued so highly.

Although some cousin marriages occurred simply because the pool of potential partners was small, most were probably intentional. Genealogical information was widely disseminated in the ranks of English landholders, and the effects of inheritance customs widely known and experienced.[74] The pleading of writs of right, for example, shows that genealogical memory could stretch back over a century to retrace the path that land ought to follow. Marriages and births formed critical junctures that could divert property in different directions. How was the property disposed of, whether as marriage portion, inheritance, or dower? Who were the children? Who was the eldest child? How many daughters or sisters inherited? Who died without heirs?—these were the questions that ultimately determined the validity of claims and preoccupied contestants and juries. They were of the utmost concern to families, not only looking back in the law courts, but also looking ahead and trying to anticipate the future descent of property. It is reasonable to assume that, within limits, families knew their kinship relations, were well aware of the possibilities of inheritance attached to them, and sought marriage alliances accordingly.

Those strategies, however, would be successful only if a couple

---

[73] *Calendar of Ancient Petitions Relating to Wales*, ed. William Rees (Cardiff, 1975), 369 (no. 220); Bliss, *Papal Letters*, 2:186; Moor, *Knights*, 3:218–219; Cokayne, *Complete Peerage*, 5:433–434, 437, 580 n. f, 9:590 n. c, 12:2:369–370, 372 n. g, 374; *Beauchamp Cartulary*, xxiii–xxiv, xlv–xlvi, lviii.

[74] Holt, "Feudal Society and the Family III," 5–7. On the issue of genealogical knowledge in complex societies, see Françoise Héritier, *L'exercice de la parenté* (Paris, 1981), 146–150, 162–166.

produced a surviving heir. That necessity, coupled with cultural pressures and personal desire to marry, meant that both men and women often remarried after the death of a spouse, sometimes spawning collateral lines of half blood. Indeed, Bracton's lengthy explanation of how to calculate the nearness of heirs is predicated on two assumptions: first, that men and women remarried and had additional children, and second, that they endowed those children with land. From Table 1.3 it is easy to see why problems arose. Of the widows who remarried, at least twelve (18.5 percent) produced a second set of children, while eight of the husbands' second wives who survived them and remarried had additional children (27.6 percent).[75] Alice, sister and heir of Robert de Tony (d. 1309), for instance, married three times and produced children by all three marriages, though the heir to the Tony estate was her son Thomas de Beauchamp. Inheritance by the half-blood could be important to the survival of an estate, for at least three baronies descended through half-blood lines after the other failed. Even with several marriages, however, the quest for a male heir could end in frustration.[76]

The high rate of remarriage can also be attributed to the eco-

TABLE 1.3 MARRIAGES AND REMARRIAGES IN 81 BARONIES

	First Marriages	Husbands' Second Marriage
N	337	62
Widowed Wives	181	52
% of N	53.7	83.9
Widows Who Remarried	65	29
% of Widowed Wives	35.9	55.8
Widowed Husbands Who Remarried	62	—
% of N	18.4	—
Survivor Not Known	94	
% of N	27.9	

[75] Bracton, 2:190–200. See also Pollock and Maitland, *History of English Law*, 2:302–305. Thirteen Clare daughters contracted a total of twenty-two marriages, and eight married more than once (Altschul, *A Baronial Family*, 44).

[76] Cokayne, *Complete Peerage*, 12:1:774 n. i, 12:2:370–372, 960. Roger de Quincy (d. 1264) married three times but failed to produce a male heir (*EB*, 61, 63; Cokayne, *Complete Peerage*, 12:2:751–754).

nomic attractions of marriage to a widow. On the death of her third husband, Henry Biset, in 1208, for example, Isolda Pantolf controlled a formidable estate built out of her inheritance, dower lands from three husbands, and the wardship and marriage of Henry's minor heirs, which she purchased from King John for 1,000 marks. It is not surprising to find men competing for her marriage.[77] The winner, William de Huntingfeld, sealed a contract with Isolda in which she granted the wardship of Henry Biset's son and heir along with his inheritance to Huntingfeld, so that he could marry the boy to his daughter Sarah. In return, Huntingfeld took over the responsibility of paying off part of Isolda's debt to the Crown.[78]

It is often assumed that the economic power of women like Isolda made them particularly attractive to younger sons hunting for an endowment. Baronial marriages, however, indicate that there was considerable competition for widows. Barons who wanted to remarry wielded greater influence than their younger relatives, and they used it to secure advantageous matches. Of those sixty-two barons in Table 1.3 who remarried, at least twenty-five (40.3 percent) chose widows. Robert de Brus, baron of Writtle in Essex and lord of Annandale, married Isabel, the daughter of Gilbert de Clare as his first wife. After Isabel died, however, Robert shifted his focus. He chose as his second wife Christian, daughter of William de Ireby, a northern knight. Christian was also the widow of two other northern landholders, Thomas Lascelles and Adam de Gesemouth.[79] The quest for a second wife was no more arbitrary than the search for the first. There, too, regional, political, and family interests played a part in the choice of partners. The Church's rules of affinity, in fact, opened the possibility of creating a fictive kinship through second marriages, which could supply crucial links in family alliances. In the case of the first diagram in Figure 1.6, Ralph de Mortimer was in a sense marrying his brother's wife's aunt when he took Gladys, the widow of Regi-

---

[77] *Pipe Roll, 10 John,* 198–199 (including the right to marry whomever she pleased); *12 John,* 80 (Richard Neville, "pro habenda petitione R. ad Ysold' Biset ut ipsum Ricardum capiat in uirum"). Richard's suit failed.

[78] *Rolls of the Justices in Eyre, Being the Rolls of Pleas and Assizes for Gloucestershire, Warwickshire and Staffordshire, 1221–1222,* ed. Doris Mary Stenton (London, 1940), 105–106 (no. 247); *Pipe Roll, 13 John,* 24; *14 John,* 177; *16 John,* 172.

[79] *EB,* 102; Cokayne, *Complete Peerage,* 2:358–360, 12:2:320–321. Altschul notes that of the eight Clare daughters who remarried, "five married relatively minor English barons" (Altschul, *A Baronial Family,* 45).

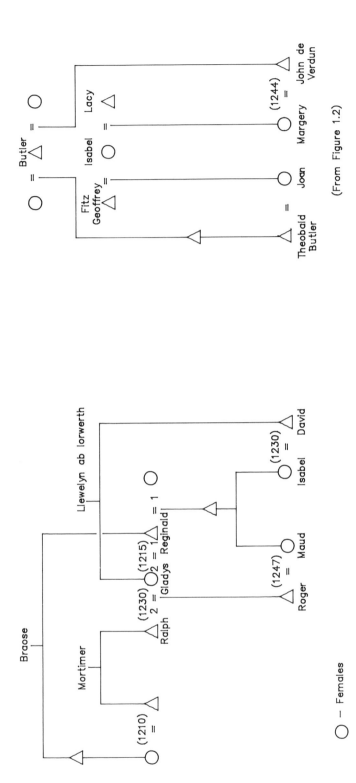

FIGURE 1.6. Linkage through Widows and Half-blood Marriages

---

nald de Braose, for a wife in 1230. The marriage between Gladys's brother David and Isabel de Braose at about the same time laid the foundation for a sibling-cousin alliance when Roger de Mortimer married Maud de Braose in 1247. In the second diagram, marriage allied two sets of parallel half-blood lines. The fictive sibling-cousin alliance was clearly intentional. Isabel's second husband, John Fitz Geoffrey, paid the Crown 3,000 marks for the wardship and marriage of Theobald Butler and married the boy to his daughter Joan by Isabel.[80]

As a result of such strategies, land fragmented by female inheritance and by family grants flowed into the hands of other baronial families. Altogether, 68 of the original baronial families acquired 115 portions of baronies, whether through grant, purchase, or marriage. Of the 57 single heiresses to baronies, 28 (49.1 percent) married other barons, leading to the merger of 16 baronies. At least 83 descendants of 61 of the original baronies married baronial heiresses. Not all of these marriages resulted in a lasting consolidation of the properties because not all produced heirs to both parts. Yet marriage potentially counteracted the centrifugal force of diverging devolution by keeping partitioned land within the ranks of baronial landholders, especially in conjunction with the right of reversion in women's inheritance. Marriage to widows acted in a like manner, keeping dowers and, later, land held jointly within the ranks of kin, of neighboring lords, or of the elite in general. For those reasons, marriage was an essential tool in the management of family wealth and in the maintenance of the power of a local group or class.

The way in which marriage, descent, and grants guided land in certain directions can be seen in the Mohun family. Reginald de Mohun (d. 1258), baron of Dunster, married twice and had a son by each wife (see Figure 1.7). His second wife was Isabel, widow of Gilbert Basset and daughter of Sibyl, one of the Marshal coheirs,

[80] First diagram: Cokayne, *Complete Peerage*, 1:22, 9:275–276, 280–281; *EB*, 7–8, 21–22. Second diagram: Cokayne, *Complete Peerage*, 2:448–449, 5:433–434, 437, 12:2:246–251; G. E. Watson, "Lacy, Geneva, Joinville and La Marche," 1–3; *CPR, 1247–1258*, 49, 200, 214, 217; *ERF*, 2:96. The king first granted the wardship to Peter of Savoy. In 1265 Theobald received the king's protection at the instance of his brother-in-law, John de Verdun (*CPR, 1258–1266*, 493). For marriage alliances through affinal relations and especially through widows' remarriage in a much different setting, see Martine Segalen and Philippe Richard, "Marrying Kinsmen in Pays Bigouden Sud, Brittany," *Journal of Family History* 11 (1986): 109–130.

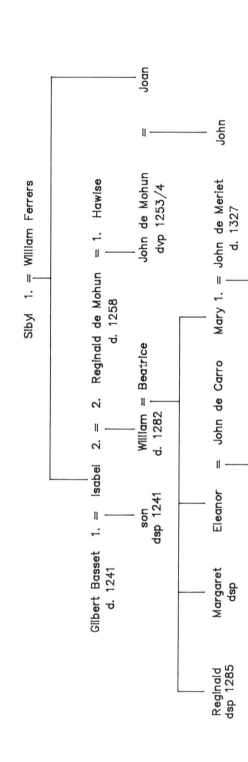

FIGURE 1.7. Descendants of Reginald de Mohun (d. 1258)

by William de Ferrers. Reginald and Isabel's son William thus stood to inherit a portion of the vast Marshal estate.[81]

That inheritance included the manors of Greywell and Mildenhall, Wiltshire. William Marshal had granted Mildenhall to Sibyl and William de Ferrers as a marriage portion. They, in turn, granted it as a marriage portion to Isabel and her second husband, Reginald. Greywell had been in royal custody when Henry III granted it to Gilbert Marshal, one of William's ill-fated sons. Gilbert granted it in marriage to his niece, Isabel, and her first husband, Gilbert Basset. Since the couple's heir did not survive them, and Gilbert Marshal died childless, the manor should have reverted to royal custody. Reginald de Mohun, however, granted both Greywell and Mildenhall to his younger son William and his wife and the heirs of their bodies. The conditional grant was significant.[82]

William de Mohun died in 1282. He had four children, but his son and one of his three daughters died underage, so that his inheritance passed to his surviving daughters, Eleanor and Mary. Eleanor's son died without issue and Mary's daughter died before her father, John Meriet. Meriet therefore held William's lands by curtesy down to his own death in 1327. At that time, the wisdom of Reginald's strategy became clear. Isabel's descendants had died out. Her property was therefore partitioned among her sisters' children, one of whom happened to be Reginald's great-grandson, John de Mohun, since John's grandfather had married Isabel's sister Joan. In other words, Reginald's son John by his first wife married the sister of Reginald's second wife, who thus became a stepmother and sister-in-law all at once. It was yet another variation on the brother-sister alliance, though instead of marrying his brother's wife's sister, John married his *father's* wife's sister. According to the terms of Reginald's grant to William, moreover, the manors of Greywell and Mildenhall reverted to Reginald's heir, John, in 1327. His grant to his younger son thus behaved as a marriage portion and kept possession of the land within the family, even though it involved the inheritance of his second wife. The convoluted strategy paid off: John acquired the two manors as well as a share of Isabel's other lands.[83]

[81] *EB*, 63, 114; Cokayne, *Complete Peerage*, 4:199.

[82] *Book of Fees*, 2:748; Cokayne, *Complete Peerage*, 9:20–21; *CIPM*, 1:500; PRO, C.132/25, no. 15; BL, Egerton MS 3724, fol. 73 (Mohun Cartulary).

[83] Moor, *Knights*, 3:163–164; Greenfield, "Meriet of Meriet," 179, 184–185; *CIPM*, 2:436, 530, 3:415, 7:46.

The marriages and settlements of the Mohuns over the thirteenth century provide an excellent illustration of the advantages of a careful marriage strategy. Marriage was of deep concern to every family. Its choices revolved around the need to produce heirs, to direct the devolution of its property, and to acquire new lands. Those choices, moreover, had important social and political repercussions. The juncture of marriage determined which way land would flow in the event of female inheritance and thus determined the distribution of wealth between families. Decisions about marriage, therefore, were never made in a vacuum and were far too important to be entrusted to the participants alone.

Choice, Consent, and the Formation
of Marriages in the Elite

Choice of marriage partners was critical. Families could do little about the sex or survival of their children. They did have the power to select marriage partners, and through that selection they could erect a framework for the descent of their lands. Each marriage balanced contrary hopes and fears: the hope that female inheritance would bring property to the family and the apprehension that the male line might fail and the patrimony be partitioned among women. Astute marriages ensured that if the latter transpired, property would be distributed within a known kin or social group and thereby reinforce the local patterns of lordship and power. Those considerations directed the hunt for marriage partners. Of course, a variety of factors entered into the plans for marrying children, and some alliances were purely coincidental. Nevertheless, there is compelling evidence that families were well aware of the effects of descent, inheritance, and diverging devolution and used marriage as a means of trying to control those forces, however imperfectly. It meant that children's marriages had to be closely supervised.

Families, moreover, had to cooperate in that supervision and in the arrangement of marriages. This cooperation can be glimpsed in the inmarrying over several generations in the descent of the Marshal, Chester, Arundel, and Huntingdon inheritances, all of which were partitioned among female heirs. Within roughly four generations, the descendants of these four families, who intermarried at a few points, contracted more than 122 marriages, including the second marriages of both men and women. In 86 (70.5 percent) of the marriages, the descendant's partner was also of baronial rank. In addition, 15 of the marriages involved two members of the descent group (related by either blood or marriage), as in the Mohun example. The marriages of the 16 original co-heiresses of the four families, moreover, were all arranged before the death of the last male heir in each line, so that the endogamy was intentional, rather than the product of random fortune hunting. In at least 10 cases, widows or husbands remarried, had children, and thereby established collateral lines of half blood. The remarriages of widows thus fit into this pattern of endogamy as well. Of the baronial widows known to have remarried, at least 8 married another baron.[84] At the level of a single family, the marriages of the Mortimers vividly illustrate how matchmaking could consolidate a patrimony and weave a powerful network of blood, lordship, and affinity.[85]

Social endogamy was not limited to the ranks of baronial landholders. Knightly families pursued similar goals, and inmarrying was common among regional or occupational groups.[86] Some of the heiresses of portions of baronies, for example, married into local society. Those marriages augmented the pool of land in the hands of middling landholders and bolstered their control over the county or region. At least forty-six portions of twenty-four baronies partitioned by female inheritance migrated via marriage into knightly families of the same region.[87] The four sisters and coheirs of Peter de Brus, baron of Skelton, married northerners, and the

[84] The figures presented here differ from those in my "Marriage, Class, and Royal Lordship," 193, because the latter did not include the marriages of the Clare family. The men who remarried were Roger de Somery (d. 1273), Alan of Galloway (d. 1233), William de Forz (d. 1260), William de Ferrers (d. 1254), William de Vescy, John de Vescy, Reginald de Mohun (d. 1258), Warin de Mountchesney (d. 1255), John de Lacy (d. 1240), Richard de Clare (d. 1262), and Gilbert de Clare (d. 1295). Among the women were Helen, daughter of Llewelyn ab Iorwerth; Constance of Brittany; Isabel and Maud, daughters of William Marshal; Joan, Eleanor, Maud, and Isabel, daughters of William de Ferrers; Joan, daughter of William Fitz Martin; Eleanor, daughter of Reginald Fitz Peter; Margaret, daughter of Roger de Quincy; Margaret, daughter of Thomas de Clare; and Eleanor, Margaret, and Elizabeth, daughters of Gilbert de Clare.

[85] Holmes, *Estates*, 10–19; R. R. Davies, *Lordship and Society*, 53–55, 281–282; Cokayne, *Complete Peerage*, 8:441 n. e, 9:599 n. d; Waugh, "Marriage, Class, and Royal Lordship," 194–195.

[86] See Holt, *Northerners*, 66–70; R. R. Davies, *Lordship and Society*, 48–60; Michael J. Bennett, "A County Community: Social Cohesion amongst the Cheshire Gentry, 1400–1425," *Northern History* 8 (1973): 28–32; idem, *Community, Class and Careerism: Cheshire and Lancashire Society in the Age of Sir Gawain and the Green Knight* (Cambridge, 1983), 26–30; Christopher T. Allmand, *Lancastrian Normandy, 1415–1450: The History of a Medieval Occupation* (Oxford, 1983), 68–69.

[87] These figures include only those husbands for whom information can be obtained in Cokayne, *Complete Peerage*, and Moor, *Knights*.

two daughters and coheirs of one of them also married northern knights. Because of the prestige that one of those knights, Walter de Faucomberg, acquired through his marriage, he was able to marry his son to the daughter of another northern baron, Robert de Ros of Helmsley, Yorkshire, thereby becoming a part of baronial society.[88]

Marriage to an heiress or a wealthy widow could also provide a younger son with a landed endowment, if he could arrange a match. As in the case of marriage to widows, younger sons and outsiders faced competition from baronial heirs. Yet, not all baronial heiresses married barons, and the tendency toward marriages between partners of like status did not altogether preclude advancement by marriage. Most nonbaronial partners of baronial heiresses came from the ranks of wealthy knights or royal ministers whose economic and social position, if not their title and ancestry, placed them near the top of the elite.

The actual formation of a marriage, or the betrothal, required careful negotiation and expression.[89] It demanded the participation and approval of the relations, friends, and dependents of the two families, all of whom were affected by the new constellation of claims created by the marriage. The influence of landholding and endogamy can thus be seen as clearly in the making of an individual match as in the overall pattern of marriages. The attention that the biographer of William Marshal devotes to Marshal's efforts to arrange marriages for his children is a case in point. He comments that William left only one of his daughters unmarried at his death and that he was troubled by the fact that she remained unmarried and hence unprovided for. On his deathbed, therefore, he stated that he wanted her to have, so his biographer relates, 30 *librates* of land and 200 marks to ensure that she would prosper.[90] Otherwise,

[88] *EB*, 77–78; Cokayne, *Complete Peerage*, 5:267–276 (Faucomberg); Moor, *Knights*, 1:68–69, 2:3–4, 39, 4:279–280, 5:62–63. The marriages of Faucomberg's son provide additional evidence of endogamy. Isabel de Ros died, and Walter Junior took as his second wife Alice, daughter of John de Killingham, a local knight. On Walter's death in 1318, she married another Yorkshireman, Ralph de Bulmer, as his second wife. In the meantime, Walter Junior's youngest son John had married Eve, Robert de Bulmer's daughter by his first wife.

[89] McFarlane, *The Nobility*, 84–86; Holmes, *Estates*, 42–45; Palmer, "Contexts of Marriage," 42–67.

[90] *L'histoire de Guillaume le Maréchal, comte de Striguil et de Pembroke, régent d'Angleterre de 1216 à 1219*, ed. Paul Meyer (Paris, 1901), 256. A bequest of land was not possible, but the statement can perhaps be taken as an instruction directed to his

he had ensured that each of his daughters had a worthy husband. The success of endogamy, moreover, depended on the control of the marriages of sons as much as on those of daughters. Marshal's biographer points out that William initiated negotiations with Baldwin de Béthune, the count of Aumale, for a marriage between his eldest son and one of Baldwin's daughters and attended closely to the details. It was an important marriage and received universal approval, including the king's consent.[91] At a much later date, the chronicler of the Mortimer family of Wigmore likewise noted the arrangements that the family made for the marriages of its sons and daughters and digressed at one point to expound proudly on Matilda de Braose's glorious ancestry on both sides of the family.[92]

These narratives relate the basic elements of marriage alliances that were legally solidified in contracts. The most essential, and best-known, feature of the contract involved property: the grant of a marriage portion and/or the guarantee of dower land if the wife survived her husband. Baldwin de Béthune, for example, gave his daughter Alice all of his lands in England in marriage with William Marshal's son. Other clauses display the intensity of a family's interest in a particular alliance and its awareness of the fragility of such arrangements. The Marshal-Aumale contract specified that if Alice died, then William Junior would marry Baldwin's other daughter, or that if William died, then Alice would marry Marshal's next heir, Richard. A marriage contract between Ivo de Dene and Fulk de Oyri offers a good example of a landholder eager to make an alliance with a certain family. The contract specified a grant of land and a marriage between Ivo's son Nicholas and Fulk's daughter Isabel, or Fulk's niece Isabel, or a daughter of Robert de Molton, Fulk's kinsman, or any other kin of

---

eldest son. William, his son and heir, did in fact arrange a marriage for her, as the biographer notes (207–208).

[91] Ibid., 208 n. 2; Cokayne, *Complete Peerage*, 1:354 n. c, 10:367; *Rot. Chart.*, 112–113 (confirmation). The biographer mistakenly reported that Baldwin had only one daughter, but the contract clearly shows that he had two. His statement that the marriage was approved by all is borne out by the witnesses to John's confirmation of the contract: the bishop of Norwich; the earls of Arundel, Chester, and Salisbury; Hugh le Bigod; Gilbert de Clare; Thomas Basset, and Peter de Stoke. The biographer does not mention it, but William also arranged marriages for his younger sons during his lifetime. See Cokayne, *Complete Peerage*, 10:365–377; and Altschul, *A Baronial Family*, 43–44.

[92] She was the wife of Roger de Mortimer (d. 1282). See Dugdale, *Monasticon*, 6:348–355, esp. 351.

Fulk without disparagement.[93] Ivo also promised that if Nicholas died, then he would grant Fulk the marriage of his son Reginald, and that if Reginald died, then his son Simon, and so forth. Like Ivo, Marshal, and Aumale, many landholders realized that there was a good chance that the partners might die before the marriage could be celebrated and so provided in their contracts for marriages between other children of the same families.[94] As a further precaution, some contracts also made arrangements for the care and custody of the new couple by one of the families while they remained underage.[95]

As these last examples illustrate, partners were often quite young at the time of their betrothal. Marshal's eldest son was probably about twelve years old when the match with the heiress of Aumale was arranged, and she was only about six or seven. The marriage itself was not celebrated until 1214, nearly eleven years after the contract was drawn up.[96] Information about the ages of landholders is not often available, so that reliable statistics about the age at marriage are hard to come by.[97] Yet marriage contracts often involved children or young adults, because the heads of most families, like William Marshal, wanted to ensure before they died that their sons and daughters were well matched and that the descent of their patrimonies was, to some extent, ensured. The marriage could be arranged, lands exchanged, and the partners safely taken care of until they reached the canonical age of consent, twelve for girls, fourteen for boys. To ensure a favorable match, some landowners turned the right of marrying their children over to a third party. The practice occurs throughout the thirteenth and early fourteenth centuries and sometimes arose out of financial need, such as when a landholder, deeply in debt, sold off his

[93] *CRR*, 9:295.

[94] PRO, E.40/376; DL.25/2028; E.326/194; E.368/47 m. 12; *Rot. Chart.*, 137; *CChR*, 2:90; *CPR, 1266–1272*, 623; *CRR*, 1:212, 9:295.

[95] *CRR*, 1:212, 9:295; *CPR, 1266–1272*, 623.

[96] *L'histoire*, 208 n. 2. Other examples of marriages between minors can be found in PRO, E.326/194; E.40/376; *Close Rolls*, 14:284; *CPR, 1266–1272*, 623; *CPR, 1281–1292*, 470; *CCR, 1272–1279*, 41, 110; *CCR, 1279–1288*, 180; *ERF*, 1:327; *CChR*, 2:90; Eyton, *Antiquities*, 4:356; *HKF*, 1:165; G. W. Watson, "Marriage Settlements," *Genealogist*, n.s. 34 (1918): 29–30; *Pleas before the King or His Justices, 1198–1212*, ed. Doris Mary Stenton (London, 1952, 1953, 1967), 3:151–152 (no. 968).

[97] Josiah Cox Russell, *British Medieval Population* (Albuquerque, 1948), 156–158; J. B. Post, "Another Demographic Use of Inquisitions Post Mortem," *Journal of the Society of Archivists* 5 (1974–1977): 110–114; Sue Sheridan Walker, "Free Consent and Marriage," 123–134.

property and at the same time made provision for the support of himself and his family for the rest of their lives.[98] Yet prominent, well-established families also granted or sold the marriages of their children to other lords on occasion.[99]

Contracts expressed the communal interest surrounding marriages by recording the participation of family and friends.[100] These friends, counselors, or administrators ("dispositores" as one contract calls them) were often individuals with a specific interest in the lands or families involved. In the early thirteenth century, for example, when one widow leased her dower lands and marriage portion and granted the marriage of her heirs to a third party, she did so with the counsel and consent of her friends and relatives as well as those of her heirs, meaning her husband's ("de consilio et assensu tam amicorum et parentum suorum quam parentum heredum suorum").[101] Both sets of relatives watched closely the widow's actions because they wanted to ensure that neither they nor the heirs would lose their reversionary rights because of her grant.

The way in which families negotiated those property interests and the way in which those interests were supervised by friends can be glimpsed in a covenant for the marriage of Henry, son and heir of Edmund de Lacy, and Margaret, daughter and heir of William Longspee, in 1256. The marriage was politically sensitive because it involved a significant realignment of wealth and territorial rights. William and Edmund agreed to place themselves at the disposal of two sets of friends who would arrange for the marriage and for the giving and receiving of lands in dower and marriage.[102] The choice of friends is notable. Edmund's mother, Si-

---

[98] PRO, Just.1/1180 m. 7; DL.25/2028 (includes a lease of dower and dowry); *Cartularium Monastarii de Ramesia*, ed. William H. Hart and Ponsonby A. Lyons (London, 1884–1893), 2:268–269; *Rot. Chart.*, 98.

[99] *CChR*, 1:186 (Marmion); PRO, KB.26/149 m. 9 (Mansell-Senevill); *Annales Prioratus de Dunstaplia, AD 33 to 1297*, in *Annales Monastici* (London, 1864–1869), 3:182–183 (Peyvre-Grey); *CPR, 1258–1266*, 495 (Lovel-Bassingburn); *CPR, 1266–1272*, 414 (Pencester-Hocton-Anulphi), 623 (Crioll-Pecche); *CIPM*, 3:473 (Noers); Moor, *Knights*, 3:219 (Mortimer-Butler).

[100] *Close Rolls*, 9:46–47 (Urtiaco-Molis); *CPR, 1292–1301*, 346 (Ros-Tibetot); *CPR, 1301–1307*, 327 (Segrave-Mohun); PRO, E.40/376; Cokayne, *Complete Peerage*, 9:261 n. b; Helmholz, *Marriage Litigation*, 47 n. 83.

[101] PRO, DL.25/2028.

[102] PRO, E.326/194; *Catalogue of Ancient Deeds in the Public Record Office* (London, 1890–1915), 1:234 (B194); *CPR, 1247–1258*, 534, 536. The property for the dowry and dower was settled in a separate instrument (PRO, C.148/109).

mon de Montfort, Hugh le Despenser, and William Ludeham acted on behalf of Edmund Lacy, while Fulk Basset the bishop of London, Stephen Longspee, Philip Basset, and John de Arundel represented William Longspee. The negotiators thus included powerful magnates as well as affinal and blood relations. The Bassets, for example, were the Longspees' in-laws; Philip was married to William Longspee's aunt, Ela. Hugh le Despenser's wife, Aline, was Philip's daughter. There was yet another family connection between the Bassets and Longspees. William's father had married Idonia, daughter and coheir of Richard de Camvill, who had married Eustachia, daughter and heir of Gilbert Basset, Philip and Fulk's uncle. (Some of these relationships can be seen in Figure 5.2.) Finally, there was a distant affinal relationship between the Lacys and the Longspees. Robert de Quincy, uncle of Margaret Edmund's mother, had married Helen, daughter of Llewelyn ab Iorwerth and aunt of Matilda de Clifford, William Longspee's wife.[103] The negotiations for the match clearly illuminate the social context within which barons formulated their marriage alliances and the way in which those social interests were brought to bear on marriage.

Control over marriage was therefore exercised on two levels. The first and most important was the family itself. Children were raised within the protection of the household and, if possible, betrothed at an early age. The second level was social. Partners were chosen and offered through negotiations that included a number of families whose interests were affected by the proposed marriage. The family, its kin, and peers acted together to make the match, so that the choice of marriage partners became a function of group interests and cohesion.

This social control did not bring lay landholders into serious conflict with the Church, at least during the thirteenth century and beyond. On the contrary, English barons probably viewed the Church as a guarantor of their marriages, not as an opponent. As in the development of royal jurisdiction over property in England at the same time, there were inconvenient aspects to the development of the canon law of marriage, but on the whole, the benefits probably outweighed the liabilities. Any rules dealing with issues as sensitive as matrimony, descent, and inheritance were bound to spark ambivalence, because they could have unintended or perhaps undesirable consequences. Yet, in general, the constitution of

---

[103] *EB*, 36, 112, 138; Cokayne, *Complete Peerage*, 4:259, 7:676–688, 11:382–385.

simple rules solidified marital arrangements and hence protected marriage strategies. Three doctrines impinged on the formulation of those strategies: the permanence of marriage, free consent, and consanguinity.[104]

It may be, for instance, that some lay landholders rankled at the fact that a marriage was supposed to be permanent and that they could not easily set aside a wife whom they did not like or who did not bear them male heirs. It certainly caused John de Warenne, the last earl of Surrey, extreme frustration in the early fourteenth century when he repeatedly tried and failed to set aside his wife in favor of the mother of his illegitimate sons.[105] Others obtained the annulments they wanted but the number is not large. Set against that inconvenience, the ease of determining legitimacy according to the Church's rules must have seemed a distinct advantage to men acutely concerned with stable property holding. They were less concerned about getting rid of partners who did not produce male heirs than about ensuring that their marriage arrangements would stand up to challenges by relatives or outsiders.[106] Furthermore, by multiplying the number of potential claimants, the easy separation of spouses would have jeopardized social order as much as or more than the failure of male heirs did. They were willing to risk the latter in favor of a stable legal environment. Englishmen made their preference clear in their determined opposition to the Church's doctrine concerning children born before wedlock; it would only have opened the door to more challenges to property holding.[107]

Consent likewise posed difficulties for marriage strategies. At the most elemental level, a valid marriage depended only on the free consent of the two partners. The consequent ease with which

[104] These are the three doctrines that Duby identifies as the core of the Church's model of marriage and that brought it into conflict with lay landholders in the twelfth century. He argues that by the thirteenth century the conflict had been resolved (*Medieval Marriage*, 20–21, 83–110).

[105] F. Royston Fairbank, "The Last Earl of Warenne and Surrey, and the Distribution of His Possessions," *YAJ* 19 (1907): 193–264; Searle, "Seigneurial Control," 28–29.

[106] Most of the dispensations relating to the marriages of English landholders were intended to uphold the marriage rather than annul it. Of twenty-nine dispensations recorded in the *Calendar of Papal Letters* issued between 1248 and 1302, only one referred to annulment (Bliss, *Papal Letters*, 1:253, 307, 323, 331, 332, 368, 369, 428, 491[2], 497, 503, 510, 512, 514, 515[2], 517, 518, 519, 520, 523, 547, 563–564, 588, 602).

[107] Searle,"Seigneurial Control," 26–27.

a marriage could be made meant that families had to be more vigilant lest their children make unwanted matches. But that degree of vigilance is itself a measure of the confidence landholders placed in the Church's authority. The lay process of marrying offered little scope for the exercise of individual choice or taste, but landholders respected the notion of free consent. Not all individuals, for instance, accepted proposed marriages. Throughout the thirteenth century, the king and barons worked together to formulate legislation providing compensation to lords whose wards married without permission or refused proffered matches, implicitly recognizing limitations on their ability to persuade children to accept their choice of marriage partners.[108] All the same, they insisted that lords could not disparage wards by marrying them to inferiors—an explicit acknowledgment that consent could be manipulated.

Marriage contracts and royal grants of marriage likewise acknowledged the importance of consent. Some contracts contained sanctions, in the form of a fine to be paid by the family of the offending partner, in case one of the parties refused the marriage on reaching the age of consent.[109] Some royal grants stipulated that the grantee had to obtain the consent of wards or widows.[110] The *Prerogativa Regis*, in fact, shows that the king used the requirement of consent to his advantage. It states that if an heiress were betrothed before the death of her parent or ancestor, and if she became the ward of the king while she was still under the age of valid consent (twelve years), then when she came of age she could choose ("eligat") whether to take the boy to whom she had been betrothed or to take another offered to her by the king.[111] The statement summarizes the relation between consent and choice. It envisions only a very narrow range of personal choice between alternatives selected by the family or lord under special circumstances. As in the cases of marriage contracts and grants, the state-

---

[108] Walker, "Free Consent and Marriage," 126–128; Plucknett, *Legislation*, 114–117; S.F.C. Milsom, "Legal Introduction," in *Novae Narrationes*, ed. Elsie Shanks (London, 1963), clv–clviii.

[109] *Close Rolls*, 14:284 (Mowbray-Clare); *CCR, 1272–1279*, 111 (Despenser-Furnival); *CChR*, 2:90–91 (Mortimer-Vere); Eyton, *Antiquities*, 4:356 (Fitz Alan–Mortimer); PRO, E.13/1D m. 6; Walker, "Free Consent and Marriage," 125 and n. 16 for additional examples.

[110] For an example, see *Patent Rolls*, 2:11.

[111] *Statutes of the Realm*, 1:225.

ment honors the requirement of free consent but does not concede a right of free choice.

This evidence makes it clear that English kings and barons largely accepted the Church doctrine of consent. The evidence about consanguinity is more ambiguous. The number of dispensations that individuals received during this period is very low compared to the total number of marriages contracted and compared to the number of known marriages in which the partners were related within the prohibited degrees. Some parties went out of their way to secure a dispensation. When Roger de Mortimer arranged the marriage between his daughter and Thomas de Beauchamp he requested a dispensation from the pope after the marriage was arranged but before it was completed. The dispensation noted that the match was intended to calm the dispute over Elfael.[112] It also noted that Roger had already secured royal consent to the marriage. Roger wanted to ensure that this crucial match would not be upset and therefore took pains to ensure the confirmation and support of the two lords who exercised the greatest authority in the case. Their consent was necessary, but also welcome because it legitimized the arrangement. A dispensation meant that a marriage would not be overturned. Families might have thus obtained dispensations for matches that they feared were invalid in order to ward off any potential or actual challenges and to protect the marriage. Because marriage was so vital to families, landholders needed to be assured that their arrangements would not be disrupted because of easily dissoluble marriages.

Although canon law gave landholders' strategies greater stability, marriage could never provide complete protection against the accidents of birth, death, and inheritance. Toward the end of the thirteenth century, therefore, landholders began to employ a variety of legal devices to supplement their family policies and to give them greater discretion over the descent of their lands. The most important of these devices, at first, were jointures and conditional grants or entails.[113] Land could be settled in such a way that a cou-

---

[112] Bliss, *Papal Letters*, 2:186. In 1289 Thomas's great-uncle, Walter, obtained a papal dispensation to remain in marriage to another Alice de Tony, whose relationship to the heiress of Elfael is not known (Bliss, *Papal Letters*, 1:503). For another dispensation obtained for a marriage designed to settle family conflict, see Bliss, *Papal Letters*, 1:515. See also Helmholz, *Marriage Litigation*, 87.

[113] Pollock and Maitland, *History of English Law*, 2:16–29; S.F.C. Milsom, *Historical*

ple had a joint tenancy and that after the death of the last tenant, the land would devolve in the way specified in the grant. The land, for example, could go to the eldest male heir of their bodies, but there was no restriction on the conditions that could be applied to the settlement. Families, in fact, did not use jointures and entails exclusively to concentrate lands in the patrilineal line.[114] One of the most important purposes of conditional grants seems to have been to ensure that lands given to daughters or younger sons would revert to the family if they did not establish lasting families of their own.[115] Jointures and conditional grants gave greater precision to conveyancing and complemented family strategies rather than redirecting them. Indeed, it became common for settlements to be made as part of marriage contracts.[116]

Marriage, therefore, remained a critical element in family strategies for the consolidation and accumulation of wealth down through the thirteenth century. Those strategies embraced a wide range of families and wove them into complex networks of kinship and landholding. The strategies depended on the proper selection of marriage partners to create socially endogamous matches. That endogamy, and the claims to land that flowed within it, sharpened the perception of a group identity and provided a sense of cohesion to otherwise disparate families. Under these circumstances, every marriage was potentially of political significance, for it always altered the distribution of wealth and the patterns of descent within the class.

This system of marriage and kinship, however, did not provide for the custody of minors or for the arrangement of their marriages. These strategies, and the cohesion they created, were therefore threatened whenever a landholder died leaving unmarried, minor heirs. It was a point of uncertainty, and it was precisely at this point that the feudal lord—in this case the king—stepped in. Having seen how important marriage was, not only to individual

---

Foundations of the Common Law (London, 1969), 140–168; Walker, "Royal Wardship," 192–219.

[114] Holmes, *Estates*, 42–45; McFarlane, *The Nobility*, 62–66; Peggy Jefferies, "The Medieval Use as Family Law and Custom: The Berkshire Gentry in the Fourteenth and Fifteenth Centuries," *Southern History* 1 (1979): 45–69.

[115] For an example of a settlement designed to compensate for the lack of a legitimate heir, see John M. W. Bean, "The Percies' Acquisition of Alnwick," *Archaeologia Aeliana*, 4th ser., 32 (1954): 309–319.

[116] Holmes, *Estates*, 44–45.

families but to the landholding elite as a whole, one can appreciate how intently tenants-in-chief attended the king's exercise of his feudal powers of wardship and marriage. These rights were not merely residual feudal incidents—they were of deep political importance to everyone concerned.

·2·

ROYAL LORDSHIP IN THE
THIRTEENTH CENTURY

The king's rights over wards, widows, and marriage grew out of the feudal customs of the eleventh and twelfth centuries. Their purpose was the maintenance of the king's control over his land and feudal assets. Yet they posed a threat to families that became evident under the Angevins, whose arbitrary exercise of lordship provoked the tenants-in-chief to rebellion in 1215. The rebels sought to reduce those dangers by restricting the king's seigniorial authority in Magna Carta. To understand how royal lordship developed in the thirteenth century, it is essential to begin with an understanding of its customary origins and the nature of the changes brought about in 1215. Challenged by Magna Carta, Henry III and, even more decisively, Edward I acted to halt any further erosion of their rights as landlords. They defined, clarified, and built on the customs that they inherited. Individual elements changed to correspond with changes in society, politics, and law, but the king's feudal authority, unlike that of other lords, remained largely intact. By the end of the century, therefore, the Crown's right to primer seisin, relief, consent to marriages and alienations, and prerogative wardship was clearly enunciated and enforced. In very real ways, royal lordship was still a powerful force in English society and politics on the death of Edward II, touching virtually every aspect of the lives of tenants-in-chief.

The Customary Foundations and Principles
of Royal Lordship

The laws and customs upon which the king's seignioral regime rested became intelligible as early as Henry's coronation charter.[1] Reliefs, consent to marriage, wardship, and escheat were logical extensions of the feudal principle that a lord accepted a man as his tenant and bestowed the tenement conditionally in return for service and only for the tenant's lifetime. The lord stepped in at death

---

[1] *Select Charters*, 116–119. The basic information about royal lordship can be found in Pollock and Maitland, *History of English Law*, 1:307–349; Bean, *Decline*, 7–20; *Prerogativa Regis*, v–xlvi; Milsom, *Legal Framework*.

of a tenant, on the marriage of heiresses, and in the case of inheritance by a child to ensure that he would have a tenant who could perform the services of the fee or would have compensation if those services could not be performed.

By 1200 English lords had lost most of their discretionary authority over free tenants and their holdings. This loss had been brought about in part by the introduction of the judicial actions of novel disseisin and mort d'ancestor under Henry II and in part by the erosion of knight service.[2] By guaranteeing the tenant's right to his land and by depriving lords of their ability to discipline tenants by distraint or disseisin—withholding or dispossessing lands— legal and social change broke the logical connection among tenure and relief, wardship, and marriage and rendered them incidental to landholding. They truly became "feudal incidents." Although their importance as devices for the enforcement of lordship declined, they gained significance as sources of revenue. Royal lordship did not suffer so much, since it was not hampered by the introduction of royal writs. Thus, the tenurial logic of feudal incidents at the level of the tenants-in-chief was relevant throughout the thirteenth century.

The first of these incidents was relief: on the death of a tenant his heir had to pay the lord a sum of money to take up his tenement. The payment was an acknowledgment of lordship. Originally an heir did not automatically succeed to the tenement, but rather had a claim to succeed that took affect only when the lord accepted him as a tenant.[3] Henry I promised that unlike his brother he would demand only "just and legitimate" reliefs from heirs, though it is well known that English kings exercised broad discretion over the amount and payment of reliefs throughout the twelfth century. A tenant-in-chief had to strike the best bargain he could with the king until Magna Carta fixed the rate of reliefs for all free tenants.[4] Magna Carta brought royal practice into line with the prevailing custom regarding reliefs in one other way as well. Glanvill noted that if an heir was a minor and his lands fell under wardship, then he was exempt from paying relief upon coming of age. In spite of this limitation, the king often demanded relief

---

[2] Milsom, *Legal Framework*.

[3] Thorne, "English Feudalism and Estates," 193–209; Milsom, *Legal Framework*, 154–164, esp. 164.

[4] Pollock and Maitland, *History of English Law*, 1:307–318; Milsom, *Legal Framework*, 162–164; Holt, *Magna Carta*, 107–108, 207–209; Wilfred L. Warren, *Henry II* (London, 1973), 386; Sanders, *Feudal Military Service*, 97–107.

from minors when they received their inheritance, until the barons demanded an end to the practice in Magna Carta.[5]

Yet, in one important respect, the king's feudal authority over inheritance was left untouched throughout the twelfth and thirteenth centuries. According to Glanvill, when a tenant died the lord had to find out who the heir was, take his homage, and only then demand relief. The lord was entitled only to a "simple seisin" or possession of the tenement.[6] Bracton also called this "common" or concurrent seisin: "a simple seisin [*simplicem*] will not be refused the lord, that he may be acknowledged as lord, provided that he takes nothing therefrom and removes no one from possession against the will of the heirs. . . . He cannot have first seisin though he may have a common seisin [*communem*]."[7] The phrasing reveals a concern for the rights of lords, whose role in inheritance had been curtailed by mort d'ancestor, which had made the seisin of an heir virtually automatic. Simple seisin was a reminder of the lord's past authority, hence like relief an acknowledgment of lordship.[8] For Bracton, "primer seisin," which he also calls "vacuam seisinam," was the possession a lord could take if the tenement were vacant at the death of the tenant or if there was some doubt about who was the correct heir.[9] By Bracton's time, therefore, Henry II's legal reforms had reduced the role of the lord in inheritance to that of a caretaker safeguarding the rights of the true heir. Nevertheless, even the right to simple seisin opened the door for mischief, and prompted Bracton to warn against the wickedness of lords. Indeed, the Statute of Marlborough (1267), cap. 16, provided the tenant with a legal remedy if the lord committed any waste or destruction during his brief occupation of the tenement.[10]

The king's rights at inheritance were more sweeping and preserved an earlier stage of feudal relations. Glanvill asserted that on the death of a baron, the king customarily seized the barony and held it until the heir paid relief, a reversal of the order in which

[5] *Glanvill* (ix.4), 107; Richard Fitz Nigel, *Dialogus* (Oxford, 1983), 94, 96–97; Holt, *Magna Carta*, 209–210; Bracton, 2:245–248.

[6] *Glanvill* (ix.1, 4, 6), 103–104, 108, 110; Pollock and Maitland, *History of English Law*, 1:310–311; Milsom, *Legal Framework*, 169–170.

[7] Bracton, 3:245–246.

[8] Milsom, *Legal Framework*, 164–174, esp. 169–170.

[9] Bracton, 3:246, 247; *Glanvill* (ix.6), 110; Milsom, *Legal Framework*, 170 n. 2. Britton also equated "primer seisin" with the seisin of vacant holdings (*Britton*, 2:52, 55).

[10] Bracton, 3:248; *Statutes of the Realm*, 1:23–24.

other lords had to take homage and relief.[11] This is the primer seisin that other lords could exercise only if there were doubt about the inheritance. Although Bracton does not mention the king's right of primer seisin, it remained unaltered through the thirteenth century. It preserved the notion that inheritance was the lord's acceptance of an heir as his tenant, even if in the wake of Magna Carta the Crown could no longer deprive an heir of his patrimony. That acceptance was confirmed in the ceremony of homage. Throughout the thirteenth century and beyond, tenants-in-chief had to perform their homage to the king personally, which meant traveling to Westminster or wherever the king might be.[12] The journey could be a burden. The king sometimes postponed homage as a favor or because the tenant was ill. For the sake of convenience, he sometimes scheduled homage to be taken at Parliament. If he was out of the realm, his lieutenants would take fealty but the tenant would have to perform homage to the king when he returned.[13] The king sometimes gave *custody* of lands to heirs before they came of age, but they obtained full possession only when the king had taken homage.[14] The performance of the ceremony stressed the personal bond of lordship that existed between the king and all of his tenants-in-chief.

Because only the lord and his court could determine a man's acceptability as a tenant, the lord had the right to consent to the marriages of female heirs and the right to arrange marriages for female wards. Although originally women could perform neither homage nor military service, families nonetheless expected that in default of male heirs their tenements would descend to women. If that happened, it would be the heiress's husband who performed homage and the services due from the land. In consenting to a marriage, the lord was declaring the prospective husband acceptable as his tenant.[15] And since female inheritance depended on the relationship between the husband and lord, who better than the lord could select a suitable husband for a female ward? Henry I promised that he would not withhold his consent for a reasonable

[11] *Glanvill* (IX.6) 110; Milsom, *Legal Framework*, 163.

[12] *Prerogativa Regis*, 63–64.

[13] *CChW*, 285; *Rot. Parl.*, 1:89, 393; *CPR, 1247–1258*, 23; *Close Rolls*, 5:86, 110; *CFR*, 1:4, and passim.

[14] For two examples, see *CFR*, 2:370–371, 378, 404; and *CCR, 1318–1323*, 411 (Clifford and Percy).

[15] Milsom, "Inheritance by Women," 60–89; Searle, "Seigneurial Control," 8–12; Milsom, *Legal Framework*, 104–105; *Glanvill* (VII.12), 85.

marriage and that if a tenant-in-chief died leaving an unmarried daughter as heir he would give the girl in marriage with her lands and with the counsel of his barons. Female inheritance at this point was not automatic. By arranging a marriage for an heiress, the king acknowledged her claim to the tenement yet also ensured that he would have an acceptable tenant to perform the required services. The issue was so critical that an heiress remained in the custody of her lord, no matter what her age, until she married with her lord's consent.[16]

A lord could not be forced to take an unacceptable tenant, and for Henry and his successors in the twelfth century, the test of acceptability was above all political loyalty. Henry I promised that he would not charge families for his consent nor withhold it unless the woman wished to marry his enemy. At the end of the century, Glanvill repeated that exception and added "or some otherwise unsuitable person."[17] Contests within the royal family over the right to rule split the nobility and strained loyalties. There was a real danger that an heiress's marriage might transfer wealth from a loyal tenant into the hands of an ally of the king's rival so that the king would lose the services of the fee as well as control over the land.[18] After the reign of John, that danger lessened except along the borders with Wales and Scotland or in times of political conflict. In most cases, it was unlikely that an heiress would marry an enemy of the Crown. Indeed, at the end of the thirteenth century, Britton commented that the "prohibition [against marrying without consent] *was first made*, lest the female heirs of our land should marry with our enemies" (emphasis added).[19] Nevertheless, the king still worried about the suitability of potential husbands and tenants, as Henry III indicated in a writ of 1243. He stated that widows had spurned the security that they were supposed to give not to marry without royal consent, had not asked for consent, and had married themselves indiscriminately to whomever they pleased.[20] In order to prevent further injury to himself and to the Crown, Henry ordered his agents to take lands of Margaret, the heiress of the earldom of Warwick and widow of John Marshal, as security that she would not marry without his license. He ex-

[16] *Select Charters*, 118; *Glanvill* (vii.12), 85.

[17] *Select Charters*, 118; *Glanvill* (vii.12), 85.

[18] Holt, "Politics and Property," 19–24, 30–32, 36–38.

[19] *Britton*, 2:23. Bracton does not treat the issue of the king's rights of consent (2:255).

[20] *Close Rolls*, 5:61. For another example, see *Close Rolls*, 12:391.

plained that because she was one of the wealthiest women in the realm and held a well-fortified castle sited near the Welsh Marches, it would not be useful to him if she married anyone he could not trust. Henry III was not so concerned as his predecessors might have been that Margaret would marry an enemy, but he certainly wanted assurance that the man who was ultimately responsible for such an important inheritance would be capable and trustworthy.

As this example indicates, the feudal logic that gave the king the authority to consent to the marriage of an heiress also gave him the power of consent over a widow's marriage. Glanvill wondered whether a widow before remarrying needed to obtain the permission of the warrantor of her dower, that is, her husband's heir who in most cases would be her son. He concluded that even though her second husband performed fealty only for the dower and was not therefore the heir's actual tenant, she indeed had to get her warrantor's consent or forfeit her dower. If, however, she held other lands as a marriage portion or inheritance, then the consent of her chief lord would suffice.[21] The king's right of consent was reinforced by the fact that during a minority the widows of tenants-in-chief held their dowers of the king. He had the responsibility of assigning dowers, but he could also withhold them if widows failed to surrender custody of the heirs or if they married without license.[22] No matter how many times an heiress married, therefore, she had to get her lord's consent to each match, and the king routinely exercised this authority down through the early fourteenth century.[23] Indeed, before Magna Carta, the king often arranged marriages for widows, as Henry I's coronation charter implies in the promise that he would not give widows in marriage against their will.

The central issue in seigniorial consent, whether in the marriages of heiresses or widows, was the control of land and services, not marriage itself.[24] Fines paid to the king for the right to marry

---

[21] *Glanvill* (vii.12, ix.4), 85–86, 108; Bracton, 2:246, 255; Milsom, *Legal Framework*, 104–105. Subsequent husbands performed only fealty to the lord.

[22] Palmer, "Origins," 17 and nn. 61, 62. For an explicit recognition that a widow held her dower of the king, see *Close Rolls*, 11:195–196.

[23] At the end of the thirteenth century, both *Fleta* and *Britton* give the impression that this ongoing right of consent no longer pertained to lords other than the king (*Britton*, 2:23, 26; *Fleta*, 29). See also PRO, SC.1/45/227: "Pour ceo qe nous avoms entendez qe vous estes en volunte de vous marier a notre cher e foial mons. Richard de Pendele, saver vous fesoms qe nous vous donoms le conge a ce faire."

[24] Searle, "Seigneurial Control," 5–7. The significance of landholding is made clear in the articles of the eyre (*Fleta*, 46–47).

either a widow or an heiress through Henry III's reign clearly show that the consent that the king gave was to take a woman with her land, "cum terra sua."[25] That the formula does not appear more often was more likely due to the practice of the Exchequer scribes than to differences in the nature of the grants.[26] What attracted the king's attention was the transfer of wealth and obligation that occurred with marriage. The marriage strategies of tenants-in-chief thus fell under the watchful eye of the king. Each of the important matches discussed in the previous chapter—between William Marshal's son and heir and Baldwin de Béthune's daughter, between Edmund de Lacy's son and heir and William Longspee's daughter and heir, and between Roger de Mortimer's daughter and Thomas de Beauchamp (Figure 1.5)—contained the potential for a significant realignment of wealth and power depending on the pattern of survival of family members. And all were subject to royal consent.[27]

The Mortimer-Beauchamp marriage, moreover, makes it clear that the king's power of consent covered the marriages of all women whether they were actually heiresses at the time of their marriage, since Mortimer had a son when he negotiated the match. That was the scope of the Crown's authority when Henry I promised not to withhold consent. With the uncertainties of survival in this society, any woman was a potential heiress. Indeed, sisters often inherited from brothers who died childless. To be effective, therefore, a lord's consent should have included all women with the potential to inherit, lest he be forced to take as his tenant an unsuitable man who happened to have married a woman who later turned out to be an heiress. Furthermore, the marriage of any of his tenants' daughters or sisters affected the lord's interests because the transfer of property through a marriage portion could

[25] For example, *Pipe Roll, 9 John*, 6. The phrase recalls Henry I's coronation charter and was used by Henry's Exchequer when recording fines in the pipe roll for permission to marry widows (*Pipe Roll, 31 Henry I*, 21, 34, 43). The Exchequer continued to use the formula into Henry III's reign, at least (e.g., *ERF*, 1:7, 35).

[26] The pipe rolls of Henry II and his sons record approximately 135 fines for permission to marry heiresses and widows, and 37 of the entries contain the formula "cum terra sua" in one form or another. The fine and pipe rolls for 6 John record only Richard de Greinville's debt of a palfrey for the king's consent, but John's confirmation contains the formula "ducendam in uxorem cum tota hereditate et feodis et pertinentiis" (*Pipe Roll, 6 John*, 86; *Rot. Ob. et Fin.*, 220; *Rot. Chart.*, 137).

[27] *Rot. Chart.*, 112–113; *CPR, 1247–1258*, 534; *ERF*, 2:249; Bliss, *Papal Letters*, 2:186.

affect the tenant's ability to perform his services.[28] Yet, by the end of the twelfth century, the authority of most lords had retreated to the point that it covered only actual heiresses. Glanvill stated that "no woman who is an heir to land may be married without the direction or consent of the lord," and makes no other mention of the power of consent. Bracton simply repeats Glanvill's position.[29] Neither treatise discusses royal consent, but the king continued to supervise the marriages of heiresses and nonheiresses alike throughout the thirteenth and early fourteenth centuries.[30]

Royal consent, however, was not one dimensional, for it served to protect the marriages themselves as well as the king's interests. Cooperation between the Crown and tenants-in-chief in the thirteenth century made it unlikely that the king would withhold his consent. Conditions in England contrast, for example, with those in the king's domains in southern France, where consent to marriage was a political issue requiring close supervision. In England the problem of political loyalty arose only in times of political unrest or rebellion.[31] At other times, the Crown could largely trust the instincts of baronial and knightly families to provide appropriate partners for women. It did not need tight supervision. The circulation of land within a narrow range of families suited the king's interests as well as those of the families themselves. Under these circumstances, royal consent served as a legitimization of marriage agreements and as a sanction for the enforcement of their terms. The Crown used the basic feudal powers that it retained from the twelfth century to promote, as well as to supervise, the marriage alliances of the families of its tenants-in-chief. For that reason, ten-

---

[28] Searle, "Seigneurial Control," 7, 8–12, 10 n. 19.

[29] *Glanvill* (VII.12), 85; Bracton, 2:255; Searle, "Seigneurial Control," 11–12.

[30] *ERF*, 1:151; *Patent Rolls*, 2:87; PRO, E.159/9 m. 13, (Clare); E.159/15 m. 13d (Warenne); Altschul, *A Baronial Family*, 32–33. For consent to marry heiresses, see *ERF*, 1:7, 35, 40. For consent involving women who were not yet heirs, see *CPR, 1247–1258*, 326 (Cantilupe-Lacy, 1254); *CPR, 1292–1301*, 346 (Tibetot-Ros, 1298); *CPR, 1301–1307*, 320 (Fitz Walter–Botetorte, 1305); *CChR*, 2:90–91 (Mortimer-Vere); G. W. Watson, "Marriage Settlements," *Genealogist*, n.s. 35 (1919): 95–96 (St. Amando–Despenser, 1313); idem, "Marriage Settlements," *Genealogist*, n.s. 36 (1920): 137–138 (Vere-Warenne).

[31] PRO, SC.1/15/31; and J. P. Trabut-Cussac, *L'administration anglaise en Gascogne sous Henry III et Edouard I de 1254 à 1307* (Geneva, 1972), 35–37, 43, 73–77, for the marriage of the daughter and heir of Gaston de Bearn. PRO, SC.1/19/81, 82, 96, for consent to a proposed match between the Joinville and La Marche families. In March 1266, Henry III allowed a coheiress to marry whomever she pleased so long as it was someone who had been steadfastly loyal to Henry and Edward in the Barons' War (*CPR, 1258–1266*, 572).

ants-in-chief would not object to the reasonable exercise of consent and would welcome it in situations in which they were eager to guarantee the fulfillment of a contract.

The king's rights of wardship and marriage were greater than those of any other feudal lord with respect to free tenants. According to the reciprocity of the feudal contract, the lord gave land in exchange for his tenant's service. If the lord could not obtain the service because the tenant was a child, it was reasonable that he should recover the payment he made for the service (that is, the land) while the tenant was incapacitated.[32] If a tenant held of several lords, each obtained custody of the tenements held of him. Right to the custody of heirs and their marriages was less clear cut. The method of determining which lord received it was in dispute through much of the thirteenth century until it was decided that it would go to the lords of whom tenants had first held their lands. The king's seigniorial rights cut through the problem. As the ultimate lord of the land, the king obtained the custody of all of the lands of a tenant-in-chief, even those held of other lords, and he exercised the right of marriage regardless of the priority of enfeoffment.[33] In practice, prerogative wardship cut deeply into the seigniorial authority of other lords.

The Crown insisted on its rights of prerogative wardship throughout the thirteenth century, much to the annoyance of mesne lords. Anyone who held some land in chief by knight service, no matter how little, fell within the scope of the king's lordship.[34] The number of those affected, moreover, tended to grow because any person acquiring land held in chief of the king became subject to prerogative wardship. That threat was sufficiently alarming to prompt Abbot Samson in the late twelfth century to exclaim that if one of his tenants married a woman who held even a mere acre in chief, then the king would seize all of the tenant's lands and the wardship of the heir and thereby enter the fee of the Abbey to the prejudice of the Abbot.[35] The danger was not

[32] Milsom, *Legal Framework*, 111–112, 155.

[33] *Glanvill* (vii.10), 84; Pollock and Maitland, *History of English Law*, 1:321; *Prerogativa Regis*, xiv; Bean, *Decline*, 9–10.

[34] For example, *Close Rolls*, 5:473; *CIPM*, 3:291, 292; Eyton, *Antiquities*, 4:253–255 (1/20th of a fee); *CIPM*, 4:106; *Rot. Orig.*, 1:131; *CFR*, 1:487 (3 acres held as 1/40th of a fee); *CIPM*, 3:369, 5:50; *CCR, 1296–1302*, 474; *HKF*, 1:93–94 (4 virgates held for 18 geese to mew the royal falcons). The Dunstaple chronicler grumbled about the king's rights in the last case (*Annales de Dunstaplia*, 3:401).

[35] *The Chronicle of Jocelin of Brakelond*, ed. and trans. Harold E. Butler (London, 1949), 58; cited by John E. Lally, "Secular Patronage at the Court of King Henry

illusory.[36] In addition, the king's right overrode any leases or grants at term that the tenant may have made in his lifetime, while down to 1327 the Crown also took custody of any lands that the tenant held in socage of another lord, overriding the customary right of the family.[37]

The king's right to a wardship depended on which parent held in chief and the order in which they died. The king lost the right in the case of "curtesy," that is, if a woman holding in chief died before her husband. Bracton explained that a lord was not entitled to custody if the homage of the ancestor continued. The homage of a male tenant was extinguished on his death, but since the husband of an heiress performed homage for her lands, if she died and her husband survived her and they had had children, the homage that her husband performed in his wife's name continued and the lord would not be entitled to the wardship if there were minor heirs.[38] The provision applied equally to second husbands. In 1281–1283, the king's justices declared that in cases in which a man's son died before him leaving an infant heir and the man held lands in curtesy that would descend to his grandchild on the man's death, the man would have the wardship and marriage of the child.[39] On the other hand, if a woman outlived her daughter and heir, so that the daughter's husband would not have performed any homage in the daughter's lifetime for her mother's lands, then on the woman's death the king could take the wardship, if her

---

II," *BIHR* 49 (1976): 164. See *Prerogativa Regis*, xii–xiii, for a summary of the ways in which subtenants could become tenants-in-chief.

[36] The earl of Gloucester lost the wardship of one of his tenants at the end of the thirteenth century precisely because the tenant's grandfather had married the heiress of a tenant-in-chief and had performed homage to the king. In fact, neither the heiress nor her descendants had actually held any land of the king. Homage alone was enough to give the Crown the right of wardship (*The Red Book of the Exchequer*, ed. Hubert Hall [London, 1896], 3:1013–1014; *CIPM*, 2:524; *CPR, 1281–1292*, 147; *CFR*, 1:204; *CCR, 1279–1288*, 273).

[37] Bracton, 2:100; *Close Rolls*, 10:190. For socage, see *Prerogativa Regis*, xvii–xviii; and *Rot. Parl.*, 2:10, 12 (no. 34). The king sometimes restored leaseholds to lessees during a minority (*CPR, 1281–1292*, 394).

[38] Bracton, 2:258–259, 4:360–361; Milsom, "Inheritance by Women," 82–88; Pollock and Maitland, *History of English Law*, 2:414–420. For examples, see *CIPM*, 2:490; and *CCR, 1272–1279*, 199.

[39] *Select Cases*, 5: lxviii–lxix, cxliii–cxliv, a judgment on John de Sandwich's petition for the wardship of his granddaughter. For further details, see *CCR, 1279–1288*, 131, 226, 244; *CPR, 1281–1292*, 113, 422; *CIPM*, 2:480; PRO, E.136/1/15 m. 8; *EB*, 45.

grandchildren were minors.[40] The rights of the husband in curtesy tempted some widowers to claim them when they in fact had not had any children by their wives.[41] Finally, if during their lifetimes, the parents sold the marriage of their heir to a third party and if they died before the purchaser completed a marriage, then the king obtained the right of marriage.[42]

Dual inheritances created further complications that are evident in the descent and custody of a portion of the barony of Kirklinton in the thirteenth century. Because the heiress to the barony died in 1272 without direct heirs of her own, the barony was partitioned among her six aunts.[43] One of the coheirs was Euphemia, wife of Richard de Kirkbride, who had died in 1267 leaving a minor son and heir, Richard. Since Richard Senior had not held any lands in chief, and since Euphemia survived him and retained lands of her own, Richard Junior became a ward of Walter de Wigeton of whom Kirkbride had held by knight service. Euphemia died sometime before 1272, so that Richard Junior was her representative when Kirklinton was partitioned. At that time, the king claimed the wardship of Richard Junior as Euphemia's heir. The escheator seized all of his lands, including those held of Wigeton. Walter protested. The king took the matter up with the royal council, and they determined that Walter was entitled to the wardship of the lands held of him and of the heir because the Kirkbride lands had not yet been united with the Kirklinton inheritance at the time of Richard Senior's death.[44] Prerogative wardship, in other words, was not retroactive. Richard had not performed homage for his wife's lands, indeed she had not inherited, by the time he died. The king therefore ordered his escheators to restore the wardship to Wigeton, though reminding everyone at the same time that in

[40] Bracton, 4:360–361. For one example, see *ERF*, 2:66, 75; *CIPM*, 1:198, 282; *Close Rolls*, 11:95–96; Cecil A. F. Meekings, introduction to *The 1235 Surrey Eyre* (Guildford, 1979), 182–183; *HKF*, 3:356–358.

[41] *EB*, 31, 45; *CIPM*, 1:563, 774; *Close Rolls*, 7:198; *CPR, 1247–1258*, 155 (Crevequer). Inquests were often ordered through writs of *scire facias* to escheators, e.g., PRO, C.245/1/24.

[42] Bracton, 2:263; *Fleta*, 1:29.

[43] *EB*, 58–59; Moor, *Knights*, 2:287–288. The estate was not actually partitioned until 1274 when the heiress's husband Eustace de Balliol died because he held by curtesy (*CFR*, 1:26, 27; *CCR, 1272–1279*, 132–134).

[44] *CCR, 1272–1279*, 171. For a similar case, in which the tenancy-in-chief descended through the mother and did not come into custody until she died, see *HKF*, 1:200; Moor, *Knights*, 1:8–9; and *CCR, 1272–1279*, 197, 269, 278; *CPR, 1281–1292*, 428; *CCR, 1288–1296*, 179.

the future he would be entitled to the wardship of *all* of Richard Junior's lands. Because of the marriage, Wigeton lost any hope of future wardships.

Prerogative wardship gave the king the opportunity to offer a marriage to the heir or heiresses. In the case of an heiress, wardship extended beyond the age at which she came of age—fourteen years—until she married with the king's approval. During the thirteenth century, that was interpreted to mean that an unmarried heiress could recover her lands if she was of age though she herself remained in the custody of the Crown. If, for example, a tenant-in-chief died leaving three daughters to partition his estate, the eldest of age and married, the middle of age and unmarried, and the youngest a minor and unmarried, the king would have no rights of wardship or marriage over the eldest or her third of the estate, only the right of marriage over the middle daughter, and the right to both the wardship of the youngest daughter's share of the estate as well as to her marriage.[45] In 1300 the three unmarried sisters and coheirs of Thomas Peverel, Margery, Joan, and Denise (aged twenty-two to twenty-five), challenged the king's right after they had been distrained to pay a fine for their marriages, claiming that they should be free to marry themselves.[46] The matter was taken up by the king's council in Parliament, and though no outcome has been found, it is clear from other cases of about the same time that the king continued to exercise control over the marriages of heiresses who were of age.[47] If, however, an heiress who was of age married someone underage, her lands fell into royal wardship since her husband would perform homage for them and be the formal tenant. In some cases, the king mitigated the rule by giving the wardship to the bride's father.[48]

The king similarly exercised the right of marriage over male heirs under twenty-one years of age, though the feudal logic be-

[45] *Glanvill* (vii.12), 85; Bracton, 2:254–255; *Britton*, 2:23. For an example of an heiress receiving custody of her lands upon coming of age but remaining under royal supervision, see *ERF*, 1:458–459, 2:15, 19, 166; *Close Rolls*, 5:415, 447, 6:70, 156, 293, 294, 366, 409, 7:120, 8:122, 216; *CPR, 1247–1258*, 206, 216, 419; Cokayne, *Complete Peerage*, 4:199, 12:2:937 (Agatha Ferrers).

[46] PRO, E.159/74 m. 34; *CIPM*, 3:599.

[47] *CIPM*, 2:605; *CFR*, 1:231; *CPR, 1281–1292*, 254 (Isolda de Bocton, 23); *CIPM*, 4:144; *CPR, 1301–1307*, 111 (Isabel de Chilton, 16); *CIPM*, 4:159; *CPR, 1301–1307*, 120, 207 (Margery de Canuz, 20).

[48] *Select Cases*, 3:liii n. 1; *CIPM*, 4:148; PRO, E.372/150 m. 42d; *ERF*, 2:425–426; *CPR, 1258–1266*, 420–421 (grant).

hind that right is not so clear as in the case of female wards.[49] In arranging a marriage for a boy the lord was not protecting his tenurial interests in the same way that he was when arranging a marriage for a girl. After all, he had an accepted tenant in a male heir, even if he was a minor. The right to the marriage of male heirs should be seen instead as the product of two other aspects of feudal lordship. On the one hand, during a minority the king assumed lordship over the family and estate of his tenant-in-chief. And since in a marriage the husband in effect became his wife's lord, by arranging a marriage for a male ward, the king, as head of the estate, was providing for a new subtenant and the acquisition of additional lands.[50] It can be thought of as a marital subenfeoffment. The lord's tenants, moreover, may have expected that when their lord arranged a marriage for the heir, he would find a bride among the other families of his court, and keep their lands within the homage.[51] On the other hand, the king as lord wanted to continue his tenant's family line. The arrangement of a marriage was an extension of the lord's acknowledgment of a tenant's patrilineal claim to a tenement. It conformed to the lord's interest as well for it was hoped that a marriage would produce an heir, provide for the continuity of services and loyalty, and reduce the possibility of family strife over the tenement.[52] These seigniorial concerns are evident as soon as the king's right of marriage over male wards appears in the reign of Henry I, and it was so well established by the time of Glanvill that he did not find it necessary to explain the logic of the right.[53]

---

[49] See the discussion of the problem in *Rot. Dom.*, xxiii–xxv; and Pollock and Maitland, *History of English Law*, 1:326–327.

[50] For husband as *dominus*, see Palmer, "Origins," 29–31. The argument is supported by Fitz Nigel's discussion of debts (Fitz Nigel, *Dialogus*, 114–115).

[51] There are indications that the king was expected to arrange marriages between his knights and women in his custody in Orderic Vitalis, *The Ecclesiastical History of Orderic Vitalis* (Oxford, 1978), 6:308–309; and in *BNB*, 2:12.

[52] Palmer, "Origins," 5–6.

[53] Although Henry's coronation charter does not mention wardship of males, the pipe roll for 31 Henry I makes it clear that he exercised the right (*Select Charters*, 118; *Pipe Roll, 31 Henry I*, 37, 66, 67, 83, 88, 94, 111, 119, 137, 155). The way in which that power was used is nicely illustrated in Henry's charter providing for the wardship of the Ridel heir and for marriages between the Ridel and Basset families (*Regesta Regum Anglo-Normannorum* [Oxford, 1956], 2:184 [no. 1389]; Frank M. Stenton, *The First Century of English Feudalism, 1066–1166* [Oxford, 1961], 34–37, and 34 n. 4). The marriage was a variation of a brother-sister linkage: in this case the heir married his sister's husband's niece instead of sister. It should be noted that the charter specifically designated a marriage between the Ridel heir and Bas-

Prerogative wardship also gave the king complete access to his tenant's resources. As Glanvill and Bracton noted, a feudal lord had "full custody" of the inheritance, that is, the lord took his tenant's place and assumed all of his tenant's rights of lordship over his demesne and tenantry.[54] The lord conferred churches that fell vacant during the custody, took the wardships and marriages of military tenants as they occurred and could grant, give, or sell them to whomever they pleased as well as consent to the marriages of female heiresses. Lords had the "power to dispose of everything to the heir's advantage, just as they would dispose of their own."[55] The king exercised the same rights during an ecclesiastical vacancy, through the forfeiture of a felon, or later when a tenant-in-chief was an idiot or incapacitated.[56]

The Crown vigorously pursued its rights to the wardships of military subtenants, through *gard per cause de gard* or a vacancy.[57] The right extended indefinitely, potentially giving the lord the wardship of any military subtenant of a tenant already in wardship, though such extended chains of wardship were rare, depending as they did on the conjunction of minorities.[58] An extent of the lands of Richard de Clare, the earl of Gloucester, in 1263 reveals the value of these windfall wardships to the king and the corresponding liabilities for mesne lords. The extent distinguished between those fees over which Clare had the right of wardship, marriage, and relief, and those held by tenants who also held of the king in chief, in which case the feudal lordship of the Clare family was restricted to the collection of reliefs.[59] Of nearly fifty fees held

---

set's *daughter's* daughter, so that it was cognizant of family linkage through female descendants. By 1176 the king had a routine system for taking custody of wards and their lands (Fitz Nigel, *Dialogus*, 94–95). For the later right, see *Glanvill* (vii.9), 82–83. By the time of the Statute of Merton in 1236, it was referred to as a "mere right" (*Statutes of the Realm*, 1:3).

[54] *Glanvill* (vii.9), 82–83; Bracton, 2:252.

[55] Bracton, 2:252. The point about consent is not clear. Glanvill states that lords had full custody, "in mulieribus si que in eorum custodiam exciderint maritandis," implying that they had consent only if there were a female heir. Bracton puts the same point somewhat differently: "et in mulieribus maritandis, et maritagiis vendendis si quae fuerint maritandae." The general statement, "in mulieribus maritandis," suggests that he accorded the lord a general right of consent.

[56] Margaret Howell, *Regalian Right in Medieval England* (London, 1962), 169–171; *CPR, 1272–1281*, 373 (felon); *CPR, 1301–1307*, 413; *CIPM*, 4:289 (idiot).

[57] *Prerogativa Regis*, xvi–xvii.

[58] I have found only one example for the entire period (*CPR, 1301–1307*, 504; *CIPM*, 4:170).

[59] *Close Rolls*, 12:284, 286–290, 292; *CIPM*, 1:530; PRO, C.132/27/5 m. 42. Es-

of Clare, nineteen were held by tenants who also held in chief of the king. Indeed, during two Clare minorities in the reign of Henry III, that of Richard between 1230 and 1243 and that of his son Gilbert between 1262 and 1265, Henry acquired the wardships of at least eleven Clare tenants and their lands.[60] There was an added danger to the lord in these wardships *per cause de gard*. If the wards married tenants-in-chief and produced heirs, then in the future the fees would be subject to prerogative wardship, augmenting the king's resources at the expense of the mesne lord. The Crown likewise acquired wardships during ecclesiastical vacancies. For example, during four of the six vacancies of Canterbury in the reigns of Henry III and Edward I, the king took in at least nine wardships. The lands and heirs of Hamo de Gravenel, a tenant of the archbishop, came into royal custody in 1228, and his descendant Richard Gravenel became a royal ward during the vacancy in 1270–1272.[61] The king was entitled to such wardships from the death of the old bishop or abbot to the grant of temporalities to the new one.[62] If a wardship fell in during a vacancy, it stayed under royal control even after the new bishop received the temporalities.[63] As can be seen in Table 2.1, the wardships brought in through vacancies and other sources accounted for only a fifth

cheators made similar inquiries after the death of Roger de Quincy in 1264 (*CIPM*, 1:776; PRO, C.132/40, no. 9, esp. mm. 6, 11, 15, 18, 20).

[60] *ERF*, 1:227, 229, 234, 235, 283; *CPR, 1232–1247*, 3, 107, 240, 383; *CPR, 1258–1266*, 267; *Close Rolls*, 4:103, 257, 12:200–201; *CIPM*, 1:554; PRO, E.159/20 m. 13d.

[61] The vacancies are calculated from *HBC*, 210–211. The Gravenel wardships can be found in *Patent Rolls*, 2:201; *CPR, 1266–1272*, 617; *CIPM*, 1:802. The other wardships can be found in *ERF*, 1:217, 229; *Patent Rolls*, 2:114, 507; *CPR, 1232–1247*, 269; *Close Rolls*, 4:398–399; *CPR, 1266–1272*, 497, 528, 568–569, 608, 714; *CCR, 1272–1279*, 23; *CIPM*, 1:803, 805. Four vacancies at Durham in the same period produced seven wardships (*ERF*, 1:156, 2:64; *CFR*, 1:47; *Patent Rolls*, 2:117, 172; *CPR, 1232–1247*, 185, 238; *Close Rolls*, 4:274, 357).

[62] Robert de Bingham, the bishop of Salisbury, died on 2/3 November 1246, and his successor, William of York, who was elected on 10 December, did not receive the temporalities until 29 January. In the meantime, a tenant of the bishop died before 28 December leaving a minor daughter and heir whose custody Henry III granted to an Exchequer clerk, though she was abducted and married someone else (*HBC*, 251; *CIPM*, 1:101; Howell, *Regalian Right*, 97; *ERF*, 2:65; PRO, E.159/1B m. 10d).

[63] For cases in which the king granted wardships after the temporalities had been restored, see *HBC*, 220; Howell, *Regalian Right*, 170 nn. 1, 2; *ERF*, 2:64; *CPR, 1247–1258*, 52; *HBC*, 220; *CFR*, 1:47. In one case, Henry III displayed some scruples about exercising his right (*Close Rolls*, 4:272, 274, 375). The tenancy can be traced in *Rot. Chart.*, 184; and *ERF*, 1:171.

TABLE 2.1 WARDSHIPS FROM VACANCIES, WARDSHIPS,
AND OTHER SOURCES

Source	N	% of all wardships
Wardships	104	7.7
Honors	75	5.5
Dowers	37	2.7
Vacancies	30	2.2
Forfeitures	20	1.5
Total	266	19.6

NOTE: The total number of wardships = 1357.

of all the wardships between 1217 and 1327, yet the Crown jealously protected its rights to them.

During a vacancy or wardship, the king's rights as lord were largely limited to those of the former lord. He did not, for instance, have the right of prerogative wardship and did not automatically obtain the marriages of subtenants. On the other hand, the king seems to have exercised the right of primer seisin during a vacancy or wardship, to judge from the escheators' accounts.[64] Finally, the king also assumed the responsibilities as well as the benefits of lordship and assigned dowers to the widows of tenants.[65]

Feudal lordship was thus not irresponsible. Ideally, the reciprocity that gave the lord the right of wardship obligated him to watch over and protect his tenant's inheritance and children during a minority. The lord could not alienate any of the inheritance and had to maintain the heirs in a state commensurate with their status. He had to see to it that some of the debts of the deceased tenant were paid and was obliged to supervise the legal affairs of the minor. He was also supposed to pay any alms or charities that the deceased had established.[66] Homage bound the lord to ensure that the estate of his accepted tenant was honorably maintained. He could not waste the estate and thereby deprive the heir of his property. During the thirteenth century, *waste* largely referred to the excessive cutting of woods or underbrush, the destruction of the buildings on the lands, and excessive demands on the unfree

[64] *Prerogativa Regis*, xvii–xviii; *Close Rolls*, 14:532; PRO, E.372/147 m. 32 (primer seisin).
[65] *Prerogativa Regis*, xxvii–xxxi. For examples, see *CPR, 1266–1272*, 252–253; *CCR, 1272–1279*, 200, 449, 472; *CCR, 1279–1288*, 268, 388, 448, 501.
[66] *Glanvill* (VII.9), 82–83; Bracton, 2:252; Fitz Nigel, *Dialogus*, 95.

tenantry.[67] The prohibition of waste provides an interesting indication of the extent to which landholders valued unfree tenants as an economic asset that had to be carefully tended. The king's officials or guardians could not levy excessive tallages, manumit villeins, or marry female villeins to free tenants. The Crown was aware of the potential harm that wardship could cause and cautioned escheators against wasting woods and instructed them to tallage the unfree "saunz grant grevance."[68]

The lord's obligation to wards extended to their marriages. He was not supposed to arrange unsuitable matches that disparaged heirs. However, the origin and precise meaning of *disparagement* are unclear. Moralists, chronicles, legal writers, and romances all expressed the ideal that men and women should marry spouses of the same status.[69] Indeed, one chronicler went so far as to claim that the king was legally empowered to separate noble girls and widows from ignoble husbands.[70] The apprehension that the king might arrange an undesirable match may explain Henry I's promise to consult his barons in arranging marriages for female heirs. Yet Glanvill did not mention the problem, and the term *disparagement* does not seem to have been used until John's reign when it first appeared as a restriction applied to royal grants of marriages. The problem was unlikely to have been frequent or widespread in the world of seigniorial courts because wardships and marriages circulated among a small group of known associates. Two changes in the late twelfth century may have disrupted that pattern and produced a need for stricter definition. The first was that Richard and John seem to have sold a far larger number of wardships to strangers, diminishing the social control over marriage by the

---

[67] Walker, "The Action of Waste," 185–206; *Rot. Dom.*, xxix.

[68] BL, Add. MS 32,085, fols. 146–146v. I owe this reference to Dr. Paul Brand.

[69] Baldwin, *Masters, Princes, and Merchants*, 1:248–249, 2:178 n. 133; Holt, "Feudal Society and the Family IV," 26. The notion also figures in the penalties for rape as discussed in both Glanvill and Bracton (*Glanvill* [XIV.6] 176; Bracton, 1:417, cited by John F. Benton, "Clio and Venus: An Historical View of Medieval Love," in *The Meaning of Courtly Love* [Albany, 1967], 20 n. 4).

[70] *Gesta Regis Henrici Secundi Benedicti Abbatis*, ed. William Stubbs (London, 1867), 2:71–72. The "law" is not mentioned elsewhere nor is the specific case, involving Henry II's seneschal of Anjou. Other chroniclers also noted, however, that Richard I took the time at his coronation, when he supposedly made the separation, to arrange several honorable matches involving heirs and heiresses. See *Gesta Regis Henrici Secundi*, 2:73; *The Chronicle of Richard of Devizes*, ed. and trans. John T. Appleby (London, 1963), 4–5, appendix A, 85; *L'histoire de Guillaume le Maréchal*, 3:95 n. 3, 115–116, 118–119; and Roger of Hoveden, *Chronica Rogeri de Houedene* (London, 1868–1871), 3:3.

court itself. Perhaps as a result, in Magna Carta, the barons did not look to the royal court for the protection of wards in marriage. Instead, they made John promise that the ward's *family* would be consulted, in contrast to Henry I's promise to consult his barons. The second change was Henry II's legal revolution, which, as it transformed free tenements to property, must have increased family concern about mésalliances. The fate of family property was intimately related to marriage, and a mésalliance became potentially more serious because of the legal distinction between free and unfree tenures. Thenceforth, a bad marriage could mean the loss of freedom and land. The first time that disparagement was explicitly defined, in the Statute of Merton (1236), it was taken to mean marriage to a villein or burgess.[71] The sanctions of the statute were directed at mesne lords; it did not deal with the king's rights. For greater tenants-in-chief, such a marriage was unthinkable, and no example has been found. At their level of society, the issue of compatible status remained paramount throughout the thirteenth century.[72] It seems likely, therefore, that as James C. Holt has speculated, the provision against disparagement was not forced on a reluctant John in 1215, and that his use of the term in royal grants reflected the Crown's desire to stabilize the pattern of marriage and property holding within the body of tenants-in-chief.[73]

[71] Holt, *Magna Carta*, 319: Magna Carta (1215), cap. 6; *Statutes of the Realm*, 1:3: Merton, cap. 6; Milsom, "Legal Introduction," clvii–clviii; Bracton, 2:264–265, repeating Merton.

[72] Matthew Paris and the baronial reformers used the term *ignoble* to describe and denounce the spouses chosen for English wards by Henry III (Paris, *Chronica Majora*, 4:628; *DBMRR*, 80–81, 270–271). The most notorious claim of disparagement in the thirteenth century was that of the friends and family of Hugh de Neville, who was married to a daughter of Thomas de Weyland, a royal justice, while Weyland had custody of the boy (*Rot. Parl.*, 1:52; Cokayne, *Complete Peerage*, 9:484–485). One chronicler called Joan of Acre's husband by a clandestine marriage, Ralph de Monthermer, a "mere knight" (*The Chronicle of Walter of Guisborough*, ed. H. Rothwell [London, 1956], 259).

[73] Holt, *Magna Carta*, 47; Milsom, "Legal Introduction," clvii–clviii. Holt's argument that statements relating to disparagement in Exchequer fines "were intended not so much to protect the heir or heiress but to state the conditions on which the proffer had been agreed and to exclude the *parvenu* not because he was a social threat (although he might well be that) but because his intrusion would alter the terms of the negotiation" (Holt, "Feudal Society and the Family iv," 26) is unconvincing for several reasons. First, it is clear from the context that disparagement referred to something that would happen to the wards ("pro maritando herede ubi non sit disparagiatus"). The government had other formulas to indicate that a wardship could not be alienated. Second, the term was soon picked up by private

Disparagement, waste, and maintenance of heirs were traditional limitations on feudal lordship intended to protect wards and
their lands, and affected the Crown's authority as well as that of
other lords. From the late twelfth century onward, however, specific restrictions on prerogative wardship developed to protect the
mesne lordship of tenants-in-chief. In one respect, the king applied the limitation himself by exempting the holders of great liberties from the provisions of prerogative lordship. Toward the end
of the thirteenth century the *Prerogativa Regis* noted that prerogative wardship applied to the fees of all tenants-in-chief except
those of the archbishop of Canterbury, the bishop of Durham, or
the Marcher barons.[74] These immunities were well established by
Edward's reign, but it is not clear when they originated. The liberties of the Welsh Marches probably took shape during the
twelfth century under the pressures of military conflict and in the
absence of royal interference in the region. Marcher lords needed
full control of their fees in order to wage war as effectively as possible against the Welsh or to extend the frontier.[75] Like the Welsh
Marches, Leinster represented a military outpost, and when King
John confirmed his grant of Leinster to William Marshal on 28
March 1208, he included the right to take the custody of fees held
of Marshal in Leinster, whether or not the tenants held of the king
elsewhere, though John retained his right to the marriage of the
heirs.[76] At one time Chester, Durham, and, in a slightly different
context, Canterbury had also been military frontiers. It seems reasonable to assume that the king would want to ensure the strength
and integrity of these vital lordships by allowing the lords custody
of their fees during minorities.

---

parties who used it in agreements that had nothing to do with the king (e.g., *CRR*,
6:7–8 [1210]; and *Rot. Chart.*, 98). Third, the Crown looked out for wards and widows in other ways, stipulating, for example, that marriages could be made only with
the consent of the widow or that the guardian could arrange a marriage only with
the advice and consent of the ward's relatives and friends (e.g., *Pipe Roll, 9 Richard
I*, 82, 114, 233; *1 John*, 178; *3 John*, 257; *6 John*, 144, 253; *9 John*, 101; *CPR, 1232–
1247*, 194).

[74] *Statutes of the Realm*, 1:226. For the rights in Durham, Chester, and the
Marches, see Constance M. Fraser, "Edward I and the Regalian Franchise of Durham," *Speculum* 31 (1956): 330–331; idem, "Prerogative and the Bishops of Durham," *EHR* 74 (1959): 474; R. R. Davies, *Lordship and Society*, 100–101, 251.

[75] R. Rees Davies, "Kings, Lords and Liberties in the March of Wales, 1066–
1272," *TRHS*, 5th ser., 29 (1979): 41–61, esp. 55–59.

[76] *Rot. Chart.*, 176, cited by Annette J. Otway-Ruthven, "The Constitutional Position of the Great Lordships of South Wales," *TRHS*, 5th ser., 8 (1958): 14 n. 2. See
idem, "The Medieval County of Kildare," *Irish Historical Studies* 11 (1959): 189–190.

Because the military threat in England had subsided by the thirteenth century, destroying the logic of immunities from prerogative wardship, the king's attitude changed. The liberties seemed only to diminish his resources. Over the thirteenth century, he occasionally tried to circumvent them, though when Henry introduced the escheatorships in 1232, he did not appoint any in Durham or Chester, perhaps in recognition of their liberties.[77] Royal intervention came to an end in 1258. After Henry granted his half-brother, William de Valence, the wardship of the lands and heir of William's in-law, Warin de Mountchesney, William occupied a fee that Mountchesney held of the archbishop of Canterbury. The archbishop complained about the intrusion, and in October 1258, the council of magnates decided that the archbishop should recover custody of the fee, that William's occupation of the fee would not prejudice the archbishop's right to the custody of his fees in the future, and that the archbishop should recover damages. The judgment temporarily ended any assault on these immunities, and thereafter the holders of the three major liberties exercised their rights without serious interruption, though escheators did not automatically respect the liberties, and the holders had to assert their claims.[78]

THE EFFECTS OF MAGNA CARTA

The most significant restrictions on royal lordship resulted from political opposition. Magna Carta restated the obligations concerning waste, disparagement, and the maintenance of the estate during a minority, but went beyond these traditional limits to fix reliefs and define prerogative wardship.[79] In more general terms, it

---

[77] *Patent Rolls*, 1:323; *Close Rolls*, 5:436; E. R. Stevenson, "The Escheator," 115. For Henry III's attitude toward liberties, see David A. Carpenter, "King, Magnates, and Society," 39–70.

[78] *Close Rolls*, 10:276, cited by F.R.H. DuBoulay, *The Lordship of Canterbury: An Essay on Medieval Society* (London, 1966), 90 n. 1, and see 89–92, for a valuable discussion of the archbishop's use of wardships after that. For the application of these rights under Edward I, see *CIPM*, 3:194 (at p. 125), 544; *CCR, 1288–1296*, 409–410, 415–416, 465, 493–494; *CCR, 1296–1302*, 270; PRO, SC.1/24/29. In 1253 Humphrey de Bohun claimed that all lands of his fee were exempt from prerogative wardship, but on what basis is not known (*Close Rolls*, 8:292).

[79] Magna Carta (1215), cap. 2 (reliefs), 3 (prohibition of relief after minority), 4 (waste), 5 (maintenance of inheritance during minority), 6 (disparagement). Magna Carta of 1225 repeated caps. 2, 4, and 5 verbatim, but slightly altered 3 and 6. Stipulations that a lord could not take custody of the lands of a minor until he took

also ended the arbitrary exercise of seigniorial authority by forbidding unjust disseisins and exactions. Those restrictions went to the heart of the king's disciplinary powers and brought his actions somewhat into line with those of mesne lords as regulated by the assizes. Magna Carta thus had a significant impact on the king's power as a feudal lord.

In the first place, it distinguished between tenants-in-chief who held directly of the Crown and those who held of the the king through an escheated lordship: *ut de corona* as opposed to *ut de honore, ut de escaeta,* or *ut de baronia.*[80] Whenever baronies, honors, or other estates escheated or lapsed to the Crown, the tenants of those lordships became tenants-in-chief. Early on it was recognized that escheats represented a special case of royal lordship and that subtenants should not have to bear the full weight of royal lordship. The Dialog of the Exchequer, for example, stated that the payment of relief by tenants of honors under royal control was governed by the customs pertaining to those honors, not by those of royal lordship, so that their reliefs were fixed.[81] Magna Carta in 1215 reiterated the distinction in tenure, adding that such tenants would not have to do any more service than they owed to their former lords. The 1225 version took the next logical step and applied it to wardships: during the minority of a tenant-in-chief who held of an honor, the king would have the wardship only of the lands held directly of that lordship, unless the tenant held elsewhere of the king. Prerogative wardship over the lands did not apply in those cases. This distinction henceforth became the standard test in determining the extent of the king's rights in lands that came under his authority, whether by escheat or forfeiture.[82]

After Magna Carta, tenants of escheated honors regularly came into royal custody, though not in great numbers, and the Crown

---

the homage of the heir and that the lord would retain the wardship of the lands of a minor until the age of twenty-one even if the heir was knighted in the meantime were added to cap. 3. The 1225 version dropped the requirement originally stated in cap. 6 that the lord had to inform the heir's kin before contracting a marriage for the minor. See Holt, *Magna Carta,* 316–319, 351–352, for both versions.

[80] Pollock and Maitland, *History of English Law,* 1:281–282; *Prerogativa Regis,* xiv–xv.

[81] Fitz Nigel, *Dialogus,* 121.

[82] Magna Carta (1215), cap. 43; (1225), cap. 36. The 1215 version stated that "nos eodem modo eam tenebimus quo baro eam tenuit," which implies a limitation of the rights of wardship and marriage, but the 1225 version made it explicit. See Holt, *Magna Carta,* 207, 328–329, 355. For a successful application of this test by tenants of mesne lords, see *Rot. Parl.,* 1:430.

generally respected the limitations that Magna Carta imposed. Altogether, between 1215 and 1330, the Crown granted out seventy-five wardships acquired through honors (see Table 2.1).[83] When it was discovered that a tenant held *ut de honore*, the king usually restored the lands held of other lords to their respective lords. In one case, an inquest held after the wardship had been granted and the heir had come of age revealed that the tenant held of the Crown only by the honor of Boulogne and that he also held of the abbey of Bury St. Edmunds. By then it was too late to restore custody to the abbot, so the king assured him that the grant would not prejudice the abbey's rights to the wardship of the lands held of the abbey or to the heir's marriage in the future.[84]

In the second place, Magna Carta theoretically limited the Crown's rights over serjeanty and socage tenures. It stated that if a tenant holding of the king by socage, fee farm, or burgage tenure died leaving a minor heir, the king could not claim the wardship of lands held by military service of other lords nor the marriage of the heir. Nor would he have custody of those lands or fee farm. Magna Carta applied the same restriction to tenants holding by petty serjeanty, defined by Magna Carta as the service of knives, arrows, or the like.[85] The king retained the full rights of prerogative wardship over grand serjeanties. Yet because the line between grand and petty serjeanties was not always clear, the king's right of wardship had to be decided on an ad hoc basis each time a serjeanty came into custody. Not surprisingly, the king often assumed the full rights of wardship in ambiguous cases and did not adhere strictly to Magna Carta's prescription.[86]

Some of Magna Carta's most far-reaching provisions were those which regulated the king's authority over widows. They stipulated that the king could not withhold a widow's *maritagium*, inheritance, and dower on her husband's death and guaranteed that a widow could not be married against her will. Widows had to give the king

[83] This should be considered a minimum figure. The Chancery enrollments of grants do not always mention the fact that lands were held of a particular honor.

[84] *CIPM*, 1:248, 350; *CPR, 1247–1258*, 469–470.

[85] Magna Carta (1215), cap. 37; (1225), cap. 27. There was no difference between the two versions (Holt, *Magna Carta*, 326–327, 355).

[86] Bracton, 2:113–114, 231, 253–254; *Britton*, 2:7; Pollock and Maitland, *History of English Law*, 1:290, 323; and Elisabeth G. Kimball, *Serjeanty Tenure in Medieval England* (New Haven, 1936), 150–198. For a dispute over the custody of a serjeanty in which the council determined that the king had no right, see *Rot. Parl.*, 1:214; *CCR, 1302–1307*, 492. Magna Carta was silent regarding personal or administrative services.

security that they would not marry without his permission, but beyond that the king could not interfere with her or her lands.[87]

These chapters enshrine two general principles. The first is that a woman could not be compelled to marry. Magna Carta went beyond Henry I's vague promise in his coronation charter not to marry a widow without her consent by prohibiting him from *distraining* a widow to marry.[88] In 1189 Richard had seized the lands of Hawise, daughter and heir of William le Gros, earl of Aumale, after the death of her first husband because she refused to marry William de Forz as the king requested. The distraint seems to have had the desired effect, for she married Forz shortly thereafter.[89] Magna Carta removed the sanction of distraint. In sharp contrast, Ireland preserved a stage of feudal lordship that Magna Carta brought to an end. In a writ of 1243, Henry III explained that Irish law still permitted him, as a last resort, to distrain widows by their lands to take husbands that he chose for them. Accordingly, he ordered his justice to distrain Emmeline, widow of Hugh de Lacy, earl of Ulster, to accept Stephen Longspee as her husband as Henry had requested. Whether or not in response to this order, she married him.[90]

After Magna Carta, therefore, there were qualitative differences in the king's rights of marriage over minor heiresses and widows in England. The king could choose a husband for his ward, but could only withhold consent to a marriage proposed by a widow. As Henry III was trying to compel Emmeline to marry Longspee, for example, he was simultaneously urging Margaret, the countess of Warwick, to marry one of his courtiers, John de Plessetis. Unlike Emmeline, Margaret could not be distrained, and Henry had to proceed cautiously lest he violate the provisions of Magna Carta.

[87] Magna Carta (1215), caps. 7, 8 (1225), cap. 7. The 1225 version gave more explicit instructions concerning the assignment of dower; see Holt, *Magna Carta*, 318–321, 352. See also Milsom, "Inheritance by Women," 63–65, for a comparison of the charters; and Walker, "Feudal Constraint and Free Consent," 97–110.

[88] "Et eam non dabo marito nisi secundum velle suum" (*Select Charters*, 118); "Nulla vidua distringatur ad se maritandum" (Holt, *Magna Carta*, 318 [1215 version]).

[89] *Pipe Roll, 6 Richard I*, 163 (receipts from goods sold in 1 Richard I); Cokayne, *Complete Peerage*, 1:353–354.

[90] *Close Rolls*, 5:60; *CPR, 1232–1247*, 352; *Close Rolls*, 5:277, 358, 363; *Rotulorum Patentium et Clausarum Cancellariae Hiberniae Calendarium* (Dublin, 1928), 287, 411, 413, 429. Magna Carta was not fully enforced right away: "Margareta de Reveres habet literas directas omnibus, quod non distringatur per regem vel aliquem de suis ad se maritandum quamdiu vivere voluerit sine marito" (*Patent Rolls*, 2:269 [1229]).

He instructed his agents to enter into a contract with Margaret, as part of the security she owed not to marry without license, in which she would agree that she would lose her lands forever if she married without Henry's permission.[91] Since the king could not force a widow to marry, he had to rely on persuasion—applied either directly or indirectly through the widow's friends—to convince her to accept his candidate. Margaret, in fact, may have resisted Henry's pleas and married someone other than Plessetis, but because of her contract with the king, Plessetis eventually acquired the earldom for his life, regardless of whether his marriage to her stood.[92]

The issue of distraint highlights the second principle contained in these chapters: that a tenant or widow should have his or her lands without hindrance from the king. Glanvill had stated that when an heiress remarried, her lord could not demand a second relief.[93] Magna Carta similarly affirmed that an heir did not have to pay a relief or fine after a wardship. The only payment to which a lord was entitled was a single relief, and anything beyond that was unjust. For some time, King John and his predecessors had demanded fines from widows for the right to take up their inheritances, *maritagia*, or dowers. Those fines duplicated, in a sense, the reliefs that had already been paid.[94] Magna Carta tried to prevent the king's hindering heirs, heiresses, and widows from entering lands to which they were entitled and unjustly mulcting them for their entry.

This protection along with the emphatic prohibition against unjust disseisin in chapter 39 also affected the king's "disciplinary jurisdiction" over marriage and consent. Like other lords, the king seized the lands of contumacious tenants to force them to perform services or fulfill their obligations to the king, and the ultimate sanction was disinheritance if a tenant refused to obey. In Glan-

[91] *Close Rolls*, 5:61. According to a later reference, Margaret promised by her own charter that she would forfeit her lands to the king if she had married without the king's consent (*CPR, 1247–1258*, 76).

[92] Cokayne, *Complete Peerage*, 12:2:365–366; *Close Rolls*, 5:9. Henry granted Plessetis Margaret's marriage on 25 December 1242 (*CPR, 1232–1247*, 352), though Margaret may have married someone else in the meantime (Mason, "Resources of Warwick," 69–70). In 1302 Edward I wrote directly to Christine de Kirkeby and her counselor to urge her to marry his knight, Bertram de Mountbouchier (PRO, SC.1/37/146; *HKF*, 2:162–163; *CIPM*, 2:91; Moor, *Knights*, 3:174–175).

[93] Milsom, *Legal Framework*, 104; *Glanvill* (ix.4), 108.

[94] Holt argues that these fines raised the expectations of tenants-in-chief that lands would pass automatically to women, but they must have been extremely aggravating nonetheless (Holt, *Magna Carta*, 46–47, 113–115).

vill's age, for example, a tenant who married off an heiress without obtaining his lord's permission thus lost his lands forever, and throughout the twelfth century English kings seized the lands of heiresses or widows who married without their consent.[95] Marriage and inheritance were of such crucial importance that even more terrible punishment might be threatened for disobedience. In July 1184, Gilbert of Plumpton was brought in chains before Henry II and accused by Ranulf de Glanvill of raping a girl in royal custody and marrying her without license.[96] Ranulf was particularly annoyed by the transgression because he had intended to marry the girl, along with her inheritance, to his steward and subsheriff in Yorkshire. Gilbert was found guilty and condemned to be hanged, but he was reprieved at the last moment, so the story goes, by the bishop of Worcester. Nevertheless, the king seized Gilbert's lands and sold all the chattels found on them. The king's concern was for his lordship, not the girl.

Yet harsh discipline was exceptional. In only 6 of the 31 cases of marrying without license recorded in the pipe rolls for the reigns of Henry II and his two sons did the king seize the property of the offenders. In the rest, he was content to levy a fine, albeit a sometimes hefty fine, for the transgression (see Table 4.4.). Indeed, the pipe rolls give the impression that violations of the king's right of consent were not frequent in the twelfth century, especially in comparison with the 135 fines for permission to marry. Disseisin or imprisonment, then, served as a warning to tenants-in-chief as to what they could expect if they violated the king's authority over marriage rather than as a routine sanction.[97] It should be noted, moreover, that widows and wards did not flout royal lordship by

---

[95] Milsom, *Legal Framework*, 1–35, esp. 11 n. 1; Searle, "Seigneurial Control," 9–10; *Glanvill* (vii.12), 85. Heiress: *Pipe Roll, 27 Henry II*, 51. Widow (Alice de Nonant): *Pipe Roll, 22 Henry II*, 150; *33 Henry II*, xxviii, 146. Rose de Dover paid Richard I £700 for her inheritance and the right to marry whomever she pleased. In 1204 John seized her lands because she married without *his* permission and charged her another 100 marks and 2 palfreys (*Pipe Roll, 6 Richard I*, 250; *7 John*, 117, 195; *Rot. Ob. et Fin.*, 229; *Rot. Lit. Claus.*, 1:7, 8).

[96] *Pipe Roll, 31 Henry II*, xxxii, 76; *Gesta Regis Henrici Secundi*, 1:314–316; *Pipe Roll, 30 Henry II*, 29, 38.

[97] *Pipe Roll, 21 Henry II*, 132; *23 Henry II*, 95, 110; *24 Henry II*, 111; *26 Henry II*, 41, 72; *27 Henry II*, 47, 51; *30 Henry II*, 17; *31 Henry II*, 72; *32 Henry II*, 9; *34 Henry II*, 15; *6 Richard I*, 79, 118, 162, 238; *7 Richard I*, 97, 110, 211, 234; *9 Richard I*, 206; *1 John*, 28; *2 John*, 19, 27, 87; *6 John*, 183; *7 John*, 195; *13 John*, 29; *16 John*, 151; *Rot. Dom.*, 23–24, 27, 75. For punishment as a warning to others, see *Rot. Ob. et Fin.*, 523–524, cited by Holt, *Magna Carta*, 114.

frequently contracting marriages without permission. Tenants-in-chief largely accepted their duties. Out of the more than 175 widows and wards listed in the *Rotuli de Dominabus*, only 2 arranged marriages without royal consent. Marriages contracted by wards without royal license were no more frequent after 1215 than they were before. Fewer than 20 were recorded over the following century.[98] The rate was higher for widows, but did not approach widespread disrespect for the king's lordship.

Magna Carta, nevertheless, forced kings to be more circumspect in their treatment of disobedient widows and wards, as the language of Henry III's writ concerning the countess of Warwick illustrates. Throughout the thirteenth century, the Crown treated violations of consent by widows as petty crimes, or "trespasses," and some men wound up in prison as a result.[99] Although the Crown still seized widows' lands for such an offense, it was clear that the seizure was a distraint to compel appearance before the king or the payment of a fine, not a forfeiture. Henry III, for example, ordered the mayor and sheriffs of London and Suffolk to seize the lands of Richard de Gosbeck and Margaret, widow of William le Breton, because they had married without his license. They were to hold the lands until Richard and Margaret paid the fine for their trespass.[100] The seizure was clearly intended as a formal

[98] This conclusion is based on evidence from the fine, close, patent, and memoranda rolls. See, for example, *Close Rolls*, 4:406; *CFR*, 1:20, 97, 133, 2:90, 3:217, 369; *CPR*, *1272–1281*, 11–12; *CPR*, *1281–1292*, 111; *CPR*, *1317–1321*, 43, 49; *CCR*, *1279–1288*, 251; Cokayne, *Complete Peerage*, 4:1–2, 9:408. Without published pipe rolls, it is more difficult to trace thirteenth-century fines. In fact, it is likely that the number of unauthorized marriages by both widows and wards is greater than these figures indicate, for some married without license after their marriages had been granted out, in which case they paid their fines to the grantees (see e.g. *CPR*, *1247–1258*, 483). Bracton noted that lords could no longer disinherit heiresses who married without their consent, but he did not discuss the king's rights. Nor did he mention the sanctions available to lords, though the cases cited in this and the following notes support Searle's suggestion that distraint for a fine became the standard penalty (Searle, "Seigneurial Control," 10 and n. 21).

[99] The term *trespass* is used in various cases: *ERF*, 1:43, 61; PRO, E.159/7 m. 8d; *CRR*, 15:272 (no. 1132); *ERF*, 1:265; *Close Rolls*, 5:431–432, 498; E.368/27 m. 4; *ERF*, 2:119, 167; *CPR*, *1247–1258*, 334; E.13/1B m. 10d; *Close Rolls*, 12:127, 391, 13:321, 14:445; *CFR*, 1:71, 149, 151; *CPR*, *1281–1292*, 111; *CCR*, *1279–1288*, 251; E.159/60 m. 8; HMC, 4th report, 4:389. Prison: *Close Rolls*, 5:534; E.159/61 m. 4d; /72 mm. 9d, 69.

[100] *Close Rolls*, 5:498, 500–501, 512. For similar cases, see *ERF*, 1:43; PRO, E.159/4 m. 9; *ERF*, 1:61; E.159/6 m. 17 (distraint "ad ostendum . . . quo warranto"); *CRR*, 15:272 (no. 1132); *Close Rolls*, 1:519; *The Memoranda Roll of the King's Remembrancer for Michaelmas 1230–Trinity 1231* (London, 1933), 88; *Close Rolls*, 8:275, 12:127,

step in a legal process rather than an end in itself. In cases in which the king had granted his right in a widow's marriage to someone else, the king generally supported the grantees in their suits if the widow married without license.[101] The issue sometimes struck close to home. When Edward I's daughter, Joan of Acre, the widow of the earl of Gloucester, married Ralph de Monthermer clandestinely, Edward was outraged and ordered her lands seized in January 1297. Most he quickly restored, though he held onto the rich honor of Tonbridge for nearly three years, collecting the revenues and exercising the rights of lordship. The marriage and distraint attracted the notice of several chroniclers, and is important for showing how the king could lose control over a vital estate as a result of a widow's marriage.[102] In the case of wards, the king was usually content to levy a fine and he conformed to the principles laid out in the statutes of Merton and Westminster I.[103]

An analogous problem, though much rarer, was a ward's refusal to accept a proffered marriage. According to one story, the king in the twelfth century allowed guardians of the wards of tenants-in-chief who refused a marriage to retain custody of the lands until the ward satisfied them of the value of the marriage.[104] The statutes of Merton and Westminster established a formula for recompensing a lord in case a ward refused a marriage. A ward, whether of the king or anyone else, could not be compelled to marry and could not forfeit his or her lands for such a refusal, so that the issue in the thirteenth century turned on money. Edward I re-

---

13:321; SC.1/45/39, 48; E.159/60 mm. 2d, 7d; *CCR, 1279–1288*, 451. Escheators accounted for such lands while they were in custody (PRO, E.372/117 m. 7; /124 mm. 19, 20, 20d; /141 m. 23; /149 mm. 32d–33). In some cases lands were restored only after the fine had been paid: *CFR*, 1:5, 71, 149; PRO, E.159/60 m. 8; /72 mm. 9d, 69d; E.143/4/6 no. 1, for the same case.

[101] Walker, "Feudal Constraint and Free Consent," 104–105.

[102] *CCR, 1296–1302*, 12, 29, 34, 39; *CPR, 1292–1301*, 288; *CFR*, 1:389; *Parliamentary Writs*, 1:296; PRO, E.372/149 mm. 32d–33; E.136/1/18, 19A (Tonbridge accounts). Edward had arranged to marry Joan to Amadeus, count of Savoy (*CPR, 1292–1301*, 243; *Foedera*, 1:2:861). Rishanger notes the restoration of the lands and implies that they had been seized "in gravem patris offensam"; see *Willelmi Rishanger, quondam monachi S. Albani, Chronica et Annales*, in *Chronica Monasterii S. Albani*, 2:173. See also *Walter of Guisborough*, 259; and *The Chronicle of Bury St. Edmunds, 1212–1301*, ed. and trans. Antonia Gransden (London, 1964), 134. The Crown acquired at least one wardship by reason of these lands being in his custody (PRO, E.159/71 m. 80; *CIPM*, 3:391).

[103] Plucknett, *Legislation*, 115–117; Milsom, "Legal Introduction," clv–clvi.

[104] PRO, KB.26/148 m. 19. The events narrated in the plea took place in the reigns of Henry II and his sons.

garded Thomas Bardolf's claim that he did not want to be married to be an insufficient excuse for refusing the marriage that Edward offered him and worried that it might be a bad example to others, so that he ordered his men to be as hard on Thomas as they could be *without breaking the law*.[105]

Magna Carta laid out broad standards for the legitimate exercise of the king's seigniorial authority. Depending on the tenure by which a tenant-in-chief held his lands, the king could have (1) full prerogative rights over all the lands and over the marriage of the heir, or (2) right to the wardship of lands held directly of him *ut de escaeta* and perhaps the marriage of the heir, or (3) rights as lord determined by the tenure of the lands held of him.[106] In the last case, he would have the wardship and marriage of the heir only if they pertained to him as lord of those lands and not in the case of socage or petty serjeanty tenures. He had to give a widow her lands once she had given him security that she would not marry without his consent and could not force her to marry by distraining her lands. In general, Magna Carta removed disseisin as a sanction for consent and marriage but did not interfere with the king's right to distrain lands to compel payment of a fine.

The Legal Refinement of Royal Lordship under Henry III and Edward I

Despite Magna Carta, many aspects of relations between the Crown and tenants-in-chief remained ill defined. Henry III and Edward I seized the opportunity presented by this uncertainty to reinforce and in some cases to extend their feudal prerogative. These efforts were of consequence not only because they protected such royal assets as wardships, but more importantly because they maintained the Crown's initiative in its relations with tenants-in-chief. Their decisive action prevented the erosion of royal lordship through neglect or the encroachment of tenants during the thirteenth and early fourteenth centuries. Henry III stated the Crown's authority over tenants-in-chief in a series of ordinances and statutes and set up a permanent system for the management of those rights in the foundation of the escheatorships. Although Henry proved to be a vigilant landlord, he did not rigorously en-

---

[105] *CChW*, 1:241; cited by Plucknett, *Legislation*, 116; and Frederick M. Powicke, *King Henry III and the Lord Edward: The Community of the Realm in the Thirteenth Century* (Oxford, 1966), 706–707.

[106] *Prerogativa Regis*, xv–xvi.

force his rights vis-à-vis the magnates and left it up to his son to put teeth into his policies.[107] As in so many other areas of relations between the Crown and tenants-in-chief, Edward pressed his feudal authority to the limit and demanded strict compliance from his tenants. The *Prerogativa Regis*, which summarizes the king's rights until about 1285, and the Articles of the Escheators (*Articuli de Escaetoribus*) demonstrate the effectiveness of the policy and the vigor of royal lordship at the end of the thirteenth century.

Henry III initiated this policy by restricting alienations by tenants-in-chief. Control of alienation had at one time been an essential aspect of feudal lordship.[108] During the twelfth century, lords wanted to be assured that tenants could perform the services of their tenements, and were concerned that a dismemberment of the tenement would reduce its value and jeopardize the services. In the thirteenth century, their concern shifted to their rights of wardship and marriage as the value of feudal services declined and that of feudal incidents rose.[109] Now they feared that alienations would deprive them of economic resources. They felt that the desire, widespread in medieval society, to grant land to the Church as alms was particularly dangerous because it removed that land from their control.[110] The way in which lords controlled alienations prior to Magna Carta is obscure, but the charter indicates that Henry II's assizes had severely hampered their efforts. In the charter, they tried to preserve a modicum of service by establishing restrictions on subenfeoffments and grants to religious institutions and turned to legal devices to prevent further alienations.[111]

Although the king's writs did not affect royal lordship, the growing freedom of alienation for subtenants was infectious, and the government grew alarmed. The king had often confirmed grants by tenants-in-chief, and in the thirteenth century it acted to inhibit unauthorized alienations. On several occasions, for example, Henry III ordered his sheriffs to prevent individuals from alien-

[107] See Carpenter, "King, Magnates, and Society," for an appraisal of Henry's policies toward the magnates.

[108] Pollock and Maitland, *History of English Law*, 1:343–344; Milsom, *Legal Framework*, 115–116; Paul A. Brand, "Control of Mortmain Alienation in England, 1200–1300," in *Legal Records and the Historian* (London, 1978), 29–30.

[109] Milsom, *Legal Framework*, 112–113, 154–156.

[110] Ibid., 114–121; Brand, "Control of Mortmain Alienation"; Sandra Raban, *Mortmain Legislation and the English Church, 1279–1500* (Cambridge, 1982), 1–28.

[111] Brand, "Control of Mortmain Alienation"; Scott L. Waugh, "Non-Alienation Clauses in Thirteenth-Century English Charters," *Albion* 17 (1985): 1–14.

ating lands.[112] In other instances, he got tenants to agree not to alienate, sell, or farm any of their holdings.[113] Yet the Crown became so worried about the problem that it began investigating alienations. In 1212 King John ordered his sheriffs to inform him about all fees and serjeanties within their counties, who held them, the service by which they were held, and whether any lands had been alienated through marriage portions, subenfeoffment, or mortmain.[114] Additional inquests were held between the 1220s and 1250s to determine, among other things, the extent of the damage to serjeanty tenures and escheats caused by alienations. The government supplemented these special inquiries through routine questions put to hundred juries in the eyres.[115]

It was in this context that Henry III acted to halt unlicensed alienations. In 1228 he ordered his sheriffs to proclaim that no one holding in chief could alienate lands to a religious house or religious person without royal license.[116] Then in 1256 he issued his sweeping prohibition against all alienations without license. The writ explained that unlicensed alienations had caused an intolerable loss of wardships and escheats and a diminution in service so that henceforth no one could enter a royal fee without special license.[117] The Crown's position was straightforward: alienations by tenants-in-chief required royal authorization.

It is less clear, however, how that authorization worked under Henry III. The Chancery rolls for Henry's reign contain occasional, but not routine, confirmations of grants. And the king sometimes personally authorized grants and final concords without issuing a formal license or confirmation.[118] Jurors on inquisi-

---

[112] *Close Rolls*, 4:299 (a marriage portion originally granted by the king, *Pipe Roll, 10 John*, 90, and *11 John*, 36); 6:98 (wife's inheritance); 7:258 (dower). On royal restrictions on alienation in general, see Pollock and Maitland, *History of English Law*, 1:335–337; and more fully, Bean, *Decline*, 40–103.

[113] *Rot. Ob. et Fin.*, 530–531: "nichil dabit vel alio modo alienabit" (the phrase is inserted in John's confirmation of a grant, *Pipe Roll, 16 John*, 160); *Close Rolls*, 6:359. This undertaking is identical to those made by subtenants to mesne lords at about the same time (Waugh, "Non-Alienation Clauses," 11–12).

[114] *Book of Fees*, 1:52. The fullest returns are for Northumberland, 1:200–205; and *Testa de Nevill*, ed. John Caley and William Illingworth (London, 1807), 392–393.

[115] Kimball, *Serjeanty Tenure*, 215–229; *CPR, 1247–1258*, 209–210 (1253); *Book of Fees*, 2:1323–1427.

[116] Bean, *Decline*, 57–60; Brand, "Control of Mortmain Alienation," 32. The order is printed in *Close Rolls*, 1:88. It emphasized the loss of services and tallages.

[117] Bean, *Decline*, 66–79; printed in *Close Rolls*, 9:429.

[118] Bean, *Decline*, 68–71. For examples, see PRO, CP.25 (1)/193/5/55, and /193/6/

tions post mortem assumed that such a confirmation was necessary for an alienation, including grants of marriage portions, but the measure must have been difficult to enforce without closer supervision.[119] Furthermore, Henry's ordinances are vague about the range of prohibited alienations. The 1228 writ stated that no portion of a tenement ("aliquid de tenemento") could be alienated in mortmain, while the 1256 ordinance prohibited anyone from entering a barony or fee held in chief without royal license. What, exactly, did these restrictions cover? The *Prerogativa Regis* from early in Edward I's reign stated that tenants-in-chief could not alienate the major portion of their lands without license but could alienate members and parcels. This seems to fall far short of Henry's provision, though it may reflect the actual practice of his administration as it attempted to cope with a difficult mission.[120]

Edward I acted more decisively. The hundred inquests that he launched on his return from the Crusade in 1274 to acquaint himself with his administration and its performance during his absence revealed that unauthorized alienations had damaged his lordship.[121] As a result, the government made a more determined effort to license alienations and to punish offenders. In a case in 1279 over a disputed advowson, the king's attorney argued not only that it was unlawful under the king's prerogative to alienate a fee without the king's license, but that if a fine had been levied, even in the past, making such an alienation without his consent, then it was void because it worked to the king's disinheritance.[122] It is an indication of how forcefully Edward asserted his prerogative concerning alienations. Orders to sheriffs and escheators to seize lands that had been alienated without license increased, and

---

8; SC.1/9/82; *Patent Rolls*, 2:328. It may be that the final concord itself represented a valid record of consent. Later, however, the parties received a letter patent as well as the foot of the fine, even if the fine noted consent (CP.25[1]/75/39/231, 240; *CPR, 1301–1307*, 131 [Brun]; CP.25[1]/194/8/22; *CPR, 1307–1313*, 213 [Fitz Warin]).

[119] *CIPM*, 1:887; PRO, C.132/45, no. 20 (no date); *CIPM*, 1:801, C.132/41, no. 14 (1271–1272).

[120] *Prerogativa Regis*, xl–xlii; Bean, *Decline*, 70 n. 2. The examples cited by Bean for the reign of Henry III (69) all involve substantial holdings. Furthermore, the *Prerogativa Regis* does not exactly follow Magna Carta (1225), cap. 32, since it explicitly prohibits alienating the *majorem partem* rather than reproducing Magna Carta's vague formula (Holt, *Magna Carta*, 356).

[121] Helen M. Cam, *The Hundred and the Hundred Rolls: An Outline of Local Government in Medieval England* (1930; reprint, 1963), 34–38, 195–199. For examples of such alienations, see *RH*, 1:60, 83, 90, 91, 102, 121, 191, 193, 197, 241, 2:31, 119.

[122] *Select Cases*, 1:48–49. The outcome is not known.

the Chancery began to enroll licenses on a regular basis, though it was not until the last ten years of Edward's reign, when the administrative apparatus was fully in place and his financial need had become overpowering, that licenses and seizures became routine. Both are signs of a more vigorous enforcement of royal lordship, likewise evident in licenses for grants to religious houses and in the quo warranto proceedings.[123]

Edward's administration specified more minutely the kinds of alienations that required royal license and delegated enforcement to the escheators. They interpreted Henry's precedent broadly to include every aspect of a tenement. The Articles of the Escheators, drawn up sometime after 1295 and confirmed by licenses to alienate, indicate that the requirement covered any alienation that diminished the tenement in any way, including subenfeoffments or substitutions; life grants and leases, burdening lands with corodies or pensions; alienations of rents, services, or advowsons; alienations by religious institutions of lands that had once been granted them by the Crown; fraudulent conveyances to religious institutions; and even manumissions of villeins or changes in their services. The government also gave escheators responsibility for enforcing restrictions on purprestures (encroachments on royal lands and highways), which were similarly viewed as diminishing the Crown's resources.[124] The breadth of control over alienations was new, a product of Edward's vigorous lordship. His restrictions on pensions and manumissions went beyond what common lawyers were willing to allow Henry VII at the end of the fifteenth century.[125] Edward's seigniorial authority far outstripped that of any mesne lord. In 1325, after the Crown had seized lands for the rebellion of 1321–1322, some tenants of forfeited estates complained to the king that whereas formerly they had been able to alienate lands without their lords' license, once the Crown had assumed lordship, escheators seized lands they alienated as though they were held in chief. Edward acknowledged the legitimacy of

[123] Bean, *Decline*, 66–79. For examples of orders to seize alienated lands, see *Rot. Orig.*, 1:19, 20 (2), 21 (2), 22, 26 (4), 28, 29, 30.
[124] *Statutes of the Realm*, 1:238–241; Huntington Library, HM. 19,920, fols. 59v–61; Stevenson, "The Escheator," 113, 129; *CPR, 1313–1317*, 512 (manumission). The scope of restrictions is evident from the escheators' records (PRO, E.136/3/10 mm. 4 [annual rents], 9 [toll]; E.372/154 m. 53 [purprestures and appropriations of the king's soil]; E.372/160 m. 50 [ovens]; E.143/4/4, no. 24 [dowry]; E.153/1956, no. 15 [rent]).
[125] *Prerogativa Regis*, 146–147.

their complaint.[126] Nothing could show more clearly the contrast between the powers of royal and mesne lordships.

Licensing, however, did not mean that the Crown tried to halt all alienations by its tenants-in-chief, only those which seriously detracted from its feudal rights or services. Mesne lords struggled throughout the thirteenth century to find a legal formula to inhibit unacceptable alienations without violating the principles enshrined in novel disseisin and mort d'ancestor. They found a partial solution with the help of Edward I in the statutes *De Viris Religionis* (1279) and *Quia Emptores* (1290). Because the Crown was not affected by its own writs, it could act on its own to achieve the same ends. Tenants-in-chief could go ahead with grants to family, Church, or strangers so long as they secured royal consent and provided the grants did not diminish the Crown's resources. That meant, for example, that family grants would have to take the form of substitutions. Edward I confirmed a grant by Ingram de Monceaus to his son John while John was still a minor in 1289. When Ingram died four years later, he held nothing of the king in chief. Yet the grant had been made in such a way that John held in chief of the king and that if Ingram died before John was of age the king would lose neither the wardship nor the marriage.[127] It is precisely that preservation of feudal incidents which Henry III had hoped to achieve through the licensing of alienations.

Henry's original pronouncement made it clear that the Crown would punish unlicensed alienations by seizing the land.[128] In practice, the seizure was only a distraint, and once a fine was paid, the lands were returned to the grantee. The delay between the seizure and restoration was usually very short, though in some cases the lands were farmed out to officials and kept in royal custody for a number of years. Neither the grantor nor the grantee forfeited the lands. Here again, Magna Carta may have inhibited royal action and prevented disinheritance. Therefore, when Edward II seized Gower in 1320 and treated it as forfeit, he violated

---

[126] *Rot. Parl.*, 1:430.

[127] *CCR, 1288–1296*, 19–20; *CIPM*, 3:53. For a family grant by subenfeoffment that deprived the Crown of a wardship, see *CIPM*, 2:802; and *CCR, 1288–1296*, 214. The Crown for some time had permitted tenants to transfer some or all of their lands to their heirs in their lifetimes: *Patent Rolls*, 2:428, 6:37, 10:51; *ERF*, 1:308, 2:13. Later, the king permitted alienations even after an inquisition *ad quod damnum* had ascertained that in the future the king would lose custody of the land (*CPR, 1301–1307*, 231, 314, 315, 319, 335, 423, 426, 464; *CPR, 1317–1321*, 219).

[128] *Close Rolls*, 9:429: "tunc terram, quam eo modo ingressus fuerit, capias in manum nostram et eam salvo custodias donec aliud inde preceperimus."

custom and aroused violent opposition. After he was deposed, the Commons complained of the practice and asked that the Crown demand only fines for the right to alienate. Although the king and council declared that such lands had never been forfeit, they made the conciliatory gesture of declaring that fines would be levied in the Chancery by due process.[129] The pronouncement restored the equilibrium between lord and tenant, based on shared principles for the enforcement of lordship, that Edward II's incompetence had upset.

The partitioning of an estate between female coheirs posed dangers to lordship similar to those of alienation. By the mid–thirteenth century, the law balanced the rights of the king and those of the family when an inheritance was partitioned.[130] Yet the details of that balance were recent and became settled only after a long legal development. Originally, only the husband of the eldest coheir performed homage to the lord and performed the services of the fee. The lord may have retained the right to the marriage of any minor coheirs, but he did not have the right of escheat if they died without heirs of their own. Instead, if one of the coheirs died without heirs, her share accrued to the other coheirs. This accrual was not an escheat, for, as both Glanvill and Bracton took pains to make clear, no homage was performed to the eldest coheir until the third generation, at which point the inheritance was divided into separate holdings. The eldest heiress, however, may have had the right to take custody of the lands of her minor sisters and in some cases secured custody of the minor heirs of her sisters.[131] The uncertainty and confusion concerning the tenurial arrangements probably reflect the tentative nature of women's inheritance down to Henry II's legal reforms.

Those reforms secured a right of inheritance for women and raised the need for some clarification, which Henry III supplied for tenants-in-chief in the so-called *Statutum Hiberniae de Coheredibus* in 1236. The statute was a writ explaining English custom con-

[129] *Rot. Parl.*, 2:9, 12 (no. 27), cited by James C. Davies, "The Despenser War in Glamorgan," *TRHS*, 3d ser., 9 (1915): 39. Edward II had treated other lands as forfeit (*CFR*, 2:197).

[130] Pollock and Maitland, *History of English Law*, 2:276–278; Milsom, "Inheritance by Women"; *Glanvill* (vii.3); Bracton, 2:226–227; *Close Rolls*, 3:375–376; Scott L. Waugh, "Women's Inheritance and the Growth of a Bureaucratic Monarchy in Twelfth- and Thirteenth-Century England," forthcoming.

[131] Pollock and Maitland, *History of English Law*, 2:277; *Novae Narrationes* (London, 1963), 265 (C211A). I owe these references to Professor Robert C. Palmer.

cerning women's inheritance to the justiciar of Ireland. Henry declared that if a father held in chief of the Crown, then each of his daughters would have to perform homage for her share directly to the king.[132] Although coheirs had been responsible to the Crown for their feudal obligations since the late twelfth century, this writ was the first explicit statement of the practice. [133] It protected the king's rights of wardship and marriage over each portion and meant that a partition had to be done in such a way that each of the coheirs received a portion of the lands held in chief, as the *Prerogativa Regis* noted. The regulation reinforced the principle that rearrangements of the family inheritance could be made only by substitution in order not to harm royal lordship. It simultaneously protected the rights of younger coheirs who might be cheated of their inheritance if they fell under the exclusive authority of their elder partner. Royal lordship could be mutually beneficial to the king and tenants-in-chief. Mesne lords, however, did not enjoy the same legal protection, and their practices remained unsettled down through the thirteenth century. [134]

That mutuality lay behind Henry's third clarification of the law. Sometime toward the end of his reign, he established the principle that the king would have the guardianship of idiots along with custody of their lands until they died so that they would not alienate their lands and disinherit their families in their infirmity. Grants by idiots were invalid, and when a tenant-in-chief was shown to be incapacitated, the king recovered lands that he had alienated and kept them in custody for the benefit of the heirs.[135] Britton told the story that Henry made the provision at the behest of his minister and favorite Robert Walerand whose nephew and heir was an idiot.[136] Although the king thus undertook to guard Walerand's

[132] *Close Rolls*, 3:375–376.

[133] The legal development is described by Milsom, "Inheritance by Women." For examples, see Pollock and Maitland, *History of English Law*, 2:277 n. 1. Glanvill does not mention the practice, but it is clear that coheirs of some tenants-in-chief held directly of the Crown while others held of the eldest coheir (Holt, "Feudal Society and the Family iv," 10–15; *CRR*, 11:174–175 [no. 869]).

[134] Pollock and Maitland, *History of English Law*, 2:278; *Britton*, 2:23, 29, 40.

[135] *CPR, 1247–1258*, 437–438, 481, 508; *CIPM*, 1:367; *CCR, 1279–1288*, 381, 383; Bracton, 2:51–52.

[136] Frederic W. Maitland, "The 'Praerogativa Regis,' " *EHR* 6 (1891): 366–370, reprinted in idem, *The Collected Papers of Frederic William Maitland* (Cambridge, 1911), 2:184–187; Donald W. Sutherland, "Peytevin v. La Lynde: A Case in the Medieval Land Law," *Law Quarterly Review* 83 (1967): 531–533; Pollock and Maitland, *History of English Law*, 1:481.

interests, he was not simply a disinterested watchman, for he acquired custody of the lands and could treat that custody like a feudal wardship, granting it out to whomever he wished and collecting the profits of the lands and lordship. On the other hand, because he was acting as a trustee in such cases, he usually commissioned only a single custodian for the lands who was often a relative of the heir and who often had to account to the king for his custodianship.[137]

Two final aspects of royal lordship received clearer definition in the later years of Henry III's reign or early in his son's reign. One was the king's right of marriage over tenants holding *ut de honore*. In limiting the king's rights of wardship to those of the lord whose lands had escheated to the king, Magna Carta did not explicitly mention the right of marriage of a minor heir. Magna Carta's identification of the king's rights with those of the former lord could be interpreted to mean that the right of marriage would fall to the lord of prior enfeoffment, giving the king no greater right in the marriage than that of any of the other lords of whom the minor held lands.[138] That, in fact, seems to have been the case. In 1270 William de Mountchesney went before the royal council seeking to recover custody of a manor that had been held of him by Hubert de Mountchesney. The escheator had seized the manor even though Hubert died holding of the king only by the honor of Rayleigh. A search of the Domesday Book proved William correct, so the council ordered the restoration of the manor to him according to the provisions of Magna Carta. At the same time, however, the king ordered an inquest to determine of which lord Hubert's ancestors had first been enfeoffed because it was not known to whom the marriage pertained.[139] Shortly thereafter, however, it

[137] *CPR, 1272–1281*, 330 (kinsman); *CPR, 1281–1292*, 446 (brother); *CPR, 1307–1313*, 115 (widow); *CCR, 1279–1288*, 383 (cousin); *CFR*, 1:127–128. Appointments of custodians for idiots were usually enrolled on the Exchequer memoranda rolls under commissions.

[138] *Prerogativa Regis*, xv.

[139] PRO, KB.26/197 m. 11d: "Et quia non constat domino Regi nec suo consilio utrum antecessores predicti Huberti primo feofati fuerunt de predicto . . . feodo . . . vel de antecessoribus eiusdem Willelmi propter quod ignoratur ad quem maritagium heredum predicti Huberti pertinet dominus Rex ex sua gratia speciali concessit quod inquiratur per patria." I have not found a conclusion to the case. An order for the inquest was issued in February 1270 (*CPR, 1266–1272*, 477). The case is puzzling because, according to other sources, Hubert had two sisters and coheirs, both of whom were married and of age (*CIPM*, 1:883 [no date]; *ERF*, 2:501–502 [homage, 18 November 1269]).

must have been settled that in such cases the king would have the right of marriage regardless of the priority of enfeoffment, for that is the position taken in the *Prerogativa Regis*.[140]

The second and more important right to be defined was primer seisin. The Statute of Marlborough (1267), cap. 16, specifically contrasted the rights of the king with those of other lords on the death of a tenant. In accordance with customary practice, the king took all of the lands of the fee into custody until it was determined whether the heir was of age and until he performed homage.[141] It was a profitable right. An early escheator's account for the county of Essex from 1257–1258 shows that he routinely collected profits from the lands before he delivered them to the heir, and an Exchequer estimate of revenues in 1284 indicated that the king could expect about 300 marks from the profits of primer seisin.[142] The right was of even greater importance legally, for it formed the foundation upon which the royal government built the machinery for the management of royal lordship in the thirteenth century.

The king's lordship, as refined by Henry and Edward, was summed up in the *Prerogativa Regis*. The origins of the document are unclear. It was not a statute and did not have legislative force, but it came to be included in statute books and was treated as legislation in the fourteenth and fifteenth centuries.[143] It seems to have been widely disseminated, though there is no indication of how it was put to use. It is cast in the form of a memorandum explaining the king's feudal rights over his tenants and was probably written early in Edward I's reign, before 1285.[144] The need for such an explanation probably arose out of the intense interest in royal lordship, expressed in the hundred inquests and experiments with stewards, that Edward generated on his return to Eng-

---

[140] *Statutes of the Realm*, 1:225.

[141] Ibid., 1:24.

[142] PRO, E.163/1/14; Mabel H. Mills, "Exchequer Agenda and Estimate of Revenue, Easter Term 1284," *EHR* 40 (1925): 229–234, citing E.163/1/23: "Exitus escaetarum Regis singulorum decedentium qui de Rege tenent in capite quorum heredes sunt pleni etatis. Videlicet a die mortis usque ad diem seisine."

[143] Maitland, "Praerogativa Regis."

[144] For the dating, see ibid., 184–188; *Prerogativa Regis*, xviii n. 47, xxi, xl; *Select Cases*, 3:lii n. 5. It should also be noted that the document does not mention lands held in jointure, a method of settling lands that became very popular after 1290 and that caused some difficulties for escheators. Furthermore, the provisions regarding the alienation of lands were not practiced in the 1290s and beyond. Chancery memoranda concerning royal prerogatives were not unusual. See *Selected Cases*, 5:lxxiv n. 4.

land in 1274. It is possible that it originated as an internal memorandum intended to explain the king's rights to officials, perhaps to the stewards when they were introduced in 1275. At that time, information about royal rights would have been useful to estate personnel and attorneys as well as to royal ministers and justices. Since these categories were not mutually exclusive and individuals moved from one position to another demanding similar kinds of skills, a single description of the king's feudal authority could have circulated widely through the ranks of a ministerial elite. The *Prerogativa Regis* is perhaps best understood as a product of the increasing professionalization of law and administration that produced other written memoranda and commentaries on law, administration, and estate management in the late thirteenth century. It is not a final statement and not completely accurate. Whatever its exact provenance, it clearly demonstrates the vitality of royal lordship at the outset of Edward I's reign and the widespread interest in its effects. Landholders and ministers alike had to be well-informed about the king's feudal rights.

From the middle of Edward I's reign, however, family settlements threatened to undercut that authority. Tenants-in-chief increasingly settled their lands on themselves and their wives in joint tenure with some stipulation about the descent of the lands after their deaths. Jointures and entails potentially deprived the king of the custody of lands during a minority, while a person who succeeded through a remainder did not pay relief.[145] The popularity of such devices was partly responsible for the growing number of licenses to alienate in the later years of Edward's reign and beyond.[146] Between 1288 and 1327, lands on at least thirty-six estates that fell into royal wardship were settled jointly on the husband and wife.[147] In a third of them, the joint settlement covered a substantial portion of the estate leaving little in wardship. The timing and impact of such settlements can be seen in the example of the Hardeshull estate. When John de Hardeshull died in 1276 leaving

---

[145] PRO, E.159/78 m. 34, for a dispute over the payment of a relief by one who entered through a remainder settled on his behalf.

[146] See the calculations of Stevenson in "The Escheator," 139.

[147] *CCR, 1302–1307*, 254, 416; *CCR, 1313–1318*, 381; *CIPM*, 3:248, 285, 597, 4:151, 176, 313, 345, 361, 400, 410, 5:200, 264, 270, 319, 350, 514, 599, 612, 6:52, 58, 93, 96, 130, 179, 285, 323, 325, 326, 339, 406, 411, 443, 593, 595, 602, 733. According to this information, the practice did not become widespread until early in the fourteenth century; only seven of the thirty-six cases fell in the reign of Edward I. For the timing of the changes at the higher ranks of the nobility, see Holmes, *Estates*, 49–50.

William, a minor son and heir, the inquisition post mortem showed that none of the family's lands were held jointly. Eustace de Hacche acquired William's marriage in 1284 and married the boy to his daughter Juliana, at which time he settled some of the Hardeshull lands along with new lands on the couple in joint tenure. When William died in 1303, his inquisition post mortem revealed the results of the settlement, which left the Crown with only a single tenement in wardship.[148] Joint tenancy, however, does not seem to have barred the king's right to the wardship of the heir.[149]

The Hardeshull case illustrates one of the difficulties facing the Crown, for all of the family lands except those held in chief were part of the settlement. The king could discourage tenants-in-chief from making settlements of lands held in chief but it had no authority over the lands they held of other lords, and those were the lands that tenants-in-chief mostly used for jointures and entails. The settlements, therefore, primarily hurt prerogative wardship. The king's control over alienations may explain why jointures, like uses, appeared in greater numbers earlier among smaller landholders than among the greater who held substantial portions of their estates in chief.[150]

All the same, the king was not openly hostile to these family arrangements and in some cases actively assisted in creating them. Even if permission for the settlement had not been obtained, the

[148] *CIPM*, 2:185, 4:176. The Crown was aware of the impact of these settlements and tried to protect its profits by fastidiously insisting that the wife had actual seisin of the lands held jointly before it would allow her to have possession after the death of her spouse (*CIPM*, 4:385; PRO, E.153/51, no. 3).

[149] For the king's rights in joint tenancy, see *Prerogativa Regis*, xviii, xxvi–xxvii, 35, 55. According to Bracton, the dual homage should have barred the king from wardship of the heir as well as of the lands held in chief, for wardship "will never be delivered as long as the homage of his ancestor continues" (Bracton, 2:258). He raises this point in a discussion about the rights of wardship when the mother, who is an heiress, dies first. In that case, the lord does not receive the land or heir because the homage continues in the husband (2:259). Constable makes a similar point about joint tenants: "Deux iointenaunts, a eux & a lez heirs lun, celui en fee devie, son heire deinz age, lauter en vie, le roy navera le gard de leire quar il ad son tenaunt" (*Prerogativa Regis*, 35). In nine of the cases of joint tenancy cited above, the subsequent grant of wardship made no mention of any rights over land and only concerned the marriage of the heir, perhaps because the lands were under the widow's control (*CPR, 1292–1301*, 304; *CPR, 1301–1307*, 34, 122, 443; *CPR, 1307–1313*, 68; *CPR, 1313–1317*, 620; *CFR*, 2:90, 299, 3:215–216, 222; *CCR, 1302–1307*, 254; *CCR, 1318–1323*, 662; *CIPM*, 3:248, 285, 4:151, 313, 338, 345, 361, 410, 6:406, 443).

[150] Bean, *Decline*, 122, 135; Holmes, *Estates*, 46–51.

king might uphold it. William de Leyburn settled lands on his wife, Juliana, and himself jointly, and when William's son Thomas married Alice, the daughter of Ralph de Tony, William settled the manor and castle of Leybourne, Kent, on them jointly without royal license. When their husbands died, both Juliana and Alice had to sue to recover custody and then pay a fine for the alienations. The king, exercising his right of primer seisin, always seized lands held jointly when one of the partners died and returned them to the survivor only after his or her right had been established.[151] On the other hand, there are many examples of settlements made with the king's license.[152] Tenants-in-chief similarly used the king as a feoffee, surrendering their lands to the king who then granted them back to the tenant and his wife jointly with a provision for heirs.[153] Indeed, with the help of their lord some tenants-in-chief created complex conditions for the descent of their lands and even disinherited one relative in favor of another.[154] These settlements and others like them recalled the method of substitution practiced in seigniorial courts centuries before. In that era, when a lord could not be forced to accept a tenant, the only way that a tenant could put another in his place was by surrendering his tenement to his lord who would then bestow it on the tenant's candidate.[155] Because the king had retained control over alienations, he continued to exercise this seigniorial authority down into the fourteenth century. Tenants-in-chief had at least to obtain his license before making a substitution or settlement, and for even greater security they surrendered their lands to the king who then regranted them.[156]

During the thirteenth century the Crown conscientiously protected and reinforced its feudal prerogatives. It confirmed and built on customs of seigniorial relations that it had inherited from

---

[151] *CIPM*, 4:410, 5:220; *CPR, 1307–1313*, 34, 68; *CCR, 1307–1313*, 26, 212–213, 217. The process of recovering lands is discussed in the next chapter.

[152] For example, *CIPM*, 5:131.

[153] For example, ibid., 4:369; *EB*, 131.

[154] Cokayne, *Complete Peerage*, 4:118–120; 10:335–336; Fairbank, "The Last Earl of Warenne," 206–217, 219–225, 234–242.

[155] Milsom, *Legal Framework*, 103–106. Such surrenders are sometimes recorded in the escheators' accounts, since the tenements came into royal possession for a short time; see, e.g., PRO, E.372/124 mm. 19, 21.

[156] Some grants were made to heirs before the death of the tenant and could take the form of a grant *se dimisit*, as described in Milsom, *Legal Framework*, 147–153. See, e.g., *Patent Rolls*, 2:428; *Close Rolls*, 6:37, 10:51; *CPR, 1247–1258*, 553; *ERF*, 1:211, 2:13; *CCR, 1288–1296*, 19–20.

the twelfth century and that the barons had modified for their protection in Magna Carta. The solidification of these customs through explicit legal definition meant that they remained not only profitable to the king but instrumental in shaping relations between the king and the most important landholders in the realm through the thirteenth century and beyond. The Crown's rights of relief, primer seisin, prerogative wardship, consent to marriage, and control of alienations gave the king extensive power over the lands and families of his tenants-in-chief. Yet, that authority could be effective only if the means of enforcing it were adequate. The legal specification of the king's rights in the thirteenth century therefore demanded a corresponding improvement in the supervision and administration of those rights.

· 3 ·

ADMINISTERING ROYAL LORDSHIP

Both Henry III and Edward I incorporated institutional changes in their program of strengthening royal lordship. As a result, in the century after Magna Carta the Crown searched out and exercised its feudal rights with greater energy than it ever had before. It replaced the ad hoc measures hitherto employed for the management of those rights with permanent institutions to administer the lands and heirs that came into its custody, to enforce its authority over marriages and alienations, to investigate and settle contested claims, and to distribute the resources of lordship according to the king's will. The changes deepened the impact of royal lordship on tenants-in-chief and forced them to keep pace with the inventiveness of royal lordship and to conform to its administrative routines in order to protect their interests. All the same, tenants-in-chief welcomed institutionalization to some extent, for they benefited from the existence of regulations, tribunals, and officials that helped them sort out complications in title and descent. Finally, institutionalization did not make royal lordship purely mechanical. During this period the king never delegated omnicompetent authority over feudal business to any single individual or office, and there was no institution, comparable to the Tudor Court of Wards, which integrated the functions of management, receipt, accounting, and jurisdiction. The king maintained his discretion over these rights so that seigniorial authority and the resources that it made available remained powerful instruments of the king's personal rule down through the early fourteenth century.

ESCHEATORS, SUBESCHEATORS, AND WARDS

The most visible changes occurred at the local level with the creation of the escheatorships. As in the administration of thirteenth-century estates, local officials were essential for the effective supervision of tenants and seigniorial dues. Escheators linked the Crown and tenants-in-chief and became the principal means by which the royal government managed and enforced its rights. Their success led to a multiplication of subofficials and duties that ranged from

105

securing wardships to seizing lands for unauthorized alienations. They were the king's feudal bailiffs, given responsibility for royal tenants and wards.

During the twelfth century, local management had been organized through the sheriff and periodic commissions. Under Henry II, the justices itinerant investigated escheats and wardships and turned them over to the custody of the sheriffs. Henry II showed some interest in removing escheats and wardships from the control of sheriffs and entrusting them to separate officials, but it was his son, Richard I, undoubtedly pressured by financial need, who instituted the most important changes.[1] In 1193 he entrusted *most* lands then in royal custody to two men, Hugh Bardolf and William de Ste. Mere Eglise. The reform, however, was neither thorough nor permanent. Sheriffs still had custody of some escheats in their counties, and Richard turned other wardships over to different keepers. John followed these measures and assigned officials to care for the king's escheats.

Henry III introduced a permanent system of management. The baronial council that had control of the government during Henry's minority began by inquiring into royal escheats in 1217 and then by establishing custodians of escheats in each county in 1218–1219.[2] Then, in 1232, as part of the general reforms of the Exchequer initiated by Peter des Rivaux, Henry set up the system of local escheatorships that would remain in place down through the fourteenth century. Two escheators had responsibility for the king's feudal incidents north and south of the Trent, and subescheators acted under their authority in each county.[3] Edward I and Edward II modified this basic structure for short periods, but in each case the government eventually returned to the original pattern of organization. The escheatorships embodied royal lordship in the county communities and made it more difficult for tenants-in-chief to evade their feudal obligations. In seigniorial matters, tenants-in-chief henceforth had to deal with the Crown through the escheators.

---

[1] Thomas Madox, *The History and Antiquities of the Exchequer of the Kings of England* (London, 1769), 1:299–300; Doris M. Stenton, introduction to *Pipe Roll, 6 Richard I*, xx–xxii; Stevenson, "The Escheator," 113–115.

[2] Madox, *History and Antiquities*, 1:300; Stevenson, "The Escheator," 114; *Patent Rolls*, 1:132, 154.

[3] Stevenson, "The Escheator," 114–116; Powicke, *Henry III*, 105–108; idem, *Thirteenth Century* (Oxford, 1962), 62–65; David A. Carpenter, "The Decline of the Curial Sheriff in England, 1194–1258," *EHR* 91 (1976): 12–16.

The escheators' work was based on the right of primer seisin, which allowed the Crown to take immediate possession of lands on the death of a tenant-in-chief. When the king found out about the death of a landholder, through either the family, an interested party, or royal officials, he ordered the escheator to take custody of the deceased's lands until further orders.[4] The procedure depended on two assumptions: first, that the deceased was a tenant-in-chief and, second, that the lands held in chief were held *ut de corona*, so that *all* of the lands were seized, not just those held of the king. The Crown retained custody until the heir paid relief, if he or she was of age, or until the escheator's inquest into the tenure, descent, and value of the lands (the inquisition post mortem) revealed that they did not pertain to the Crown. Tenants-in-chief, unlike the tenants of mesne lords, could not obtain seisin until their feudal obligations had been met. If the heir was a minor, the king would relinquish custody of the lands or heir only if an inquest found that the tenant did not hold in chief or *ut de corona*, and even then the king often held onto the lands until the proper tenants or lords petitioned to recover custody. The escheator could neither deliver the lands to anyone nor assign dower to the widow until he had received a writ from the king ordering him to do so. In the meantime, he collected the issues of the property.[5] Furthermore, through the escheators, primer seisin enhanced the Crown's ability to investigate and to assert its lordship over subtenancies. Escheators thus enumerated the tenants' advowsons and knights' fees, enabling the king to exploit any opportunities to make presentations or to take wardships *per cause de gard*.[6]

As exercised by the escheators, therefore, primer seisin emphasized the power of royal lordship and made clear the subordination of tenants-in-chief to the royal administration. Neither heirs nor mesne lords nor widows could get possession of their lands without complying with their lord's regulations and routines, for he had their lands. In this context, the importance of the Statute of Marlborough can be fully appreciated: by reiterating the king's right of primer seisin, it not only highlighted the distance between

---

[4] Stevenson, "The Escheator," 120–129. The writ was usually a *diem clausit extremum*, but the Chancery used a variety of writs; see Walker, "Royal Wardship," 98–104.

[5] *Rot. Parl.*, 1:91–92; *Statutes of the Realm*, 1:142–143; Ludwik Ehrlich, *Proceedings against the Crown (1216–1377)* (Oxford, 1921), 60–61.

[6] For examples of such inquests, see *CIPM*, 2:128, 154, 3:285, 472, 597, 4:163, 235, 296.

his lordship and that of other lords, but it reinforced the administrative structure that Henry III had erected for royal lordship.

As part of this authority, the escheator took charge of minor heirs. No matter what the age of the child or children, the Crown was entitled to physical possession.[7] The *Tres Ancien Coutoumier* in Normandy argued that wards should be raised in their lords' household to instill in them and in the lord a sense of mutual fidelity and to give them a proper education.[8] That reasoning does not seem to have been important to English kings during the thirteenth century.

If the wards were very young, the Crown returned them to their mother's care until they were old enough to be granted to a guardian.[9] By and large, the personal attitude of individuals subject to the king's lordship is invisible to us, screened by the terse formality of the royal records. Against this bland background, the aggressiveness that mothers displayed in taking and keeping charge of their children stands in stark relief. The government, in fact, did not entirely trust widows, fearing that they might send the wards away or marry them without royal permission.[10] Its fears were justified. Mothers occasionally refused to give up custody of their young children when their wardship and marriage had been given to a royal guardian. The king had to force them, by seizing their dowers, to surrender the wards.[11] To forestall such problems, the king demanded that a widow provide security that she would not deprive him of his rights as lord when he gave her temporary custody of her children. In one case, the escheator took the ward into custody, returned ("rebailla") her to her mother, and took security. The widow then had to travel to Westminster, appear before the treasurer and barons of the Exchequer, and go through the same routine of delivery and recovery. She later repeated it with the

[7] For an example, see *CCR, 1272–1279*, 235.

[8] Pollock and Maitland, *History of English Law*, 1:326.

[9] For example, *CCR, 1288–1296*, 336; *CPR, 1281–1292*, 418; PRO, SC.1/16/70; 45/55, 57, 61; 62/35; 19/141 (Mountchesney).

[10] Problems in recovering wards: PRO, SC.1/39/138; *Close Rolls*, 4:385–386, 11:88; *CCR, 1313–1318*, 198 (falsely accused). In six cases in which wards were turned over to their mothers, the children were aged between two and fourteen (*Close Rolls*, 11:195–196; *CCR, 1272–1279*, 324; *CPR, 1281–1292*, 418; *CPR, 1292–1301*, 71–72; *CCR, 1288–1296*, 336; PRO, SC.1/39/138; *CIPM*, 1:471, 2:184, 770, 3:90, 6:16). In the twelfth century, a widow was fined for making her son a knight while he was in royal custody (*Pipe Roll, 14 Henry II*, 29, Avelina de Ria).

[11] *Patent Rolls*, 1:146, 179 (Vescy); *CPR, 1232–1247*, 229; *Close Rolls*, 4:92, 257, 267; *ERF*, 1:408–409; *CCR, 1272–1279*, 324; *CPR, 1281–1292*, 418.

king's council.[12] It is clear that there was a deep attachment between a widowed mother and her infant children and that royal lordship was a harsh intrusion into that relationship, especially whenever the king or guardians wanted personal custody of the wards.

If wards were old enough at the death of their parent, they could be entrusted to royal officials or lodged in the royal household. Escheators, for example, often paid for the sustenance of wards out of their revenues. At least one was turned over to a monastery for safekeeping.[13] At any given time, a few wards of noble or knightly descent could be found alongside the royal children in the household, though not for long periods.[14] Between 1242 and 1244, for example, Windsor Castle housed at different times Henry III's children, the daughters of John de Lacy, and the eldest son of Nicholas de Molis, the seneschal of Gascony, though the three heirs were there only two to three months.[15] Six wards aged eight to twenty were in the household between 1316 and 1318. One of them, Thomas Wake, had been in wardship since his father's death in 1298 and had been successively in the custody of his mother, Gaveston, and the queen before coming into the household. But he married without Edward's permission, and Edward as a concession to the bride's father, Henry of Lancaster, granted him custody of his lands soon after, though he was not yet of age.[16] Some wards stayed on and became the king's companions, but only rarely. Most only paused there before they were shipped

---

[12] PRO, SC.1/16/70. One widow promised to support the heirs and not to marry them or alienate the king's rights, under pain of losing her dower (*Close Rolls*, 11:195–196).

[13] *CCR, 1272–1279*, 72; *CCR, 1302–1307*, 357, 518; *CPR, 1272–1281*, 171; *CIPM*, 2:46; PRO, E.372/149 m. 38 (expenses of the escheator south of the Trent, 30–32 Edward I). Disputes sometimes arose over the issue of who should bear the cost of sustenance (e.g., E.159/84 mm. 34, 65).

[14] Walker, "Royal Wardship," 166–176; Parsons, *CHEC*, 88 n. 125, 112 n. 170; Hilda Johnstone, *Edward of Carnarvon, 1284–1307* (Manchester, 1947), 37, 43, 73–74; PRO, E.136/1/15 mm. 8, 8d.

[15] *Close Rolls*, 5:30, 54, 76, 120, 153; *CPR, 1232–1247*, 351, 391, 397, 423, 425. The length of stay has been based on a comparison of the original orders for custody and grants of wardship. Molis was appointed on 17 June 1243, and the order concerning his son, which included provisions for a valet, was issued on 27 June (*CPR, 1232–1247*, 380; *Close Rolls*, 5:30). The provision for these children was apparently part of the arrangements that Henry made for the governing of England while he was away in Gascony between May 1242 and September 1243.

[16] Stapleton, "Wardrobe Accounts," 340–341; Cokayne, *Complete Peerage*, 12:2:302–304.

off to a guardian to whom the king granted their marriage. The guardian became responsible for their care and raising. Indeed, the Household Ordinance of 1318 emphasizes the limitations of the king's *financial* responsibility to wards and implies that they resided in the household only a short time. It states that wards would receive wages and livery according to their status, but that payment would stop "as soon as they had their lands, or until the king had given or sold [their wardship]. And then they would be at the cost of those who had them by gift or purchase."[17] Though little is known of their life at court, no special office or official was responsible for feudal wards. It is clear that, in contrast to the assumptions of the *Tres Ancien Coutoumier*, the king of England did not feel any special need to cultivate the loyalty of his tenants' heirs by keeping them around court. Patronage was far more important.

The escheators' work lay primarily in taking custody of lands, holding inquests into tenures, rights, and ages of heirs, and accounting for receipts from lands in their custody.[18] That business increased sharply whenever women inherited, for the escheator was responsible for overseeing the partition of the lands among coheirs, a task that in many cases had to be done several times before each was satisfied.[19] The escheator similarly assigned dowers once widows had given security not to marry without license, sometimes collected reliefs or took security for the payment of relief, sometimes sold wardships, and usually took custody of the lands of vacant religious institutions. As the overseer of the king's seigniorial rights, the escheator was given the authority from the reign of Edward I to seize lands alienated by tenants-in-chief without royal license or lands into which an heir had entered before performing homage and to conduct inquisitions *ad quod damnum*.[20] They conducted much of their work ex officio, without explicit

---

[17] Thomas F. Tout, *The Place of the Reign of Edward II in English History* (Manchester, 1914), 280.

[18] BL, Add. MS 32,085, fols. 145v–150: "Le Office le Escheytur."

[19] Stevenson, "The Escheator," 132.

[20] Ibid., 129–130, 139–140; Bean, *Decline*, 74–75; Brand, "Control of Mortmain Alienation," 37–38. References to the seizure of alienated lands are not common before 1290. One of the articles in the hundred inquests related to the seizure of lands by escheators, but I have not found any reference in the returns to an escheator seizing lands for an unauthorized alienation. Jurors in Northamptonshire, for example, reported that escheators had taken various lands into custody, but they all related to inheritance (*RH*, 2:9, 10; *CIPM*, 2:17, 49, 61, 69, 781, for corresponding inquisitions post mortem). One example in 1283–1284 can be found in PRO, E.159/58 m. 21.

warrant from the king. Escheators and especially the subescheators, for example, often learned of the death of a tenant-in-chief
sooner than the king or Chancery and could seize lands ex officio
to prevent anyone from entering them and depriving the king of
his rights.[21] Escheators were likewise well placed to watch for the
alienation of lands without license, and they spent a lot of time
making such ex officio seizures. From the late thirteenth century
onward, moreover, the escheators periodically conducted general
inquests into royal rights. The Articles of the Escheators show that
the government expected them to investigate thirty-three separate
items including alienations, the marriages of wards and widows,
treasure trove, liberties, and purprestures, though it is evident
from their accounts that most of their work went into enforcing
restrictions on alienations.[22] The government also charged them
with the responsibility of ensuring that the lands in their custody
were properly maintained and that no rights or assets were sub-
tracted.

The surge of interest in royal lordship in the second half of the
thirteenth century dramatically increased the escheators' work,
which in turn prompted a proliferation of subofficers and associates. It is evident from the hundred rolls that an administrative
structure devoted to caring for the king's feudal rights was fully in
place by 1274. The escheators were drawn from the growing pool
of professional administrators who served in a wide variety of positions in both royal and baronial administrations. They were not
trained specifically for the job of escheator, but rather drew on a
variety of legal, ministerial, and financial skills that could be applied to their feudal duties. Some, like Henry de Bray, John de
Hotham, John Walwayn, or Henry de Wingham, rose to powerful
prominence within the courts or administration. Most served tours
of duty in local offices.[23] Beneath the two chief escheators, subes-

[21] Stevenson, "The Escheator," 128–130. An example can be seen in PRO, SC.1/
16/70.
[22] Huntington Library, HM. 19,920, fols. 59v–61; *Statutes of the Realm*, 1:238–241.
A writ of *certiorari* (1291) asking why an escheator had seized certain lands is endorsed "quia per generalem inquisitionem ex officio escaetoris captam" (PRO,
C.257/1/36). The escheator's account for 1327–1328 shows that in a single day in
one county, he seized lands alienated by several tenants-in-chief, indicating some
kind of inquest (E.357/2 m. 29 [Devon, 28 June; Dorset, 29 June]; m. 30d [Here-
ford, 1 July]).
[23] For information about some personnel, see Stevenson, "The Escheator," 156–
167; Noël Denholm-Young, "The Authorship of the Vita Edwardi Secundi," *EHR*

cheators in each county commanded a staff of clerks, bailiffs, and associates.[24] These men performed the routine tasks of feudal administration. After officially taking lands into custody, for example, escheators usually turned them over to assistants to keep until the escheator received further instructions.[25] This large personnel enabled the Crown to sharpen its vigilance over tenants-in-chief and lessened the possibility of losing wardships, marriages, or escheats. The different elements of the royal administration, once they had matured, functioned automatically and complementarily to safeguard the king's right to wardships and marriages.

For all of the formality of these institutions, moreover, the administration still operated on such informal channels of communication and information as word of mouth, hearsay, and rumor. These channels connected all elements of the administration and gave the king direct access to his ministers. They also gave interested parties access to and influence over the administrative process. The treasurer and barons of the Exchequer, having heard a rumor while Edward I was overseas that an heiress had married without license, ordered the couple to come before them to answer the charge. The king issued instructions by word of mouth concerning the care of wards in royal custody.[26] Royal ministers heard about conditions within their bailiwicks and related the information to their superiors, while interested parties brought news of the death of a tenant-in-chief to the notice of the government, hopeful of a grant of wardship.[27] Of course, hearsay could be wrong, and that is often why it has come to light. The economic and social importance of wardship and marriage meant that individuals had a stake in providing information, including false information.[28]

---

71 (1956): 189–211 (Walwayn); *State Trials of the Reign of Edward I (1289–93)*, ed. Thomas F. Tout and Hilda Johnstone (London, 1906), xxxii–xxxiii, 17–18 (Bray).

[24] The hundred rolls name more than a hundred men who conducted the king's feudal business in twenty-one counties between 1265 and 1274. This figure is a low estimate since presentments of escheators varied from county to county; e.g., Kent 25 (*RH*, 1:200–235), Derbyshire 3 (1:58, 59, 60), Cambridgeshire 2 (1:50, 52), and Dorset 1 (1:98). Some, however, worked in more than one county, e.g., Thomas Pyn, subescheator in Devon and Somerset (1:64–65, 90, 2:146; *List of Sheriffs for England and Wales, to 1831* [London, 1898], 34).

[25] PRO, SC.1/29/206; *CPR, 1301–1307*, 85; *Rot. Parl.*, 1:91. Information about their work can be culled from disputes over the responsibility for accounting; e.g., PRO, E.159/94 mm. 109, 110.

[26] Rumor: PRO, E.159/61, m. 4d (1287, Edward was overseas at the time). Word of mouth: *CPR, 1272–1281*, 171, *CCR, 1288–1296*, 338.

[27] Stevenson, "The Escheator," 125; PRO, SC.1/10/157.

[28] *CPR, 1272–1281*, 320–321; *RH*, 1:239; *CIPM*, 6:388.

Hence, behind the activities revealed in the formal Chancery writs, there existed a complex network made up of informal contacts and communications, on which the king's officials relied to help keep track of tenants-in-chief and the tenures by which they held their lands.

Inquests and Eyres

The successful administration of the Crown's seigniorial rights depended on accurate knowledge about the terms by which tenants held their lands. This was especially true after Magna Carta because it established specific criteria for the proper exercise of royal lordship. Yet confusion over the nature of these obligations continually recurred as partitions, marriage portions, and grants of all kinds altered the tenurial map and rendered earlier versions obsolete. The Crown, therefore, relied on various kinds of inquest to try to keep abreast of its changing tenantry.[29] By the late twelfth century, the Domesday Book had long been out of date in respect to military obligations and subtenancies. Recognizing that problem, Henry II had attempted to bring tenurial information up to date through the *Cartae Baronum* in 1166. Nineteen years later he undertook an ambitiously thorough inquest into the lands of widows and wards in royal custody, which resulted in the *Rotuli de Dominabus*.[30] During the thirteenth century, the Crown instituted periodic inquests, on the model of the 1166 inquest, to gather information about its tenants-in-chief and their lands. In 1212 John sought information about services and alienations. When his son, Henry III, issued his prohibition against alienations in mortmain in 1228, he also ordered an inquest into alienations that had already been made.[31] Then, late in 1242, Henry ordered an extensive series of inquests into knights' fees and tenures throughout England in conjunction with his overseas expedition that year.[32] Two years later the government conducted another investigation, this time into concealed wardships, marriages, and escheats and

---

[29] The problems of record keeping have been discussed in John S. Critchley, "Summonses to Military Service Early in the Reign of Henry III," *EHR* 86 (1971): 79–95; Waugh, "Reluctant Knights and Jurors," 952–958; and Michael T. Clanchy, *From Memory to Written Record: England, 1066–1307* (Cambridge, 1979), 19–20, 132–147.

[30] Warren, *Henry II*, 275–281.

[31] *Book of Fees*, 1:52; *Close Rolls*, 1:88. No returns for the 1228 inquest have survived, if it was ever held.

[32] *Book of Fees*, 2:637–639; Powicke, *Henry III*, 89–91.

into alienated serjeanties.[33] In 1250 and again in 1253, just as he embarked on his campaign in Gascony, Henry III sent his chief escheator, Elerius, abbot of Pershore, to all of the king's manors, cities, and boroughs to inquire about alienations from demesnes and escheats, advowsons belonging to the king, and other rights that pertained to the king.[34] Edward I initiated an even more ambitious investigation of tenures, services, and alienations in the hundred inquests of 1274–1275, and authorized additional surveys in 1279 and 1284.[35]

Although the government often undertook inquests and consulted the Domesday Book and other surveys to settle issues of custody arising out of tenure, the usefulness of surveys was limited by the fact that they captured only a single instant in a constantly shifting landscape of tenure and tenancy.[36] They dated rapidly and had to be renewed often. Their data, moreover, were never summarized or indexed, making it difficult to retrieve and use.[37] Nor were they revised to account for changes in landholding.

The inquisitions post mortem simplified the government's task. They provided immediate information about tenure and a tenant's holdings upon which the Crown acted. While not infallible, the inquests usually provided a good indication of the scope of the Crown's rights over a particular estate. They were not, however, the final word. Petitioners seeking to recover custody of lands or wards from the Crown often challenged the jury's judgment. In that case, other records had to be consulted and new inquests held. From the Crown's standpoint, the most authoritative records were those which showed that it had exercised the rights under dispute at some point in the past thereby establishing a precedent for its claim. The data provided by inquisitions post mortem, therefore, were often tested against that of other sources. By the late thirteenth century the Crown had a comprehensive reservoir of data about the tenants-in-chief and their holdings on which it relied to enforce its rights of feudal lordship. The actual process of compiling the information, both in surveys and inquisitions post mortem, reminded tenants-in-chief of their obligations while simultane-

---

[33] Kimball, *Serjeanty Tenure*, 217–218; *Book of Fees*, 1142–1147.

[34] *CPR, 1247–1258*, 71, 95, 209–210.

[35] Powicke, *Thirteenth Century*, 359–360; Donald W. Sutherland, *Quo Warranto Proceedings in the Reign of Edward I, 1278–1294* (Oxford, 1963), 17–19, 166–167.

[36] For example, *Red Book*, 3:1013–1014; PRO, KB.26/197 m. 11d (Domesday).

[37] For the government's ability to use the information, see Clanchy, *Memory*, 138–147; and Sutherland, *Quo Warranto*, 172–173.

ously keeping local officials familiar with the feudal tenantry of their bailiwicks.

The eyres complemented this system of officials and surveys and adjudicated infractions of royal lordship, though their value in this respect declined over the thirteenth century.[38] The refinement of royal lordship increased the work of the eyres. After the Assize of Northampton in 1176, queries about wards and widows who ought to be in royal custody formed a regular feature of the eyre.[39] Bracton's list of the chapters of the eyre includes questions about escheats and serjeanties as well as wards and widows. By the end of the thirteenth century, the list had grown to include questions on felons, demesne manors, alienations by tenants-in-chief, as well as on the work of the escheators themselves.[40] This expansion mirrors the Crown's increasing concern over feudal rights in the thirteenth century and the new legal precision that Henry III and Edward I brought to that concern. But it also made the eyre too cumbersome and inefficient for the routine enforcement of royal lordship. The presentments of hundred juries in these new areas are meager compared to the government's expectations. Most dealt with the marriages of widows, a function that had not changed since the time of the *Rotuli de Dominabus*.[41] The knowledge of hundred juries was, moreover, localized and limited. They often knew, for example, that widows had remarried, and they confidently appraised their lands. Marriage was common, public knowledge. Yet, they usually did not know whether a widow had obtained royal permission for her marriage. They could not answer the crucial question from the Crown's standpoint, Quo warranto? As a result, the husbands had to come before the court to show their license, or pay a fine if they could not produce one.[42]

[38] Examples of the enforcement of royal lordship can be found in PRO, Just.1/ 623 m. 13 (1284–1285, Northamptonshire), and /739 mm. 50, 57d, 66, 67 (1291– 1292, Shropshire).

[39] *Rot. Dom.*, introduction by J. H. Round, xviii–xix; *Select Charters*, 179–180.

[40] Bracton, 2:330–333; *Fleta*, 1:46–54; *Book of Fees*, 2:1323–1427.

[41] David Crook, "The Later Eyres," *EHR* 97 (1982): 246–247; *Crown Pleas of the Wiltshire Eyre, 1249*, introduction by C.A.F. Meekings (Devizes, 1961), 37–40. For an example of a presentment for alienation, see PRO, Just.1/623 m. 13: "quo warranto . . . intraverunt feodi domini Regis."

[42] Juries often replied "nesciunt quo warranto" when asked about widows' marriages (*RH*, 1:90, 239, 463; PRO, Just.1/278 m. 46). Jurors in Shropshire in 1290– 1291 named ten widows who had remarried but did not know by what warrant. Five of the seven husbands who appeared produced the appropriate license, and

The long intervals between eyres reduced their usefulness in pre-
venting widows from marrying without license, though they uncovered some unauthorized marriages and punished some widows. Even in respect to widows' marriages, however, the eyres were
not so efficient as the escheators. By the late thirteenth century,
therefore, the eyres were no longer at the forefront of the enforcement of lordship.

The "inquest system," to use Helen Cam's term, was thus multi-
layered. According to the Articles of the Escheators, the Crown
expected its local agents to be on the lookout for violations of feudal obligations and to conduct general inquests into the king's seigniorial rights. Occasional commissions like the hundred inquests
supplemented their work, while the eyres punished some violations and provided a means of overseeing the work of the escheators. Violators were also hauled before the assizes or *coram rege*,
and later the Crown directed commissions of oyer and terminer to
look into escheats, alienations, and the subtraction of feudal rights
in certain areas. Finally, the government also conducted special investigations into concealed dues or the obstruction of the king's
lordship by other lords.[43] In other words, the royal administration
devoted a considerable proportion of its resources and energy to
enforcing the king's feudal lordship.

The impact of this institutionalization on tenants-in-chief is
plainly visible in the treatment of widows. By the end of the thirteenth century, a widow had to follow a fixed procedure after the
death of her husband to obtain her dower and inheritance. Magna
Carta required her to provide security that she would not marry
without royal license, which in practice meant swearing an oath to
the king that she would not marry. Only *after* she had fulfilled that
requirement did the king permit the assignment of her dower, and
the escheator did so only after receiving a writ from the king. The
government evidently expected that many widows would travel to
Westminster to render their oaths personally at the Exchequer or
Chancery. After Brian de Brompton died in December 1294, the
escheator reported to the chancellor that Brian's widow, Matilda,
had been sick and unable to come before the king's court so that,
on the king's order, he had taken her oath and had assigned her

two were fined for marrying without authorization (PRO, Just.1/739 mm. 50, 57d,
66, 67, 74d).
[43] Cam, *The Hundred*, 27–33; Huntington Library, HM. 19,920, fols. 59v–61;
CPR, 1292–1301, 433; *CPR, 1301–1307*, 238; PRO, C.47/1/18; SC.1/12/181; Carpenter, "King, Magnates, and Society," 65.

dower.[44] The sheriff or escheator could thus stand in the place of the king to receive a widow's oath. Once she had obtained her lands, the king might grant the right of consent to her marriage to someone else or might give her permission to marry whomever she pleased. Finally, the eyres carefully scrutinized widows' marriages to see if they had adhered to their oaths. Local and central officers worked together to supervise widows and their marriages, so that a widow had to follow a prescribed administrative procedure and work through the institutions of royal lordship in order to recover her dower and to marry. The Crown did not interfere in her rights, but they were clearly subordinated to the routines of government.

CHANCERY, EXCHEQUER, AND PETITIONS

As the treatment of widows indicates, the establishment of a system of local management necessitated changes at the center of government. Since the twelfth century, the responsibilities of seigniorial management and accounting had been divided between the Chancery and Exchequer—fiscal matters going to the Exchequer and administrative ones to the Chancery. In the thirteenth century this work multiplied as the local administration became more efficient. Complaints about royal lordship likewise swelled. Primer seisin was a powerful tool in the hands of the escheators, and it was not always exercised properly. Many lands were seized unjustly, triggering a process of petition and inquest that added significantly to the work of the central offices.

The Exchequer was largely responsible for receiving and accounting for fines offered for wardships and marriages, for amercements for violations of feudal obligations, for issues of lands held by escheators or custodians, and for rents or farms paid by guardians. Until the reign of Henry III, receipts from escheats were separated from the shrieval accounts and isolated on the pipe rolls, while fines offered for wardships or violations continued to be turned over to sheriffs for collection and accounting.[45] Once

[44] PRO, SC.1/27/20; *CCR, 1288–1296*, 409, 411. For other examples of oaths taken by local officials, see *Close Rolls*, 9:348, 10:212, 14:183–184, 227; *CCR, 1279–1288*, 197; *CCR, 1307–1313*, 195, 249; *CIPM*, 2:411. The usual manner of rendering an oath is related in BL, Add. MS 32,085, fol. 146v; PRO, E.159/5 m. 2; /64 mm. 13, 13d; *CCR, 1288–1296*, 170, 174, 256, 323–324 (Audeham).
[45] D. M. Stenton, Introduction to *Pipe Roll, 6 Richard I*, xx–xxii; Madox, *History*

the escheators were established, they rendered their accounts separately in the Exchequer, and from about the period of baronial reform, the accounts were regularly enrolled along with other foreign accounts on the pipe rolls, though it could be years before a final audit was made.

There was no fixed system of receipt for feudal dues through the early fourteenth century. The flexibility of the domestic system of government allowed the king to assign revenues as he pleased to any one of several different offices, including the Exchequer, wardrobe, and chamber. Under Henry III, for instance, grantees and escheators occasionally, though regularly, paid small sums to the wardrobe.[46] In the year after Edward I returned to England, between 18 October 1274 and 16 November 1275, the keeper of the wardrobe, Master Thomas Bek, accounted for a total receipt of £17,823 10s. 10 1/2d., of which he received £1,313 7s. 8d. from escheators and sheriffs (7.4 percent).[47] Until the final years of Edward's reign, however, the escheators sent most of their receipts to the Exchequer. As the fiscal pressures of war mounted, they paid more to the wardrobe or directly to creditors. During the reign of Edward II, the rents and fines for some wardships were paid into the chamber.[48] Thus, while the Exchequer managed the bulk of the funds derived from feudal lordship, the royal government made little effort to centralize feudal receipts. That such centralization was possible is clearly evident in Edward III's plan in 1349 to direct all of the income from wardships to the wardrobe. Even though the experiment lasted a short time, it was comprehensive, involving the receipt of revenues as well as the valuation of wardships by special commissioners who answered directly to the wardrobe.[49] In attempting to bolster the revenues of the wardrobe, Edward consolidated authority over feudal resources in a single office in a way that his predecessors had never tried. The effort stands in stark contrast to the measures employed by the government over the preceding century and a half when the assignment of rev-

---

and Antiquities, 296–302; *Roll of Divers Accounts for the Early Years of the Reign of Henry III*, ed. Fred A. Cazel (London, 1982), vi, 74–90.

[46] PRO, C.47/35/1, nos. 7 (*ERF*, 2:403), 27, 67, 106, 162, 174, 181, 189, 204; E.372/115 m. 11d.

[47] PRO, E.101/350/20. Of the total, the escheator north of the Trent paid £627 4s. 4d. (PRO, E.372/119 m. 21).

[48] *CPR, 1313–1317*, 636; *CFR*, 2:151 (wardrobe), 322.

[49] Tout, *Chapters*, 4:122–128.

enues depended on the immediate needs and convenience of the Crown, rather than on a prearranged fiscal system.

The task of coordinating the work of escheators, sheriffs, and central officers fell to the Chancery. By the reign of Edward I, the Chancery routinely supervised the escheators, collected inquisitions post mortem, authorized most grants of wardships and marriages, and handled conflicts involving royal lordship, the assignment of dowers, and the delivery and partitioning of inheritances. Exceptions, because the Chancery was traveling with the king or for other reasons, were duly noted.[50] Some of that business was performed on behalf of the treasurer and barons of the Exchequer, the courts, the royal council, or private petitioners. Because it was the hub of the royal administration, the Chancery mediated lord-tenant relations at the highest level of society. Through the chancellor the king directed the activities of the escheators and other local officials responsible for enforcing his feudal authority over the tenants-in-chief. Those officials wrote to the chancellor asking for clarification of their duties or pleading for relief, while the tenants-in-chief addressed some of their grievances concerning the weight of lordship as well as their requests for feudal resources to the chancellor. Royal favors, justice, and commands flowed outward from the court through Chancery writs, and information, complaints, and supplications flowed back.

A substantial portion of the business of the Chancery and Exchequer involved the settlement of disputes over the scope of royal lordship. As the efficiency of the administration improved, a larger number of lands were taken into the king's hands on the presumption that the tenant held in chief *ut de corona*. Prudence dictated that an escheator seize all of the property of a deceased landholder regardless of the tenure of a specific parcel because it was possible that the tenant held lands elsewhere of the king by military service, in which case the king would be entitled to prerogative wardship. Furthermore, the Crown's rights were based on a few general principles, and particular cases were not spelled out a priori, so that exceptions to those rights had to be established on an ad hoc basis. Thus, lands held of other lords, lands held in socage or petty serjeanty, lands held *ut de honore*, lands held in jointure, lands under entail, lands held by lease or life tenure, and even lands of individuals who held nothing in chief were routinely taken into custody.

[50] *CIPM*, 3:330.

Common-law remedies were available and occasionally used. In at least one case, a donee relied on the action of replevin to recover custody of a manor that had been taken into royal custody because he had been accused of entering it without license. The subsequent trial vindicated his claim that he had entered with royal permission.[51] The Statute of Westminster (I) in 1275 gave plaintiffs the option of using the writ of novel disseisin or a bill of complaint to recover lands that had been unjustly seized by escheators, sheriffs, or other royal bailiffs. It covered only cases in which the officer acted ex officio, that is, without writ or direct authority from the king. It was a limited remedy, and only a few parties seemed to have availed themselves of the action in subsequent years.[52]

Most petitioned to recover lands, basing their claims on tenure. Families claimed that lands were held in socage or petty serjeanty rather than by knight service; mesne lords asserted that the tenant-in-chief held *ut de honore* or by serjeanty or socage; and widows argued that they had joint seisin with their husbands. A specific procedure developed, therefore, to determine claims. The Crown seized lands on the death of a landholder or after they had been alienated without license; an individual such as a mesne lord, heir, or relative petitioned for the custody or possession of the land; the king ordered an inquest or search of the rolls; and once the information had been collected, a judgment was made. Only by following these steps could claimants recover lands, whatever the merits of their cases.[53]

Although the king or chancellor occasionally ordered the escheator to turn lands over to the appropriate person immediately after they had been informed of the tenure by the inquisition post mortem, most individuals had to go through the petitioning procedure in order to recover possession. In twelve cases between 1291 and 1296 in which a widow recovered lands she had held jointly with her husband, nine were initiated by the widow's petition.[54] Once the king or chancellor received the petition, he issued

[51] PRO, E.143/5/1 (no. 2); *Placita de Quo Warranto Temporibus Edw. I, II, et III* (London, 1818), 115. I owe the last reference to Dr. Paul Brand.

[52] *Statutes of the Realm*, 1:33; *Rot. Parl.*, 1:117; PRO, Just.1/1370 mm. 23, 23a; E.159/94 mm. 109, 110; Ehrlich, *Proceedings against the Crown*, 25, 51, 111.

[53] Ehrlich, *Proceedings against the Crown*, 61–64; *Prerogativa Regis*, xviii–xxi.

[54] Except as noted, the paired references are to (a) *CIPM*, 3, for the number of the inquisition post mortem and/or the inquest on the *certiorari*; and (b) *CCR, 1288–1296*: (1) 24, 210–211; (2) 36, 214 and *CFR*, 1:199; (3) 101, 283; (4) 75 and 76, 286; (5) 107, 306; (6) 198, 354 and *CFR*, 1:337; (7) 175 and 197, 358; (8) 280, 417; (9) 263, 419, 421; (10) 247, 422; (11) 331, 496; (12) 370, 496 and *CFR*, 1:369.

a writ of *plenius certiorari* to the escheator that directed him to conduct a second inquest. On average, eight of the widows waited a little over a month before petitioning, though three displayed real enterprise by petitioning for their lands within days of their husbands' deaths, while another delayed six months before doing so.[55] When the difference was a matter of days, the widow probably anticipated the seizure of lands and acted as soon as her husband died. Indeed, in those cases, the inquisition post mortem had not even been taken. Obviously, the problems of recovering lands were widely known, and these widows astutely tried to minimize them. After the second inquest was returned, the lands would be restored, if the inquest upheld the plaintiff's claim. In the nine cases of jointure, the average time between the issuance of the writ of *plenius certiorari* and of the writ to deliver the lands was 2.4 months, but it ranged from 4 days to 10 months.

Royal officials were extremely cautious in making judgments and were obviously reluctant to reach decisions that might prejudice the king's rights. Whether because of bureaucratic caution or personal influence, cases could drag on for a considerable time. Some mesne lords of whom Thomas d'Audeley held lands in Chester had to wait four years before they recovered the wardships to which they were entitled by the liberty of Chester.[56] The potential for delay stands out clearly in the elaborate maneuvering over the Traneys wardship. John de Traneys died in 1311 leaving as his heir his brother Thomas, nine years old. He held his lands of the bishopric of Durham, which was vacant, so that Edward II took custody of the lands and heir.[57] On 25 July, Edward granted the wardship of the lands and Thomas's marriage to the king's yeoman, Nicholas de Chilham, at the request of Queen Isabella. The following day, Edward ordered a second inquest into the lands held of the bishop. That inquest repeated the finding of the inqui-

---

[55] The delay is calculated between the date of the writ to the escheator and the date of the writ *plenius certiorari*. In one case, the writs were issued on the same day (*CFR*, 1:369; *CIPM*, 3:370; *CCR, 1288–1296*, 496, 14 January 1296). It is assumed that the delay between the death of the tenant and the issuance of the writ to the escheator and that between the widow's petition and the issuance of the *certiorari* would be roughly the same. In one case the widow (Peche) waited seven years before petitioning (*CFR*, 1:199, 12 February 1284; *CIPM*, 3:36, 11 December 1291; *CCR, 1288–1296*, 214, 20 January 1292).

[56] *CIPM*, 5:62; *CCR, 1307–1313*, 80, 99, 408.

[57] The writ *diem clausit* was dated 13 April. Antony Bek died on 3 March, and the new bishop did not receive the temporalities until 20 May (*CIPM*, 5:300; *HBC*, 220).

sition post mortem that Traneys did not hold of the bishop by military service and that he only owed a money rent—socage tenure. Consequently, on 14 February 1312, Edward ordered his escheator to deliver custody of the lands to Idonia, Thomas's mother, as the nearest relative.[58] Chilham, however, was determined to have the wardship. He complained to the queen, who convinced Edward to order another inquest, which reported that the bishop had never had the wardship of the Traneys lands because the heirs had always been of age, but that the bishop had had the wardship of other lands held by the same tenure. On receiving that report, Edward ordered the escheator to resume custody of the lands until the next parliament, when it would be decided what should be done with them.[59] The judgment must have been favorable to Chilham, for he recovered custody. Yet Idonia was just as persistent, and she petitioned Parliament in 1314 to have the wardship of the lands in socage. The council in Parliament referred the case to the Chancery, and yet another inquest was held, on 25 July 1315. This one reported that the bishops had never had wardship of the Traneys lands and that they had never had the wardship of lands of similar tenure. Edward duly ordered the escheator to deliver custody of the lands to Idonia on 1 September.[60] The case was unusually protracted, but wardship disputes could drag on, particularly if a series of inquests had to be held.

The procedure, moreover, might be conducted generation after generation. As a new corps of royal officials took charge, they did not necessarily follow the precedents established by their predecessors. In 1233 Henry III took into custody a manor that had been held by Robert de Hugham of Warin de Mountchesney because Robert's heir was a minor and he held some land of the king by service of finding a horse, saddle, and bridle for the king's army when it went to Wales.[61] Mountchesney protested on the grounds that this serjeanty tenure did not give the king the right to prerogative wardship. The issue came before the king and his council, who supported Mountchesney's argument and so ordered the

---

[58] *CPR, 1307–1313*, 379; *CCR, 1307–1313*, 401. The second inquest was probably held at Idonia's request.

[59] *CIPM*, 5:300 (inquest on a writ of *plenius certiorari*, 5 April 1312); *CCR, 1307–1313*, 426 (6 June).

[60] *Rot. Parl.*, 1:325; *CIPM*, 5:610; *CCR, 1313–1318*, 247–248. For a similarly convoluted dispute, see *Rot. Parl.*, 1:306–307; *CCR, 1313–1318*, 307.

[61] *BNB*, 2:743. It was the manor of Boughton, Kent, which was at stake (*Book of Fees*, 2:664, 679).

manor restored to Mountchesney's custody. Bracton, in fact, used the case to illustrate his point that petty serjeanties did not entitle the king to prerogative wardship.[62] That judgment set a precedent but it did not inhibit Crown practice. When the heir died around 1259 leaving another minor heir, Robert, royal officials apparently did not even take custody of the serjeanty and allowed the lords of the other lands the wardship and marriage of the heir.[63] Robert in turn died in 1301, and the escheator once again seized custody of *all* of Robert's lands. The seizure forced Hugh de Vere, the husband of Denise de Mountchesney, granddaughter and heir of the Warin who made the earlier complaint, and Alexander Balliol, lord of another of Hugham's manors, to petition the king for the wardship of the lands that Robert held of them.[64] The issue went to Parliament but was not settled before Edward I's death. Edward II then ordered the treasurer and barons to search their rolls and finally authorized a restoration of the lands to Balliol and Vere in 1310, specifically citing the decision of 1233 as the basis of the restoration.[65]

The case amplifies the point made above: the government did not routinely determine the scope of its rights before acting. It operated on the presumption that the Crown was entitled to prerogative wardship and so took custody of all lands to which it potentially had a right. This presumption protected royal lordship in a way that the feudal lordship of others could not, because it put control of land in the king's hands. The king respected the tenurial limitations imposed on his lordship by Magna Carta, the liberties

---

[62] Bracton, 2:113, 254.

[63] That is the implication of an inquest held around 1274 (*CIPM*, 2:58). The Robert Senior to whom the inquest refers died around 1259, leaving a widow, Beatrice (*ERF*, 2:298). The inquest states that one manor was in the custody of William de Mountchesney for eleven years and that William de Wilton, lord of Chilham, had custody of another along with the marriage of the heir. Wilton, a royal justice, died around 1264, while Mountchesney, heir of Warin, came of age in 1256 and died in 1287 (*EB*, 111, 144; Edward Foss, *The Judges of England* [London, 1848–1864], 2:519–520). It is not clear why the inquest was held, except that the escheator reported in his account for that year that Mountchesney had not allowed him entry to the manor of Boughton (PRO, E.372/124 m. 22).

[64] PRO, SC.1/28/173; *EB*, 144, for the descent of the Mountchesney family.

[65] *CIPM*, 4:36; *CFR*, 1:450, 463–464, 468; Maitland, *Memoranda de Parliamento*, 110–111 (no. 182); PRO, E.159/82 m. 27d; *CCR, 1307–1313*, 196, 197. The last Robert died without children of his own in 1317, so that his inheritance fell to the children of his aunt, Beatrice. She had two daughters, Helen and Benedicta, and the Hugham property was partitioned between Benedicta and Waresius, Helen's minor heir (*CIPM*, 6:20; *CFR*, 3:30–31).

that he had bestowed on some tenants, and the property settlements such as jointures and entails into which his tenants sometimes entered, but he did not automatically honor them. Any exception to his rights had to be asserted and until it was proven, the
Crown retained the lands.[66]

The treatment of socage and serjeanty tenures provides an excellent illustration of this process. In spite of the fact that Magna
Carta and Bracton laid out fairly clear guidelines for determining
the king's rights of wardship when tenants held of him by small
serjeanty or socage, throughout the thirteenth and early fourteenth centuries each instance was determined on an ad hoc basis
and, in regard to serjeanties, the king did not necessarily adhere
to these criteria, as the Hugham case demonstrates.[67] Since the
king stood to lose both the wardship and marriage, the government proceeded cautiously, taking custody of the lands on the
death of the tenant and undertaking an investigation only when
an interested party petitioned. Indeed, in some cases, the king pro-
visionally granted the wardship to someone else pending the outcome of the investigation.[68] One case involving service by rendering a pair of gilt spurs began with the death of the tenant in 1269
and was not settled for another two years, at which point the Exchequer concluded that the king had no right to the custody of the
lands.[69] The judgment confirmed the requirements of Magna
Carta, but only after a long delay.[70] Each time that lands held by

[66] See *CIPM*, 2:284, where an inquest revealed that the king had no right to the
wardship of certain lands, but had retained custody because no one had challenged
his right (cited by Walker, "Royal Wardship," 36). The king granted the wardship
to someone else, though four years later restored custody to the heir, who was still
a minor, on condition that he pay the issues to the guardian (*CCR, 1279–1288*, 165,
175, 275).

[67] Kimball, *Serjeanty Tenure*, 150–198.

[68] *CIPM*, 1:383; *Close Rolls*, 10:81–82, 103.

[69] *CPR, 1266–1272*, 341; *CIPM*, 1:714; PRO, E.368/43 m. 10; *Close Rolls*, 14:68–
69, 319–320, Bussell wardship.

[70] Kimball's argument that the king treated petty serjeanties as socage only after
1306 is clearly wrong (Kimball, *Serjeanty Tenure*, 177). She placed too much faith in
Britton. His statement that in cases of socage and burgage tenures, as well as petty
serjeanty, the king took the wardship and marriage of the heir is not borne out by
actual practice (*Britton*, 2:7; Kimball, *Serjeanty Tenure*, 171–172, 185–186). Practice
varied. One petty serjeanty (Noel) fell to the Crown in successive generations in
1236 and 1279. In the first instance, the king sold the wardship and marriage of
the heir to the widow for 100*s.*, while in the second the lands were declared to be
socage and turned over to the widow, though the king saved the right of marriage
(*ERF*, 1:308; *CIPM*, 2:330; *CCR, 1272–1279*, 523, 535; *Book of Fees*, 2:1344, 1346,

socage or petty serjeanty came into royal custody, claimants had to go through the same process to recover custody. Even if their claim was justified, if the Crown could show that it had once exercised the right of wardship or marriage, then it would continue to do so in the future.[71]

Claimants addressed their petitions to the king, council, chancellor, treasurer, and other officials, and they were heard in a variety of tribunals including the Exchequer, Chancery, and Parliament.[72] The procedure in each forum was the same. It was essentially an administrative process though it contained a kernel of judicial disputation and legal significance since it involved the determination of the extent of the king's rights.[73] The collection and interpretation of tenurial information were the most crucial components of this procedure. As repositories of information about tenure and lordship, the Chancery and Exchequer constituted the king's feudal memory, so that it was logical that they should handle the bulk of this business. The Exchequer retained fiscal information while the Chancery stored surveys, inquisitions, writs, and, of course, the enrollments of writs. They supplemented this core of knowledge with a steady stream of writs *certiorari* asking local officials to supply details about specific lands or actions by escheators.[74] This was the evidence the government marshaled to settle disputes. In 1270 Warin de Mountchesney asserted in king's bench that the escheator had been unjustified in taking custody of certain lands held of Warin because the tenant had held in chief of the honor of Rayleigh, and a search of the Domesday Book proved him correct. Gilbert de Clare disputed the king's claim to the custody and marriage of the heir of one of his tenants in 1275,

---

1381). For a similar case, see *CCR, 1296–1302*, 424; and *CCR, 1307–1313*, 430, 514 (Sauvage).

[71] PRO, E.159/72 m. 13d.

[72] Petition, PRO, SC.1/25/30; referral of cases to treasurer and barons, PRO, E.368/32 m. 14d; *Rot. Parl.*, 1:214, 326; and private disputes, E.13/1B m. 10d; /18 mm. 8d, 69d; PRO, SC.1/7/162, 199, 200; 8/127, 138; 9/53; 10/107; 31/101. The development of the court of Chancery in this period, based in part on the hearing of petitions, is summarized in *Select Cases*, 5:lxvii–xcvii.

[73] *Select Cases*, 5:lxxv: "legal disputation was latent in all acts of administration." A good example of the way in which an administrative procedure (assignment of dower) could shade off into a legal judgment can be found in PRO, C.133/39, no. 5; and *CIPM*, 2:528.

[74] See, for example, PRO, C.257/1, nos. 36–40; /2, nos. 3, 4, 5, 7, 11, 12 16, 17, 19, 20, 21 22, 24, 25, 27–30; /3, nos. 1, 6, 7, 8A, 10, 11, 13, 18. Similar writs can also be found in the Escheators' Files, E.153. Most related to alienations without license.

but he was overruled by the pipe rolls and other records that showed that the tenant's ancestors had performed homage to the king.[75] Finally, when a dispute over custody of lands that the plaintiff contended were held in socage rather than by knight service reached the king's council in the parliament of 1306, the council ordered a new inquest into the tenure but also commanded the chancellor to search the Chancery rolls and earlier inquisitions post mortem concerning the property, and the barons of the Exchequer to search their rolls for precedents. In this case, the investigation supported the plaintiff so that the king directed the Chancery to send a writ to the keeper to turn over custody to the claimant.[76]

The most important differentiation in the disputes was between those which could be settled through routine bureaucratic procedure and those of greater complexity which required weightier counsel. It was basically the same as the discrimination made by the receivers of petitions in Parliament who allotted the most difficult to the king and council and directed the rest to the appropriate office.[77] Simple cases, like claims by widows for lands held in jointure, could be determined on the merits of the evidence presented and did not usually require extensive debate. Cases, on the other hand, that involved difficult issues or potentially affected the king's lordship not only required greater documentation but had to be deliberated by a more influential tribunal comprising officials and justices. This could be done in the Exchequer or Chancery or Parliament. By the early fourteenth century it appears that Chancery was considered the most appropriate forum for disputes over royal lordship, perhaps because it commanded most of the evidence used to settle such disputes. The king sent cases to Chancery, individuals were summoned before the king or council in Chancery ("coram nobis in cancellaria nostra"), and Parliament sometimes directed cases to Chancery for deliberation.[78] Yet there were no rigid jurisdictional boundaries between these "courts,"

[75] PRO, KB.26/197 m. 11d (*Crown v. Mountchesney*); *Red Book*, 3:1013–1014.

[76] *Rot. Parl.*, 1:214; *CCR, 1302–1307*, 492.

[77] Maitland, *Memoranda de Parliamento*, lv–lxiv.

[78] PRO, E.159/88 mm. 58, 156–157; C.245/1, nos. 3, 5, 7, 9, 14, 21, 22, 24. Some were ordered to come before the king and council (no. 10), to Chancery (no. 11), before the king and council in Parliament (no. 13), and before the council (no. 23). See also *Rot. Parl.*, 1:325. For a case heard by the king in Chancery, see *CFR*, 2:203. By the fifteenth century, cases were routinely referred to Chancery (*Prerogativa Regis*, xix).

and their composition was roughly the same, the members having been drawn from a pool of officials, justices, and magnates closest to the king. The important thing was that expert opinion be brought to bear on a case so that the king's rights would be protected and the claim receive a fair hearing. Whatever the tribunal, decision making was centralized in the hands of the most powerful officials in the government.

When hearing cases involving wardships, these tribunals were acting as a seigniorial court, adjudicating lord-tenant disputes in the lord's court. The tenants-in-chief were at a distinct disadvantage in such cases. Not only did their lord have possession of the lands in question, but the cases were decided according to the procedures and standards set by the lord. Information about tenure was crucial, and to a great extent tenants-in-chief were dependent on the royal administration for the collection of that information, as John Filiol learned in the reign of Edward I. John de Dagworth died sometime in 1290 or 1291, at which point the the king claimed the wardship of his lands and the marriage of his heir, John. Filiol, of whom Dagworth held a manor by military service, contested the king's claim, and the dispute came before the treasurer and barons. Filiol argued that his family had long taken custody of Dagworth's ancestors who held only a petty serjeanty of the king *ut de honore*. The king, therefore, could claim custody only of that tenement.[79] A search of the Exchequer, however, turned up the fact that John's ancestor had offered a fine for a quarter of a knight's fee in 1242. Challenged to counter that evidence, Filiol could only repeat that his family had long been seised of the wardship ("nichil dixit nisi quod prius quod semper tam post quam ante fuerunt in seisina de predicta custodia et maritagio qui acciderunt"). Finally, the barons also discovered that in John's reign William de Huntingfeld had purchased the wardship and marriage of a Dagworth heir from the Crown.

The type of evidence made a difference. Filiol's reliance on seisin time out of mind was anachronistic in the thirteenth century when the Crown could support its case with written evidence. He failed to perceive the issue in those terms. The transformation wrought by institutionalization, in other words, was partly the product of new standards of record keeping. That change was an essential prerequisite to the hostility displayed by royal justices in

[79] PRO, E.159/64 mm. 5d, 9d.

127

the 1280s to prescriptive claims in quo warranto cases.[80] By the late thirteenth century, the royal government could expect that its tenants would have the same kinds of proof that it so assiduously preserved. The tenants-in-chief overturned that expectation in quo warranto, but Filiol's case was crushed by the weight of Exchequer record, and he learned in a bitter way that prescription could not stand up to written record in his lord's court.

Yet the barons had been selective; they did not tell the full story contained in the records. The same issue had arisen in 1260 on the death of Osbert Dagworth, grandfather of the heir in 1291. The inquisition post mortem reported that Osbert held a tenement in chief of the king of the honor of Rayleigh, but a second inquest told a more elaborate tale. It explained that Osbert's father, Richard, had been a minor in the custody of his lord, Baldwin Filiol, but that because of some offense that Baldwin had committed, King John had seized the wardship and heir and had sold them to Huntingfeld.[81] Furthermore, when Richard died, Osbert had been a minor and had also been in the custody of the Filiol family. At the time of the inquest, Osbert's son and heir was in the custody of John Filiol. Henry III, with the assent of the magnates of the council, granted Osbert's widow the wardship of the lands held of the king by serjeanty, the only lands that pertained to him.[82] In other words, Filiol's contention in 1291 was correct, and it was borne out by royal records. Nevertheless, as in the Hugham case, the precedent did not mean anything, and in 1292 Edward granted the marriage of the Dagworth heir to the eldest daughter of William Fitz Warin.[83]

Whether the oversight was deliberate or simply due to a lack of communication between the Exchequer and Chancery is unimportant. Since it was royal officials who conducted the search, they would tend to be satisfied with evidence that supported the king's cause and not necessarily seek out all relevant information. The case clearly demonstrates the overwhelming advantage that the Crown enjoyed in dealing with its tenants because of the information and precedents that it could marshal and the selective way in which it could use them. That superiority allowed the king to be generous at times and to relinquish custody of lands even though

---

[80] Sutherland, *Quo Warranto*, 71–85, 182–184.
[81] *CIPM*, 1:466, 521.
[82] *CPR, 1258–1266*, 128.
[83] *CPR, 1281–1292*, 498–499.

his records indicated that he had a right to the wardship.[84] Knowledge was power, or, more accurately, knowledge backed by acceptable proof was power, and such proof was not easily obtained. Nevertheless, the data did not always support the Crown's case, and for the most part the government did not act arbitrarily. The candidate favored by the king and queen did not prevail in the Traneys case, for example. Yet it took skill and persistence to combat the Crown. Lords like Filiol who did not keep pace with changes brought about by royal institutions could be penalized. Families and mesne lords had to conform to the practices of the royal administration and courts and to the standards of proof that they set or risk losing their rights.

By the end of Edward I's reign, therefore, tenants-in-chief were forced to follow similar bureaucratic procedures whether as heirs to secure their inheritance; as widows to secure their dowers; as conveyancers to alienate lands; as beneficiaries to acquire lands, wardships, or widows' marriages; or as mesne lords, immunity holders, or families to recover their rights. Anyone who had a claim to lands taken into royal custody went through an identical process that varied only according to length.[85] Royal lordship had become institutionalized, and these institutions mediated relations between the Crown and the landholding elite. They were not distant and exceptional, but rather an ordinary and universal consequence of feudal landholding for tenants-in-chief. Since they affected the vital processes of inheritance and marriage, they were unavoidable, and tenants-in-chief had to learn to conduct their business with the Crown according to the routines of those institutions.

Institutionalization, however, did not have to be forced on tenants-in-chief for two reasons. First, they benefited from the existence of routines, tribunals, and sanctions that regulated landholding and relations between families. These institutions lessened the risk of conflict within the ranks of the landholding elite and provided a largely disinterested forum for resolving difficult issues. In

---

[84] *CCR, 1296–1302*, 281, Sudington wardship.

[85] For individual examples, *ut de escaeta*, see *CIPM*, 2:26, 77; *CCR, 1272–1279*, 102; *RH*, 1:172; *ut de honore*, see *CIPM*, 4:315; *CCR, 1302–1307*, 261; *CPR, 1301–1307*, 413; liberty of the Welsh Marches, see *CIPM*, 3:544; *CCR, 1296–1302*, 270; socage, see PRO, E.368/43 m. 10; *CIPM*, 1:796; *Close Rolls*, 14:560; *CCR, 1272–1279*, 6; *CIPM*, 5:251; *CCR, 1307–1313*, 376–377; serjeanty, see *CIPM*, 2:685, 3:37, 69; *CFR*, 1:255; *CPR, 1281–1292*, 300; and ward by right of wardship, see *CIPM*, 3:563; *CPR, 1292–1301*, 187, 194.

the partitioning of estates among coheirs, for example, the royal administration provided a means of achieving an equitable distribution of resources as well as procedures for adjudicating the claims of disgruntled coparceners. By the fourteenth century, landholders relied entirely on the institutions of the law and royal courts to protect their property arrangements and they identified the stability of those arrangements with the stability of the institutions.[86]

In the second place, the institutions developed slowly and were not alien to the experience of tenants-in-chief. They grew out of the ideology and practices of the seigniorial court, so that the king and tenants-in-chief agreed on basic principles governing their respective rights and obligations. The centralization of royal lordship had been powered by the king's desire to conserve and to enforce his seigniorial rights. To do so he built on and elaborated practices, such as quo warranto, which were part of the common experience of feudal landholding. As a result, the institutions were recognizable and simple, though as they grew, they became more and more pervasive. The difference between the seigniorial court and the royal government in this respect was one of scale, not quality. Even with an expansion of business, the system preserved the ideal of a personal reciprocity between lord and tenant. That ideal comes closest to explicit expression in homage and fealty, in the oaths of widows not to marry without license, and in the language of petitions and letters dealing with issues of lordship. The sense of personal obligation and contact that animated lord-tenant relations can be seen, for example, in a letter written by Denise de Mountchesney to Edward I in 1297. She has to restore her granddaughter, a royal ward whom she had been caring for, to the king, and she writes to explain that she cannot come herself to render the girl into the hands of the king's lordship ("venir a vous en ma propre person de cele garde rendre en les meyns de votre seygnureurie").[87] The personification of obligations and authority evident in this passage was typical of seigniorial relations and helped to temper, or perhaps palliate, the institutionalization of royal lordship. This did not mean that tenants-in-chief merely acquiesced in the process or never expressed annoyance at the procedures they had to undergo. Yet it did provide a wide field of agreement within

[86] Robert C. Palmer, *The Whilton Dispute, 1264–1380: A Social-Legal Study of Dispute Settlement in Medieval England* (Princeton, 1984), 3–27.
[87] PRO, SC.1/19/141.

which the king and tenants-in-chief could bargain without coming to blows.

PERSONAL LORDSHIP AND THE EXPERIMENT WITH STEWARDS

Institutionalization in no way diminished the king's personal control of his feudal rights. Although they delegated considerable authority to their subordinates, kings did not allow their bureaucracy complete discretion over the exercise of royal lordship. They retained control of the administration, took an active part in deliberations about disputed rights, decided how to distribute the benefits of lordship, and even took a hand in arranging marriages. Edward I proved to be especially attentive to the details of lordship and launched an ambitious scheme to reorganize his local administration. The plan failed, but it is nonetheless indicative of the personal control and interest that kings exercised over their seigniorial institutions and of the important place those institutions occupied in the royal administration.

The king made his interest in his lordship clearly evident while he was overseas, for even though absent the king kept in close contact with the administration and personally authorized the disposition of widows, wardships, and marriages. Feudal lordship was too important to be delegated entirely to subordinates. During his campaign in Gascony in 1253, Henry III wrote to his regents, Queen Eleanor and his brother Richard of Cornwall, instructing them about the disposal of the wardships of the Urtiaco and Vescy families.[88] Edward was as vigilant as his father. When he was in France in 1286, for instance, Edward conducted a wide variety of feudal business by letter with his lieutenant in England, Edmund of Cornwall. A rumor that Pernell, the eldest daughter and coheir of John de Vaux, had married without license reached the king overseas, so that he ordered the treasurer and barons of the Exchequer to investigate the matter.[89] A similar rumor must have prompted Edward to order Edmund on 5 October 1286 to inquire secretly if Isabel de Mortimer, widow of John Fitz Alan, had married without license. The letter set the administration in motion. Isabel's lands were seized, she had to appear before the barons of the Exchequer to defend her marriage, and finally recovered her lands in June 1287, eight months after Edward wrote to Edmund.

[88] *CPR, 1247–1258*, 287, 463; *ERF*, 2:295; *EB*, 84; *CIPM*, 1:315, 785.
[89] PRO, E.159/61 m. 4d. Edward even specified a fine of £230 for the trespass.

It turned out that Henry III had granted the right of her marriage to her father, that after he died his executors accepted her fine for the right to marry whomever she pleased, and that she had married Robert de Hastang on 2 September 1285.[90] Edward likewise monitored the Mountchesney wardship that fell in at about the same time, and closely circumscribed his lieutenant's authority in the matter. Edmund could act in these cases only by the king's special order.[91] Furthermore, while on campaign in Scotland in the summer of 1296, Edward demanded that escheators' accounts and the inquisitions post mortem of several tenants-in-chief be sent to him, after which he issued orders concerning the wardships.[92] Edward's reach was long, and he kept a close watch on his tenants-in-chief and seigniorial rights even during a military campaign.

Nevertheless, the Crown was forced to give its local agents some responsibility for disposing of wardships and marriages. Because of the efficiency of the administration, the growing numbers of tenants-in-chief, and the new enforcement of different aspects of royal lordship the number of lands and wards falling into royal custody increased rapidly from the middle of the century. The king could not hope to have a hand in decisions concerning every wardship, widow, marriage, or alienation, even when he was in England. Nor was it necessary that he do so. Wardships of small estates, which would be of interest only to neighbors or family, would be more easily sold by the king's local agents than by the central administration.[93] The government, therefore, began to distinguish between major and minor wardships, that is, between those of political or financial importance, of which the king or his council would dispose, and those of lesser value, which could be entrusted to the discretion of local officials. It drew the line at estates valued between £20 and £50 a year. The distinction allowed the king to exercise his personal authority over the wardships and

[90] PRO, SC.1/45/39 (5 October 1286); E.159/60 mm. 2d, 7d (memoranda concerning Isabel's appearance before the barons and the proof of the grant of her marriage, November 1286); SC.1/45/48 (acknowledgment by Edward, 15 May 1287); CCR, 1279–1288, 451.

[91] PRO, SC.1/16/70. Edmund kept him well informed about the wardship (PRO, SC.1/45/55, 57, 61, 62/35). In the Mortimer case, Edward told Edmund that "sine speciali precepto nostro sub privato sigillo nostro terre ille et tenementa non deliberantur" (PRO, SC.1/45/48). For a general discussion of the administrative arrangements while the king was overseas, see Tout, Chapters, 1:276 and n. 5, 290–293.

[92] CCR, 1288–1296, 500, 512.

[93] CIM, 1:93.

marriages of the most important families among the tenants-in-chief while leaving the rest to the routine operation of the administration. It was a question not only of economic value but also of prestige. The disposition of the lands and marriages of the heirs of powerful families potentially affected the entire network of relations within the landed elite and was therefore politically sensitive. It was the subject of close scrutiny by the elite as well as by the king and his ministers.

Henry III employed these criteria in 1242–1243 and again in 1253–1254 for the regency councils he set up in England while he campaigned in Gascony. On 5 May 1242, he placed the kingdom in the hands of William de Grey, the archbishop of York; Walter Mauclerc, the bishop of Carlisle; and William de Cantilupe, a household steward, and gave them power to sell all wardships worth less than £50 a year that fell in during his absence.[94] The council accordingly sold some minor wardships, but kept others in custody for the king's judgment, while Henry issued orders from France concerning several important wards.[95] Henry's order for his lieutenants in 1253–1254, Queen Eleanor and Richard of Cornwall, did not explicitly contain the same criteria, but they conformed to the practice of the earlier council.[96] They granted a few minor wardships and left others to await the king's return, while Henry himself disposed of the lands and heirs of several baronial families from Gascony.[97] Henry clearly delimited the sphere of the regency's responsibility to routine tasks and preserved to himself discretion over politically and financially important wardships, marriages, and widows.

This discrimination between wardships was adopted by the barons during the period of reform after 1258. The Provisions of Oxford thus prohibited the chancellor from sealing any grant of a great wardship ("grant garde") without the approval of the council. Accordingly, in July 1259, the escheator south of the Trent, William de Wenling, was given authority to farm all wards and es-

[94] *Foedera*, 1:244; *CPR, 1232–1247*, 290. Henry also gave the council the power to authorize elections in abbeys and priories under the value of 50 marks. Henry actually departed on 17 May.

[95] *ERF*, 1:382, 384, 389, 394, 398, 404, 407; *CPR, 1232–1247*, 376, 383, 391, 397, 412. Writs issued by the regents are listed in *ERF*, 1:378–404, and *CPR, 1232–1247*, 298–396. After he returned on 27 September, Henry also confirmed a grant that Grey had made (*CPR, 1232–1247*, 415).

[96] *Foedera*, 1:291; *Close Rolls*, 7:480; *CPR, 1247–1258*, 200, 206, 209, 214.

[97] *ERF*, 2:176, 186, 192, 195; *Close Rolls*, 8:162; *CPR, 1247–1258*, 268, 271, 276, 285.

cheats that fell in worth £20 or less.[98] The reformers' use of the distinction shows that there was a consensus about the importance of certain wardships based on the value of the lands and the status of the family. In fact, the attitude spilled over into private estates.[99] Within the feudal tenantry of an estate, whether at the level of barony, earldom, or kingdom, there were distinctions in wealth and status that the lord of the estate had to recognize. He could profit from wardships and marriages, but he had to be careful how he disposed of the heirs and lands of his most important tenants. Effective lordship from the lord's standpoint did not preclude good lordship for tenants. On the contrary, the two went hand in hand and reinforced one another.

From the outset of his reign, Edward I understood the benefits of feudal lordship and sought to improve the administration he had inherited from his father. He was a particularly energetic landlord and demanded a high level of competence from his ministers. When he returned to England in 1274, he found that some tenants had flouted his seigniorial authority and had abused his agents, so that he introduced changes in the administration. As in other areas, Edward did not overturn his father's practices, he simply applied them more forcefully. The changes demonstrate his interest in his seigniorial rights and the degree of discretion over wardships and marriages that he was willing to concede to his ministers.

Since Edward was still on Crusade when Henry III died in 1272 and did not return to England until 1274, provisions had to be made for wardships and marriages that fell in during his absence. When he departed in 1270, Edward had entrusted his affairs in England to three agents, and once he became king, though in absentia, they took over the machinery of royal lordship on his behalf. At first, they managed his rights as a private lord and gained experience handling feudal business, which they transferred to

[98] *DBMRR*, 102–103, cap. 7, "grant garde"; *CPR, 1258–1266*, 29. Escheators had sold wardships before (*ERF*, 2:237).

[99] In an agreement between Roger de Mortimer and Robert de Vere in 1268 for the redemption of Vere's lands after the Barons' War, Vere, with Roger's consent, appointed a steward to receive the issues of his lands on Roger's behalf until the redemption was fully paid. The steward was instructed to sell any wardship worth £10 or less to help pay the debt, but he could sell more valuable ones only with the consent of both lords (*CChR*, 2:89–90, also cited by Clive H. Knowles, "The Resettlement of England after the Barons' War, 1264–67," *TRHS*, 5th ser., 32 [1982]: 31–32).

royal lordship after Henry III died.[100] They proceeded cautiously, however, and did not dispense major wardships. When the lands and heirs of several important tenants-in-chief fell into their hands between 1272 and 1273, they kept them in custody until Edward returned and dealt with them himself.[101] He personally authorized each grant and distributed the wardships to individuals close to him.[102] Edward even took a hand in minor wardships, though his lieutenants usually granted and sold them on their own.[103] In one case, Edward ordered a manor that his agents had granted out taken back into custody and gave it to one of his ministers.[104] Finally, the authority of Edward's lieutenants covered all aspects of royal lordship, including the punishment of marriages contracted without royal license.[105]

Although these ministers adequately performed routine administrative duties, they could not project the king's personal prestige and so could not command a high level of compliance with his lordship. Edward's absence thus prompted an outbreak of disobedience among tenants-in-chief and mesne lords. In their accounts for these years, the escheators reported again and again that they were unable to answer for the issues of certain lands that should have been in their custody because someone had entered them without license and had ejected the escheator or prevented him from taking custody. The bailiffs of great lords like the earls of Gloucester and Norfolk or the countess of Warwick seized lands, heirs entered their inheritances without license, and even the men of the queen and the earl of Cornwall ejected ministers.[106] In several cases, it was the mesne lord who denied the escheator's taking

[100] The agents were Walter Giffard, the archbishop of York; Roger de Mortimer of Wigmore; and Robert Burnell, then archdeacon of York. For an example of their work, see *CPR, 1272–1281*, 110. These grants were recorded on the patent roll for 1275 because the grantee requested that they be resealed with the king's seal. See also *CPR, 1266–1272*, 650.

[101] *CIPM*, 2:14, 16, 17, 56; *CPR, 1272–1281*, 64, 87, 93, 112, 139. The wardships involved Ralph Musard, Thomas Fitz Otto, George Cantilupe, and Roger de Somery among others.

[102] Musard: *CPR, 1272–1281*, 79, 134, 281. Edward's lieutenants had committed lands to custodians who were supposed to account for the issues (*CFR*, 1:1; PRO, E.372/124 m. 19).

[103] PRO, E.372/120 mm. 24–24d; /124 mm. 19–22; E.136/1/3–7; *CPR, 1272–1281*, 44, 45, 46.

[104] PRO, E.372/120 m. 24; E.136/1/3.

[105] *CPR, 1272–1281*, 11–12; *CFR*, 1:2, 10, 20; *CIPM*, 2:11; *EB*, 26–27 (d'Aubigny).

[106] PRO, E.372/124 mm. 20d, 21, 21d; E.136/1/3; *CIPM*, 2:98, 109.

custody of the lands and so prevented him from exercising prerogative wardship.[107] Some of these reports may have been contrived in an attempt to reduce the escheator's financial obligations to the king. The general picture of tenant unruliness before Edward returned, however, was borne out by the hundred inquests and by a special investigation that Edward ordered to name those who prevented the escheators from doing their job.[108] For example, when Robert de Sutton, lord of Aston, Northamptonshire, died in 1273 his heir was only eight years old.[109] Though the Crown should have had custody of the manor, the earl of Gloucester's bailiff acted first. He ordered an associate to seize the manor while he arranged to sell it to someone else for 10 marks. It was only then that the subescheator stepped in and took possession in the king's name.[110] Heirs likewise tried to defraud the administration. When his lands came into custody in 1273, Remegius Melling was just over eighteen years old, but he asked for an inquest to prove his age. He did not take any chances. He gave Thomas le Chapman a virgate of land to help him suborn the inquest. Thomas fulfilled his part of the bargain by serving as chief juror at the inquest, which not surprisingly declared Remegius to be of age. The Chancery duly ordered the escheator to give Remegius his inheritance.[111]

Tenants clearly exploited the new king's absence to sidestep their obligations. The returns of the hundred inquests also demonstrated that the royal administration had not prevented alienations prejudicial to the king's rights or unlicensed marriages by

[107] PRO, E.372/120 m. 24d; /124 mm. 21, 21d.

[108] PRO, C.47/1/18, no.15: "Nomina magnatum qui deforciant escaetori domini Regis citra Trentam seisinam terrarum et tenementorum que deberent esse in manu domini Regis eo quod tenentes tenuerunt de domino Rege in capite." The return is undated and torn, but the tenants whose lands ought to have been in royal custody, such as Robert Walerand, Jordan de Sakeville, and others, all died between 1271 and 1273. The returns list lands of eight tenants-in-chief in the custody of at least six magnates. There is no evidence in the accounts or elsewhere that the escheators were punished for making false claims.

[109] *CFR*, 1:3; *CIPM*, 2:61; Christopher J. Holdsworth, introduction to *Rufford Charters* (Nottingham, 1972), cx.

[110] The escheator sold the full wardship to Stephen de Sutton, the heir's great-uncle and a canon of York, for 650 marks (PRO, C.47/1/18, no. 15; *RH*, 2:9; *CFR*, 1:49; *CCR, 1272–1279*, 59; *CPR, 1272–1281*, 97; Holdsworth, *Rufford Charters*, cx–cxi).

[111] *RH*, 1:239; *CFR*, 1:28. For a fine of 5 marks, Remegius also gained the right to marry whomever he pleased. For another case of concealment of age, see *CIPM*, 2:15; *CFR*, 1:3; and *CPR, 1272–1281*, 320–321.

widows.[112] In addition, they revealed that although during the same period, escheators had committed a variety of minor malfeasances such as waste, selling goods from lands in royal custody for their own use, extorting money from wards and others, and taking custody of lands that did not pertain to the king, their activities did not engender nearly so much complaint as those of sheriffs and royal bailiffs.[113] Nor were the escheators guilty of corruption that deprived the king of his rights. When asked about the taking of bribes to lower the value of wardships, or about suborning juries to report heirs of age when they were not, or about concealing wardships from the king, the hundred jurors had little or nothing to report.[114] From the hundred returns, royal lordship does not appear to have weighed too heavily on local communities and landholders. It was a private, rather than public, issue: a question of lord-tenant rather than Crown-community relations.

On the basis of the evidence that it collected from escheators and juries, therefore, the government's primary concern regarding the administration of royal lordship must have been that it was not efficiently enforcing and managing the king's rights. As a result, Edward reorganized his seigniorial administration. The so-called Statute of the Exchequer issued in Parliament at Westminster in October 1275 outlined the new system. Henceforth, the sheriffs would be responsible for the wardships and escheats in their counties and would perform the functions of subescheator on their semiannual tourns.[115] In respect to these duties, the statute put them under the authority of three stewards who were assigned to survey the wardships and escheats in each county as well as to take custody of the king's demesnes throughout England. The sheriffs

[112] Alienations: *RH*, 1:60, 83, 90, 91, 102, 121, 191, 193, 197, 241; 2:31. Widows: *RH*, 1:90, 231, 237, 239, 463; 2:28, 40, 63, 71, 94, 105.

[113] Taking goods: *RH*, 1:45, 52, 60, 64, 65, 90, 114, 157, 160, 172, 182, 185–186, 192, 239, 337, 366, 370, 384, 463, 500; 2:10, 11, 17, 20, 23, 24, 35, 88, 95, 128, 160, 194, 206, 207, 223, 248, 254, 316. Extortion; *RH*, 1:115, 118, 200–201, 239, 293, 346, 445, 457; 2:24, 128, 129, 146, 206, 212, 216. Taking custody: *RH*, 1:11, 38, 45, 47, 359; 2:14. For similar conclusions based on the same evidence, see Cam, *The Hundred*, 199–202; and Walker, "Royal Wardship," 96–97.

[114] The three articles are printed in Cam, *The Hundred*, 254–255. My search of the hundred rolls did not turn up a single case relating to these queries. Walker similarly concluded that the escheators were generally honest ("Royal Wardship," 97).

[115] Stevenson, "The Escheator," 119; *Statutes of the Realm*, 1:197a. The statute did note that sheriffs should perform these duties "au meins de grevaunce del people kil porrunt."

were supposed to consult with the stewards about the farming or sale of wardships and escheats and then account to the Exchequer for the revenues during their customary audits. In essence, the change abolished the offices of escheator and subescheator, amalgamated responsibility for the royal demesnes and royal lordship in the hands of three new officers, and gave the sheriffs the work of the subescheators.[116] The relationship between the steward and the sheriff was the same as that between the chief escheators and the subescheators. Orders concerning lands in custody, the assignment of dowers, or alienations were addressed either to the stewards or to the sheriffs who, for these purposes, were called escheators. The intention behind this rearrangement seems to have been to simplify and to strengthen the administration of royal lordship: a whole layer of administration—the subescheators—was removed; sheriffs accounted for all revenues in their bailiwicks; authority for all royal assets including demesnes, forests, and feudal resources was centralized in the hands of the stewards; and the sheriffs lent the weight of their authority to the exercise of royal lordship at the local level.

The reform was put into effect with the appointment of the stewards in November 1275. The country was divided into three bailiwicks with a separate steward assigned to each.[117] The statute gave the stewards the power to lease small manors and demesnes, then minor wardships worth £20 to £30 a year and to receive from widows who held dower lands of the same value fines for the right to marry whomever they pleased of the king's allegiance.[118] This echoed a similar order to the escheators in January 1275 empowering them to sell all custodies and marriages in their bailiwicks worth less than £20 a year.[119] The stewards routinely sold minor wardships and marriages, though the sales were often confirmed by the king, chancellor, or other official.[120] As stipulated by the statute, sheriffs sold or demised wardships only on the instruction

[116] The position of the sheriffs is made clear in the heading to their accounts as escheators, PRO, E.372/125 m. 2: "Compotus Alexandri de Kirketon de exitibus escaetarum Regis in comitatu Ebor' dum idem Alexander fuit vicecomes in predicto comitatu et escaetor per provisionem factam per Regem quod vicecomes essent excaetores in ballivis suis."

[117] Stevenson, "The Escheator," 117.

[118] CPR, 1272–1281, 314.

[119] CPR, 1272–1281, 77; Rot. Orig., 23. For sales by the escheator south of the Trent, see CFR, 1:47; CPR, 1272–1281, 83.

[120] CPR, 1272–1281, 255, 310, 312, 376, 403, 415, 422, 438, 458; CPR, 1281–1292, 168; CCR, 1272–1279, 460; PRO, SC.1/26/48A.

of the stewards.[121] The sheriffs had to inform the stewards about the wardships and lands in their custody, and the stewards commanded the sheriffs to carry out the routine business associated with the custody of lands.[122] Furthermore, the sheriffs accounted for wardships and escheats taken into royal custody, while the stewards accounted for only demesne lands.[123]

The reform, therefore, hinged on the relationship between the stewards and the sheriffs, and it fell apart when that relationship proved unworkable. The problem was partly that the division of labor and authority was never clarified. The Chancery addressed writs indifferently to stewards and sheriffs, sometimes producing conflict.[124] One of the stewards complained to the chancellor that the Chancery had instructed him to take custody of certain lands, but that it had sent an identical order to the sheriff of Lancashire, who carried it out and then would not let the steward's men have possession.[125] A sheriff made the same complaint about a steward.[126] This lack of cooperation between sheriffs and stewards undermined the system. A particularly disgruntled steward wrote to the treasurer in late 1282, pleading that his burden of work be lightened.[127] He complained not only that the work was too heavy,

[121] PRO, E.372/134 m. 2. William de Hamelyn, sheriff of Warwick and Leicester, "liberaret dictum manerium Johanni de Monte Alto per preceptum Ricardi de Holebrok senescalli dominicorum Regis et sicut idem Ricardus recognovit et per breve Regis directum eidem Willelmo in quo continetur quod in hiis que officium escaeterie predicte in predicto comitatibus contingunt sic intendens et respondens secundam formam eidem Ricardo per Regem traditam et injunctam." Both the stewards and the sheriffs paid money into the Exchequer, and the sheriffs' receipts from escheats were identified separately from their other payments (PRO, E.401/ 97, 101, 102, 103).

[122] Richard de Holebroke ordered the sheriff of Lincolnshire to deliver a wardship after he had sold it (PRO, SC.1/48/48), while the sheriff of Bedfordshire and Buckinghamshire informed Holebroke about the wards he had in custody (SC.1/ 48/32).

[123] A few of the sheriff's accounts as escheators are enrolled in PRO, E.372/125 mm. 2 (Yorkshire, 6–9 Edward I), 2d (Somerset and Dorset); /127 mm. 2 (Somerset and Dorset, 10 Edward I, also in E.136/1/10), 2d (Lincoln, 9–11 Edward I); /128 m. 32 (Lincoln, 7–9 Edward I); and /134 m. 2 (Warwick and Leicester, 4–6 Edward I). Some of the stewards' accounts are enrolled in E.372/128 mm. 28d–31 (Richard de Holebroke, 8–11 Edward I), and m. 35 (Ralph de Sandwich, 9–10 Edward I). An audit of Normanville's account is enrolled in E.159/54 m. 4d; /65 m. 12d.

[124] Stevenson, "The Escheator," 118.

[125] PRO, SC.1/24/30; *CIPM*, 2:420.

[126] *CIPM*, 2:219, cited by Walker, "Royal Wardship," 111.

[127] PRO, SC.1/10/157: "A cher seignur le seon Lyge a ses comandemenz ceo ke il poet de honur e de reverence. Sachez Sir se vous plest ke ieo esteie alant vers Sal-

but also that the authority the king had given him was insufficient to guard wardships as well as they should be. He must have been referring to his authority vis-à-vis the sheriffs, for he also fretted about his relations with the sheriffs in the counties in which he worked, claiming that they retained money that they had received from wardships. He even admitted that he dare not undertake his duties in several counties, probably out of fear of the sheriffs. Finally, he told the treasurer that he had heard that men had once again entered the king's fee and had appropriated goods and the marriages of widows and heirs so that no money could be levied from them, perhaps as a result of all of the conflict with the sheriffs. His lament pinpoints the weaknesses of Edward's reforms.

The government gradually gave up the experiment in 1282 and 1283 and reverted to the earlier system of escheators. In July 1282 Edward ordered John de Kirkby to sell or demise all the wardships that came into royal custody in all counties, thereby circum-

---

lopebyr oue deners e retornay a Brehulle por ceo ke ieo ne esteye mye en bon estat e enveiay les deners avant a Sallopebyr par les mens [miens] e de yllockes feusse venuz a vous por vous mustrer ke mon estat ne me soeffre mye travayler entaunz de counteez por les gardes estendre e vendre sicome le Rey me manda / ne la baylye ke ieo ay du Rey nel me soefre mie se ele deit estre ben garder. Por quei ieo vous pri come cher seignur ke de cel travail me voilez aleger / Et se votre volunte est ke ieo me entremettre en les parties ob ieo suy repeiraunt. Volunters le fray a menz ke ieo saveray e purray [Od] porceo ke ieo ay oy Sire par akone genz ke les viscontes ont seisy plusors choses e unt recevmuz deners les quels il retenent vers eus e ke akone gent sont entre le fee le Rey de novel e unt aproprie choses endreit de ceo e des mariages de vedues e des heyrs dont hom poreit en akon lyu lever deners e des autres choses se vous plest votre volunte me maundez. Et sachez Sir ke ieo ne osereye enprendre en nule manere cest chose a fere en le Counte de Nicol, Warr' ne Leyc', mes en les autres countez fray ceo ke vous me maunderez solung mon poer. Mes ke les viscontes seient par mei charge des deners. Et ceo ke vous volez ke hom face des gardes de graunz seygnurs come de Sire Johan le Mareschal ensement si vous plest me maundez. Honur e bone vie." The counties were part of Holebroke's bailiwick. The letter is undated, but the writ *diem clausit extremum* for John le Marshal was issued 4 December 1282, and his wardship was granted to John de Bohun on 4 June 1283 (*CIPM*, 2:471; *CFR*, 1:185; Cokayne, *Complete Peerage*, 8:258–259). The Exchequer seems to have been at Shrewsbury in the fall and winter during Edward's Welsh campaign. Edward held a parliament there on 30 September 1282, and the sheriff of Bedfordshire was ordered to appear there to render his account on 14 January 1283 (*HBC*, 508; PRO, E.159/56 m. 1d). The letter, therefore, was probably written in the winter, sometime before Henry de Bray's appointment as escheator south of the Trent on 23 February 1283, though Bray accounted for the issues of the Marshal lands from 11 December (Stevenson, "The Escheator," 118, for Bray's appointment; E.372/133 m. 31, Bray's account). The sheriffs of Lincolnshire, Norfolk, Bedfordshire, and Staffordshire were all involved in the Marshal wardship and were all still acting as local escheators early in 1283 (*CIPM*, 2:471).

venting the stewards. He most likely issued the order to raise money for his campaign in Wales that summer.[128] Thomas de Normanville was made escheator north of the Trent, while the government appointed Henry de Bray as escheator south of the Trent in February 1283.[129] In 1285 Edward once again gave escheators discretion to sell minor wardships and marriages to the king's use, under the supervision of the Exchequer.[130] He attempted no other reform of the institutions, and the system of escheators was retained down through the reign of Edward II.

The disappointing results of the reforms of 1276–1283 exemplify some of the problems facing the Crown in the exercise of its seigniorial authority. The imperfections of the administration hampered enforcement. As a result, some magnates retained custody of lands that pertained to the king because of prerogative wardship, some widows failed to obtain license to remarry, and some individuals disregarded the prohibition against alienating lands without license. Part of the problem lay in the procedure of the "inquest system." Jurors were not always knowledgeable about the facts in the case or about the proper application of royal lordship.[131] The problem was also due, however, to the burden of work, as the steward complained. In spite of the remarkable institutional growth over the thirteenth century, it was hard for the Crown to keep track of all of its tenants and their activities, and royal lordship, as defined by Henry III and Edward I, affected a wider range of those activities than it had the century before. The government, for example, discovered many unlicensed alienations by tenants-in-chief only when the escheators took custody of the lands on the death of the tenant.[132] Under the administration created over the thirteenth century, the Crown demanded a great deal from a small corps of officials in each county.

Because the escheators and subescheators formed the essential links between the king and his tenants, the king supervised their

---

[128] *CPR, 1281–1292*, 30.

[129] Stevenson, "The Escheator," 118.

[130] PRO, E.159/59 m. 22d.

[131] *RH*, 2:230: "Dicunt quod Agnes filia Ade Kok est vidua et tenet x libratas terre in isto hundredo de domino Rege pro 6 d. reddenda domino Rege 6 d. per annum . . . set dicunt quod nesciunt utrum debeat maritari per dominum Regem pro tale servicio vel non." The difficulty of obtaining accurate information from local jurors and its impact on decisions about royal rights can be seen in *Rot. Parl.*, 1:17–18; and *CIPM*, 2:778. Jurors were also fined for "concealing" information (*Book of Fees*, 2:1383–1384).

[132] For example, *CPR, 1321–1324*, 325, 366; *CIPM*, 6:515.

activities closely and came down hard on any laxity or any infringe-
ment of his seigniorial rights. When Edward II, for example,
heard in 1315 that because of the slackness of his ministers the
manor of a tenant-in-chief had not been taken into custody, he
ordered the matter corrected immediately.[133] Conversely, the king
did not want ministers to act on their own authority, as the punishment of a subescheator and a royal justice in 1293 illustrates. Geoffrey de Howell held of Ralph Basset of Weldon by military service,
and when he died leaving a minor heir, his lands and heir came
into Basset's custody. Ralph in turn died leaving a minor heir, so
that the Howell wardship should have come to the king, since Basset held in chief of the king. Yet, according to the proceedings in
Parliament in 1293, the subescheator, William de Mere, contrary
to his assignment, allowed the Howell heir to enter his inheritance.
The justice, Reginald de Legh, then arranged a marriage for the
boy.[134] Both men were committed to the Tower, and Reginald had
to pay for the marriage. The harsh sentence drove home the point
that royal ministers were expected to act only in the king's interests. William had transgressed his official responsibilities because
escheators could not deliver an inheritance to an heir without an
explicit order from the king.[135] Reginald's error was worse. He had
taken it upon himself to make a judgment that deprived the king
of a wardship, whereas it was the responsibility of royal ministers,
especially judges, to *maintain* the king's rights.[136]

With the beginnings of a bureaucratic state in the thirteenth century, the honor and dignity of the Crown came to rest in part on
the performance of its ministers. A memorandum concerning the
duties of the escheator in the late thirteenth century emphasized
this dependence when it cautioned that he should "take nothing
through which the king shall lose something or anything else contrary to his right, for it is often seen that *through taking too little,
dishonor is greatly increased*" (emphasis added).[137] Laxity in the bureaucracy produced dishonor because it eroded the authority that
was expected of a lord or king as well as the specific rights on

[133] *CChW*, 428.

[134] *Rot. Parl.*, 1:91–92.

[135] *Statutes of the Realm*, 1:142–143.

[136] Ehrlich, *Proceedings against the Crown*, 64–65; Gerald L. Harriss, *King, Parliament and Public Finance in Medieval England to 1369* (Oxford, 1975), 161–162.

[137] BL, Add. ms 32,085, fol. 148r: "Estre ceo sey avise le Escetur que ryen de nuly
prenge par quey le Rey seit ryen perdant ne nul autre areryz de seon dreit kar
souent est aparceu que pur poy de prise sy encrest grant deshonur."

which that authority was built. It was the duty of the king's agents to uphold his honor and to assert his seigniorial rights as fully as possible. In England, therefore, the transformation from a feudal to a bureaucratic monarchy did not mean that its feudal authority atrophied. On the contrary, it was a powerful force behind institutionalization in the first place, and it accounted for a significant proportion of the administration's business in the thirteenth century. Nor did institutionalization lessen the king's discretion over wardships and marriages. Royal lordship remained the king's personal prerogative. He distinguished between those wardships of which he wanted personally to dispose and those he allowed his ministers to sell, but that was all that he gave up. Otherwise, royal lordship was exercised at his command and under his supervision. Indeed, the enforcement of feudal authority became more rigorous as tenants-in-chief were forced to conform to the practices of royal institutions. That conformity demonstrated the differences between mesne lordship and royal lordship and how much the power of the bureaucratic state owed to the king's dignity as a feudal lord.

·4·

THE USES OF ROYAL LORDSHIP

Law and administration preserved the king's feudal incidents and placed them at his disposal. He then used them in two ways: as revenue and as patronage. The latter proved to be more compelling, and financial considerations usually gave way to the desire to reward friends, support the royal family, or reciprocate service and loyalty. The king, in fact, turned virtually all of these assets over to others, keeping only a few in his own hands. Nevertheless, he tried to reap some financial benefit from his lordship. The government collected whatever profits it could while lands were in its custody, sold and leased wardships and marriages, and gave some to its creditors as payment for loans. The complete command that the king had over these resources allowed him to adjust their use according to his particular needs, to the needs of the recipients of his favor, or to changing external circumstances. Feudal lordship was thus a highly versatile instrument of rule. Grants were not standardized and individuals received wardships and marriages under a variety of terms. Finally, however he distributed his feudal incidents, the acts of taking custody of his tenants' heirs and lands and bestowing them as rewards to others served to reaffirm his honor and authority. They were concrete demonstrations of his power as a feudal lord. An analysis of the nature of the grants, the revenues produced by feudal lordships, and the way in which the king distributed this wealth brings to light the importance of royal lordship in the king's rule.

Before examining the grants themselves, however, it is important to get some idea of the scale of the resources that feudal lordship made available to the king. Depending as it did on the accidents of birth and death among tenants-in-chief, the incidence of wardship and marriage was unpredictable but regular. Between 1216 and 1327, the lands and heirs of more than 1,357 landholders fell into royal wardship, most of whom held *ut de corona*.[1] The

---

[1] The figure of 1,357 probably underestimates the actual number of wardships. It has been compiled primarily from grants recorded in the Chancery or Exchequer rolls and from escheators' accounts. Yet some grants were not formally enrolled—70 have been discovered through indirect references: proof of age, crown pleas, complaints of waste, debts for the purchase of a wardship, confirmations of re-grants, or miscellaneous writs (e.g., *CIPM*, 2:158, 651; PRO, Just.1/739 m. 57; *CFR*, 1:277–278, 437; *CPR, 1247–1258*, 496; *CPR, 1258–1266*, 252). In other cases,

value of these wardships varied considerably, since tenants-in-chief came from all parts of the social spectrum. The most valuable were those involving the baronies, which also give a clear picture of the frequency and impact of minorities. Of the original 192 baronial families in 1200, 105 (54.7 percent) fell into royal custody one or more times down to 1330, producing 192 wardships, of which 22 involved earldoms.[2] Expressed in terms of the 635 generational changes over the period as a whole, minorities occurred 30.2 percent of the time. Yet the burden of wardship was not shared equally by all of the 105 families: 49 fell into custody only once, 33 twice, 16 three times, 6 four times, and the unlucky Wake family, of the barony of Bourne in Cambridgeshire, came into royal wardship in each of its five generations between 1205 and 1330. In other words, 12 percent of all of the baronies accounted for 40.1 percent of the wardships by producing minor heirs in three or more generations. Judging by the baronial sample, the Crown might have expected its tenantry to produce a regular supply of wardships, but it could not have anticipated which lands or heirs would come into custody at any given time.

The exact value of the wardship depended on the survival of widows and the length of the minority. The right of wardship did not include dower lands. That meant that in most cases the Crown obtained custody of two-thirds of the estate, though sometimes less if more than one widow was still living. Dowers, coupled with other charges on the estate, could significantly reduce the value of the wardship.[3] The length of minorities varied, as can be seen in Table 4.1, where 534 male wards are grouped according to their age at the time of the inquisition post mortem.[4] The results are not surprising. The children were spread fairly evenly between the ages

though it is known that heirs were in royal custody, there is no record of what the king did with the wardship (*CFR*, 2:324; *CPR, 1313–1317*, 100; *CCR, 1313–1318*, 399 [Chancy]). Furthermore, because record keeping improved during the thirteenth century, there is more information concerning wardships for the later period. Finally, some sales by local officials were never enrolled (*CFR*, 1:77 [Erley]; *CPR, 1272–1281*, 310 [Bleyz]).

[2] For the baronial sample, see above, Chapter 1, n. 10. Minorities are compiled from *EB* and from royal sources, and those in *EB* have been included here only if confirmed by the record of a grant or other evidence of royal custody. Conversely, the total given here includes some minorities that Sanders did not mention. When the minorities of fragmented portions of baronies are included, there were a total of 269 baronial wardships.

[3] PRO, E.159/78 m. 34: Henry de Rihull's lands were valued at £13 6s. 8 1/4d., but rents, annuities, and dowers reduced it to 23s. 11 1/4d.

[4] An heir to a knight's fee came of age at the *end* of his twenty-first year (Bracton, 2:250; Walker, "Proof of Age," 306–323).

TABLE 4.1 DISTRIBUTION OF MALE WARDS BY AGE

Age	N	%
1 year or less	23	4.3
2–7 years	140	26.2
8–14 years	189	35.4
15–19 years	171	32.0
20 years or more	11	2.1
Total	534	100.0

of two and nineteen, with the bulk of them (65.9 percent) fourteen years old or younger. When wards were that young, the advantage to the Crown lay not only in the fact that the minority lasted longer, but that the heir was below the age of valid consent. The king got the right of marriage along with the lands if the child had not been betrothed. In fact, a substantial proportion of the boys were below the age of making a valid betrothal (seven years).[5] The Crown was thus supplied with a steady stream of wardships and marriages, many of them involving the wealthiest families in the kingdom. Expressed in averages, the king could expect about twelve wardships to occur each year, two of which would involve baronial families, and the wardships of male heirs would last roughly eleven years.

THE NATURE OF ROYAL GRANTS OF WARDSHIP

The Crown took the same care dispensing its feudal rights that it took enforcing and administering them. It did not simply dump them onto a market to be sold to the highest bidder. Since neither custom nor law bound the king to any particular form of grant, he adjusted the content and terms to accommodate the needs of policy, patronage, and influence around the court.

A hopeful suitor could secure a wardship or marriage in one of several ways. A number petitioned the king directly.[6] Some asked for specific lands or individuals, while others anticipated the deaths of tenants-in-chief and either requested wardships as soon as the tenant died or even before.[7] On a few occasions, the king

[5] See Helmholz, *Marriage Litigation*, 98–99, for age of consent. At least eighty-four female wards twelve years old or younger fell into custody during this period.
[6] *CCR, 1302–1307*, 486 (grant to Suthewell).
[7] For example, *Rot. Parl.*, 1:162, 310, 467; Maitland, *Memoranda de Parliamento*,

146

granted wardships before notifying the escheator of the death of
the tenant-in-chief, which may indicate that the recipient had already petitioned for the favor.[8] Finally, there was sometimes a
queue of individuals, to whom the king had promised future wardships, waiting for grants and pressuring the king to find resources
quickly.[9]

Instead of approaching the king directly, individuals asked influential courtiers or ministers to intercede with the king on their
behalf. They wrote to ministers such as Hubert de Burgh or Robert Burnell, or to royal favorites such as Piers Gaveston or the Despensers, seeking their help in obtaining wardships or marriages.[10]
The competition for royal wards was fierce, so that it was advisable
for supplicants to be well connected and as swift as possible. In a
reply to a retainer's plea for a particular wardship, Piers Gaveston
made it clear that speed was of the utmost importance. Edward II
had granted the wardship to Hugh le Despenser, Sr., three days
before the request arrived.[11] Chancery enrollments sometimes indicate that grants had been made at someone's request. Officials
such as the treasurer, chancellor, or controller of the wardrobe,
and courtiers like Gaveston, or, most often, the queen urged the
king to make particular gifts.[12]

The purpose and process of enlisting influence at court are revealed in two letters written in support of John de Beauchamp's

---

244, 250 (nos. 425, 437); *Ancient Petitions Relating to Northumberland*, ed. Constance
M. Fraser (London, 1966), 10–11 (no. 11); *CPR, 1232–1247*, 210.

[8] For two examples, see *CIPM*, 5:270, 278; and *CPR, 1307–1313*, 291, 326
(Braose and Russell). For the relationship between inquests and grants, see Stevenson, "The Escheator," 122–137.

[9] See, for example, the backlog of promises that Henry III created in 1266 and
his difficulties in fulfilling them (*CPR, 1258–1266*, 580, 591, 604, 666, 668; *CPR,
1266–1272*, 50, 51, 61, 100, 116, 167, 168, 171, 178, 182–183, 187, 202, 218, 250,
251).

[10] PRO, SC.1/1/198, 202, 211 (to Hubert de Burgh); 2/19 (to Jocelin de Wells,
bishop of Bath and Glastonbury); 22/100 (to Robert Burnell); 49/112 (to Hugh Despenser, Jr.).

[11] Maddicott, *Thomas of Lancaster*, 78–79, and appendix 1, 335. Despenser resold
custody of the lands to his own retainer, Ingram de Berenger, and the marriage to
Adam de Welle (*CPR, 1307–1313*, 94, 95; *CIPM*, 5:61; Greenfield, "Meriet of Meriet," 116–120). For a similar case, see Maitland, *Memoranda de Parliamento*, 244 (no.
425).

[12] A large number of grants, for example, were made at the queen's request
(*CPR, 1266–1272*, 242, 608; *CPR, 1281–1292*, 420; *CPR, 1301–1307*, 56, 245, 416,
496; *CPR, 1307–1313*, 379; *CPR, 1313–1317*, 119, 254). Others are listed in
Walker, "Royal Wardship," 132–133.

effort to secure the wardship of the Mohun lands in 1282. They provide a rare opportunity to penetrate the terse statements of royal records and see the kinds of negotiation that swirled around every major wardship. William, the younger son of Reginald de Mohun, died in 1282 leaving a five-year-old son, Reginald (see Figure 1.7).[13] Beauchamp wanted to farm the lands during the minority. To further his cause, he enlisted the assistance of William de Valence and Robert de Tibetot. Valence wrote to Robert Burnell, the royal chancellor, asking him to intercede with the king on Beauchamp's behalf.[14] His letter shows that Valence was sufficiently well informed to know when Mohun's inquisition post mortem had been held and returned to Chancery. He also recognized Burnell's pivotal position: the chancellor not only received the inquests, he also had influence with the king. It was thus worthwhile to try to win him over to the project. Tibetot, a knight active in royal service, took a different tack in his letter to Burnell.[15] Whereas Valence had urged the grant on the basis of Beauchamp's proven and promised service to the Crown, Tibetot argued that it would be more profitable for the king to farm the lands to Beauchamp than to keep them in his own hands.[16] The effort was in vain. In spite of these arguments and the impressive support that Beauchamp was able to marshal for his cause, Edward granted most of the Mohun estate to his queen, Eleanor, the marriage of the heir to the queen mother, Eleanor, and a manor and hundred to the steward of the household, Robert Fitz John.[17]

Beauchamp's disappointment underscores two important points: first, that the king retained ultimate authority over the disposal of his feudal rights; and second, that he often exercised that authority himself. Valence's letter demonstrates his appreciation of that fact and his concern to present as strong a case as possible to the king. He certainly realized that the grant of the wardship depended on Edward's authorization, and that even someone as influential as he could not automatically count on receiving what he asked for. Because the Chancery enrollments of grants only occasionally name the authority for a particular grant, the king's role in dispensing wardships is not readily visible. Nevertheless, it is ap-

[13] *CIPM*, 2:436, 530; *CFR*, 1:168; Moor, *Knights*, 3:163–164.

[14] PRO, SC.1/24/158.

[15] Tibetot had previously acquired the marriage of John de Mohun, William's half-blood cousin (*CPR, 1272–1281*, 318).

[16] PRO, SC.1/24/138.

[17] *CPR, 1281–1292*, 52; *CCR, 1279–1288*, 254.

parent from other sources that the king retained a lively interest in many of the wardships that came into his hands and that he personally directed their distribution.[18]

The king could dispense a single wardship in several different ways. When the lands of a tenant-in-chief came into royal custody, the king assumed the lordship of the estate, which gave him the power to confer churches and to take the wardships of tenants in knight service. He also reserved the right of wardship over lands held in dower.[19] Now, as Glanvill had noted, the king could grant either the full rights of wardship, including advowsons, fees, and dowers, or only a portion of it.[20] This ability to break up the wardship into its constituent elements enhanced its usefulness to the king. Out of the 1,357 wardships that fell in between 1217 and 1327, the Crown made more than 1,815 separate grants, while 269 baronial wardships were divided into 477 grants.[21] The king exercised his powers selectively and grants of wardship and marriage did not follow a simple form.

The surrender of all of the king's rights was a significant concession, which, in fact, kings did not often make. The king conferred this privilege in only 5 percent of all of the grants between 1216 and 1327 (Table 4.2).[22] The majority of such grants, moreover, occurred in the politically troubled years between 1260 and 1267, as Henry III and his opponents tried to rally support for their causes.

[18] On 18 October 1284, the treasurer sold the marriage of a ward "in presencia et ex assensu domini Regis" (E.159/91 m. 110d).

[19] Bracton, 2:252.

[20] Glanvill (vii.10), 84; cited by Lally, "Secular Patronage," 163.

[21] For the baronial wardships, see n. 2 above. Any transfer of a wardship from the king to someone else has been recorded as a grant. If a wardship was granted and then surrendered to the king and regranted, each grant has been counted. If a widow died while the heir was underage, any grant of the custody of dower lands has also been counted separately.

[22] The grants related to seventy-six wards. In two cases, two sisters and coheirs were granted separately as full wardships, and in three instances, a single ward was granted to different individuals on separate occasions under the terms of a full wardship (CPR, 1313–1317, 162, 617; CFR, 2:242, 247; CCR, 1313–1318, 166; Moor, Knights, 1:230–231 [Comyn]; CFR, 3:357, 358; Moor, Knights, 2:78 [Foliot]; CPR, 1258–1266, 349, 451 [Hemmgrave]; CPR, 1307–1313, 380, 393, 396, 408, 512; CCR, 1307–1313, 365–366, 372, 435, 534; CFR, 2:120–121; EB, 38–39 [Pointz]; CPR, 1324–1327, 95, 341; EB, 8, 63 [Hastings]). In six instances, the original grant was later enlarged to the full rights of wardship as a favor to the recipient (e.g., CPR, 1327–1330, 22, 326, 377, 546–547). The wording of grants was not consistent: one enrollment stated that a grant was with "dotibus cum acciderint et omnibus aliis ad custodiam illam spectantibus," while another mentioned only the dowers (PRO, E.372/141 m. 26; CPR, 1281–1292, 472 [Middleton]).

TABLE 4.2 TYPES OF GRANTS OF WARDSHIPS

Type of Grant	Baronial Sample	Others	Total	%
Full rights (land and marriage)	36	55	91	5.0
Full rights (land only)	18	10	28	1.5
Lands with marriage (limited rights)	128	763	891	49.1
Land only	197	322	519	28.6
Marriage only	66	159	225	12.4
Custody	32	29	61	3.4
Total	477	1,338	1,815	100.0

Henry, for example, granted full rights of wardship to his brother, Richard of Cornwall, to his two sons, Edward and Edmund, to his half-nephew, Guy de La Marche, to royal ministers such as John Mansell and Walter de Merton, and to political allies such as Hamo Lestrange. While he was briefly in power after the battle of Lewes, Simon de Montfort likewise gave full rights as rewards to his supporters: John Fitz John; John de Havering, Eleanor de Montfort's yeoman; and Thomas Fitz Thomas, the mayor of London. By the end of 1267, twenty-eight grants of this kind had been made, nearly a third of all of those granted out over the century as a whole.[23] At other times, kings made such grants to members of the royal family, trusted ministers, and royal favorites.

The minority of a tenant-in-chief offered the king a variety of ways in which to distribute patronage. He was most likely to give someone custody of the lands along with the right of marriage while reserving for himself the other benefits arising out of the wardship.[24] Grants of custody and marriage accounted for about half of all of the grants. In a significant number of cases, the king gave the lands to one person and the marriage to another. When Francis de Audeham, heir to the barony of Chiselborough in Somerset, came into the king's hands on the death of his father in

[23] *CPR, 1258–1266*, 72, 82, 97, 153, 156, 175, 200, 254, 277, 291, 304, 341, 349, 351, 353, 392, 435, 451, 527, 532, 574; *CPR, 1266–1272*, 8, 13, 63, 258, 467. For the alliance between Fitz Thomas and Montfort, see Gwyn A. Williams, *Medieval London: From Commune to Capital* (London, 1970), 221–227.

[24] *CPR, 1266–1272*, 82; *CPR, 1272–1281*, 100, 134; *CPR, 1292–1301*, 527; *CPR, 1307–1313*, 62, 85, 220; *CFR*, 3:35–37. The king sometimes granted the lands and marriage to one person but at different times (*CPR, 1307–1313*, 95, 99, 100).

1291, for example, Edward chose to grant the wardship of his lands to the royal knight Eustace de Hacche and the boy's marriage to Roger la Warre, a knight with interests in Somerset.[25] If an heir was married or betrothed when he or she came into custody, then the king gained only custody of the lands, which he could dispose of as he pleased.[26] The custody of lands might include the full rights of lordship, as Edward's grant to Hacche demonstrates; he received power over advowsons, knights' fees, and parks along with the lands. If the grant of a wardship did not include the right to dower lands, then as they fell in, the king could give them to others.[27] Finally, though he often obtained the custody of land without the right of marriage, he seldom obtained the marriage alone. That usually occurred when lands had been held in jointure and the widow survived.

The king could apportion custody of the lands of a particular estate among several recipients, spreading his patronage as widely as possible and using his resources to their maximum advantage. That is what Henry III chose to do with the wardship of the Hastings estate in 1250. He granted the marriage of the heir of Henry de Hastings to his half-brother Guy de Lusignan and rewarded a number of family members, ministers, and favorites with the wardship of the lands. The Hastings family, for example, held the hereditary stewardship of the Abbey of Bury St. Edmunds, and when it came into royal custody, Henry granted it in turn to Walter de Thurkelby, Thomas de Hemmgrave, and Guy de Lusignan.[28] Henry likewise granted custody of Hastings' lands and manors to Guy; to his other half-brother, Geoffrey de Lusignan; to his knight and minister, Guy de Rocheford; to his servant, Stephen Bauzan, in place of his fee of £20 a year; to John de Schipton, the prior of Newburgh; to another minister, William de St. Ermino in place of his fee; to Robert Walerand in place of his fee of 20 marks; and to Stephen Spineto, Imbert Guidonis, and John Frethorne in place of their fees from the Exchequer.[29] The lands given to Frethorne

[25] *CCR, 1288–1296*, 179 (lands); *CPR, 1281–1292*, 428 (marriage); *EB*, 34; Byerly and Byerly, *RWH*, passim, for Hacche; Moor, *Knights*, 5:158–159, for Warre.

[26] See, for example, *CIPM*, 3:326, 4:28; *CPR, 1292–1301*, 190 (Tany).

[27] *CPR, 1258–1266*, 291; *CPR, 1272–1281*, 105; *CCR, 1272–1279*, 319; *EB*, 11, 146; Cokayne, *Complete Peerage*, 9:375 (grant of the dower lands of Maud, Roger de Mowbray's widow, to her second husband, Roger Lestrange).

[28] *Close Rolls*, 6:64; *CPR, 1247–1258*, 72, 80, 200.

[29] *CPR, 1247–1258*, 77, 83, 86, 93, 99, 103, 126, 129, 134, 220; *Close Rolls*, 7:39; *ERF*, 2:110–111, 175.

came out of a dower, while the grants to Guy de Lusignan and Guy de Rocheford included the full rights of lordship. Henry gave John de Mery the full wardship over a manor, but demanded that Mery pay a rent of £10 a year to another royal yeoman, Maurice de Rocheford, brother of Guy.[30] Henry made the wardships even more attractive by permitting the custodians of those lands which were of ancient demesne to tallage the tenants.[31] The exceptional size of the Hastings estate allowed an unusually broad distribution of favors, but even in the case of smaller estates the Crown sometimes distributed the resources among several individuals. In nearly eighty cases (4.4 percent), the king divided up a single wardship among three or more people.

One resource over which the Crown often retained control during a minority was the right of presentation to churches. The Crown was particularly interested in advowsons and husbanded them carefully because they provided support for royal clerks. Escheators thus assessed advowsons and knights' fees separately when large estates fell into custody.[32] Subescheators quickly notified their superiors whenever churches fell vacant on lands in wardship, and with equal dispatch escheators wrote to the chancellor asking for instructions.[33] The opportunity to exercise these rights occurred irregularly. While the Cantilupe lands were in royal custody at the beginning of Edward I's reign, for instance, Edward made 6 appointments.[34] Between 1232 and 1327, the Crown made over 600 appointments through wardships, which represents approximately 20 percent of all presentations recorded in the patent rolls during that time.[35]

A wardship, moreover, could include the custody of other children in the family besides the heir presumptive. Bracton pointed

---

[30] *CPR, 1247–1258*, 91, 96.

[31] *Close Rolls*, 7:111, 133.

[32] BL, Add. MS. 32,085, fol.147v. E.g., PRO, C.134/35, nos. 15, 16, 17 (valuation and partition between the king and widow of Patrick de Chaworth's advowsons in England and Wales, worth 357 marks, 16s. 8d).

[33] PRO, SC.1/6/112. For a guardian who made a presentation illegally, see *CPR, 1266–1272*, 654–655.

[34] *CPR, 1272–1281*, 58, 61, 75, 160, 234, 417.

[35] Altogether, 3,093 presentations of one kind or another are recorded in the patent rolls, 1,129 because of vacancies (36.5 percent) and 1,352 (43.7 percent) for other reasons. The figures should be regarded as only broadly comparative because they included instances in which individuals surrendered livings and the king reappointed and because appointments were sometimes entered twice in the records. Moreover, the patent rolls do not cover all appointments.

out that a chief lord retained the right to the custody of the lands and the marriage of each heir to the lands, one after another, no matter how many times the heirs died within age.[36] Thus, the wardship could last until the youngest child came of age, if that child were the only surviving heir. Two related issues were involved. One was the right of marriage of children besides the heir and the other was the right to the custody of lands and heirs if the first heir died while still a minor. The enjoyment of these rights depended on the wording of the grant. Henry III's grant to Guy de Lusignan in 1251, for instance, was explicitly limited to the marriage of Henry, son and heir of Henry de Hastings. As a result, Guy did not have any right to the custody or marriage of Henry Junior's three sisters, Ada, Hillary, or Margery, two of whose marriages Henry III sold to William de Cantilupe in 1252, while Hubert Houel abducted Ada and married her without royal license.[37] In contrast, Edward I's grant of the marriage of Francis de Audeham to Roger la Warre in 1291 promised that if Francis died before he came of age, then Roger would have the marriage of Francis's sister Isabel.[38]

Down to the reign of Edward II, most grants were not so explicit, and it is not always clear what claims guardians had to other marriages or to the lands once an heir died.[39] It is clear, however, that the Crown did not automatically relinquish its authority over successive wardships. When an heir died while still a minor, the king usually directed the escheator to take custody of the new heirs and their lands. It was left up to guardians to petition the king if they thought that their grants entitled them to successive wardships. They sometimes lost their rights, though the king could ex-

---

[36] Bracton, 2:257.

[37] *Close Rolls*, 7:87, 215, 356, 441; *CPR, 1247–1258*, 191. William also purchased the right to Henry Junior's marriage from Guy and then married the boy to one of his daughters (*CChR*, 1:390; *EB*, 40; Cokayne, *Complete Peerage*, 6:345).

[38] *CPR, 1281–1292*, 428. Other examples can be seen in *ERF*, 1:35; *CPR, 1258–1266*, 201–202; and *CPR, 1281–1292*, 464.

[39] The *Rot. Dom.* shows guardians with custody of all of the children and arranging marriages for them (29). According to a rough count, grants of lands and *heirs* in *ERF*, as opposed to *heir*, made up nearly three-quarters of the total. Under such grants, the king sometimes delivered all of the children to the grantee (*ERF*, 1:407; *Close Rolls*, 5:51–52), or the grantee obtained custody of the new heir if the original heir died (*ERF*, 2:45, 198; *CPR, 1247–1258*, 33, 394; *ERF*, 1:187; *CPR, 1232–1247*, 301); unless, of course, the new heir was of age, (*CPR, 1266–1272*, 642; *CIPM*, 2:112; *CFR*, 1:53, 62 [Malore]). Chancery practice may not have been all that precise (*ERF*, 2:49, 61, for conflicting references to the same grant).

tend the wardship as a special favor.[40] Though the phrasing of grants thus determined whether wardships would fall to the Crown or the recipient, governmental practice under Henry III and Edward I was not consistent. Edward II's grants were more explicit.[41] In various ways they specified that some grantees would have the marriage of the heir and of successive heirs if the first died while in custody. The formulas were probably intended simply to clarify the rights of grantees, and if a grant did not contain a guarantee of future wardships, the recipient lost custody when the heir died.[42] As profligate as he was, even Edward II did not entirely loosen his grip on the feudal reins.

Early in the thirteenth century, the Crown also seems to have tried to limit the transfer of wardships. Royal licenses to give, assign, or bequeath wardships thus appear in the Chancery rolls of the 1240s and 1250s, or formed part of royal grants of wardships.[43] Unless specified otherwise, the right of wardship pertained only to the individual, or individuals, named in the grant. As a result, wardships did not always descend to heirs or assignees if the guardians died. They returned to royal control and could be granted once again. In fact, when that happened, the king often regranted the wardship to an assignee or relative.[44] On the other hand, to judge by the Articles of the Escheator, the Crown was not particularly concerned in the late thirteenth century about the alienation of wardships, and it is evident that executors sometimes retained possession of the deceased's wardships without explicit license.[45] Incidental information, often revealed at an inquest for the proof of age or in legal suits, shows that wardships had come into the hands of third parties without any official recognition of

[40] *ERF*, 2:126; *Close Rolls*, 9:348, 10:87–88 (Ingoldesthorp); *CPR, 1307–1313*, 291; *CIPM*, 5:270, 6:706; *CCR, 1323–1327*, 430; *CPR, 1324–1327*, 261–262; PRO, SC.1/49/112 (Braose); *CPR, 1292–1301*, 229; *CCR, 1288–1296*, 372–373.

[41] *CPR, 1307–1313*, 61, 62, 95, and passim.

[42] *CFR*, 2:286, 289, 292; *CPR, 1313–1317*, 515; *CPR, 1317–1321*, 262; *CIPM*, 5:603; *EB*, 27–28, 68 (Molis wardship).

[43] *Rot. Chart.*, 1:48; *ERF*, 1:234; *CPR, 1232–1247*, 275, 347, 460, 486; *CPR, 1247–1258*, 219; *CPR, 1258–1266*, 499–500; *CPR, 1266–1272*, 13; Sheehan, *The Will*, 286.

[44] To the recipient's brother: *CPR, 1272–1281*, 264; *CCR, 1302–1307*, 454. Assignee: *CCR, 1279–1288*, 451. Recipient's widow: *CPR, 1232–1247*, 481; *CPR, 1247–1258*, 102, 148; for the original grants: *CPR, 1232–1247*, 422, 431, 469; *Close Rolls*, 5:232, 379–380, 473.

[45] *CPR, 1272–1281*, 360; *CCR, 1279–1288*, 197; *ERF*, 1:460–461. For the transfer of wardships by testament, see Sheehan, *The Will*, 286–287.

the fact.[46] Those who obtained wardships from the original guardians may have secured confirmations in order to protect their claims.[47] Since disputes could erupt over the right to a wardship, it was prudent for all concerned to have clear evidence of their title.[48] In most cases, though, the transaction occurred out of sight of royal records. Any change in the number of confirmations is more likely due to a relaxation or change in administrative practice than to a change in the behavior of guardians. Furthermore, the king could take back a wardship and grant it to someone else.[49] While the Crown did not behave capriciously, it did use its discretionary authority to distribute wardships as it pleased. For the recipients, that meant that their titles to wardships could be precarious. Approximately 148 wardships were surrendered because of death, forfeiture, resumption, or an error in the grant. The king then granted out at least 100 of those to someone else and most of the rest were restored to the original recipient for one reason or another.

The king also dictated the terms on which guardians held their wardships. Those terms fell into five categories. In the first place, the Crown made some outright gifts without any fee or rent. In that case, the recipient collected the full profits from the lands during the minority and from the sale of the marriage of the heir, if he was entitled to it and if he chose to sell it. The Crown, second, sold wardships and marriages. A third category was comprised of grants of wardship in return for an annual rent, usually paid in the Exchequer, leaving guardians whatever profits they collected above the rent. Custody of lands granted to ministers or favorites to take the place of fees they received from the Exchequer can be placed in this category. In a few cases, the king made a fourth arrangement, levying a fine for the marriage and collecting a rent for the lands. Finally, the king occasionally appointed custodians who simply accounted for the issues and expenses of the lands at the Exchequer. The king or escheator usually assigned a custodian

[46] Walker, "Royal Wardship," 122.
[47] For a transfer of a wardship by grant and regrant, see *CPR, 1266–1272*, 13, 42.
[48] For example, PRO, E.159/78 m. 40.
[49] *CPR, 1272–1281*, 306, 314; *CPR, 1281–1292*, 51, 60; *CFR*, 1:109, 174, 175, 179; *CIPM*, 2:234 (Dive wardship); *CFR*, 1:255; *CCR, 1288–1296*, 373; *CIPM*, 2:685 (Wassingley); *CPR, 1313–1317*, 614, 673; *CFR*, 2:332; *CIPM*, 5:599 (Brianzon); *CCR, 1272–1279*, 396, 407, 440, 444, 464, 475, 559; *CIPM*, 2:265, 269, 323; *CPR, 1272–1281*, 310 (Wyger and Ripariis).

immediately after the death of a tenant-in-chief to care for the property before it was granted out.

Complications could of course arise in the process of making a grant, which delayed the benefits for either the Crown or the recipient. Once the king had granted a wardship or the grantee had offered a fine, the government ordered the appropriate official to deliver seisin of the lands or heirs to the recipient, though obtaining seisin was not always easy.[50] Conversely, like most Crown debtors, purchasers of wardships occasionally fell behind in their payments and had to be reminded of their obligations. The Crown usually set a schedule for the payment of the fine at the time of the grant. That does not mean that the grantee observed the schedule: Eudo de Shelfhanger's payments on a fine of 80 marks levied in 1251 trickled into different departments over the next fourteen years.[51] Some recipients, in contrast, never got hold of the wardships promised to them. After the grant it might turn out that the tenant did not hold in chief, or the heir died in custody or married without license.[52]

THE PROFITS OF LORDSHIP

The king could use his feudal resources either as direct or as indirect contributions to his finances. In the former, feudal revenues flowed into the household or treasury from three basic sources: payments to the Crown such as reliefs, fines, and amercements; leases or farms of lands held in wardship; and the direct management of such lands. The foundation of the escheatorships in the 1230s strengthened the Crown's ability to profit from lordship, though the full potential of the system was not realized until the end of the century when the costs of Edward I's military ambitions drove him to extract as much as he could from all possible sources. Furthermore, administrative shortcomings, policy considerations, and political constraints limited the amount that could be raised from feudal incidents. As a result, the king granted wardships, marriages, and widows' marriages to creditors and others as payment for debts or expenses. This constituted an equally important,

---

[50] PRO, SC.1/25/104 (order for seisin); /31/101 (refusal to pay installment of fine unless seisin delivered).

[51] *ERF*, 2:121; PRO, E.368/41 m. 2d; *Close Rolls*, 12:4, 13:273.

[52] *CCR, 1272–1279*, 545 (Ripariis); *CFR*, 1:395; *CCR, 1296–1302*, 146 (Mortimer); *CPR, 1301–1307*, 515, 520 (Clavering); *CFR*, 3:202, 217; *CPR, 1258–1266*, 448; *CPR, 1266–1272*, 568–569 (no explanation).

though less visible, contribution to royal finances. The Crown thus realized only a fraction of the potential value of wardships in cash, and cash receipts fluctuated greatly from reign to reign. Their contribution to royal finances, moreover, was always far below that of other resources.

That fluctuation is plainly evident in the feudal income recorded in the pipe rolls through the end of John's reign. Because Angevin policies excited a political reaction that limited in some ways what the Crown could henceforth derive from its lordship, it is worth looking at that income in some detail. It can be seen in Table 4.3 that the modest revenue that Henry II collected from fines for wardship and consent increased considerably under his financially hard-pressed sons, Richard and John.[53] Although it is clear that

TABLE 4.3 FINES FOR WARDSHIPS AND CONSENT TO MARRY,
HENRY II TO JOHN

Nature of Fine	Henry II	Richard I	John
Consent[a]	1,008.5	1,046.0	13,796.5
N	10	6	44
(avg. p/A)[b]	144	523	862
(avg. fine)	101	174	314
Wardship	3,876.5	11,579.5	49,082.5
(avg. p/A)[b]	176	1,158	3,068

John's Fines for Wardships			
Large fines	(500+)	Small fines	All fines
N	29	131	160
% of All Fines	18	82	100
Total Receipt	33,040	16,042	49,082.5
% of All Fines	67	33	100
Avg. Fine	1,139	122	307

NOTE: All fines are expressed in marks, and averages have been rounded to nearest whole mark.

[a] Excluding widows' marriages.

[b] Only those years in which fines were levied have been used to calculate the annual average.

[53] The figures in tables 4.3 and 4.4 are all taken from the pipe rolls except for those of 15 John, which are taken from *Rot. Ob. et Fin.* The analysis rests on two rather generous assumptions: first, that the Exchequer routines for collecting and recording feudal fines did not change over the period as a whole; and second that no significant variation occurred in the number of fines or amercements collected outside of the Exchequer, for example, in the chamber. Offers of palfreys or other

Henry I and his successors received fines for their consent to marriages contrary to Henry's promise on his coronation, the fines were neither heavy nor frequent until the reign of John, especially in comparison with the total number of marriages that must have been contracted between tenants-in-chief. The Crown did not simply tax marriage. The pipe rolls for the reign of Henry II, for example, record only ten fines for Henry's consent, or approval for a marriage contract. Henry, in fact, supervised marriages more closely than the pipe rolls indicate, though supervision did not necessarily mean levying fines.[54] John, however, charged dearly for his consent. Fines were not only more frequent but also larger than those offered in his father's reign. Indeed, a marriage contract drawn up around 1195 between Thomas de Verdun and Hugh de Lacy in Ireland, providing for a marriage between Hugh and Thomas's sister, concluded with the telling stipulation that Thomas had sworn to do all that he could, by giving money or in any other way, to obtain Lord John's consent to the marriage.[55] It signaled the changes that would take place in the exercise of royal lordship.

Offers for wardships followed an identical path: rising when Richard came to the throne, then shooting up in his brother's reign. The sharp escalation was due to an increase in the size as well as the number of fines charged. At times royal lordship became extortionate.[56] In a similar vein, Richard and John not only charged excessive rates for relief, they demanded it even after lands had been in royal custody during a minority.[57]

It is the revenue collected from widows, however, that shows how truly mercenary royal lordship could become in Richard and John's hands. Widows, of course, were in a more vulnerable position than supplicants for royal favors since they depended on their lord to secure their dower rights and inheritances. As seen in

---

horses were often included in the fines, and they have been calculated at 5 marks each, though this probably underestimates their true worth (see *Pipe Roll, 8 Richard I*, xxiv; *2 John*, xvi–xvii; *7 John*, xxv). See also Walker, "Feudal Constraint and Free Consent," 99–101, esp. n. 28, where the count of widows' fines is greater than mine because Walker has included old as well as new fines under 1 John.

[54] *Rot. Dom.*, xxiv, 38–39, 55, 77; Lally, "Secular Patronage," 165–167; *CRR*, 11:174–175 (no. 869); *Rot. Chart.*, 36. Fines were sometimes levied but not recorded on the pipe rolls, as, for example, in *Rot. Dom.*, xxiv, 26.

[55] *Calendar of the Gormanston Register*, ed. James Mills and M. J. McEnery (Dublin, 1916), 144, 192–193.

[56] For an example of Richard's charging twice for the same wardship (Setvans), see *Pipe Roll, 2 Richard I*, 110; *4 Richard I*, 171 (paid); *6 Richard I*, 36.

[57] Holt, *Magna Carta*, 107–109, 207–210; Warren, *King John*, 183.

Table 4.4, the Crown collected a steady but unremarkable number of amercements from widows for marrying without license down to 1198. The Crown likewise collected modest amounts from widows for the right to marry whomever they pleased, for the right not to be distrained to marry, or for the king's consent to a specific marriage proposal. By 1198, however, Richard's financial difficulties had mounted to the point that his justiciar launched an eyre in which he instructed the justices to scour the countryside for widows whom they could mulct. The 1,689 marks that the government managed to squeeze from them in a single year was unprecedented.[58] Yet John kept up the pressure on widows and

TABLE 4.4 FINES FOR WIDOWS' MARRIAGES, HENRY II TO JOHN

	Henry II (1165–1189)[a]	Richard I (1189–1198)	10 Richard I (1198–1199)	John (1199–1216)
Consent to Marry[b]	1,258	980	330	16,475
N	14	8	2	56
Right Not to Marry or to Marry Whomever the Widow Pleased[b]	838	2,431.5	1,359	25,015
N	5	18	40	93
Total	2,096	3,411.5	1,689	41,490
N	19	26	42	149
Avg. Fine	110	131	40	278
Amercements for Marrying without License	1,451	137[c]		442
N	13	9		9
Avg. Fine	112	15		49

NOTE: All fines are expressed in marks, and averages have been rounded to the nearest mark.

[a] This begins with the earliest fine recorded in the pipe rolls.

[b] Some fines included the right to the wardship of lands or heirs or permission to take up dower lands, doweries, or inheritances.

[c] These fines are from 1193–1195 and 1196–1197 (in *Pipe Rolls, 6, 7, 9, Richard I*) only. No other fines have been found for Richard's reign.

[58] Doris M. Stenton, introduction to *Pipe Roll, 10 Richard I*, xxviii; idem, introduction to *Pleas before the King or His Justices, 1198–1202* (London, 1952–1953), 1:34–35. A comparison of the returns (*Book of Fees*, 2:1323–1331) and the pipe roll shows how the inquest generated income; e.g., *Book of Fees*, 2:1324, and *Pipe Roll*,

substantially increased both the number and level of fines. And Table 4.4 does not even include the enormous fine of 20,000 marks that John charged Geoffrey de Mandeville for the marriage of Isabel, countess of Gloucester.[59]

Richard and John thus derived most of their feudal revenue from fines. For a period in the later years of their father's reign, the government had experimented with the direct management of lands held in wardship through special keepers who restocked and farmed the lands.[60] In a few instances, Richard made sure that the Crown profited once again when it restored the lands to the proper heirs. William d'Aubigny and Eustace de Vescy, for instance, had to pay fines of 2,000 and 1,200 marks respectively to recover their lands from Richard I.[61] Yet Richard largely abandoned Henry's managerial scheme. He and John preferred selling their rights to collecting direct receipts.

The impressive revenue that they extracted from feudal fines ultimately had a political cost, though it is important to tally it accurately. Magna Carta imposed specific limits on the king's seigniorial exactions in only two cases: reliefs and widows' lands. In addition, the baronial denunciation of "unjust" fines in the Articles of the Barons (cap. 37) and in Magna Carta (cap. 55) probably inhibited the Crown's collection of large fines for the king's consent to women's marriages.[62] In an age in which legal change was giving the free tenants of mesne lords a proprietary grip on their tenements, the Crown's fines in these areas had the effect of underscoring how precarious the tenure of tenants-in-chief was and how little things had changed for them.[63] Indeed, fifty-nine (39.6 percent) of John's fines on widows were simply for the right not to be compelled to marry. The exploitive supervision of marriage, in

---

10 *Richard I*, 94 (Countess Gundreda), 165 (Countess Margery). Eyres had been used before to raise feudal revenue (J. H. Round, introductions to *Pipe Roll, 22 Henry II*, xxii; and *23 Henry II*, xxii–xxiii).

[59] Holt, *Magna Carta*, 107, 123.

[60] J. H. Round, introductions to *Pipe Roll, 29 Henry II*, xxvii; *30 Henry II*, xxviii–xxix; *31 Henry II*, xxviii; *32 Henry II*, xxiii–xxv; *33 Henry II*, xxvii, xxxi–xxxii, xxxvii–xxxviii; and *Rot. Dom.*, xxvii, xxxii–xxxiii. In 1183–1184, this enterprise raised more than £1,647 (Round, introduction to *Pipe Roll, 32 Henry II*, xxviii–xxix). Not all of the lands were in wardship, e.g., the honor of Arundel (Cokayne, *Complete Peerage*, 1:235–236).

[61] *Pipe Roll, 2 Richard I*, 68, 129; *EB*, 2; *HKF*, 3:10–12.

[62] William S. McKechnie, *Magna Carta: A Commentary on the Great Charter of King John* (Glasgow, 1919), 454–456; Holt, *Magna Carta*, 256–258.

[63] Palmer, "Origins," 390.

particular, must have smacked of villeinage, which was often determined on the basis of merchet, a fine for marriage.[64] Magna Carta thus eliminated the king's power to force widows to marry, and as a result fines for not marrying gradually dwindled in the thirteenth century though they did not die out altogether. The Crown also persisted in selling its right of consent to widows' marriages, though at a far lower rate than before, while other fines for consent almost disappeared. In Henry III's reign, for example, forty-four fines levied for widows' consent to marry or for the right to marry whomever they pleased totaled only 3,809.5 marks, or an average of 87 marks per fine, a dramatic departure from John's practice. Such fines were more important individually as instruments of control or as a recognition of lordship than collectively as revenue. The Crown's recognition that it could not levy fines for tenurial obligations arbitrarily was an important concession to tenants-in-chief that brought their tenure more closely, though not completely, into line with that of other freemen. The Crown never conceded the obligations themselves; it threw the full weight of the administration against those who failed to pay reliefs or married without license. Henry III thus continued to seize the lands of widows or wards who married without his permission, largely, as was discussed in Chapter 2, in order to compel them to pay their fines. In twenty-two cases in which widows' amercements are known, they totaled 2,515.5 marks, or about 114 marks per fine. Through such measures, the Crown upheld its seigniorial honor and forcibly reminded tenants of their obligations, though it no longer sought to profit unduly from its authority. As a consequence, the proceeds of seigniorial enforcement trickled into the Exchequer in a volume greatly reduced from that of Richard and John.

In contrast to these involuntary payments, Magna Carta did not specifically mention what the Dialog of the Exchequer called "voluntary offerings *in rem*"—that is, fines for wardships and marriages.[65] The barons probably found these fines less objectionable for several reasons. As the Dialog makes clear, the process of making an offer for a specific benefit was an acknowledged aspect of relations between Crown and tenant or subject, and it expressed a sense of the Crown's dignity and superiority. More concretely, the

[64] Searle, "Seigneurial Control." For thirteenth-century fines, see above, Chapter 2, n. 98.
[65] Fitz Nigel, *Dialogus*, 119.

fine compensated the Crown for the revenue it lost in giving up a wardship. An individual, moreover, freely entered into a contract with the king ("conventione cum principe"). The king might set the price, but the recipient could choose whether to accept it, unlike a relief or marriage fine.[66] Finally, as a practical matter, it would have been difficult to set rates for voluntary offerings since they were subject to many variables.

Magna Carta, therefore, did not dictate the level of fines, though it is possible that chapter 55 may have influenced the levying of large fines of 500 marks or more. Fines and the decision whether to demand them were determined by the specific circumstances surrounding each wardship. Every supplicant had to make the best bargain that he or she could, and subjects did not mind paying reasonable fines for benefits the king made available. As Table 4.5 makes clear, there were several periods after Magna Carta (1222–1226, 1242–1246, 1257–1261, 1282–1286, 1307–1311, 1317–1321) when either the average annual income or the average fine exceeded those of John's reign. In fact, in the five years after 1241, the barons suggested that Henry III was not collecting enough by way of such sales.[67]

Yet it is noticeable that the general level of fines receded from that set by John, that fines fluctuated greatly from year to year, and that the Crown levied large fines only half as often as John had (compare Tables 4.3 and 4.5).[68] What this seems to mean is that in the absence of explicit prescriptions concerning fines, the Crown changed its policy. Income was only one, and not the most important, consideration in exercising royal lordship in the thirteenth and early fourteenth centuries. The fact that the average fine (both with and without large fines) declined slightly meant that receipts from the sale of wardships remained relatively stagnant in periods of rising prices and land values. After a century, the Crown was charging roughly the same or even lower rates for lands that had significantly appreciated in value. Such income was further restricted by the fact that the Crown levied fines on only about one-third of all of the grants it made.[69]

[66] Cf. Holt, *Northerners*, 178.

[67] Paris, *Chronica Majora*, 4:181–186, 372–374.

[68] There were some exceptionally large fines (*Patent Rolls*, 2:87; *ERF*, 1:151, 271, 461, 2:96; *CFR*, 1:185, 2:121, 401–402, 3:202, 367). See also Chapter 5, n. 11, below.

[69] The government charged fines in 566 grants, 31 percent. The actual total is higher because in some cases the enrollment does not specify the amount of the

TABLE 4.5 FINES FOR WARDSHIPS, 1217–1326

Total Fines		N	Avg. p/A	Large Fines[a]	N	Avg. Fine[b]
1217–1221	1,476.0	19	295.2	500	1	77.7
1222–1226	13,325.0	24	2,665.0	11,000	2	555.2
1227–1231	2,605.0	23	521.0	1,000	2	113.3
1232–1236	11,215.0	47	2,243.0	6,900	7	238.6
1237–1241	4,729.5	23	945.9	2,500	2	205.6
1242–1246	18,297.5	37	3,659.5	16,200	8	494.5
1247–1251	10,492.5	51	2,098.5	4,500	3	205.7
1252–1256	1,889.0	22	377.8	0	0	85.9
1257–1261	7,432.5	20	1,486.5	5,200	3	371.6
1262–1266	2,045.0	13	409.0	700	1	157.3
1267–1271	1,307.0	10	261.4	500	1	130.7
1272–1276	3,485.0	35	697.0	1,550	2	99.6
1277–1281	1,739.0	16	347.8	0	0	108.7
1282–1286	11,484.0	14	2,296.8	10,500	3	820.3
1287–1291	2,887.0	12	577.4	2,000	1	240.6
1292–1296	628.0	12	125.6	0	0	52.3
1297–1301	5,990.5	40	1,198.1	2,400	3	149.8
1302–1306	5,568.0	33	1,113.6	3,645	4	168.7
1307–1311	8,662.5	16	1,732.5	7,200	3	541.4
1312–1316	9,922.5	40	1,984.5	5,425	4	248.1
1317–1321	8,983.5	22	1,796.7	7,100	4	408.3
1322–1327	7,507.0	35	1,501.4	4,850	4	214.5
Total	141,671.0	564	1,287.9	93,670	58	251.2

NOTE: All fines are expressed in marks.
[a] Large Fines = 500 marks and more.
[b] The average fine less large fines = 94.9 marks.

The most significant change in practice occurred between 1267 and 1297 (Table 4.6). In the early years of his reign, when his treasury was relatively solvent, Edward I levied few large fines and demanded much less than his father and son for grants of important wardships and marriages. Indeed, a fine of 7,000 marks charged to Edmund of Cornwall in 1282 represents nearly one-third of the total amount levied in these years.[70] In contrast, Ed-

---

fine. Fines were recorded in the fine rolls, originalia rolls, and memoranda rolls. Additional fines may have been recorded in the pipe rolls, but a random check of some rolls for the thirteenth century did not uncover any fines not recorded in the other sources.

[70] *CPR, 1281–92*, 35, 163. See Scott L. Waugh, "The Fiscal Uses of Royal Wardships in the Reign of Edward I," in Coss and Lloyd, *Thirteenth Century England I* (Woodbridge, 1986), 53–60.

TABLE 4.6 COMPARISON OF FINES FOR WARDSHIPS,
HENRY III TO EDWARD II

	1222–1266	1267–1296	1297–1326
Total Fines	72,031	21,530	46,634
N	260	99	186
Avg. Total p/A	1,601	718	1,555
Avg. N p/A	6	3	6
Avg. Fine	277	218	251
Total of Large			
Fines	48,000	14,550	30,620
N	28	7	22
Avg. Total p/A	1,067	485	1,021
Avg. Fine	1,714	2,079	1,392
Avg. Fine less			
Large Fines	104	76	98

NOTE: All fines are expressed in marks and have been taken from Table 4.5.
Averages have been rounded to nearest whole mark.

ward treated minor wardships, those worth less than £20, as purely economic resources to be sold for income. The sudden jump in the number of fines levied between 1272 and 1276 can thus be attributed to the fact that in 1272–1274 escheators sold most of the minor wardships then on hand. Neither the number of wards in royal custody, nor the volume of grants changed during Edward's reign, so that the lowering of fines on major wardships must reflect a deliberate change in policy, in which Edward bestowed wardships on favorites without stringent financial conditions. An exception to this policy occurred in 1282–1283 when Edward, probably impelled by the need to raise money for his Welsh campaign, ordered his clerk, John de Kirkby, to sell *all* wardships and marriages in the king's hands. In 1283 fines rose to 4,338 marks compared to none in 1282 and only 20 marks in 1284.[71] Beginning in 1296, when war became more continuous and financial pressures were particularly severe, Edward resumed sales of major as well as minor wardships. During the last years of his reign, the Exchequer also seems to have been more assiduous in demanding the payment of reliefs.[72]

[71] *CPR, 1281–1292*, 30, 6 July 1282. The delay in receipts may be due to accounting. Edward sold one wardship for 2,500 marks (*CFR*, 1:185 [Marshal]). For the Welsh war, see John E. Morris, *The Welsh Wars of Edward I* (1901, reprint, Oxford, 1968), 149–197.

[72] PRO, E.159/71 mm. 25, 37d, 39d; /73 mm. 25, 30.

Leases were less common than sales or outright grants, levied only 10 percent of the time. Nearly half fell in the years after 1310. Under Henry III, the government collected a handful of rents, while Edward I's administration required more than fifty recipients to pay rent. Edward II seems to have relaxed the practice in the first few years of his reign, but was then forced by the Ordainers to put his feudal incidents to fiscal use. The third clause of the Ordinances of 1311 declared that profits from escheats, wardships, and marriages should be used to pay the king's debts.[73] Even then, Edward did not really put the plan into effect before 1315 when Thomas of Lancaster gained control of the government, determined to enforce the Ordinances.[74] Thereafter, the government levied rents more frequently than it had in the past, applying them to more than a third of the grants made between 1315 and 1326 (75 of 208). Thus, even though political pressure to observe the Ordinances had abated after 1318, Edward continued to charge rents for wardships until the end of his reign, out of his desire to hoard as much wealth as possible. The farms he levied after 1321 amounted to more than £1,575 a year.[75] The actual receipts at any given time, however, were lower than the nominal value because the king reduced rents for patronage, for deductions of debts or expenses, or for dowers or payments for the sustenance of heirs.[76]

Finally, the king profited from the issues of lands while they were in his custody and until he either restored them to the proper heir, if he or she was of age, or granted them out (see Appendix). He probably could have earned the greatest profits by selling the marriages to the highest bidder and retaining the direct management of the lands until the heir came of age, in much the same

[73] *Statutes of the Realm*, 1:158.

[74] For Lancaster's policy in 1314–1316, see Maddicott, *Thomas of Lancaster*, 160–189. Between 1307 and 1315, only nine grants of wardship involved rents. For an example of Lancaster's influence in 1315, see *CPR, 1313–1317*, 162, 617; *CFR*, 2:242, 247; *CCR, 1313–1318*, 166; *CIPM*, 5:499; Moor, *Knights*, 1:230–231 (Comyn wardship).

[75] *CFR*, 3:95–96, 131, 177, 183, 187, 188–189, 190–191, 195, 214, 217, 243, 275, 277, 279 (2), 282, 310, 334, 336, 350, 354, 356, 358, 365 (2), 378, 386, 387 (2), 405, 416; *Calendar of Memoranda Rolls (Exchequer), Michaelmas 1326–Michaelmas 1327* (London, 1968), 20, 22, 23 (nos. 98, 109, 122). For Edward's efforts to exploit all sources of income, especially traditional ones, see N. Fryde, *Tyranny*, 87–105; and Mark Buck, *Politics, Finance and the Church in the Reign of Edward II* (Cambridge, 1983), 163–196.

[76] PRO, E.159/84 mm. 34, 65; /87 m. 78; /90 mm. 27, 50, 61d.

way that he handled the lands of religious houses during vacancies.[77] Such a policy, however, would have been unrealistic in the face of demands from ministers and landholding families for royal wardships. The king sold, farmed, or granted the vast majority of the lands and heirs that came into his custody. The administration, therefore, had to concentrate on collecting short-term profits. Escheators always controlled a pool of lands—composed of a few wardships, lands under primer seisin, lands seized because alienated without license or because widows married without permission, lands forfeited by felons, lands belonging to idiots, and so forth—whose dimensions and value constantly fluctuated as it was diminished and replenished by grants, deaths, and forfeitures and from which the government derived some profit.

Escheators collected income from several sources. They took custody of all of the agricultural equipment and stock and either used it to cultivate the lands or sold it to the guardian for the same purpose, but they do not appear to have alienated oxen, plows, and other stock essential to agriculture. They did sell whatever grain they found in the grange or growing in the fields as well as any wood or underbrush that could be sold without waste.[78] The king was also entitled to the products of any animals taken into custody such as dairy goods, wool, and lambs.[79] Escheators tallaged unfree tenants as soon as the lands were seized, and these "recognitions" (*recognitiones*) of the change in lordship constituted a significant portion of the income when lands were in custody only a short time.[80] If lands were in custody for an extended period, then the escheator received the usual profits from rents, services, and agriculture. If an estate as a whole was retained in custody, then

[77] According to the 1225 version of Magna Carta, the king could not sell the custody of ecclesiastical lands during a vacancy (Holt, *Magna Carta*, 272, 351–352). In 1241, perhaps as part of his financial reforms, Henry ordered that the revenues from several estates then in custody, as well as from vacant bishoprics, be paid into the Tower (*Close Rolls*, 4:277; Carpenter, "Decline of the Curial Sheriff," 21–22, for the reforms).

[78] BL, Add. MS. 32,085, fol. 146v. Most escheators' accounts included a grain account; e.g., PRO, E.372/82 m. 4d; (22 Henry III); or E.372/133 m. 31d (11–13 Edward I); or E.136/3/8. The sale of goods on the Wake and Clifford lands netted £689 9s. 2d. in one year (E.372/128 m. 34d). Valuation of wardships included the grain on hand (*CIM*, 1:93, 1091). Agricultural stock and produce sometimes formed part of the grant (*CCR, 1288–1296*, 338). See also Walker, "Royal Wardship," 120–122.

[79] BL, Add. MS. 32,085, fol. 148v.

[80] Ibid., fol. 146; PRO, E.136/1/2; E.372/149 mm. 30d–31d; and other escheators' accounts; *RH*, 1:200–235, passim.

the government kept the estate management intact and allowed estate officials to manage the lands as they had under the tenant-in-chief. The escheator appointed manorial officials and was responsible for their conduct. He likewise appointed bailiffs to oversee the work of manorial officials and to collect the receipts.[81] Some lands were farmed out. In general, the administration hoped to keep expenses of management as low as possible.[82]

Edward I increased the proceeds from this pool by increasing the interval during which the lands were in his custody and by retaining custody of portions of estates or small tenements. The Crown had always kept a few wardships under direct control.[83] On average, though, Henry kept wardships in custody only eight months. Edward doubled that time to sixteen months and kept a significant portion longer than a year (Table 4.7).[84] The change in practice is evident in the escheators' accounts, which show that of the wardships that fell in each year, the escheators retained several

TABLE 4.7 LENGTH OF TIME THAT WARDSHIPS WERE HELD
IN ROYAL CUSTODY

	0	Less than 1 Month	1–6 Months	7–12 Months	More than 1 Year
Henry III	4	14	55	24	14
(N = 111)	3.6%	12.6%	49.5%	21.6%	12.6%
Edward I	14	21	87	31	79
(N = 232)	6%	9%	37.5%	13.4%	34.1%
Edward II	17	13	87	18	20
(N = 155)	11%	8.4%	56.1%	11.6%	12.9%

[81] BL, Add. ms. 32,085, fol. 146r–v. For examples of tenants paying fines not to become reeves, see *RH*, 1:203, 205.

[82] Between 28 February 1283 and 29 September 1285, Henry de Bray hired thirty-nine men at 2*d.* a day to oversee various lands, fifteen men at 1 1/2*d.* a day, and one horseman with his horse and page at 3 1/2*d.* a day (PRO, E.372/133 m. 31d). Their wages and other management costs totaled £272 17*s.* 1 1/4*d.*, or about 18 percent of the revenues collected over that time.

[83] *ERF*, 1:317 318; Eyton, *Antiquities*, 3:164–166.

[84] The length of custody has been calculated by comparing the dates of the writ *diem clausit extremum*, in the inquisition post mortem or the fine rolls, and the grant of the wardship. I have used only those cases in which a full date for both exists, and because of gaps in the inquisitions, the sample for the reign of Henry III is much smaller than for Edward I. The first column (0) refers to grants made before the writ *diem clausit* was issued. Grants made within a month of the demise of the tenant-in-chief have been uniformly counted as half a month.

in custody for a number of years.[85] The majority of these were small holdings belonging to minor tenants-in-chief. In January 1298 the escheators had in hand the lands of at least forty tenants-in-chief, valued at £273 2s. 4d. a year. Most were worth on average only £5 9s., and some had been in custody for five years or more.[86] Yet the escheators also held onto portions of larger estates.[87] And the escheators north of the Trent seem to have kept custody of lands even longer than their counterparts in the south, especially toward the end of Edward's reign when he badly needed such revenues.[88] In several cases from the north, Edward did not bother to grant the wardship at all, preferring instead to collect the profits from the lands.[89] Part of the reason that the escheator in the north retained custody of such lands may have been that he was unable to find buyers for minor wardships, since some lay perilously near the border with Scotland and were sometimes destroyed by the Scots.[90] Whatever the reasons behind the policy, however, it was short-lived. In Edward II's reign the average interval between the writ *diem clausit* and the grant dropped to ten months. Direct receipts from feudal lordship thus reached a peak at the end of the thirteenth century, when Edward I's urgent need for cash impelled his ministers to squeeze profits from every resource (see Appendix).

What Edward did was to place the emphasis in his management of feudal resources on direct receipts. Table 4.8 provides a rough estimate of the average annual receipt from fines, farms, and escheators for three periods. What is striking is that the potential receipt from all feudal sources was particularly high under both

[85] The change may have been ordered before Edward returned from the Crusade. An escheator noted that he had been instructed to retain in custody lands worth £100 out of the estate of George de Cantilupe who died in 1272 (*CIPM*, 2:17; PRO, E.372/124 m. 19d).

[86] PRO, E.101/506/8. This is an account by the executors of Edmund of Cornwall of the wardships transferred to his custody on 3 January 1298 (*CPR, 1292–1301*, 326). The Doynel lands had been in custody since 1293 (*CIPM*, 3:97).

[87] PRO, E.372/133 mm. 31–31d; /141 mm. 23–24d. Between 1285 and 1289, the escheator south of the Trent retained the lands of thirty-nine tenants in custody for a year or more.

[88] PRO, E.136/3/8; E.372/136 m. 25; /141 mm. 26–26d; /147 mm. 32–32d; /150 mm. 32–32d, 41–43d; /153 mm. 33–35. Some lands were still in custody in 6 Edward II, though the escheator was by then ignorant of the cause ("qua causa ignoratur") (E.372/160 mm. 48, 50, 50d).

[89] For example, *CIPM*, 2:597; PRO, E.136/3/3, 4, 5 (Sutheyk).

[90] PRO, E.372/147 m. 32d, escheator unable to account for any issues because lands had been burned by Scots.

TABLE 4.8 COMPARISON OF FEUDAL RECEIPTS, EDWARD I AND EDWARD II

	1282–1296	1297–1307	1312–1322
Total Fines	7,999[a]	11,558.5	26,413
Fines p/A[b]	533	1,156	1,761
Farms p/A[c]	177	43	323
Receipts p/A[d]	1,134	3,246	1,326
Total p/A	1,844	4,445	3,410

NOTE: All figures are expressed in marks, and averages have been rounded to nearest whole mark.

[a] This figure does not include Edmund of Cornwall's fine of 7,000 marks for the Wake wardship.

[b] From Table 4.5.

[c] This is an average of the total farms levied over the period.

[d] From Appendix.

Edward I and Edward II, yet the composition of the income differed greatly. Edward I probably preferred direct receipts because he needed the money to pay for his wars and because it was more certain to be collected, while the emphasis on fines and farms after 1312 was probably the result of the enforcement of the Ordinances. Edward II's reorganization of the escheatorships into eight bailiwicks after 1322 restored the emphasis on direct receipts, and in the three full years from 1324 to 1326, escheators' revenues averaged £2,131 a year, only slightly below that attained by Edward I.

Even in the best of times, however, the cash contribution from feudal sources made up only a fraction of the king's revenues. They were certainly greater than the Exchequer estimated in 1284.[91] It put feudal receipts at £533: £333 from wardships if they were retained in the king's hands plus another £200 from primer seisin. Around this date, escheators' receipts averaged about £650 a year (see Appendix, 11–13 Edward I). After that, feudal revenues increased appreciably. Yet at the end of the century, when Edward was doing well to squeeze about £3,333 a year from fines, farms, and escheators, the total annual wardrobe receipts alone averaged about £59,000. Nor could feudal sources compete with taxation, which produced an average £39,359 each time it was levied in Edward's later years, though at that point Edward welcomed any contribution.[92]

[91] Mills, "Exchequer Agenda," 233.

[92] The averages for Edward's receipts and taxes have been computed from the

These figures emphasize the fact that neither the king nor the baronage regarded feudal incidents solely as fiscal assets. For the king, the exercise of lordship was a complex function of power, favor, and economics. Conceivably, he could have gotten more out of his lordship. Yet, the need to reward friends and honor service, the constraints of custom and politics, and the shortcomings of the administration meant that feudal resources would be put to a variety of uses rather than subordinated entirely to finance. The king, for example, never adopted the direct management of the Crown lands to increase his revenues, even when financial inducements were particularly strong at the end of the twelfth century.[93] Periodically, in the reigns of Henry II, Edward I, and Edward III, the administration ventured to manage its wardships and escheats as an economic enterprise. Each time the venture was abandoned. Because feudal lands came into and went out of custody in so many different ways and at such different times, management and accounting were difficult and expensive.[94] It was usually easier to sell or to farm or to give the lands away. Richard gave up his father's management of wardships in favor of quick sales. Overwork and administrative confusion were two reasons that Edward I's experiment with the stewards floundered in 1282. And Edward III's attempt to subsidize wardrobe expenses through wardships seems to have come unraveled partly because of the complexity of the task and partly because Edward could not resist granting favorable leases as patronage.[95] In general, therefore, the Crown lacked the will and the means to carry out a purely financial exploitation of its feudal resources. Financial considerations were offset by several factors.

Above all, there was patronage. Even under Richard and John, the government never regarded fines strictly as sales. William Bard offered Richard 200 marks to marry the daughter of Amaury Despenser, a household official. Despite this offer, Richard chose to give the girl to another member of his household, charging him

---

figures given in Michael Prestwich, "Exchequer and Wardrobe in the Later Years of Edward I," *BIHR* 46 (1973): 1–10; and idem, *War, Politics and Finance under Edward I* (London, 1972), 179.

[93] Harvey, "The English Inflation," 9–15. See also Bertram P. Wolffe, *The Royal Demesne in English History: The Crown Estate in the Governance of the Realm from the Conquest to 1509* (London, 1971).

[94] Wolffe, *The Royal Demesne*, 37. See also Harriss, *King, Parliament and Public Finance*, 166–167, for the conflict between finance and patronage.

[95] Tout, *Chapters*, 4:122–127.

only 100 marks.[96] Fines also were useful devices for controlling loyalty, because the Crown could decide whether to demand payment depending on the individual's behavior.[97] Conversely, the king often pardoned fines as a sign of favor. Henry III and his successors pardoned more than 3,800 marks out of 19 fines totaling more than 6,627 marks.[98] The king could likewise respite the payment of fines and sometimes respited the collection of the deceased's debts to the Crown so that guardians would not suffer from the confiscation of goods on the estate. The government, therefore, collected less than the amounts recorded in Table 4.5, which are only *offers* of fines for wardships and marriages, not receipts. It faced the additional problem, as it did with most debtors, of getting those who offered fines to pay. Even the collection of the revenues due from its own ministers could be a problem.[99]

Another impediment to any effort to maximize the income from royal lordship was the lack of an accurate assessment of its resources. From at least the time of the *Rotuli de Dominabus*, feudal incidents were evaluated by local juries, a process that was routinized in the early thirteenth century with the creation of the inquisitions post mortem, taken on the death of each tenant-in-chief. That assessment became the essential figure used to levy fines or farms of wardships and marriages, to audit the escheators' accounts, to assign dowers, and to partition inheritances. The inquisitions post mortem probably had their origins in the articles of the eyre. From the eyre of 1198 onward, justices inquired into wards and widows in the king's gift and into the value of their lands. The hundred juries also indicated the tenurial reason for the king's right over an individual. Those three elements—the ward, tenure, and value of the lands—formed the core of the inquisitions post mortem. They did not, however, settle into a formal form for several years and were also influenced by seigniorial extents.[100]

---

[96] *Pipe Roll, 1 John*, 7, 12; *8 Richard I*, 39; *10 Richard I*, 107. Peter married the girl (*Rot. Chart.*, 1:148). For Stokes, see Jolliffe, *Angevin Kingship*, 156, 213, 217.

[97] Holt, *Northerners*, 175–193.

[98] PRO, E.368/30 m. 10d, /43 m. 11; *CPR, 1258–1266*, 38, 351; *CPR, 1266–1272*, 497; *CPR, 1272–1281*, 99–100; *CPR, 1301–1307*, 233, 243; *CPR, 1307–1313*, 397, 520; *CPR, 1327–1330*, 244; *Close Rolls*, 3:458, 4:232, 367–368, 12:321, 326; *CCR, 1296–1302*, 473; *ERF*, 1:3, 405; Moor, *Knights*, 1:177. In three cases, neither the amount of the fine nor the amount pardoned is known.

[99] For an example, see Eyton, *Antiquities*, 3:164–166.

[100] Doris Mary Stenton, introduction to *Pipe Roll, 10 Richard I*, xxviii; *Book of Fees*, 2:1323–1336; Stevenson, "The Escheator," 114–115; H. C. Maxwell Lyte, introduc-

One problem with these inquests was that they were taken piece-meal and were based only on local knowledge. Jurors had diffi-culty estimating the overall value of estates, which could be a seri-ous limitation when the government tried to levy fines for marriages. The value of a marriage was related to the value of the lands pertaining to the ward, but inquests often gave conflicting figures. When asked, for example, the value of the marriage of Amice, widow of Anker de Freschville, jurors in Nottinghamshire declared that her dower there was worth £8 17s. 4d., but that they could not say what her marriage was worth because the major part of the tenement lay in Derby, while jurors in Derbyshire supplied two different figures.[101]

A further problem was undervaluation. The difference between the assessed and real values of lands could be quite significant, which meant that the government would not realize the full value of its assets through sales or farms.[102] Officials, of course, could err in the opposite direction as well, but they seem to have under-estimated the value of lands more often than they overestimated it.[103] The wardship of the lands and heirs of Ralph de Luddington, for example, fell into dispute between Edward I and the earl of Warwick and so was sold by each on different occasions for differ-ent amounts. The escheator first sold it to the husband of one of the four coheirs for 20 marks. After the earl recovered the ward-ship, he sold it to the widow for 60 marks.[104] Wardships resold by guardians, moreover, often fetched more than the fine originally charged by the Crown. Prices could rise spectacularly, as will be seen in the next chapter. To ensure that it received a fair price, the Crown sometimes stipulated that a guardian had to pay as much as anyone else would offer, but valuations, fines, and farms were

---

tion to *CIPM*, 1:vii–ix; Dorothea Oschinsky, introduction to *Walter of Henley and Other Treatises on Estate Management and Accounting* (Oxford, 1971), 67–72.

[101] PRO, C.132/36 no. 20; *CIPM*, 1:707. This inquest makes it clear that jurors assessed a marriage on a notional market value, that is, the rate at which they thought it could be sold. The problem can also be seen by comparing the valuations of Richard I's eyres with the fines in the pipe rolls; jurors valued the lands of Countess Gundreda at £20 but she paid £100 for the right not to marry (*Book of Fees*, 2:1324; *Pipe Roll, 10 Richard I*, 94). For other examples, see *CIPM*, 3:34, 181, 397, 398.

[102] Stevenson, "The Escheator," 137; Wolffe, *The Royal Demesne*, 61; Hilton, *A Me-dieval Society*, 42. Underassessment was likewise a problem with inquisitions *ad quod damnum*. See Raban, *Mortmain Legislation*, 64–66.

[103] *CFR*, 2:211, 212; *CIPM*, 5:520.

[104] *CIPM*, 2:26, 77; *CCR, 1272–1279*, 102; *RH*, 1:172.

always subject to negotiation or bargaining.[105] The government usually calculated sale prices, rents, and the receipts due from escheators on the value contained in the inquisition post mortem, a practice that was clearly understood by those asking or bargaining for wards.[106] Because of the tendency of these inquests to undervalue lands, farms and grants were really beneficial leases, another form of patronage.[107]

Prodded by his political opponents to make better use of his lordship, Edward II tried to overcome these difficulties by routinely charging guardians an increment above the assessed value for their rents.[108] The increments were neither uniform nor based on a fixed percentage of the assessed value, which ranged from 2 to 69 percent. In fact, in most cases the increment was simply the amount necessary to make the rent a round figure, though it was not always rounded off to the nearest amount. The sums that Edward charged for sales of wardships, broken down to an annual rate based on the length of the minority, also exceeded the assessed value of the lands. When Edward III came to the throne, however, he dropped the effort and once again charged only the extended value for rents.[109]

Given the administrative difficulties the king faced, it is understandable that he often chose not to try to collect direct receipts, but instead to assign feudal rights to repay debts, defray expenses, or compensate individuals for losses incurred in royal service. That left it up to the guardian to recoup his money out of the wardship. The treasury benefited because, even though it did not receive the income, the grants reduced the outflow of cash and helped to underwrite royal expenses and debts.

The tendency toward indirect financing is especially apparent in Edward I's assignment of escheators' revenues and in payments of

---

[105] For an apparent example of one guardian's outbidding another, see *Pipe Roll, 9 John*, 61, 149, and *Rot. Chart.*, 176. For examples of the stipulation, see *ERF*, 2:365; *CPR, 1258–1266*, 197–198; and *Close Rolls*, 11:242. Significantly, both of these occur during the period of baronial reform.

[106] PRO, SC.1/21/35; 22/100; 24/138, 158; 48/48. Furthermore, the king sometimes promised individuals a certain amount in wardships, such as the fees they received, and assigned a wardship in fulfillment of the promise, carefully noting any differences between the promised amount and the assessed value so that he could either demand the difference from the recipient as an annual rent or make it up to him in additional grants (e.g., PRO, E.372/141 m. 24).

[107] For beneficial leases as patronage, see Wolffe, *The Royal Demesne*, 60–65.

[108] *CFR*, 2:233, 256, 284, 294, 306.

[109] Stevenson, "The Escheator," 135–137.

amercements, fines, and rents. Either he or the keeper of the wardrobe instructed escheators to pay receipts to royal falconers, to the keeper of the king's horses, and to various officials responsible for victualing and wages on his campaigns in Scotland and elsewhere.[110] His use of feudal receipts to defray certain expenses stands out clearly in the account of Walter de Gloucester, the escheator south of the Trent, for 1302–1304. Walter was responsible for a total receipt of £7,544 14s. 11 1/2d.[111] Of that, he paid £2,086 19s. 1d. into the treasury in twelve tallies, though some of that most likely went to the wardrobe or creditors. He took £100 as his fee for two years and paid out more than £433 in gifts to different individuals for their laudable service to the Crown. Amadeus, count of Savoy, received 675 marks in partial payment of 10,000 marks that Edward had promised him for his faithful service. Henry de Beaumont received £200 to pay off his Italian debts, while Queen Margaret collected £3,966 13s. 4d. to help her with her debts. Walter paid another £200 to Edward's daughter, Mary, the nun of Amesbury. Finally, Walter claimed more than £140 in miscellaneous expenses including sustenance for royal wards. The king similarly directed guardians to pay fines and farms to royal creditors or favorites and even assigned reliefs to others.[112]

Kings also used wardships to pay expenses or debts. Wardships were extremely useful in this regard. Through five grants out of a single wardship, Edward II, for example, managed to raise 310 marks in cash from fines and simultaneously to write off debts and fees of nearly 720 marks.[113] Henry III made only a few such grants before the 1260s, and the rise in numbers thereafter can perhaps be attributed to the baronial demand during the period of reform

[110] PRO, E.153/51/4–9, 10, 11–17, 23–26 (writs to the escheator north of the Trent); E.136/249/1, nos. 1, 2, 3, 5, 6 (receipts from individuals testifying that they had been paid by the escheator on instruction of the keeper and letters from the keeper requesting payments). The system of wardrobe debentures and assignments becomes even clearer under Edward II (PRO, E.136/249/2, 3, 4, 5).

[111] PRO, E.372/149 m. 38. Other payments are recorded in E.159/81 m. 32; and E.136/429/1, nos. 2, 3, 5.

[112] CPR, 1258–1266, 37; CPR, 1266–1272, 63, 82, 190, 361; CPR, 1281–1292, 292, 334, 465, 497; PRO, E.101/506/8.

[113] CIPM, 5:345; CFR, 2:150, 151, 341; CPR, 1307–1313, 468–469, 492, 511, 517; PRO, E.153/52, no. 23 (Grey of Rotherfield). The grantees were Despenser, Sr.; Despenser's client, John de Haudlo; Thomas Wale; Adam de Orleton; and Henry le Scrope. See also Cokayne, Complete Peerage, 6:144–147; Scott L. Waugh, "For King, Country, and Patron: The Despensers and Local Administration, 1321–1322," Journal of British Studies 22 (1983): 47.

and rebellion that the king put his wardships to good fiscal use.[114] Edward may have learned from that experience, for he granted many more wardships for that purpose than his father had. The Household Ordinance of 1279, for example, notes that one of the two stewards received no wages because the king had granted him the wardship of lands worth £50 a year and that the other had received a wardship worth £25 to supplement his fee.[115] Indeed, Edward made even more complex financial arrangements using his feudal resources. In 1305, for example, he granted wardships to repay two men who had paid money to Italian bankers and merchants on Queen Margaret's behalf, and he ordered a third to pay his fine for a wardship to Florentine merchants on her behalf.[116] By the end of his reign, Edward I was so deeply in debt to creditors, ranging from foreign bankers to his own family, that he relied heavily on wardships to help bail him out. Royal lordship for the first time became almost totally subsumed in the system of finance. Between 1298 and 1307, he thus promised creditors wardships or issues of the escheatorships totaling 39,707 marks. He assigned the lands and money, in order of the promises, to Edmund of Cornwall; Henry, count of Bar; Amadeus, count of Savoy; Henry de Beaumont; Queen Margaret; John and Gilbert de Segrave; Henry de Lacy; and Hugh Despenser, Sr.[117] Not all of the promises were fulfilled, but the records of grants of wardships and marriages in these years, as well as the escheators' accounts, show that the administration took them seriously and strove to satisfy Edward's needs. It is notable, however, that Edward rarely gave wardships directly to foreign merchants or creditors. His hesitation may be another legacy of the period of reform and rebellion, when the barons had expressed so much opposition to Henry's grants to foreigners.[118]

---

[114] *DBMRR*, 150–153, 220–221, 226–229, 260–261. For examples of such grants by Henry III, see *CPR, 1247–1258*, 151, 214; and *CPR, 1258–1266*, 341.

[115] Tout, *Chapters*, 2:158. For other examples, see *CPR, 1301–1307*, 535; *CPR, 1313–1317*, 620.

[116] *CPR, 1301–1307*, 369, 372, 374–375, 410.

[117] *CPR, 1292–1301*, 326, 399, 425; *CPR, 1301–1307*, 59, 60, 113, 238, 239, 410, 412, 481; *CPR, 1307–1313*, 78; *CFR*, 1:532; PRO, E.372/149 mm. 30, 32, 37d–38. Though Edward II made the promise to Despenser, it was for Edward I's debts. Other creditors, like the abbot of Westminster, received wardships at the same time (PRO, E.372/155B m. 8).

[118] Waugh, "Marriage, Class, and Royal Lordship," 181–207. Edward granted some wardships to foreign creditors (*CPR, 1292–1301*, 77, 158; *CPR, 1301–1307*, 142–143). Mesne lords also granted some wardships to foreign creditors (*CPR,*

The creditors stood to gain handsomely. As in rents and fines, the Crown based its grants of wardships for debts on the value of the lands as assessed in the inquisitions post mortem. That is, it deducted the value of the wardship, prorated for the length of the minority, from the amount owed to the individual. Because of the tendency toward undervaluation, the creditor could potentially reap much more than was due. In that sense, it may have been a sign of favor for the king to grant a creditor the wardships and marriages themselves rather than cash from fines or escheators.

The intricacies and consequences of this system can be seen clearly in Edward's arrangements to repay the loans of his cousin, Edmund of Cornwall. Edward owed him a total of 9,840.5 marks and 10 1/4d. for various loans made before 1298.[119] On 3 January 1298, Edward promised Edmund all wardships and marriages then in royal hands and all that fell in, until the debt was satisfied. The lands were to be valued by a reasonable extent under the supervision of Edmund's deputy, while the marriages were to be appraised by the treasurer and barons of the Exchequer, likewise in the presence of Edmund's deputy. If Edmund refused the valuation of a marriage, then it was to be sold within a month and the proceeds delivered to him. If it was not sold, then the marriage was to be given to Edmund to sell himself within a year. Edmund also received the fines of widows for the right to marry and all rents then paid to the Exchequer for wardships. Finally, Edward gave Edmund the right to sell or bequeath the wardships and marriages he received but saved the right to advowsons, wardships, and so forth. The entire arrangement demonstrates how the Crown's financial difficulties placed the king at the mercy of certain well-placed creditors. As promised, Edward immediately delivered all wards and their lands then in custody and made additional grants to make up the debt. In fact, the account of Edmund's executors for the debt revealed that by 1304 Edmund had received 11,760 marks, 2s. 11d., nearly 2,000 marks more than had been owed him.[120] The executors therefore returned the lands

---

1307–1313, 493), while recipients of royal wardships occasionally did the same (CCR, 1272–1279, 502). The only foreign merchant to benefit substantially under Henry III was Poncius de Mora, who received three wardships in 1271–1272 as partial satisfaction of the king's debt to him (CPR, 1266–1272, 550, 623; CCR, 1272–1279, 31; PRO, E.368/46 m. 13; EB, 97–98; G. A. Williams, Medieval London, 247). His interest in these wardships was purely financial, so he sold them off for cash.

[119] CPR, 1292–1301, 326.

[120] CPR, 1301–1307, 463; PRO, E.372/149 mm. 27–27d, 29; E.101/506/6, 7, 8; E.159/71 m. 66. Edmund had died by 26 September 1300 (CIPM, 3:604).

of sixteen wards that were still in their custody. The sum in the executors' account, moreover, was based on a projection of the appraised value of the wardships, not on the actual receipts, so that it seems likely that Edmund had in fact received much more from the lands.[121]

A final category of grants that can be considered subsidies of royal expenses were those made to members of the royal family. The king used his feudal rights, like his demesne lands, to support his relatives.[122] More than 11 percent of his wardships went to relatives or in-laws (of which nearly a quarter went to Edmund). The greatest number, seventy-six, went to support queens. The king allocated wardships to help with the sustenance of his heir, to pay the queen's household expenses, or to support the queen's servants.[123] Henry III made generous grants to his children and siblings, giving at least fifteen wardships to his son Edward, seven to Edmund of Lancaster, and six to Richard of Cornwall along with the marriages of various widows.[124] Once he came to the throne, Edward also used his feudal powers to endow some of his children, though he relied on wardships less often than his father had.[125] Unlike his father, for example, he did not grant a single wardship to his eldest son, Prince Edward. Edward II cut back even more, granting only seven wardships to immediate family members: six to Queen Isabella before 1321 and one to Thomas de Brotherton.[126]

The distribution of these favors by both Henry and Edward I, moreover, makes it clear that their notion of the royal kin ex-

[121] PRO, E.372/149 m. 37d; /150 m. 43. Cf. Stevenson, "The Escheator," 126–127.

[122] Wolffe, *The Royal Demesne*, 52–58.

[123] PRO, SC.1/16/207; *Close Rolls*, 6:44 ("in auxilium sustentacionis Eadwardi filii Regis"); *CPR, 1232–1247*, 283; *CPR, 1266–1272*, 617, 682; *CPR, 1272–1281*, 79, 134; *Close Rolls*, 14:465–466. This includes wardships transferred to Queen Margaret to help pay her debts to Italian merchants and to defray the marriage expenses of Matthew de Monte Martini's daughter (PRO, E.372/149 mm. 37d–38; / 155B m. 9; *CFR*, 1:532; *CPR, 1301–1307*, 410, 412).

[124] *Patent Rolls*, 2:428; *CPR, 1232–1247*, 89; *CPR, 1247–1258*, 285, 287, 423, 501, 545, 622; *CPR, 1258–1266*, 97, 139, 153, 156, 238 (a full wardship to Edmund to maintain himself and his household), 291, 316, 527; *CPR, 1266–1272*, 242, 314, 360, 436, 533, 624; *Close Rolls*, 8:278–279, 280–281, 319; 9:6, 22–23, 41, 44. Widows' marriages: *CPR, 1247–1258*, 540 (2), 614, 622; *CPR, 1258–1266*, 275, 316; *CPR, 1266–1272*, 303.

[125] Kenneth B. McFarlane, "Had Edward I a 'Policy' towards the Earls?" *History* 50 (1965): 145–159, reprinted in idem, *The Nobility*, 248–267; Michael Prestwich, "Royal Patronage under Edward I," in Coss and Lloyd, *Thirteenth Century England I* (Woodbridge, 1986), 52.

[126] *CPR, 1313–1317*, 81, 658; *CPR, 1317–1321*, 66–67, 130; *CPR, 1321–1324*, 10.

tended beyond close blood relatives to include cousins and in-laws. Henry's lavish generosity to his Poitevin half-brothers and half-sisters is well known, indeed notorious.[127] He also generously granted at least thirteen wardships and marriages, as well as several widows' marriages, to his wife's Savoyard relations.[128] Despite the fact that Henry was denounced for lavishing such wealth on his wife's relatives, Edward continued his father's practice, granting at least five wardships to his mother's cousin, Amadeus, count of Savoy.[129] More strikingly, Maurice de Craon, Edward's half-blood relation through Isabel of Lusignan, daughter of Edward's grandmother by her second husband, Hugh de Lusignan, received four valuable wardships in 1275.[130] Finally, Edward extended the same generosity to the relatives and favorites of his first wife, Eleanor of Castile.[131]

This display of favor to the network of royal kin did not spring from a single motive or policy. Both Henry and Edward were determined to promote the interests of their family and to ensure that their children and relatives were adequately provided for. Grants of wardships and other favors also helped to reduce an ordinary part of the king's expenditure. And the beneficiaries often served the king in other capacities and would expect some kind of payment for their services.[132] All the same, family sentiment and finances were not the only considerations. Politics also played a role in these efforts to bind Continental relations as closely as possible to the English Crown. The desire to secure loyal alliances in a politically troublesome region that was of strategic importance in

[127] Harold S. Snellgrove, *The Lusignans in England, 1247–1258* (Albuquerque, 1950), 43–55; Carpenter, "King, Magnates, and Society," 39–70; Waugh, "Marriage, Class, and Royal Lordship."

[128] *CPR, 1232–1247,* 259, 261, 377, 420; *CPR, 1247–1258,* 11, 15, 148, 205, 207, 268, 271 (grant to Sanchia, countess of Cornwall, called the king's sister); *CPR, 1258–1266,* 616; *CPR, 1266–1272,* 732; *ERF,* 2:64; G. E. Watson, "Lacy, Geneva, Joinville and La Marche," 1–16.

[129] *CPR, 1281–1292,* 24, 64; *CPR, 1292–1301,* 457, 481; *CPR, 1301–1307,* 46, 113, 212; *CCR, 1279–1288,* 163, 316. For complaints against Henry's grants, see Paris, *Chronica Majora,* 3:477.

[130] *CPR, 1272–1281,* 93, 112, 422; *CCR, 1272–1279,* 221; *EB,* 3, 100; Moor, *Knights,* 1:245; Parsons, *CHEC,* 68–69 nn. 53, 54 (Montalt, Fitz Alan of Wolverton, Paynel, and Fitz Otto).

[131] Parsons, *CHEC,* 28–56. Giles de Fiennes received three wardships in 1278 (*CPR, 1272–1281,* 281; *CCR, 1272–1279,* 440, 444; *CFR,* 1:437).

[132] Craon was Edward's lieutenant in Gascony, 1289–1293, and Fiennes served Edward and Eleanor in various capacities (Parsons, *CHEC,* 53, 69 n. 54; Moor, *Knights,* 1:245; 2:20–21).

the defense of Gascony partly explains Henry's generosity toward his half-siblings. Similar calculations combined with indebtedness induced both Henry III and Edward I to grant wardships, marriages, and other favors to the duke of Brittany. The duchy had long been associated with the English Crown, and John (d. 1305) was married to Henry's daughter Beatrice.[133]

This cultivation of loyalty within the royal family seems to have ended with the death of Edward I. Edward II granted far fewer wardships to his relatives. He gave a wardship to his cousin John, son of the duke of Brittany, one to Aymer, son of Maurice de Craon, in return for an annual rent, and two to Henry de Beaumont, his mother's relative.[134] But the number of grants declined sharply, and the range of kin likewise shrank. Preoccupied by internal upheaval and wars in Scotland, Edward perhaps had less use to seek Continental allies for much of his reign. His wife's relatives, moreover, were securely bound to the throne of France, and, in any case, his relations with Isabella turned frosty after 1323. His own children were not yet old enough to benefit from grants of wardships. And the influence of the Ordinances, coupled with Edward's own greed, emphasized the fiscal aspects of royal lordship. Whatever the precise cause of this change, it is apparent that Edward did not make a conscientious effort to support his kin through grants of wardships and marriages.

During the thirteenth century, royal lordship had not yet become "independent of chance and change" and had not yet acquired the degree of bureaucratic rigidity that it would under the Tudors.[135] Indeed, the absence of a fixed policy regarding feudal revenues is striking, for the king did not exercise his lordship according to a general principle of maximizing cash receipts, nor had he ceded all of his authority to ministers or institutions. Kings valued the versatility of feudal resources. They could use them in

---

[133] *CPR, 1258–1266*, 203; *CPR, 1266–1272*, 28, 115, 178, 202, 258, 299; *CPR, 1281–1292*, 348, 464; *CPR, 1292–1301*, 77. Henry also granted Beatrice herself the full rights of wardship and marriage over John de Peyvre (*CPR, 1266–1272*, 221, 250; *CCR, 1272–1279*, 178; *EB*, 128; *HKF*, 1:8). See also Prestwich, "Royal Patronage," 43–44.

[134] *CPR, 1307–1313*, 335; *CPR, 1317–1321*, 500; *CPR, 1321–1324*, 35; *CCR, 1307–1313*, 409; Moor, *Knights*, 1:77; Parsons, *CHEC*, 46, 52.

[135] Elton, *Tudor Revolution*, 222. It should be noted that even under the Tudors feudal receipts could not match other sources of revenue and that they, too, used the resources largely for patronage of one kind or another; see Joel Hurstfield, "The Profits of Fiscal Feudalism, 1541–1602," *Economic History Review*, 2d ser., 8 (1955–1956): 53–61.

different ways to meet different needs as they arose. The increased proceeds under Richard, John, and Edward I thus resulted from deliberate policies to meet specific problems and were only temporary. Even at those times, the king also had to pay attention to political needs and above all to the demands of patronage.

PATRONAGE

Versatility was especially desirable in respect to patronage. The pressure on the Crown to give away its wealth was more or less constant. Friends, allies, and potential clients expected gifts; ministers expected rewards; and family members expected promotion. Gift giving was not only a fundamental aspect of social relations in feudal England, it was also an accepted practice of government. And, as the Dialog of the Exchequer pointed out, it glorified the king by ennobling those who served him.[136] Though irregular in terms of amplitude, patronage can be considered a routine expenditure that cannot be separated from the king's ordinary finances. Feudal incidents were ideal as patronage for several reasons. They allowed the king to shift some of the burden of expenditures off of the treasury, while the grant of a wardship did not commit the Exchequer to a lifelong payment or the king to a lifelong association. Furthermore, they were constantly replenished, and the variety of feudal rewards allowed the king to exercise his patronage in different ways. What was given, the terms on which it was given, and to whom thus varied with changes in royal policy and taste.

The feudal wealth given away as patronage can be classified according to two purposes: ministerial patronage given to officials for past service or in expectation of future service to the Crown, and political patronage given to favorites or political allies for their loyalty and support. Contemporaries did not recognize such distinctions, and the two categories were not mutually exclusive. Rewards given to some ministers, such as Hubert de Burgh for example, were more than simply payments for service; they were interwoven in a complex web of administrative and political considerations. Yet of the two, ministerial patronage was by far the more important. An obvious contrast between medieval and modern governments was the lack in the Middle Ages of a single form

---

[136] Fitz Nigel, *Dialogus*, 61.

of remuneration, a cash salary, systematically computed on the basis of work, seniority, and status.[137] The Crown paid some officials handsomely, but a cash fee was only one of several kinds of rewards that a loyal minister could expect.[138] The king often gave wardships, marriages, and widows to officials as supplementary benefits. Officials also had access to information concerning wards and widows and could bid for wardships or marriages sooner than others. As has been seen, speed could be essential in obtaining a grant. Officials, moreover, were well positioned to influence the mechanism of granting feudal rights and to divert them into their own hands. Not all ministerial grants, therefore, resulted from an intentional desire to reward good service, but they do reflect the influence exercised by administrators and courtiers.

It is not surprising, therefore, that royal ministers constituted the largest group of recipients and received a significant portion of the king's wardships. The identification of an individual's status and the consequent categorization of the recipients can only be fairly crude for this period, but they do provide a general picture of who benefited from the king's feudal patronage, as seen in Table 4.9.[139] Among those whose status can be identified, the

---

[137] This point is made for a later period by Penry Williams, *The Tudor Regime* (Oxford, 1979), 94–99, and by G. E. Aylmer, *The King's Servants: The Civil Service of Charles I, 1625–1642* (London, 1974), 160–182. The only comparable survey for the medieval period is Thomas F. Tout, "The English Civil Service in the Fourteenth Century," *Bulletin of John Rylands Library* 3 (1916–1917), reprinted in *The Collected Papers of Thomas Frederick Tout* (Manchester, 1934), 3:191–221. Information on remuneration can also be found in studies of individual offices and officers; e.g., W. A. Morris, *The English Government at Work, 1327–1336*, 1:200–203, 238–240.

[138] Henry III gave escheators south of the Trent, for instance, an annual fee of £40, and Edward I raised that to £50 and £40 for the escheators north of the Trent, though they usually received the money as an allowance on their accounts rather than as a direct payment (PRO, E.372/114 m. 19; /115 m. 11d; /117 m. 7; /149 mm. 32d, 38; /158 m. 36d; /162 m. 34d; /164 m. 37d; /167 m. 2d; /168 m. 45; /177 m. 38d; Stevenson, "The Escheator," 158–159).

[139] Recipients have been identified as royal family members, earls, barons, knights, royal knights (household knights), ministers (holding important offices at the center or in the counties), royal valets (including those described as royal servants, valets, yeomen, huntsmen, etc.), royal clerks, ecclesiastics (abbots, bishops, or important church officials), clerks, Londoners, private officials, and widows. The identification is based on references in grants themselves; *Calendar of Liberate Rolls*; Tout, *Chapters*; James C. Davies, *Baronial Opposition to Edward II, Its Character and Policy: A Study in Administrative History* (Cambridge, 1918); *Liber Quotidianus Contrarotuloris Garderobae* (London, 1787); Byerly and Byerly, *RWH*; Parsons, *CHEC*; Foss, *Judges of England*; Moor, *Knights*; *List of Sheriffs*; *DNB*; J. L. Grassi, "Royal Clerks

TABLE 4.9 THE STATUS OF RECIPIENTS OF ROYAL WARDSHIPS

	Recipients	All Wardships	Baronial Wardships
Earls and Barons	123	202	120
% of total	10.8	11.1	25.2
Knights	169	206	54
% of total	14.8	11.3	11.3
Royal Family	26	204	84
% of total	2.3	11.2	17.6
Ministers			
Royal knights	77	184	49
Ministers, etc.	349	552	117
Total Ministers	426	736	166
% of total	37.3	40.6	34.8
Miscellaneous	57	80	17
% of total	5.0	4.4	3.6
Status Unknown	340	387	36
% of total	29.8	21.3	7.5
TOTAL	1,141	1,815	477
Widows[a]	119	120	23
% of total	10.4	6.8	4.8

[a] Widows and grants to widows have been included in the categories above, their status taken as that of their husbands.

trend toward rewarding ministers and others around the king stands out. Since it is likely that many of those counted as knights served the king on local commissions, the number of officials is actually greater. It is also noticeable that members of the royal family received a disproportionate share of the wardships, though it is inflated by forty-five grants made to Edmund of Cornwall in 1298 and after to repay the king's debts. Thus, nearly half of all of

from the Archdiocese of York in the Fourteenth Century," *Northern History* 5 (1970): 12–33; Cokayne, *Complete Peerage*; Meekings, introduction to *The 1235 Surrey Eyre*; William A. Shaw, *The Knights of England* (London, 1906); *HKF*; and *EB*. In calculating the numbers of recipients, executors have been counted with the deceased, if he/she had received a grant in his/her lifetime, as in the case of Edmund of Cornwall, whose executors received a number of wardships after he had died. As can be seen from these references, the figures are heavily weighted for the reigns of Edward I and II, for which there is more information concerning knights and officials than there is for the first half of the thirteenth century.

the wardships and marriages that the king granted out circulated through the hands of royal ministers and family members. And that figure does not include grants of widows' marriages. This pattern of allocation is slightly clearer in the fate of baronial wardships, since the status of the recipient is more often known in such cases. Once again, roughly half of the grants went to men at court, and that portion is probably greater since many of the earls and barons were serving the king when they obtained their wardships. The point has been made before, but it is worth emphasizing, that the Crown used much of its feudal wealth to reward and subsidize its officials.[140]

The king accomplished this in various ways. He sometimes granted officials the custody of lands or heirs as a form of maintenance during their service.[141] The king also granted wardships in recognition of past service, and escheators paid various sums out of their receipts to compensate individuals for their losses in royal service, to pay their wages, or to honor their service.[142] Furthermore, the king used wardships and marriages to subsidize the cost of annual fees or pensions. In the 1250s, Henry III made a large number of such grants because he had been so profligate in his promises of cash fees to officials and favorites and was trying to save specie so that he could buy gold.[143] Henry used the Hastings wardship in 1250, for example, to give lands to ten pensioners in place of their annual fees.[144] As a result, Henry saved the Exchequer payments of nearly £350 a year. Grants made for fees or service thus represented a hidden savings for the government and can be considered an important part of royal finance.

Members of the court and central administration used their proximity to the king to obtain wardships for themselves or their associates. As might be expected, queens exerted considerable in-

[140] Stevenson, "The Escheator," 136.

[141] *ERF*, 1:65, 105; *CPR, 1232–1247*, 278, 283; *CPR, 1272–1281*, 133.

[142] *CPR, 1232–1247*, 210 (grant of right of marriage to ward in consideration of father's service); *ERF*, 1:458; *Close Rolls*, 13:290–291; *CPR, 1272–1281*, 109 (for service to king and queen), 462; *CPR, 1281–1292*, 174; *CPR, 1292–1301*, 336; *CPR, 1301–1307*, 247, 257, 500; *CPR, 1307–1313*, 494; *CPR, 1313–1317*, 574; PRO, E.372/115 m. 11d; /149 m. 38.

[143] David Carpenter, "The Gold Treasure of Henry III," in Coss and Lloyd, *Thirteenth Century England I* (Woodbridge, 1986), 61–88.

[144] *CPR, 1247–1258*, 83, 86, 93, 103, 126, 129, 134, 163, 220; *ERF*, 2:110–111, 175; *Close Rolls*, 7:39. One grant was made to Geoffrey de Lusignan, on condition that he pay out of the issues of the lands the fees of three men totaling £24, 20 marks.

fluence on the disposal of patronage and made sure that their servants and friends were well rewarded.[145] Princes likewise guided rewards into the hands of their servants. At Prince Edward's urging, Henry III granted wardships to Edward's yeomen, valet, butler, and cook, while in his turn, Edward I, despite his misgivings about his son's companions, granted wardships to several of them, including Piers Gaveston.[146] The king's household knights served in various capacities in both peacetime and war and consequently received occasional rewards besides their annual fees and robes.[147] Edward I was particularly generous to this group in the first half of his reign. His household steward, Robert Fitz John, for example, received six wardships between 1279 and 1287.[148] Later, financial strains made it more difficult for Edward to display the same kind of generosity. Of about thirty bannerets and fifty knights in the household in 1300, for example, only four received wardships between 1299 and 1301.[149] Officials of the household, Exchequer, and law courts were equally well placed to garner wardships. Some they received as rewards for their work, while others they obtained by manipulating the administrative machine they headed. From the time of William Longchamp, at the latest, powerful ministers used their authority over the the king's seigniorial administration to profit themselves and to promote their families.[150] Of the 121 individuals who served as chancellors, treasurers, keepers of the

[145] *CPR, 1232–1247*, 423; *CPR, 1247–1258*, 106, 632; *CPR, 1258–1266*, 353; *CPR, 1266–1272*, 608; *CPR, 1272–1281*, 79, 134, 310; *CPR, 1281–1292*, 120; *CPR, 1301–1307*, 36; *CChRV*, 325; Parsons, *CHEC*, 70 n. 63. Queens also sold wardships to officials; see, for example, Queen Margaret's sales to John de Droxford, *CPR, 1301–1307*, 97, 236, 321, 535.

[146] *CPR, 1247–1258*, 134, 639; *CPR, 1258–1266*, 466, 618; *CPR, 1266–1272*, 409, 740; *Close Rolls*, 7:95; *CPR, 1281–1292*, 339, 371, 393; *CPR, 1292–1301*, 582; *CPR, 1301–1307*, 14, 111, 244, 326, 430, 431, 504. For the prince's household and his relations with his father, see Johnstone, *Edward of Carnarvon*.

[147] For a description of their careers, see J. C. Davies, *Baronial Opposition*, 220–222; and Byerly and Byerly, *RWH*, introduction xv–xliv.

[148] *CPR, 1272–1281*, 334, 397; *CPR, 1281–1292*, 184, 214; *CFR*, 1:119, 120, 176; *CCR, 1279–1288*, 380; Byerly and Byerly, *RWH*, xvii–xviii.

[149] *Liber Quotidianus*, 188–195; Prestwich, *War, Politics and Finance*, 47.

[150] For Longchamp's use of feudal rights to promote his family, see William of Newburgh, *Historia Rerum Anglicarum*, in *Chronicles of the Reigns of Stephen, Henry II, and Richard I*, ed. Richard Howlett (London, 1884–1889), 1:335; *Chronica Rogeri de Houedene*, 3:142; A. E. Conway, "The Owners of Allington Castle, Maidstone (1086–1279)," *Archaeologia Cantiana* 29 (1911): 16–20. Hubert Walter also used the office of chancellor to accumulate wardships (Charles R. Young, *Hubert Walter, Lord of Canterbury and Lord of England* [Durham, 1968], 155–158, 165).

wardrobe, stewards, or chamberlains of the household between 1217 and 1327, 68 persons (56.2 percent) received one or more wardships, marriages, or widows at some point in their careers.[151] Likewise, 71 percent of the chancellors, 66 percent of the stewards, 61 percent of the treasurers, and only 35 percent of the keepers received wards. Some ministers, like Hubert de Burgh or John de Sandall, profited handsomely.[152] A significant number of wardships and marriages thus circulated through the hands of the king's family and the personnel most closely attached to them, contributing thereby not only to the king's finances but to the cohesion of the court as well.

Ministerial patronage was so important that the king sometimes allocated the lands and marriage of a ward exclusively to ministers. Edward II, for instance, used the the wardship of Roger Huse, the five-year-old kinsman and heir of John de Berwick, to reward several administrators. He granted two manors to William de la Beche, a valet and knight of the household; some land to Ingram de Berenger, a sheriff; a manor to Hugh Despenser, Jr.; land to James de Ispannia, a chamberlain of the Exchequer and nephew of Edward's mother, Queen Eleanor; and land to John de Sandall. He also sold Roger's marriage to Walter de Norwich, an Exchequer official who acted as treasurer, for the nominal sum of 50 marks for Walter's good service to the king.[153] Edward thus doled out the wardship to a small cohort associated through administrative service. They all stood to profit from the favors. Though Edward levied fines for the custodies, they hardly matched the potential income from the lands. According to the values given in the grants, for example, Despenser could have made £204 and Berenger £105 over and above their fines, if they retained the lands for the full term of the wardship.

---

[151] The list of ministers is taken from *HBC*, 82–84, 99–101; and Tout, *Chapters*, 6:4–11, 18–21, 25–26, 38–42, 45. It includes individuals who temporarily served in those positions as well as regular appointees. Sixteen men, such as John de Benstead, Peter Chaceporc, John Chishull, John de Droxford, John de Hotham, and John de Lexington, served in more than one post at different times.

[152] De Burgh: *Patent Rolls*, 1:323, 2:176, 187, 201, 230, 412, 434; *ERF*, 1:205, 255, 271; *Pipe Roll, 14 Henry III*, 95–96; *Close Rolls*, 1:377; *CChR*, 1:126; *EB*, 2, 45, 92, 103–104, 146; *HKF*, 3:289; Cokayne, *Complete Peerage*, 1:238; Powicke, *Henry III*, appendix C, 760–768. Sandall: *CPR, 1313–1317*, 651; *CFR*, 1:506; 2:293, 400; Tout, *Chapters*, 2:214–216.

[153] *CIPM*, 5:397; *CPR, 1307–1313*, 494, 564; *CFR*, 2:155, 200, 266; J. C. Davies, *Baronial Opposition*, 144, 146, 196, 222, 232; Moor, *Knights*, 1:81–82; Tout, *Chapters*, 2:343–345; *VCH, Surrey*, 3:519–520, 4:294.

The only significant variation in this ministerial patronage occurred under Henry III. Whether because of lax supervision or an
exaggerated sense of generosity, Henry gave more wardships to
his higher officials than either Edward I or Edward II gave to
theirs. He granted 4 or more to 25 men, while Edward I did the
same for 16 and Edward II for only 10. Those 25 men received a
total of 152. Henry, for example, granted 6 wardships to Matthew
Bezill, 7 to William de Cantilupe, 6 to Bertram de Crioll, 5 to Richard de Ewell, 12 to John Mansell, 5 to Ebulo de Montibus, 11 to
Ralph Fitz Nicholas, 6 to Robert Passelewe, 6 to Peter of Savoy, 9
to William de St. Ermino, and so forth. The only ministers to do
as well after Henry's reign were Peter de Champagne, Robert Fitz
John, John de Sandall, and Roger d'Amory.[154] Thus, Edward I
and even Edward II, in spite of his reputation as a "careless, lazy,
and indifferent king," seem to have exercised much greater restraint in distributing rewards to their officials than Henry III.[155]

The distribution of feudal incidents to officials such as these enhanced the power of the monarchy: practically by retaining
needed service and symbolically by raising the status of royal servants.[156] Officials depended on the grants to augment their incomes or to marry themselves or their family members to wealthy
tenants-in-chief—alliances that served to integrate the landholding
and ministerial elites. The language of Edward II's gift of 1,000
marks out of the sales of wardships to his treasurer, Walter de Norwich, emphasizes this particular use of feudal patronage. Edward
made the grant in recognition of Walter's good service to the
Crown ("pro bono et laudabili servicio quod idem Walterus in officio illo et alibi Regi gratanter impendit") and to maintain Walter
honorably in the king's service ("pro statu suo honorificencius
manutendo in obsequio Regis").[157] He made it, moreover, with the
approval of Walter's associates on the royal council, showing the
intense, corporate interest in the king's patronage shared by those
in his administration. The king's discretion over such patronage
had been limited to the extent that influential ministers *expected*
rewards. He depended on them to run his government and in return they expected a more or less regular stream of favors. The

---

[154] Edward II's favorite, d'Amory, received nine wardships: *CPR, 1313–1317*,
622, 631, 649; *CPR, 1317–1321*, 125, 237, 379; *CPR, 1324–1327*, 53; *CFR*, 2:230,
234, 237, 294, 316–317, 322, 391, 399, 405; 3:378; Moor, *Knights*, 1:11.

[155] Tout, *Chapters*, 2:215, for the quote.

[156] Fitz Nigel, *Dialogus*, 61.

[157] PRO, E.352/111 m. 27d.

pattern of grants of wardships shows that they were not often disappointed. As a result, gift giving had been institutionalized along with other aspects of feudal lordship and had lost some, but not all, of its conditional characteristics. In the long run, only the king chose whom to exalt or bypass. By honoring someone with feudal incidents, he demonstrated his liberality as a prince, his authority as the head of a powerful bureaucracy, and his prerogative as the ultimate feudal lord. Once again, feudal lordship undergirded the bureaucratic monarchy of the thirteenth century.

A diverse group of officials beyond the small circle at the top of the government likewise benefited from feudal grants. Royal clerks in the Exchequer and Chancery as well as royal valets and yeomen acquired a share of this patronage. Typical of them was Oliver of Bordeaux, a royal valet and squire who moved from one household office to another under Edward II, received custody of some lands of John de Meriet and Fulk de Penbridge, and whom Edward assisted in marrying a widow.[158] Local officials also acquired wardships. It might be thought that because of their close involvement with enforcement of the king's feudal rights, escheators would have gained a disproportionate share of wardships, but the inference is false. Only a few of the escheators received royal grants, and fewer still at the time they held office.[159] Peter des Rivaux obtained a valuable wardship the same day he became custodian of the king's escheats in 1232, though Henry III seized it on Peter's fall two years later and transferred it to Richard of Cornwall.[160] Others received one or more wardships during their tenure, though it is not clear that there was a connection between officeholding and the grants.[161] Altogether, fourteen out of the fifty-three major escheators from 1234 to 1327 received wardships from the Crown at one time or another, and more obtained wardships by purchasing them from the recipients of royal grants. The king clearly did not regard a grant of wardship as an ordinary

---

[158] J. C. Davies, *Baronial Opposition*, 222; Tout, *Chapters*, 2:322; *CPR, 1307–1313*, 66; *CFR*, 2:70; Eyton, *Antiquities*, 2:236–237; Stapleton, "Wardrobe Accounts," 339.

[159] *CPR, 1247–1258*, 473, 586–587 (Wingham); *CPR, 1301–1307*, 142 (Oysel), 163 (Abel), 374–375 (Abel), 410 (Abel); *CFR*, 2:136 (Hotham), 3:5 (Wayte).

[160] *Patent Rolls*, 2:491; *CPR, 1232–1247*, 89; *EB*, 108; Cokayne, *Complete Peerage*, 2:302; Powicke, *Henry III*, 84–89, 105–108, 136–137; Stevenson, "The Escheator," 115 (Braose wardship).

[161] *CPR, 1232–1247*, 132, 220 (Fitz William); *ERF*, 1:458 (Crepping, £100 fine), 2:317 (Latimer, 1,200 mark fine); *CFR*, 2:376 (Sapy, farm), 3:279 (Burgh, farm); *CPR, 1313–1317*, 511, 514 (Sapy); PRO, E.159/94 m. 40d (Rodeney); *CPR, 1324–1327*, 346 (Trussel).

method of rewarding his escheators and probably did not want to encourage any notion that the officials responsible for managing these resources had a right to them.

A high proportion of royal wardships, marriages, and widows secured by escheators and other local officers can be attributed to the fact that these men were closely connected on the one hand to the localities in which the feudal incidents arose and on the other to the administration of the king's feudal rights. Both connections could provide them with information regarding the deaths of ten-ants-in-chief and the availability of wards. Administrators must not be viewed as detached from local communities. Their interests were tightly interwoven with those of other landholders of their rank, with whom they shared a desire to intermarry and to acquire property, as well as to hold office. As in the kingdom at large, au-thority, family, and landholding commingled in the hands of the elite. Grants of wardships and marriages to officials, therefore, did not necessarily remove them from the community by placing them in the hands of a distant caste. On the contrary, those rights cir-culated back into the community through marriages and grants arranged by administrators. They used them to strengthen their local connections and landed interests. For example, after Brian de Brompton, a knightly tenant-in-chief in Shropshire, died at the end of 1294, Edward I granted the wardship and marriage of one of Brian's daughters and coheirs to Edward's clerk and escheator south of the Trent, Malcolm de Harley, specifically for the use of Malcolm's nephew Robert, son and heir of Richard de Harley, an-other Shropshire landholder.[162] In granting wardships to this group, the king was not so much implementing a policy as re-sponding to the desires of his tenants and subjects at the local level. Ministerial patronage merged with the social matrix out of which the wardship arose.

The king also used wardships to win support for his policies, though political patronage was less important than reward for service. To begin with, it is notable that English kings did not deem it politically necessary to heap feudal rewards on their magnates. Between 1217 and 1327, twenty-five earls received only fifty-one wardships or marriages. The number of barons who obtained wardships was greater (ninety-six), but still far below that of knights, ministers, and the royal family. Furthermore, many of those barons were active in the government and probably received

[162] *CIPM*, 3:291, 292; *CPR, 1292–1301*, 191; Eyton, *Antiquities*, 4:240–255, 6:233.

their grants as a result of their service rather than their status, as in the case of three barons to whom Edward I granted wardships to honor their participation in the Welsh campaign of 1282–1283.[163] The king usually allocated most of his feudal patronage to those who served him and did not routinely honor magnates with grants of wardships. There were, however, two important exceptions to this general practice. The first occurred in periods of political conflict, most notably in the period of baronial reform and rebellion between 1258 and 1266 and again in the reign of Edward II. At such times, political considerations dictated the distribution of wardships. Factions manipulated royal patronage to build support for themselves, so that it was more narrowly focused than at other times. The second related to the disposal of baronial wardships, of which earls and barons received a more conspicuous share (25.2 percent, counting widows) than they did of other wardships (4.5 percent). Indeed, if the status of the recipients of baronial wardships is considered, aside from their functions as ministers and so forth, then 71 percent of the grants went to men and women of knightly status or higher. At the opposite end of the social spectrum, minor officials who were not of knightly status, such as yeomen, valets, and clerks, received 12.6 percent of all grants other than comital or baronial wardships but only 6.3 percent of the latter. In other words, the king did not ignore status altogether in distributing patronage and displayed some sensitivity to the social snobbery of his elite by discriminating between greater and lesser wardships and by returning most of the former to the social ranks from which they came. Nevertheless, grants to social equals did not guarantee social harmony, as was shown by the conflict between the earls of Hereford and Gloucester, who had custody of Hereford and his lands until 1270.

Status seems to have influenced royal grants in other ways as well. It has already been noted, for example, that the king granted few wardships directly to foreign creditors. He likewise gave very few to Londoners. Only six men specifically identified as citizens of London received important wardships over the entire period, and at least some of those occurred under unusual circumstances. Thomas Fitz Thomas, for example, received a wardship when Simon de Montfort held power after Lewes, probably as a recognition of his support for Simon; William de Combemarton received one in 1305 to repay him for paying part of Queen Margaret's

---

[163] *CPR, 1281–1292*, 179–180.

debt to the merchants of Lucca, and Edward II granted one to John de Triple, an Italian merchant enfranchised in London, as part of a series of favors that the king bestowed on him.[164] Land-holders' prejudice against alliances with merchants and foreigners, coupled with the fact that lands close to London only occasionally fell into royal custody, probably accounts for the low number of wardships given over to Londoners.[165]

Otherwise, kings granted a few wardships or arranged marriages to enlist support. Henry III, entangled in a variety of foreign and domestic commitments, used his feudal resources in this way. In 1246, for instance, Henry entered into an alliance with his in-law, Amadeus, count of Savoy. Henry promised Amadeus an annual fee of £1,000 and a suitable husband for one of his daughters, either John de Warenne or Edmund de Lacy, heirs to the earldoms of Surrey and Lincoln.[166] The promises grew out of Henry's diplomacy. He and his brother, Richard of Cornwall, had married two of the four daughters of Raymond-Berenger, count of Provence, who did not have a son. Even though Raymond had bequeathed the county to his youngest daughter, Beatrice, the English, after his death in August 1245, entertained hopes of acquiring a share of the inheritance or at least some role in Beatrice's marriage. Indeed, the marriage aroused competition among the leaders of Europe; Louis IX (married to Marguerite, Raymond's eldest daughter), the pope, Frederick II, and the king of Aragon all wanted a say in the devolution of the territory. It was in this atmosphere that Henry concluded his treaty with Amadeus, on 16 January 1246, seeking to enlist his assistance in the bidding for Beatrice. Although such hopes were dashed when Beatrice married Charles of Anjou, Henry went ahead with his promise and married Edmund de Lacy to Alesia, Amadeus's granddaughter, in May 1247.[167] Henry's diplomatic ambitions stretched across Eu-

[164] CPR, 1258–1266, 341, 353; CPR, 1301–1307, 372; CFR, 3:193; CCR, 1318–1323, 642, 658–659; G. A. Williams, Medieval London, 216–217, 221–225, 274. The others were John de Gisors, Richard de Betonia, and Richard de Chigwell (CPR, 1281–1292, 60; CFR, 3:222; PRO, E.159/66 m. 29d).

[165] For the attitudes of landholders toward alliances with merchant families, see Sylvia L. Thrupp, The Merchant Class of Medieval London, 1300–1500 (Ann Arbor, 1962), 262–269. The wardships received by Chigwell, Betonia, and Triple all lay near London.

[166] Foedera, 1:264. At that time, Peter of Savoy had custody of the Warenne lands (CPR, 1232–1247, 259; CPR, 1247–1258, 11).

[167] Cokayne, Complete Peerage, 7:681. When he learned of the marriage, Henry appealed to the pope. He refused to intervene, since the marriage suited his inter-

rope and the British Isles. Stymied by lack of funds and military success, he tried to further his aims by cementing the loyalty of the Savoyard, Poitevin, and Scottish dynasties using the lands and marriages of the English nobility, as well as the marriages of members of his own family.[168]

Kings arranged some marriages to strengthen the court and to promote an identification of interests between the court and tenants-in-chief. By giving heiresses in marriage to his courtiers, for instance, Henry II not only rewarded his associates but bridged the worlds of the court and local community.[169] At other times, the king or queen played an even more active role in developing a social network at court or within the administration. It was clearly in their interest on the one hand to reward faithful service and on the other to foster an environment of stable family relations among those who served them. A court or administration strengthened by interrelationships enhanced its ability to execute policy and thereby bolstered the Crown's authority. This was certainly one of Henry III's goals in giving so many wardships to his relatives and in-laws. They in turn demonstrated the strength of the bonds created in Henry's lifetime by intermarrying and transferring wardships and marriages among themselves long after Henry's death.[170] Edward I's first wife, Eleanor of Castile, likewise used wardships to arrange marriages for her servants and relations, though her arrangements proved to be more successful than her father-in-law's because her relatives were not considered foreigners.[171] She did not ship wards off into alien families, but, like Henry II, astutely wedded landholding families with those who served at court. Edward, for example, granted wards from the Haversham, St. Amando, and Wake families to Eleanor, who then married them to her cousins in the Plaunche, Pecquigny, and

est in having a powerful principality in a sensitive region (Eugene L. Cox, *The Eagles of Savoy: The House of Savoy in Thirteenth-Century Europe* [Princeton, 1974], 145–152; Elizabeth M. Hallam, *Capetian France, 987–1328* [London, 1980], 215, 246; Noël Denholm-Young, *Richard of Cornwall* [Oxford, 1947], 51–52). Sometime before 1285, Alesia's niece, Alasia, married Richard Fitz Alan, the heir to the earldom of Arundel, perhaps bringing Henry's policy to a close (Cokayne, *Complete Peerage*, 1:241).

[168] Waugh, "Marriage, Class, and Royal Lordship."

[169] Lally, "Secular Patronage," 165–167; *Rot. Dom.*, 23 n. 1, 38–39, 77.

[170] PRO, SC.1/19/81, 82, 96; G. E. Watson, "Lacy, Geneva, Joinville and La Marche," 76–77.

[171] Parsons, *CHEC*, 42.

Fiennes families.[172] Humphrey de Bohun, earl of Essex and Hereford, and Edmund de Mortimer of Wigmore also married Fiennes women, while the Plaunche family provided a partner for John de Montfort, whose marriage Eleanor obtained directly from John's father, Peter de Montfort. Eleanor similarly helped to arrange a marriage between Peter de Montfort's daughter, Elizabeth, and William, son and heir of Simon de Montagu, as well as marriages for two successive heads of the Vescy family with her cousins, the Beaumonts.[173] Edward himself wanted to have a hand in his servants' marriages and sometimes took the initiative in arranging matches.[174]

Most of the time, therefore, the exercise of royal lordship was not intentionally political, in the sense that it did not aim at furthering particular policies or building up a particular faction. The primary goal was patronage. Most wardships, marriages, and widows went to the king's family, ministers, and courtiers. Though he also tried to profit from lordship, income was clearly subordinate to the need to bestow rewards. This pattern of use of feudal incidents remained remarkably constant over the thirteenth and early fourteenth centuries. Of course, it also had broad political repercussions. At all times, the exercise of royal lordship and the distribution of feudal patronage signaled the unparalleled position that the king occupied as the supreme feudal lord. They affected a broad range of people, and everyone involved from tenant to official to grantee was dependent on the king's seigniorial authority in one way or another. Much of the wealth that was given away, moreover, came to the king through his right of prerogative wardship depriving mesne lords of its use. The entire process served to reinforce the existing bonds of lordship, whether between lord

[172] Most of the marriages are described in ibid., 41–55. Eleanor was undoubtedly responsible for the marriages, but one document describes the St. Amando and Haversham wards as "maritatur per Regem" (PRO, E.136/1/15 m. 8). According to this and another source, Matilda de Haversham married John, not James, Plaunche (CCR, 1288–1296, 11; cf. Parsons, CHEC, 50 n. 182).

[173] Cokayne, Complete Peerage, 9:82 n. n; CPR, 1281–1292, 496. Simon surrendered his inheritance to the king, and two years later received it back as an entail on his son William, just at the time that his son was married (CPR, 1281–1292, 169, 341, 479–480, 485; Kenneth B. McFarlane, "The English Nobility in the Later Middle Ages," in XIIe Congrès International des Sciences Historiques, vol. 1, Grands Thèmes [1965], reprinted in idem, The Nobility, 271). For the Vescy marriages, see Parsons, CHEC, 46–48; Cokayne, Complete Peerage, 12:2:280; and CCR, 1279–1288, 67–68.

[174] Charles L. Kingsford, "Sir Otho de Grandison, 1238?–1328," TRHS, 3d ser., 3 (1909): 131, 188–189; CPR, 1301–1307, 443 (Despenser-Clare).

and tenant, king and minister, or king and court. Feudal gifts, like all patronage, could also be controversial depending on how those outside the favored ranks perceived them. Yet in this case the issue was particularly sensitive because of the very nature of the gifts themselves: children and family lands. However wisely the king distributed feudal patronage, it was always potentially harmful to the families of England's elite. The way in which the grantees used these rights was therefore of the utmost concern.

· 5 ·

GUARDIANS AND WARDS

Guardians used royal wardships to arrange marriages, to reward their clients, or to supplement their income by leasing or selling their rights to others. Since the king channeled most wardships to a privileged group around his court, outsiders often had to apply to courtiers for particular lands, wards, or widows. There was thus a secondary distribution of wardships and marriages, and some passed through several hands before a marriage was arranged or the custody settled. While this secondary distribution offered guardians the opportunity to profit, it did not necessarily harm the wards or their families, for the matches set up by guardians generally conformed to marital patterns within the landholding elite. Indeed, royal lordship became essential to the maintenance of the cooperative framework of marriage, kinship, and tenure that gave the elite its cohesion.

Royal Lordship and the Family

Minorities were profoundly troubling to families. Politics, law, and literature reveal their misgivings about the power of lords over minors and argue that kin should be consulted about guardianship and marriage. The sources, however, indicate an equivalent distrust of kin as guardians, and there is no evidence in the thirteenth or early fourteenth centuries of a widely shared sentiment that relatives alone should have charge of wards. Caught between these alternatives, landholders were wary of royal lordship, but they largely accepted it. For his part, the king was not indifferent to family sentiment and deviated from the prevailing course of patronage to grant wardships or widows' marriages to relatives, to other lords, and to the wards and widows themselves. Although only a small proportion of the total, these grants were significant precisely because they were exceptional favors made in response to requests from families.

One version of the romance of Havelock the Dane vividly dramatizes family apprehension about minorities. It turns on two parallel stories relating the betrayal of two wards, an heir and heiress to separate kingdoms, by unscrupulous guardians. The heir,

Havelock, witnessed the hideous murder of his two sisters and narrowly averted death himself at the hands of his guardian before
he was taken into exile in England where he became a mere cook,
ignorant of his true status. The heiress, meanwhile, was in the
clutches of a guardian who kept her in custody and unmarried
even though she had come of age. The two stories are joined when
the girl's guardian marries her to the cook, hoping by an apparent
mésalliance to gain her inheritance for himself and his son.[1] By
exaggerating the dangers of wardship, the romance builds on the
inherent tension between aristocratic hopes for the smooth descent
of lands and the proper marriage of heirs and fears about the consequences of a minority. Similarly, in the early thirteenth century,
an English member of Peter the Chantor's circle in Paris, Robert
of Courson, denounced the venality of feudal lordship and argued
that it led to the disparagement of wards.[2]

A product of this fear was the request that a ward's relatives be
brought into the process of guardianship or marriage. The idea
surfaced in Henry I's coronation charter, where he promised to
consult his barons in marrying heiresses and to give mothers custody of their children and lands. It reappeared in Magna Carta in
John's promise to inform relatives about marriages proposed for
wards. And it came up again in 1340 when Parliament enacted that
during a minority, custody of lands should be entrusted, in the
fashion of socage tenure, to the nearest friends of the ward who
could not inherit.[3] Otherwise, widows provide the strongest evidence of family opinion regarding royal wardships. Occupying
successive yet overlapping roles within families as daughters, potential heiresses, wives, and mothers, women were deeply involved
in marriage alliances and the disposition of family lands. Some
tried to extend that involvement during widowhood by obtaining
the custody of family lands and the marriages of their children.
The maternal bond must have been fairly strong, for widows are
conspicuous in acquiring rights of wardship, taking custody of in-
fants, and sometimes refusing to surrender their children.[4]

Society, however, did not necessarily favor kin as guardians. The

---

[1] *The Lay of Havelock the Dane*, ed. Walter W. Skeat (Oxford, 1915). For this and
other romances, see the comments in Holt, "Feudal Society and the Family IV," 25.

[2] Baldwin, *Masters, Princes, and Merchants*, 1:248–249.

[3] *Select Charters*, 118; Holt, *Magna Carta*, 307, 319; Bean, *Decline*, 25–26.

[4] For some examples, see Constance M. Fraser, "Four Cumberland Widows in the
Fourteenth Century," *Transactions of the Cumberland and Westmoreland Antiquarian
and Archaeological Society*, n.s. 64 (1964): 130–137.

Laws of Henry I stated flatly that no one, including kin, who claimed an inheritance should be given custody of a minor, and Glanvill echoed the prohibition later in the century. Henry III gave it a melodramatic twist in his explanation of English custom regarding women's inheritance in 1236, when he likened giving elder sisters custody of minor coheirs to entrusting sheep to wolves. In Normandy, the *Tres Ancien Coutoumier* was equally lurid, explaining that relatives, even widows, might kill the children.[5] The case was probably put in these terms not actually to explain the origins of the seigniorial right but rather to rationalize it in an age in which legal change had rendered its logic less obvious. Other sources make it clear that kin were not trusted on their own, and the law took care not to give them unrestricted power over orphans.[6] Indeed, in the earliest version of Havelock the heiress's guardian was her maternal uncle.[7] The romance contrasts his treason with the ideal of the king and lord as the defender of widows, orphans, and maidens. The poem draws on a familiar motif, based on Biblical precedents but uniquely appropriate to feudal kingship, to set up the theme of the betrayal of heirs by their guardians.

The king responded to family sentiment by granting some wardships to widows and kin, though the practice seems to have declined between the twelfth and thirteenth centuries. During the reign of Henry II, 32.7 percent of the fines for wardships recorded in the pipe rolls were offered by widows and 28.8 percent by other kin. These figures are distorted by the fact that they reflect only the small number of wardships (52) for which fines are recorded in the pipe rolls. A truer picture of his practice can be found in the *Rotuli de Dominabus*, which records 82 grants involving 76 wards. Widows obtained 13 (15.9 percent), other kin 12 (14.6 percent), while strangers secured 39 (47.6 percent) and the Crown retained custody of 18 (21.9 percent). In the reigns of Richard and John, when the number of recorded fines was much greater (224), 15.6 percent were offered by widows and 12.9 percent by other kin. After 1217, although widows represented more than a tenth of all of the recipients of wardships, their grants constituted only

[5] *Close Rolls*, 3:375–376; Pollock and Maitland, *History of English Law*, 1:326.

[6] *Leges Henrici Primi*, ed. and trans. L. J. Downer (Oxford, 1972), 223 (no. 70, 12); *Glanvill* (vii.11), 84–85; Bracton, 2:254; *ERF*, 1:228 (grant of lands to brother of deceased and heir to nearest relative of the heir's mother). For examples of family conflict in an earlier period, see Holt, "Feudal Society and the Family iii," 16–20.

[7] *Le Lai d'Haveloc and Gaimar's Haveloc Episode*, ed. Alexander Bell (Manchester, 1925).

about 7 percent of the total. Widows of barons and earls received just under 5 percent of the grants of baronial wardships in the same period.[8] A few others purchased the wardship of their children from the initial recipients of royal patronage.[9]

If the demand from widows remained constant, then the Crown must have altered its policy concerning the sales of wardships to widows shortly after John's reign.[10] Such a change was consistent with those noted in the last chapter. If the government's primary goal was profit, then one of the simplest means of raising money would have been to sell the right of the custody of children to those who had it—widows. As the emphasis shifted toward patronage, grants to widows would decline. Henry III and his successors, moreover, did not exploit widows' desire to keep their children in order to extract excessive fines. It charged widows more often than other grantees, levying a total of 28,582.5 marks on 61 percent of the grants, but 22,000 marks (77 percent) was charged to 6 women in fines ranging from 1,000 to 10,000 marks. The average fine levied on the remaining 70 widows was only 94 marks,[11] which was slightly below the average of all small fines (see Table 4.5).

Grants to brothers, uncles, or cousins were likewise not common in the thirteenth century. They made up just over 3 percent of the total, while wards and guardians shared the same surname in only 30 cases, excluding grants to wards or widows. Only about 20 of the 477 baronial wardships went to close kin. It is possible, indeed likely, that names mask grants to more distant kin, yet the very fact that such relations are not easily established shows that the government did not routinely grant wardships and marriages to the immediate family. The grants took a variety of forms. A father might obtain the wardship of his children when property descended to them through their mother, if the mother had not received the inheritance in her lifetime and if the father had not done homage

---

[8] These are the figures for grants or sales of the king's right of wardship and do not include those cases in which the care of children was temporarily given to their mothers. For examples of grants to widows and stepfathers, see *ERF*, 1:70; *CCR, 1272–1279*, 88; *CCR, 1279–1288*, 490; *CFR*, 1:312.

[9] *CPR, 1258–1266*, 291, 304; *CPR, 1266–1272*, 13; *Close Rolls*, 14:284–285; Altschul, *A Baronial Family*, 36; *EB*, 146; Cokayne, *Complete Peerage*, 9:375 (Mowbray).

[10] Between 1217 and 1246, widows received 10.5 percent of all of the grants (36 of 342). Between 1277 and 1316, grants to widows reached their lowest point: 40 of 805 (5 percent).

[11] For the large fines, see *ERF*, 1:342, 364–365, 2:308; *Patent Rolls*, 1:341; *CPR, 1281–1292*, 292; PRO, E.368/21 m. 2.

for it.[12] The king might also grant a widow's marriage to her parents, as Henry III did in 1272 when he gave William de Valence the marriage of his daughter Agnes, widow of Hugh de Balliol.[13] Finally, the king gave some maternal and paternal uncles, collateral kin, and grandparents custody of wards or their lands.[14]

A ward's in-laws or potential in-laws had as great, if not greater, stake in a wardship as the blood relatives, and many tried to acquire rights of guardianship. Such grants fell into one of two categories. The first was a grant to the parents of the ward's marriage partner. When the king acquired custody of heirs who had been betrothed though not yet married when their parents died, he usually honored the arrangement and turned the children over to the custody of their prospective in-laws to complete the marriages.[15] Because parents often arranged marriages while their children were still very young, this situation was not uncommon.[16] A second, though rarer, form involved giving the custody of coheiresses or their descendants to the elder coheir or her husband, the kind of situation that Henry III warned against in 1236. Henry, for example, promised Warin de Bassingburn, the husband of one of Emery de Sacy's two daughters and coheirs, that if Emery died on campaign in Gascony in 1253, then Henry would grant the ward-

[12] *ERF*, 2:66, 75; *Close Rolls*, 11:95–96; *CIPM*, 1:198, 282 (Clere-Rus); *ERF*, 1:155 (Gersingham); *CFR*, 3:5 (Wayte).

[13] *CPR, 1266–1272*, 615; *EB*, 25.

[14] *CPR, 1301–1307*, 50, 233; Charles W. Segrave, *The Segrave Family, 1066 to 1935* (London, 1936), 17, 25–26; Cokayne, *Complete Peerage*, 10:545–551 (Segrave-Plessetis); *Patent Rolls*, 2:106, 116–117, 276 (d'Aubigny); *CPR, 1232–1247*, 210 (Despenser); *CPR, 1258–1266*, 307, 532 (Mauduit to Bassingburn, maternal uncle); *CPR, 1272–1281*, 299 (Burnell); *CPR, 1281–1292*, 88 (d'Aubigny-Corbet), 497, 501 (Clare); *ERF*, 1:156, 215, 219, 2:15–16 (coparceners of Eton, *EB*, 117); *CFR*, 1:49 (Oliver de Sutton, great-uncle of heir, Holdsworth, introduction to *Rufford Charters*, cx–cxi), 115; *CFR*, 3:49–50, 203–204 (coparceners of Curry Malet, *EB*, 39). Grandparents: *ERF*, 1:205 (Sauvage to Despenser); *CPR, 1266–1272*, 358 (Aumale to Devon); *CPR, 1292–1301*, 422 (Gousle to Fitz Warin); *CPR, 1307–1313*, 68 (Leyburn to Leyburn); *CFR*, 3:190–191 (Audeley to Martin).

[15] *CPR, 1292–1301*, 451; *CIPM*, 5:62; *CPR, 1307–1313*, 26–27, 29; Cokayne, *Complete Peerage*, 1:338–339; *CCR, 1307–1313*, 535 (Audeley-Despenser). For two other examples under Edward I, see *CPR, 1292–1301*, 323; *CCR, 1296–1302*, 298, 301; *EB*, 108, 146–147; Cokayne, *Complete Peerage*, 9:376–380 (Mowbray-Braose); and *CPR, 1292–1301*, 346, 480, 522; Cokayne, *Complete Peerage*, 12:2:88–89 (Tibetot–Ros of Helmesley).

[16] In eleven cases in which it is known that an heir was already married and in which an inquisition post mortem survives, the age of the heir averaged 15.3 years and ranged from 10 to 19.

ship of Emery's unmarried daughter to Warin, which he did.[17] Even under the watchful eye of the king, however, guardians were tempted to cheat heiresses. In 1299 the escheator south of the Trent sold the wardship of the two daughters and coheirs of Walter de Gouiz to John Latimer, who married one of the girls. The other died unmarried in 1310, whereupon Latimer was summoned to appear before the king in Chancery to show why no partition had been made and why no homage had been performed.[18] Latimer was evidently keeping the land for himself. In this case the king was primarily concerned to ensure the preservation of his own rights of lordship but it nonetheless helps to explain why the Crown may have been reluctant to grant wardships to relations.

Some individuals anticipated their own death and arranged for the guardianship of their lands and children. Less than a month before he died in 1315, for example, the earl of Warwick, Guy de Beauchamp, obtained from Edward II a promise that if Guy died leaving a minor heir, Guy's executors would have the wardship of his lands until his heir came of age. They would have to render the assessed value of the lands to the king annually, they were restricted in the disposal of certain strategic castles, and Edward reserved to himself all wardships, advowsons, and dowers that fell in, but they would presumably be able to use the revenues of the lands to pay Guy's debts.[19] Guy may have also been concerned about his estate. Guy and Edward had been opponents from the time of Edward's coronation, and Guy's responsibility for the death of Gaveston had only deepened their enmity.[20] Edward nonetheless at first honored his promise when Guy died in August 1315 and turned custody of the estate over to Guy's executors.[21]

---

[17] *CPR, 1247–1258*, 205; *ERF*, 2:168; *CIPM*, 1:272; *VCH, Hampshire*, 4:417; *VCH, Cambridgeshire*, 8:15, 16. For other examples, see *HKF*, 3:236; *CIPM*, 2:60; *CFR*, 1:32; Moor, *Knights*, 2:76–77 (Foliot); *CFR*, 2:367, 368; *CCR, 1318–1323*, 7; *CPR, 1317–1321*, 500; *CIPM*, 6:111 (Merlaw); *CFR*, 3:213, 243, 245; PRO, E.159/86 m. 3; *CPR, 1272–1281*, 202; *CIPM*, 1:811, 5:330, 6:101, 429, 2:26, 77; *EB*, 58; *RH*, 1:172; *CCR, 1272–1279*, 65, 102; PRO, E.372/124 m. 21 (grant voided).

[18] *CPR, 1292–1301*, 399; *CIPM*, 3:541, 5:234; *CFR*, 2:72, 75; *EB*, 99. Edward seized the lands and gave them to his former nurse, but since Latimer was serving faithfully in Scotland, Edward soon restored them.

[19] *CFR*, 2:255.

[20] *Vita*, 11, 25–27, 30, 32, 62: John H. Trueman, "The Personnel of Medieval Reform: The English Lords Ordainers of 1311," *Mediaeval Studies* 21 (1959): 265–267.

[21] *CIPM*, 5:615; *CFR*, 2:265. For a similar example, see *CPR, 1281–1292*, 173; *CCR, 1288–1296*, 335–336; and Cokayne, *Complete Peerage*, 12:1:507–511 (Vere).

Kings at various times made similar promises, especially to tenants traveling overseas on his business or on Crusade and leaving minor heirs.[22] Kings did not lightly surrender their feudal rights, but they were pleased to grant occasional favors.

Tenants-in-chief also looked to the king to advance marriage negotiations and to uphold bargains once they had been struck. The same authority that allowed him to interfere in family arrangements could be harnessed for the family's benefit. He sanctioned matches, endorsed parents' sales of the marriages of their children, and allowed some parents to provide for the custody and marriage of their heirs in case the parents died. Hopeful suitors sought the king's assistance in obtaining marriage partners.[23] He provided lands or funds for dowries and helped families obtain dispensations.[24] He promised others to carry out planned marriages in case the parents died while the partners were still underage.[25] After making the arrangements described in the first chapter for a marriage between Henry de Lacy and Margaret Longspee in 1256, for example, Edmund de Lacy paid 10 marks of gold for Henry III's confirmation of the pact. The confirmation provided that if Henry died, then his younger brother John would take his place. The king, moreover, ensured that if the parents died before the children reached a marriageable age, the contract would remain valid. Precisely as feared, William Longspee died shortly after the marriage was agreed upon, and the king, as promised, ordered that Margaret be delivered to Edmund's custody for carrying out the marriage.[26] At every stage of this marriage, the participants called on and trusted in the king's cooperation.

Furthermore, if one of the parties to a marriage agreement hesitated, the other might call on the king to prod the reluctant party

[22] *CPR, 1266–1272*, 441; *CPR, 1301–1307*, 154; *CPR, 1307–1313*, 267; *CPR, 1317–1321*, 391.

[23] Bartholomew de Multon paid John 100 marks for a wardship, and Robert de Tateshal offered him 20 marks to urge Bartholomew to grant him the marriage (*Pipe Roll, 4 John*, 231; *6 John*, 78; *7 John*, 212; *Rot. Ob. et Fin.*, 210, 254–255). For similar cases, see *Pipe Roll, 5 John*, 148; *6 John*, 76; *7 John*, 58; *10 John*, 155.

[24] *RH*, 2:13–14, 133; *Close Rolls*, 6:167; *CCR, 1302–1307*, 264; Stapleton, "Wardrobe Accounts," 338–339. The Crown was particularly helpful to Roger de Mortimer (d. 1330) in arranging marriages for several of his daughters (Cokayne, *Complete Peerage*, 6:190 n. f, 8:441 n. e, 9:599 n. d, 10:390 n. m; *Foedera*, 2:1:387).

[25] *CPR, 1232–1247*, 417; *CPR, 1247–1258*, 25, 484.

[26] *CPR, 1247–1258*, 534, 536; *ERF*, 2:249. He gave Queen Eleanor custody of the Longspee lands.

into action.[27] In 1252, for example, Henry III confirmed a contract between his powerful minister John Mansell and Matthew Huse that provided for two marriages: the first between Matthew's son and heir Henry and Mansell's niece Joan, daughter of Alard le Fleming and Mansell's sister Emma, and the second between Matthew's eldest daughter and Mansell's unnamed nephew. But Matthew seems to have balked, perhaps fearful that the contract would not be honored if he died. In the contract he had already displayed some distrust of Mansell. It stipulated that the lands assigned as Joan's dower would be entrusted to the care of a third party, not Mansell, if Matthew died before the couple came of age. In December 1252 Henry urged Matthew to complete the bargain and assured him that he would not only guarantee the terms of the contract but would, if necessary, compel Mansell to observe them.[28] As it turned out, Matthew died the following February, before the marriages were completed. Henry duly turned the dower lands over to the designated guardian and sold the wardship of the remainder, along with the right of marriage, to Mansell for 300 marks.[29] Similarly, a decade later when Alard le Fleming died, Henry sold Mansell the wardship along with the marriage of the widow, Mansell's sister.[30]

The king, therefore, was not a distant spectator of his tenants' matrimonial arrangements, intervening only to assert his financial interests. On the contrary, he participated in various ways at different levels, and his activity could be a crucial factor in the foundation and stability of family alliances. When exercised in that manner, feudal authority served to bring the king and his tenants-in-chief together over their common interest in stable landholding and inheritance.

The king likewise assisted widows. He augmented their dowers by giving them custody of their husbands' lands during a minority.[31] He granted them the freedom to marry whomever they pleased along with the custody of their children. In general they easily secured the right of remarriage during the thirteenth cen-

---

[27] *Pipe Roll, 7 John*, 58; *10 John*, 155; *12 John*, 177.

[28] *Close Rolls*, 7:435–436. See also *Close Rolls*, 7:324; and *CPR, 1247–1258*, 170.

[29] *CPR, 1247–1258*, 181, 410; *ERF*, 2:154; *Close Rolls*, 7:324; Cokayne, *Complete Peerage*, 7:1–3; *HKF*, 3:33–34, 85–86.

[30] *ERF*, 2:395; *CPR, 1258–1266*, 254; *CIPM*, 1:562. Mansell acquired two other marriages to find partners for his sister and nephew (*Close Rolls*, 4:54; *CPR, 1247–1258*, 167, 168).

[31] *ERF*, 1:282; *CPR, 1232–1247*, 216; *Close Rolls*, 4:42, 282.

tury, although there were significant exceptions.[32] Conversely, the king sometimes granted the right to a widow's marriage in conjunction with a grant of the custody and marriage of wards.

The king extended his protection to heirs as well, though his help was never disinterested. By March 1266 Geoffrey Lutterel was no longer competent to watch over himself and his lands, so that his relatives and friends asked the king to step in and to protect Geoffrey's children from any rash acts on Geoffrey's part.[33] Henry III instituted a guardianship for Geoffrey, his children, and his property. He entrusted care of the estate jointly to Geoffrey's brother Alexander and to Geoffrey's father-in-law, William de Grey. Alexander had responsibility for caring for Geoffrey, while William had custody of Geoffrey's son and two daughters, William's grandchildren. He authorized the two guardians to use the estate to support their charges and to arrange suitable marriages for the girls, with the counsel of relatives and friends. In establishing this guardianship, Henry took care not to turn the children over to the custody of their uncle, who had a stake in the inheritance, and provided a corporate control over the property and marriages that mimicked customary family procedures. Once again, however, Henry looked out for his feudal interests, for he retained right to the wardship if Geoffrey died leaving a minor heir. The guardians evidently had no authority to arrange a marriage for the heir, so that when Geoffrey finally died in 1270, Henry took custody of the lands and heir and granted them to Robert de Tibetot, lord of some of the Lutterel lands in Yorkshire.[34] Tibetot, moreover, had been a staunch royalist in the Barons' War and continued to act as a royal administrator.

As this example indicates, families expected assistance from their friends, and that role could carry over into the custody of wards or their lands.[35] Relationships between the guardian and the ward's family are not always obvious, and it may be that in many more cases a royal grantee was actually a friend of the family. Such

[32] Walker, "Feudal Constraint and Free Consent," 97–110.

[33] *CPR, 1258–1266*, 564; Cokayne, *Complete Peerage*, 8:285–286; *EB*, 55–56; PRO, E.13/17 m. 25.

[34] *CPR, 1266–1272*, 407; *HKF*, 1:237–238; Moor, *Knights*, 5:20–24.

[35] For examples of friends or executors playing a role in wardships, see *CPR, 1266–1272*, 611, 650; *Close Rolls*, 7:90, 340 (St. Amando), 14:467–468, 544 (Staundon); *CIPM*, 2:435, 483; *CFR*, 1:184, 197 (Neville); and *CPR, 1292–1301*, 38, 381, 522 (executor as guardian of lands, which may have facilitated his responsibilities in paying debts).

was the case in 1249 when Odo de Hodonet, a Shropshire knight, acquired the wardship of Ralph, son and heir of Richard de Sandford, another Shropshire landholder, from the original grantee. Odo had previously witnessed at least one Sandford charter and witnessed additional family charters after Ralph came of age, as did Odo's son and heir, after Odo's death in 1284. Another frequent witness was Robert de Say of Morton, whose sister eventually married Ralph's son and heir.[36] While the recipients of wardships in cases such as these certainly had some pecuniary interest in their rights, they were also lending their assistance to their friends. It was one way in which the network of kinship, tenure, and clientage could benefit families and individuals.

The full panoply of interests that revolved around a given wardship and the way in which kings selected from an array of possibilities stands out clearly in the descent of the Mountchesney family. The process began in 1225 with the death of Nicholas de Anesty. At that time, William Marshal the Younger wrote to Jocelin de Wells, bishop of Bath and Wells and an influential justice, imploring Jocelin to assist him in procuring the wardship and marriage of Nicholas's daughter and heir, Denise.[37] Henry III, however, granted the wardship to Stephen de Langeton for the use of Stephen's brother Walter, whom she married. Walter died childless in 1234, and Denise offered 100 marks to marry whomever she pleased. Her surety for the fine was Warin de Mountchesney, baron of Swanscombe, Kent, and he married Denise as his second wife.[38] His first wife had been Joan, daughter and eventual coheir of William Marshal, Sr. Joan died in 1234, leaving a daughter, Joan, and a son who died without children in 1247. His mother's share of the Marshal inheritance therefore fell to his unmarried sister. Henry immediately took custody of the girl and married her to his half-brother, William de Valence.[39] When Warin de Mountchesney died in 1255, his minor son and heir, William, by his second wife, Denise, inherited the Mountchesney lands in Kent and frustrated any hopes that his half-sister, Joan, may have entertained of inheriting her father's property as well as her mother's. Henry III, however, granted the wardship of the lands to William

---

[36] *CPR, 1247–1258*, 47; *CIPM*, 1:170; Eyton, *Antiquities*, 9:229–230, 232–233, 235, 236. It is not known whom Ralph himself married.

[37] PRO, SC.1/2/19; *HBC*, 205; Foss, *Judges of England*, 2:514–515.

[38] *Rot. Lit. Claus.*, 2:57; *ERF*, 1:268; *HKF*, 3:265–266; *EB*, 144.

[39] Paris, *Chronica Majora*, 4:628; Cokayne, *Complete Peerage*, 10:377–382.

de Valence.[40] William and Joan still harbored thoughts of acquiring control of the Mountchesney property, and when her half-brother died in 1287, they mounted a campaign to get the wardship and marriage of his daughter and heir, another Denise. They obtained a bull from the archbishop of Canterbury giving them custody, but Edward I firmly quashed the maneuver as prejudicial to his rights.[41] He sold the wardship of the girl's lands to her grandmother, Denise, and Ralph de Coggeshall for 2,000 marks. In 1290 he granted the girl's marriage to his yeoman, Hugh de Vere, on condition that he marry Denise himself. Ironically, Denise died in 1313 without heirs of her own, so that the barony reverted to Joan's son, Aymer de Valence.[42]

Percentages can be deceptive because they strip away the field of choices, influences, and possibilities in which each wardship and grant was enmeshed, and that field becomes most visible in comparisons of grants. In the Mountchesney example there were two family grants in successive generations, one to an in-law and another to a widow. Yet the first to Valence was a product of Henry's interest in the advancement of *his* family and had little to do with the interests of the ward, while in contrast, Edward I made the second partly to protect an heiress from the machinations of her cousins. Within this field of possibilities, the king had two interests that remained constant throughout the period and that stand out in these examples. One was patronage. Most of the grantees mentioned here were associated with the Crown in one way or another. Yet the examples also show that royal patronage was an unpredictable variable in strategies of advancement and marriage. The grant to Langeton frustrated the younger Marshal's hopes, but his sister and her descendants were taken care of. Valence was promoted by marriage into a leading family but frustrated in plans for further enhancement. A second concern was the smooth descent of property. All of these actions, in one way or another, seek to provide a stable continuity between generations by ensuring, insofar as it was possible, that legitimate heirs would inherit and marry. But there was no rule dictating the method of achieving these goals and they could be accomplished in different ways. The king had to balance the competing interests that were brought to bear

---

[40] *CPR, 1232–1247*, 508–509; *CPR, 1247–1258*, 419. William was married in his father's lifetime, so that Henry did not obtain the marriage.

[41] PRO, SC.1/45/55, 61; /62/35; *Rot. Parl.*, 1:16–17; Cokayne, *Complete Peerage*, 9:423–424.

[42] *CIPM*, 2:610; *CPR, 1281–1292*, 292, 362, 376; *HKF*, 3:107–108; *EB*, 144.

on a wardship, with the result that royal power and patronage were not played identically on every occasion.

The same complex interplay of influences underlay grants to the heirs themselves. In nearly thirty cases, the king gave a ward custody of lands that he or she would inherit or the right to marry whomever he or she pleased. The reasons for such grants varied. In order to defend the north against the Scots in 1318, Edward II gave Roger de Clifford and Henry de Percy, heirs of two great northern baronies, custody of their lands and castles though they were only eighteen and nineteen years old.[43] Patronage may have also played a role, as in Edward II's grant in 1321 of the custody of the Montagu lands to the heir William, whose father had been a steward of the household and a close ally of the Despensers.[44] In many cases, it was merely convenient for the administration, since the heir was nearly of age or was already married and the government could not hope to sell its rights or to manage them profitably in a short period.[45] As this last statement implies, less generous motives than grace or patronage prompted some grants to wards. Magna Carta had cut back the Crown's fiscal opportunities by declaring that the king could not demand relief from an heir who had been in wardship and by fixing reliefs themselves. Edward I had to remind his overly zealous Exchequer of the ward's rights and order it to cease demands for relief in cases of minority.[46] The king could bypass these restrictions, in a sense, by charging a fine for the right of a ward to take up his or her lands before coming of age or for the right to marry. There were no limits to such fines, and some could be quite steep: Henry de Percy paid 900 marks in 1249 for his lands and marriage, John Fitz John 450 marks in 1259 for his lands, Ralph Basset of Drayton 1,000 marks in 1300 for his lands and marriage, and James le Botiller 2,000 marks in 1325 for his marriage alone.[47]

Besides keeping the interests of his tenants-in-chief as families in mind, the king was also aware of their position as mesne lords whose rights were deeply affected by prerogative lordship. He oc-

[43] CFR, 2:370–371, 378, 404. Robert de Ufford likewise received his lands in 1318 though underage (CCR, 1313–1318, 542).
[44] CCR, 1318–1323, 287, 294; Maddicott, Thomas of Lancaster, 194.
[45] PRO, E.159/73 m. 40d: sale of custody of lands to ward "qui in hoc presenti anno plene etatis erit."
[46] CCR, 1296–1302, 44.
[47] ERF, 2:47–48, 294–295; CPR, 1292–1301, 495; PRO, E.372/149 m. 31; CFR, 3:367.

casionally acted to mitigate those effects by relaxing his rights. In 1208, for example, King John consented to a marriage between the daughter of Elias Croc, a royal forester, and Michael Columbars, a tenant of the earl of Pembroke.[48] The marriage meant that in the future, if the couple produced heirs, the earl would lose his rights of wardship over the Columbars's fee. John, therefore, promised William Marshal, the earl, that in the future he would not lose that right on account of the marriage.[49] In other cases, the king granted the wardship of lands held of a mesne lord that had come into his custody through prerogative wardship back to the lord of those lands.[50] The king also gave a few wardships to mesne lords when the tenant held of the king by petty serjeanty.[51] The king had no intention of undercutting his authority through a wholesale abandonment of his rights of prerogative wardship.

Because mesne lordship and family were only two of several considerations in the allocation of wardships and marriages, they do not appear more prominently in grants, and family was by far the more significant of the two. Opportunity, circumstance, and influence helped to keep the numbers low. Grants to individual families, however, may not have been so important to landholders as the overall pattern of the use of royal wardships by guardians. If, in general, lands were not wasted, if wards married well, and widows' lands and rights were respected, then families probably concluded that royal lordship was favorable to their interests. The loss of control over marriage and descent, that is, would not be considered dangerous if surrogate lords and parents fulfilled the family's aims. Families, moreover, may not have been so concerned as one might assume about the loss of control per se, since their marriages were corporate acts involving friends and relations and never matters between parents and children alone. Under those circumstances, it mattered less that a wardship or widow went to a

---

[48] *Pipe Roll, 9 John*, 149; *Rot. Ob. et Fin.*, 567.

[49] *Rot. Chart.*, 176. It is not clear from the wording whether the grant applied solely to the children of the marriage or to subsequent generations as well. After Michael's death in 1235, Henry III took the homage of Elias's daughter Avice and delivered custody of his lands to her (*Close Rolls*, 3:73–74; *CPR, 1232–1247*, 100). There is no mention of Michael's lands at that time, though when Avice died in 1259, Henry took the homage of her son and heir, Matthew Columbars (*ERF*, 2:313).

[50] For two examples, see *ERF*, 1:133; *CIPM*, 2:470; *CPR, 1281–1292*, 175–176 (Pippard); and *CPR, 1307–1313*, 331; *CIPM*, 5:306 (Rivers).

[51] Kimball, *Serjeanty Tenure*, 182–184. In one instance the king gave a wardship to a lord who disputed the king's right (*Select Cases*, 3:88–95).

minister, favorite, royal family member, or tenant-in-chief than what happened to them after the grant, particularly since each of these groups belonged to landholding society and the lines dividing them were so indistinct. It is vital, therefore, to see how royal grantees used their rights.

GUARDIANS' USE OF WARDSHIPS: MARRIAGE

Like the Crown itself, the recipients of royal patronage had two basic options in using wardships and marriages: either to supplement their income or to cultivate social ties. They could accomplish the latter by arranging marriages for widows or wards with members of their own families.

One hundred thirty marriages of wards are known. That is a small percentage of the overall number of grants of marriages, and is probably a serious underestimate of the actual number arranged. In the baronial sample, fifty-seven marriages made by recipients have been found (24.8 percent of the wardships that included the right of marriage), thirty-one of them in cases where the grant involved only the right of marriage (47 percent).[52] Guardians made matches to promote themselves or family members, to make social alliances, or to make profits. Indeed, the king often noted that he granted a marriage to make a specific match.[53] In such cases it was advisable for a guardian to get the couple married as soon as possible. Only thirty-eight wards are known to have died in custody, but worries about the health of heirs prompted quick marriages. William de Chauncy was seventeen years old on his father's death in 1307, but he may have been in poor health. Edward II granted his wardship to the royal yeoman, Bernard de Ferandi, who passed it on to William de Doncaster. William married the boy to his daughter Margaret sometime before October 1311. William de Chauncy had died by then, leaving Margaret a widow at age eleven with dower lands worth more than £11.[54]

It is by now a cliché that marriage was an important door to advancement in English society, but it is less widely appreciated that during the Middle Ages royal lordship served as a powerful lever in opening it to individuals. Men like William de Valence, Roger d'Amory, and Piers Gaveston advanced rapidly as a result

[52] See Table 4.2 for the grants.
[53] *Rot. Chart.*, 1:48; *ERF*, 1:252; *CPR, 1292–1301*, 179; *EB*, 45, 97–98, 111.
[54] *CIPM*, 4:430; 5:275; 6:333; *CPR, 1307–1313*, 56, 61, 65; *CCR, 1307–1313*, 304; *CCR, 1318–1323*, 438.

of marriages arranged for them by the king, while other royal knights or ministers like John de Botetorte, Geoffrey de Joinville, and Elias de Rabayn advanced by marrying the baronial heiresses whose marriage the king granted them.[55] The ministerial family of St. Amando relied on a series of marriages arranged through wardships to promote itself into the ranks of baronial landholders and to link itself to families like the d'Aubignys, Montagus, and Keynes, as can be seen in Figure 5.1.[56] A successful bid for a wardship could thus result in substantial economic or social improvement for the grantee. It did not always matter who the ward was, so long as he or she had sufficient lands to improve the position of the potential partner.[57] John Latimer, a younger son in the Yorkshire family, was looking for advancement in the 1290s. To help him along, Edward I in 1297 gave him the marriage of the heiress of a Kentish knight. Before Latimer could marry her, however, she ran off with Henry de Leyburn. Edward ordered their lands seized and instructed them to pay their fine to John as compensation for his loss, though they did not do so until 1300.[58] In the meantime, Edward had found another heiress for John: one of the daughters of William de Gouiz, who held a portion of the barony of Winterbourne St. Martin in Dorset. As has been seen, John married the eldest, who was only about fifteen. He left the other unmarried so that on her death her portion of the estate fell to John's wife. The marriage lifted John into the ranks of the county gentry, and he became a prominent figure in local government, serving as knight of the shire for Dorset on three occasions, far from his origins.[59]

If a family underwent a minority generation after generation, its matrimonial alliances and the consequent patterns of descent

[55] For Rabayn, see *CPR, 1247–1258*, 62, 65; *ERF*, 2:286; *EB*, 88–89. For the others, see *EB*, 11, 96.

[56] *CPR, 1232–1247*, 53, 476; *CPR, 1266–1272*, 467, 469; *CPR, 1281–1292*, 54; *CFR*, 1:177; *Close Rolls*, 2:441, 457, 14:299–300; *CIPM*, 1:807, 2:433; *CRR*, 15:xxxi; *EB*, 26–27, 146; Cokayne, *Complete Peerage*, 11:295–297, and 297 n. f. Henry III sold the wardship of Amaury, Ralph's son and heir, to another minister, Paulinus de Peyvre, for 1,000 marks, a sum that reflected the new standing of the family (*ERF*, 1:450; *CPR, 1232–1247*, 476; *Close Rolls*, 5:406, 410, 454).

[57] The financial dimension is apparent in Henry III's promise to Nicholas de Boneville of a wardship worth £30, if the ward was a girl, for the use of Nicholas's son (*CPR, 1232–1247*, 243; *ERF*, 1:365; 2:237; *Close Rolls*, 4:267, 385–386).

[58] *CPR, 1292–1301*, 257; *CCR, 1296–1302*, 70, 136, 139, 183; PRO, E.159/72 m. 22d. The entry in the patent roll refers to William Latimer, but all subsequent references are to John.

[59] *CIPM*, 3:541; *CPR, 1292–1301*, 399; *EB*, 99; Moor, *Knights*, 3:19–20.

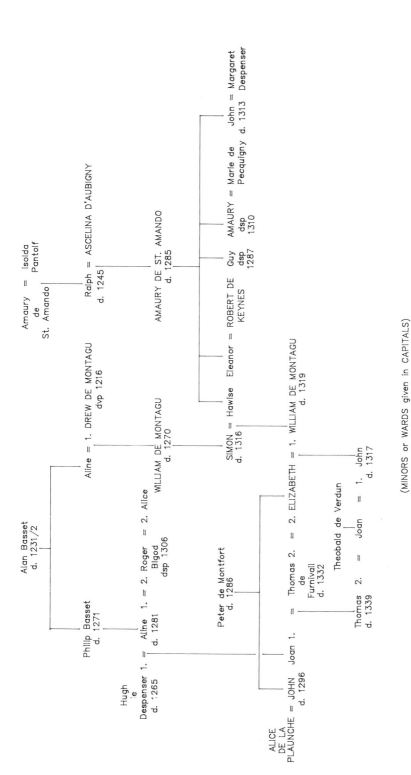

(MINORS or WARDS given in CAPITALS)

FIGURE 5.1. Minorities and Intermarriage in the Montfort, Montagu, and St. Amando Families

would have been dictated exclusively by the choices of royal guardians. In fact, such families did not usually suffer. The Mohun family, barons of Dunster, married well despite four successive minorities during the thirteenth century. The guardians of the Wake family, which suffered five minorities over same period, formulated alliances that were compatible with the status of the Wakes and that in two cases enhanced their financial position because they involved heiresses.[60] The same point is clear in the marriages formed for twenty baronial wards out of sixty-six cases in which the guardian received only the right of marriage. Eight married royal knights or ministers; the sons and daughters of men like John Fitz Geoffrey, Walter de Beauchamp, and Hugh d'Audeley. Seven married the children of other baronial families, often from the same region, such as the union brought about between the heir to half of the barony of North Cadbury, Somerset, and the daughter of Richard Lovel of Castle Cary in 1316. Three married offspring of the powerful knights Ralph Basset of Drayton, Henry de Grey, and Robert de Tibetot, whose wealth and influence made them the social equivalent of most baronial families. Finally, two wards married royal relatives: Maud de Chaworth married Henry, son of Edmund of Lancaster, while John de Hastings was married to William de Valence's daughter Isabel.[61] So long as the king granted marriages to persons of acceptable social rank, and that is an important assumption, then the marriages that those recipients made for their wards would have been consistent with the family's expectations for their children. It must be remembered that guardians had a definite interest in protecting wards—an interest that extended to protecting the ward's lands through property settlements.[62] Their own families, after all, depended on the wisdom of their actions.

The use of wardships often conformed to the social endogamy practiced within the landholding elite. They figured prominently in marital strategies and under the right conditions, for example,

[60] Cokayne, *Complete Peerage*, 9:19–23; 12:2:297–304; H. C. Maxwell Lyte, *A History of Dunster and of the Families of Mohun and Luttrell* (London, 1909), 1:1–58.

[61] *CPR, 1232–1247*, 53, 319; *CPR, 1258–1266*, 606; *CPR, 1266–1272*, 323; *CPR, 1272–1281*, 318; *CPR, 1281–1292*, 108, 125, 445, 464, 483; *CPR, 1292–1301*, 179, 304; *CPR, 1301–1307*, 152; *CPR, 1313–1317*, 574; Dugdale, *Monasticon*, 6:1:352; *CFR*, 2:245, 292; *EB*, 8, 86, 125; Cokayne, *Complete Peerage*, 3:358, 4:324, 5:436–439, 6:109, 190 n. f, 8:528 n. i, 9:7, 22, 407, 484–485, 12:1:173, 652–653; Eyton, *Antiquities*, 9:173; PRO, E.136/1/15 m. 8.

[62] For an example, see *CIPM*, 4:176; *CPR, 1281–1292*, 115.

formed the basis for brother-sister or cousin alliances.[63] The choice
of partners for wards or widows was thus neither random nor accidental, and even marriages that aimed narrowly at one's advancement forged family alliances. Since the stability of landholding society, as well as the survival of families, depended on
contracting marriages and producing heirs and since minorities
were frequent, wardships had to play a key role in alliances. That
importance can be seen in the descent of part of the Basset family
as pictured in Figure 5.2.[64] To begin with, the Basset brothers en-
ergetically acquired the wardships of relatives. At one time or another and in one combination or another they gathered the wardships of their cousins Robert de Grelley, Walter de Dunstanville,
and William de Montagu, son of Alan's daughter Aline (see Figure
5.1).[65] They also relied on royal lordship to form marriages. Gilbert got the king's permission to marry his daughter Eustachia to
Thomas de Verdun, while Thomas purchased the wardship of the
young earl of Warwick, Henry de Newburgh, to provide a match
for his daughter Philippa. Their sister Isabel married Albert de
Grelley, and after his death in 1180, Guy de Craon paid 200 marks
for the right to marry her. Gerard de Camvill similarly bought
Eustachia's marriage after her husband died to provide a wife for
his son.[66] The alliances made possible by royal lordship provided a
basis for further development in subsequent generations. The
wardship of Robert de Grelley went to his Basset uncles, who may
have been responsible for his marriage to Margaret Longchamp as
part of a half-blood alliance.[67] William Longspee purchased the
wardship of Eustachia or Idonia, daughter and heir of Richard de
Camvill, for his son William and arranged a marriage between his

[63] *Close Rolls*, 4:4, 17, 8:130. For a wardship leading to a marriage between a sister
and her brother's wife's uncle (d'Aubigny-Beauchamp), see *Patent Rolls*, 1:317–318;
ERF, 1:259–260; and C. G. Chambers and George Herbert Fowler, "The Beauchamps, Barons of Bedford," *Bedfordshire Historical Record Society* 1 (1913): 10–18.

[64] Information on the Basset family has been taken from Cokayne, *Complete Peerage*, 4:261, 11:381–382 n. k, 383, 12:2:364–365; *HKF*, 2:25, 3:38–39; *VCH, Buckinghamshire*, 3:123; *VCH, Oxfordshire*, 6:21–22, 222, 8:148; 11:94; *Rot. Dom.*, 4 n. 2,
8 n. 2.

[65] William Farrer, "The Feudal Baronage," in *VCH, Lancsashire*, 1:326–334; Cokayne, *Complete Peerage*, 9:76; *Rot. Dom.*, 4, 8, 14, 48; *Pipe Roll, 2 John*, 27; *4 John*,
127; *8 John*, 189; *Rot. Ob. et Fin.*, 349; *Rot. Lit. Claus.*, 1:313.

[66] *Rot. Dom.*, 4 n. 2, 14; *Pipe Roll, 6 Richard I*, 94 (Verdun); *7 John*, 32 (Newburgh);
Rot. Ob. et Fin., 64, 293, 348; Cokayne, *Complete Peerage*, 12:2:356–366; *EB*, 93–94.

[67] For the marriages of William and Margaret de Longchamp, brother and sister,
see E. M. Poynton, "The Fee of Creon," *Genealogist*, n.s. 18 (1902): 220; *Book of Fees*,
1:134; *Patent Rolls*, 1:65; *EB*, 47.

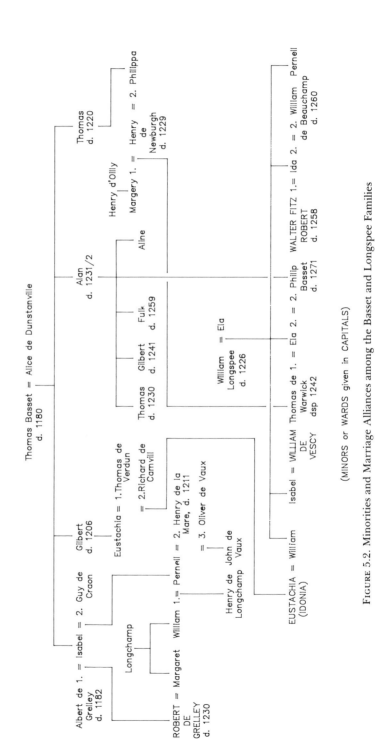

(MINORS or WARDS given in CAPITALS)

FIGURE 5.2. Minorities and Marriage Alliances among the Basset and Longspee Families

daughter Ela and the future earl of Warwick, Thomas de New-burgh. In addition, he obtained the wardship of William, son and heir of Eustace de Vescy in 1216, to provide a husband for yet another daughter, Isabel.[68] As this example demonstrates, the greatest opportunities for creating this kind of network existed within the favored circle of the king's associates who grabbed the bulk of wardships.

Wardships also furthered marital alliances among royal officials. These marriages created or reinforced an identity that bound royal administrators into a distinct group in landholding society.[69] That such an identification operated on several levels is readily apparent in the circulation of the Fitz Otto wardship. Edward I granted the wardship to his kinsman, Maurice de Craon, saving £40 worth of land for Hugh Fitz Otto, the ward's uncle and steward of the household. Within two days, Maurice regranted his right to Hugh, who in turn sold his nephew's marriage to John de Neville for £200. John intended to marry the ward, Otto, to one of his daughters, but it seems that the contract was never put into effect. Both Neville and Otto died before June 1282. Otto's lands passed to his three sisters, Joan, Matilda, and Beatrice, aged four-teen, eleven, and eight.[70] Hugh evidently retained custody of the girls, and within a year the eldest had married Guy Ferre, the Queen Mother's steward who later became a household knight.[71] Unfortunately, Joan died childless by 1285, leaving as her heir her sole surviving sister, Matilda, who was still a minor. The king therefore acquired the wardship one more time and granted it to another household knight, John de Botetorte, who married the ward himself.[72]

These knights were all connected through service in the royal household and landholding in Essex, where the Fitz Otto estate was centered. John de Neville, for instance, held land and served

---

[68] *Rot. Lit. Claus.*, 1:265, 337, 350, 364; *Rot. Lit. Pat.*, 1:178; *Patent Rolls*, 1:134, 159, 2:34; *Book of Fees*, 1:253, 254, 262, 272, 2:1065; *Close Rolls*, 10:54–55; Bliss, *Papal Letters*, 1:307, 312, 345; Cokayne, *Complete Peerage*, 11:381–382 n. k, 12:2:276.

[69] Waugh, "Reluctant Knights and Jurors," 976–979.

[70] *CPR, 1272–1281*, 93, 95, 113, 357, 449; *CCR, 1272–1279*, 391–392; PRO, DL.25/184; *CIPM*, 2:56, 430, 438; Tout, *Chapters*, 2:25–28, 34, 158; Moor, *Knights*, 3:250.

[71] *CPR, 1272–1281*, 125; *CCR, 1279–1288*, 217; Byerly and Byerly, *RWII*, 1073, 1182, 1721–1722, 1725, 1805; Parsons, *CHEC*, 32–35.

[72] *CPR, 1281–1292*, 180; Moor, *Knights*, 1:122–123; *EB*, 10–11; Byerly and Byerly, *RWH*, passim. Hugh Fitz Otto had died by 1285 (*CIPM*, 2:464).

on royal commissions in the county.[73] The witnesses to Neville's marriage contract had like connections. Robert Fitz John was Hugh's associate in the household, Peter de Chauvent had long been an influential royal knight, and Bartholomew de Brianzon was yet another household knight who held lands in Essex and was active in local administration. Two other Essex knights and commissioners, John le Breton and John Filliol, witnessed the agreement.[74] The members of this social network relied on it to sanction and enforce their agreements. It provided as well a basis for the transfer of the rights of wardship and for the formation of family alliances. Within it, Ferre and Botetorte, assisted by royal lordship, found heiresses for wives. Their marriages not only helped them to enlarge their holdings, but they also reinforced existing bonds of residence and occupation by adding a layer of family association.[75]

In this respect, it is worth looking in greater detail at a few of the marriages arranged by Eleanor of Castile early in Edward I's reign. They provide a striking demonstration of how wardship and marriage could advance the interests of both wards and guardians and cement relations between curial families. Figure 5.1 illustrates this process. Alan Basset used the wardship of Drew de Montagu, from another courtier family, to provide a husband for Aline. After Philip Basset acquired the wardship of Simon de Montagu in 1270, he granted it to yet another household figure, Amaury de St. Amando, who married the boy to his daughter.[76] The process drawing curial families together went a step further in subsequent generations in the hands of the queen, a consummate matchmaker. When Amaury's younger son, Amaury, came into royal custody in 1287, Edward granted the wardship of the lands to two household knights, Robert Fitz John and William de Montravel, but evidently gave the marriage to Eleanor. Amaury married Eleanor's relative, Marie de Pecquigny. Eleanor similarly provided a partner for Amaury's nephew, William de Montagu, through a

[73] Moor, *Knights*, 3:250–251.

[74] Byerly and Byerly, *RWH*, passim; Moor, *Knights*, 1:140, 146–147, 2:24–25.

[75] Matilda inherited a share of the barony of Bedford through her mother, Beatrice, one of the coheirs of John de Beauchamp (*EB*, 10–11). For other examples of cohesion through local marriages and service, see Ormerode, *History of Chester*, 1:58, 2:36–38, 3:290 (Orreby, Montalt, Ardern); and G. G. Astill, "Social Advancement through Seigneurial Service? The Case of Simon Pakeman," *Transactions of the Leicestershire Archaeological and Historical Society* 54 (1978–1979): 14–25.

[76] Cokayne, *Complete Peerage*, 9:76–80, 11:295–297; *CPR*, *1266–1272*, 467, 469; *Close Rolls*, 14:299–300.

convoluted transaction. In 1280 Peter de Montfort sold Eleanor the marriage of his eldest son, John, so that Eleanor could arrange a marriage for him. Simon de Montagu likewise gave Eleanor the power to arrange his son William's marriage. Eleanor married John de Montfort to her relative, Alice de la Plaunche, before 1287, and then in 1292 granted William de Montagu's marriage to John so that he could marry William to his sister Elizabeth de Montfort.[77] Eleanor's activities continued and reinforced interrelations that curial families like the Montagus, Bassets, and St. Amandos had practiced before.

By placing their lands and families in the hands of the king and queen, Montfort and Montagu demonstrated a remarkable degree of trust in royal lordship and of confidence in their judgment. Indeed, families often favored attachments to the royal family and looked with pride on such marriages.[78] Marriage into the queen's family remained an attractive proposition through the fifteenth century, when John Paston went to considerable lengths, fruitlessly, to marry one of the Wodeville relatives. His mother advised him to seek such a match in order to obtain political influence for their quest to secure title to their lands.[79]

These genealogies, moreover, emphasize the critical role played by remarriage and half blood in shaping family alliances. Since the king commanded the right of consent to a widow's marriage, individuals wrote to him seeking matches for themselves, their friends, or family. He thus added to the already considerable pressure on widows to remarry, either directly by urging them to accept a specific partner or indirectly by granting his right of consent to someone else.[80] That consent could be important in forging

[77] Cokayne, *Complete Peerage*, 9:82, 127–130, 11:297–298; Moor, *Knights*, 3:184; Parsons, *CHEC*, 48–52; Byerly and Byerly, *RWH*, passim; *EB*, 26– 27; *CPR, 1281–1292*, 169, 214, 221, 479–480, 485, 496; *CCR, 1279–1288*, 52, 380, 493. Peter promised that as soon as the marriage took place, he would enfeoff the couple of a manor and agreed not to alienate any of his lands in any way, under penalty of a 2,000 mark fine. Simon surrendered his patrimony to the king, who regranted it to Simon with remainders to William or his next heirs.

[78] Dugdale, *Monasticon*, 6:351, chronicle of the Mortimer family, referring to the marriage of Edmund Mortimer and Margaret de Fiennes.

[79] *Paston Letters and Papers of the Fifteenth Century*, ed. Norman Davis (Oxford, 1971), 1:lviii–lix, 381, 471, 504–505 (nos. 228, 282, 308).

[80] PRO, SC.1/1/211 (request); /37/146 (Edward I to widow to take a husband); *Rot. Lit. Claus.*, 1:168; *CPR, 1313–1317*, 44 (grant to John de Mortimer at request of Roger de Mortimer), 131 (to widow of Aymer de Valence's retainer at Aymer's request).

marital strategies, as in the remarriages noted earlier of Isabel, widow of Albert de Grelley and Eustachia, widow of Thomas de Verdun (Figure 5.2). Property rights help to explain the eagerness with which men sought out widows and their willingness to pay steep fines for the right of marriage, as can be seen in one example from Figure 5.1. In 1205 Pernell, daughter of Guy de Craon, heiress to the barony of Freiston, and the widow of William de Longchamp, was in a particularly advantageous position. Henry de la Mare therefore offered King John 500 marks for the right to marry her, and Oliver de Vaux made an equivalent offer for her marriage after Henry died in 1211. Oliver's investment paid off. He married her, and Pernell passed a portion of her inheritance, including the manor of Freiston, on to her youngest son, John de Vaux, the half-brother of Pernell's heir, Henry de Longchamp.[81] Royal consent, however, could be a nuisance to someone impatient to make a particular match, as is evident in Figure 5.1. Thomas de Furnivall was so eager to marry Elizabeth de Montfort, widow of William de Montagu, that he was willing to incur a fine of £200 for marrying her without royal license.[82] Marriages to widows thus brought men handsome dowers, complemented existing kinship relations, and provided starting points for future ties between families. These factors made the king's right of consent all the more important. Those who could obtain the right to the marriage, or the widow's right to marry whomever she pleased, got a head start on their competitors. The only recourse open to the latter was to marry without license and place themselves at the king's mercy. There was no hope that the king would not find out. News or rumors of marriages reached him in many ways, and he invariably took action.[83]

Of course, matrimonial strategies hinged on the consent not only of the Crown, but of widows and wards as well. In the eyes of the Church, consent was the essential criterion for a valid marriage. For families and lords, it could prove troublesome. The penalties established by the statutes of Merton and Westminster II for refusing marriages or marrying without license grew out of the individual's right of consent.[84] The issue arose because some wards rejected marriages offered by the king or guardian, while other wards and some widows simply ignored their lord and married

[81] Poynton, "The Fee of Creon," 220–225.
[82] Cokayne, *Complete Peerage*, 5:582, 8:463, 9:82 n. e.
[83] For examples, see PRO, E.159/61 m. 4d; and SC.1/45/39.
[84] Walker, "Marrying of Feudal Wards," 220–222; Plucknett, *Legislation*, 115–117.

without permission. Similarly, in some of its grants of marriage, the Crown explicitly recognized the necessity of proper consent.[85] Acceptance of an offer, therefore, was not a foregone conclusion. Although Church doctrine did not dramatically alter the pattern of arranging marriages, it did introduce an element of unpredictability into those arrangements.

The process of securing an individual's consent sometimes becomes visible. To forestall possible claims by wards that they had not been offered suitable marriages, and hence could not be fined for refusing, guardians began making offers in the Chancery or Exchequer.[86] Once Eve, the widow of William de Cantilupe, had obtained the marriage of her son William Junior in 1314, for instance, she offered, before witnesses in the Chancery, to marry him to the daughter of either John de Grey or Robert de Strenle. He refused them both, declaring that he would not have any woman for a wife.[87] His refusal, it should be noted, was a matter of personal taste. It did not imply any objection to lordship or to the fact that a choice had been made for him. Others did not object at all. When Thomas de Longvillers came before the treasurer and barons of the Exchequer in 1300 to prove his age, the king offered to marry him to one of the daughters of Adam de Creting, who were in royal custody. In contrast to Cantilupe, Thomas stated that he was willing to take any daughter that the king assigned him. The Exchequer, therefore, ordered the girls' aunt to choose one of them and send her along to the Exchequer to complete the marriage. John de Warenne proved to be equally pliant when he came before Edward I in Edward's chamber at Westminster during Parliament in 1305. Edward offered to marry him to his granddaughter, Joan of Bar, and Warenne accepted.[88] These examples demonstrate once again the bounds of consent. It gave the ward the

[85] For example, *Rot. Lit. Claus.*, 1:168; *CPR, 1232–1247*, 194.

[86] Milsom, "Legal Introduction," clvi–clvii. One ward specifically acknowledged his liability under the terms of the statute (*CCR, 1288–1296*, 36). One guardian offered a ward "quandam nobilem puellam" in marriage, but the ward asked for time to think it over, after which he offered the guardian 200 marks for his marriage and lands (PRO, KB.26/131 mm. 3d, 7d, 14).

[87] *CCR, 1313–1318*, 87; *CPR, 1307–1313*, 94. He evidently never married (Cokayne, *Complete Peerage*, 3:112).

[88] PRO, E.159/73 m. 31d. The marriage may not have taken place, for in 1301 the king sold the right of Thomas's marriage to William de Glay for £60 (*CIPM*, 3:424, 620; PRO, E.101/506/8; Moor, *Knights*, 3:119; Cokayne, *Complete Peerage*, 8:130; Charles Clay, "The Family of Longvillers," *YAJ* 42 [1967]: 50). For Warenne, see *CCR, 1302–1307*, 321.

right of refusal, not the right of choice. Complete refusal, moreover, like the younger Cantilupe's, seems to have been rare. Most wards, like Warenne and Longvillers, accepted suitable offers. Arranged marriages, whether by parents or guardians, were the norm, and the children of landholding families were raised in an environment in which it was expected that they would consent to the choices made for them. Whether they liked those choices was another matter.

Widows could be more recalcitrant. Since they were of age and had their own landed endowment, they could afford to act independently. Furthermore, after Magna Carta, the king could not coerce them into marrying. He could only fine them for disobedience, as Joan de Peyvre found. When the royal minister Paulinus de Peyvre died in 1251, Henry III sold the wardship of his heir to Paulinus's widow Joan for 500 marks. Joan then sold the wardship to another royal minister, John de Grey, so that Grey could arrange a match between the ward and his daughter. Henry granted the right to *Joan's* marriage to one of his foreign favorites, Stephen de Salinis. But Joan, upset at the prospect, married herself to John de Grey by the advice of her friends. Henry III was so furious with her that he fined her 500 marks.[89] More than forty years later, Edward I was equally infuriated when his own daughter, the earl of Gloucester's widow, married Ralph de Monthermer without permission.

Because a widow's marriage could be so valuable yet her consent so problematic, some grantees simply regarded the right as a source of profit.[90] They were not interested in marriage, only the cash it could produce. Sometimes the king simply ordered widows to pay fines for the right to marry whomever they pleased or amercements for marrying without license to royal officials, creating an indirect form of cash patronage.[91]

Others had a deeper interest in a widow's marriage and used force to get what they wanted. There were two related problems.

[89] *CPR, 1247–1258*, 104, 105; *ERF*, 2:112, 119, 167; *Annales de Dunstaplia*, 3:182–183.

[90] Walker has summed up grants of marriage as imposing on widows a "substitute lord who would sell them a license to marry or would enjoy their forfeiture if they married without license" (Walker, "Feudal Constraint and Free Consent," 104). For the marriages of two widows (Vivonia and St. John), which netted grantees 60 and 120 marks, see *CPR, 1266–1272*, 332, 404; *Close Rolls*, 14:121–122, 395.

[91] For examples, see *CPR, 1247–1258*, 95, 145, 298, 334, 395, 407, 543; *Close Rolls*, 9:376–377, 14:377.

One was rape without marriage. The second was an abduction and marriage, which deprived the lord of his right of marriage, whether over a ward or widow.[92] Tales of abduction were not frequent but were common enough to spark legislative remedies and to be a reminder that violence was never far removed from the realm of social relations in medieval England.[93] Maud de Clifford complained that John Giffard abducted her from her castle at Canford, Dorset, and took her to his castle at Brimpsfield, Gloucestershire, where he married her. As the heir of Walter de Clifford and the widow of William Longspee, she represented a wealthy prize, though she had avoided remarriage for seventeen years before Giffard acted (see Figure 1.4).[94] Impatient men struck more quickly. In 1316 Theobald de Verdun forcibly removed Elizabeth de Burgh, one of the three sisters and coheirs of Gilbert de Clare, from Bristol Castle, where Edward II had just installed her for safekeeping to await the partition of the Clare lands. He married her on the spot without Edward's permission.[95] Both Theobald and Giffard denied that the marriages had been forced. They both, however, undercut their protestations of innocence by offering the king hefty fines to amend any wrongs they may have committed against his lordship.

Another famous abduction in Edward II's reign arose out of personal disappointment and politics. Arranged marriages did not necessarily produce domestic bliss. Despite his acquiescence in a marriage with Joan of Bar in 1305, John de Warenne was seeking an annulment by the spring of 1313 when Joan would have been about seventeen years old.[96] The couple had not produced the heir that John expected and needed, but he had two sons by another woman, Maud de Nerford. John wanted to marry Maud and use their sons as his heirs, so he turned to his lord for assistance.[97] He

[92] *Glanvill*, (xiv.6), 176; Bracton, 1:417; *Statutes of the Realm*, 1:3 (Merton, cap. 6), 29, 33 (Westminster I, caps. 13, 22), 87–89 (Westminster II, caps. 34, 35).

[93] Examples of the abduction of wards can be found in *Close Rolls*, 5:500–501; and PRO, E.159/1B m. 10d.

[94] *Close Rolls*, 10:33, 14:294–295; Cokayne, *Complete Peerage*, 5:642. Henry had granted her marriage to Geoffrey de Lusignan in 1256 (*CPR, 1247–1258*, 536, 537).

[95] *Rot. Parl.*, 1:352–353; Cokayne, *Complete Peerage*, 12:2:177–178, 250–251.

[96] Fairbank, "The Last Earl of Warenne," 193–217; Cokayne, *Complete Peerage*, 12:1:511 n. i.

[97] This follows the interpretation put forth in Searle, "Seigneurial Control," 28–29. It is interesting to note that two actions seem to have been brought, one by Warenne claiming consanguinity and one by Maud claiming a precontract, or mar-

surrendered his lands to the king who granted them back with remainders to the two boys. He was frustrated, however, in his desire for a new marriage. Now, one of those who sat on the council that denied him a divorce was Thomas of Lancaster. Warenne, probably with the connivance of Edward II, vented his frustration on Lancaster by having Lancaster's wife, Alice de Lacy, abducted. She was the granddaughter of Maud de Clifford and like Maud she was seized at Canford, evidently a castle of porous defenses. One of Warenne's knights boasted that he had known Alice carnally and that she should in fact be his wife. But what must have especially galled Lancaster was that the knight claimed Alice's inheritance of the earldoms of Lincoln and Surrey, a prime component of Lancaster's wealth and prestige.[98] The enterprise, however, was futile. Warenne eventually died without the heir he wanted, as did Lancaster, while Alice married twice again.

Abduction was an extreme case of the quest for a fruitful marriage. It is important here for the light it casts on the profound significance of women's inheritance in this society. In each of these cases, it was hoped that a marriage would open the door to a rearrangement of property holding. Men intent on personal gain preyed on the vulnerability of women and pushed aside the rules of lord, Church, and social decency to get what they wanted. Warenne's abduction of Alice de Lacy was a largely symbolic insult to Lancaster, but there was a more sinister undercurrent in the possibility, however remote, that she might be married to someone else. The rivalry centered on and was enacted through women and marriage, demonstrating once again how essential they were to the maintenance of power and wealth. Yet the exceptional nature of these acts shows how widely accepted those rules were and what a sturdy framework they created for inheritance and descent.

Because those ends could be achieved more peacefully through royal lordship, it became a crucial element in personal or social strategies. It enabled individuals to advance themselves or family members through marriage, to form alliances, and to ensure the continuation of their own stock. When the chances for the birth and survival of children as well as the survival of parents to see

---

riage, with Warenne (Fairbank, "The Last Earl of Warenne," 203–206). If Maud's claim were accepted, then her children by Warenne would be his legitimate heirs. If not, and if Warenne's plea succeeded, then the children would not have been legitimized by a subsequent marriage between Warenne and Maud. In any event, all of Warenne's efforts failed.

[98] Cokayne, *Complete Peerage*, 7:392, 395–396, 687–688.

their children married were so uncertain, royal lordship assumed a critical importance. Grants of wardships helped somewhat to overcome those uncertainties and so occupied an essential place in strategies for marriage and descent. As a result, the allocation of the king's rights over wards and widows to a great extent determined the direction and complexion of social relations within landholding society. It served in some cases, moreover, to erode whatever barriers of status and identity existed between those inside or outside of court by bringing the groups together in marriage and giving them a common bond of kinship. For all of these reasons, the king's right of marriage was of the utmost importance to tenants-in-chief and to their relations with the king.

GUARDIANS' USE OF WARDSHIPS: PROFIT AND PATRONAGE

Recipients also discovered profits in royal wardships. Not every guardian used his or her rights to arrange marriages; they could be sold to someone with a greater interest in marrying the widow or ward. All guardians, moreover, valued the custody of land as a supplementary source of income and sometimes worked it themselves. Wardships helped to stock the pool of land from which families drew the temporary acquisitions they needed to protect their patrimonies. Yet, since rights of wardship were treated as movable property, guardians also sold or leased them, bequeathed them, or applied them as collateral for loans. In addition, recipients realized the value of wardships by passing them on to their followers; using royal patronage, in other words, as patronage of their own.

Those who received a wardship thus often kept the lands in custody and collected the revenues themselves. Unfortunately, little is known about the management of lands after they passed into the hands of guardians. Once they leave royal custody and the glare of public records, they disappear into the relative obscurity of private estate administrations. There are several reasons for thinking that many individuals worked the lands they held in wardship for a profit. First, only a small number are known to have been regranted. Second, it is known that in at least one instance the custodian purchased goods from the deceased's executors to stock a manor in her custody, though the custodian in this case was the queen.[99] Third, guardians often bequeathed their rights or di-

---

[99] *CCR, 1272–1279,* 67, 109.

rected their executors to use wardships for different purposes. When Edmund of Cornwall's executors, to take an exalted example, accounted for the repayment of the king's debts to him, it turned out that they still held the lands of several wards, which they had to restore to the king. Edmund and his executors had not given up custody but had instead used the wardships for income. Finally, there is miscellaneous evidence of wardships retained in the guardian's custody for several years.[100] Many guardians, for example, were from the same county or region in which the lands were located and seem to have acquired the lands with the intention of supplementing their own holdings. Edward II in 1312 sold custody of the manor of Levisham, Yorkshire, to a Master Thomas of Levisham for £100. Thomas later accounted for another £41 for the sale of oxen and sheep on the manor, though it seems likely that he purchased the stock himself. It could have been a good investment. The manor had been valued at 14 marks a year and the heir was only twenty-nine weeks old when he came into custody, so that on the basis of the escheator's estimate, if Thomas had retained possession for the full twenty years and more of the minority, he would have earned at least £190.[101]

In a few cases, the tenant-in-chief's own tenant acquired the wardship, or a consortium of local residents or tenants on the estate purchased or farmed the lands during a minority.[102] Such an arrangement could simplify the problem of managing wardships for the king or for grantees interested in taking quick profits. Gilbert de Clare received the wardship of the lands and heirs of Robert de Welle from Edward II in 1311 as partial fulfillment of Edward's promise to provide Gilbert 5,000 marks in wardships, for his service in Scotland and elsewhere. It was valued at more than £106 a year, and on 7 April 1313, Gilbert sold his rights to a group consisting of Richard le Vavassour, parson of Wytherne, Robert de Saltfleteby of Wytherne, and Peter de Scremby. Withern, Lincolnshire, was the principle holding in the Welle estate. A second group, which included Richard le Vavassour once again, purchased the wardship of the dower lands of Robert's widow directly

---

[100] *CRR*, 16:363–364 (no. 1799). In a case of waste alleged against a guardian, it was revealed that the guardian had kept the land for ten years and that it was valued at £15 a year.

[101] *CPR, 1307–1313*, 412; *CFR*, 2:151; *CIPM*, 5:266. For a similar sale of stock, see *Close Rolls*, 3:41.

[102] *CFR*, 2:162, 226.

from the king for £140 in 1315.[103] Such an arrangement suited the
needs of both Clare, whose only interest in the wardship was financial, and the local residents, who gained the opportunity to supplement their incomes.

Wardships were thus treated as chattels and changed hands in a
variety of ways that brought economic benefits to guardians.[104] A
few grantees can be found pledging their rights as security for
loans.[105] More frequently, they used them for bequests. William
Longspee, for example, married the Vescy and Camvill wards to
his own children but kept their lands in his possession until his
death. In his will, he directed his executors to use the issues of
those and other lands he held in wardship to help pay debts, religious bequests, and the expenses of his servants.[106] It is an interesting indication of baronial attitudes, showing how such rights
served a multiplicity of goals for landholders as they did for the
king. Guardians also relied on wills to transfer wardships to family
members. In spite of the fact that he was violating his own dictum
against turning sheep over to wolves, Henry III granted custody
of two of the three daughters and coheirs of Gilbert de Lesteneston to the husband of the eldest of the three, William de Saundon,
the king's cook. William bequeathed the wardship to his wife, who
bequeathed it to her son John. John then sold the marriage of at
least one of the two girls to a William de Haverberg, who married
her.[107] Of course, most wardships passed from one guardian to another through sales, leases, or grants. At least 11 percent of all of
the wardships granted out are known to have been regranted,
though this figure almost certainly underestimates the true extent
of the practice.[108]

The majority of regrants were outright sales or leases. Many of
the foreign or ecclesiastical beneficiaries of royal patronage, for
example, quickly sold off their rights. Foreigners, especially, had

---

[103] *CPR, 1307–1313*, 409–410, 560; *CFR*, 2:228; *CIPM*, 5:352, 526; *Book of Fees*,
2:1058. A similar case can be found in PRO, E.159/78 m. 40.

[104] Pollock and Maitland, *History of English Law*, 2:116–117, 148.

[105] PRO, E.368/50 m. 9; *CPR, 1232–1247*, 194.

[106] *Rot. Lit. Claus.*, 2:71; *Patent Rolls*, 2:12. For the right to bequeath wardships,
see Sheehan, *The Will*, 286–287.

[107] *ERF*, 2:231–232, 437; *CPR, 1247–1258*, 492; *CIPM*, 4:258 (Haverberg); PRO,
E.13/18 m. 69d. For another example of infrafamilial bequests, see George Wrottesley, ed., "The Chetwynd Chartulary," *William Salt Society* 12 (1891): 246–249,
251–252.

[108] I have found references to 201 regrants; 58 of the 477 (12.2 percent) baronial
wardships were regranted.

little interest in the arrangement of marriages and would have found it difficult to manage the lands themselves while they were out of the realm. Their agents in England therefore disposed of their rights as profitably as possible. Similarly, King John's confirmation in 1199 of his brother's grants of wardships to Hubert Walter assumed that the archbishop would demise them to others.[109] Given the rising demand for land during the thirteenth century, money could easily be raised by leasing lands held in wardship. After Edward I granted Imbert Guy custody of the manor of Warminster, Imbert farmed it to Bogo de Knoville for 100 marks a year for five years, at the end of which Imbert made the same arrangement with Peter de Scudmore. Imbert was a Poitevin who served as seneschal in Limousin. The lease clearly simplified his task of getting the value out of the king's patronage.[110] Henry de Percy in the early fourteenth century may have used a royal wardship to pay off a loan from Italian bankers for the purchase of Alnwick.[111]

Since wardships and marriages were much sought after, their price could increase noticeably as they changed hands. Unlike the Crown, recipients were quick to take advantage of the rising land values whenever they chose to sell their rights to wardships. The potential for inflation was noted by Jocelin of Brakelond and realized by a number of guardians.[112] A year after Philip Burnell, the baron of Castle Holgate, died in 1294, for example, Edward I granted the marriage of Philip's son to William de Valence, who arranged to grant it to Hugh Despenser. Yet Valence died before the transfer took place, and the marriage fell to Valence's executors who sold it to Antony Bek, the bishop of Durham, for 500 marks. Bek held on to the marriage for another six years before he finally sold it to Despenser for 1,000 marks, so that Hugh could marry the heir to his eldest daughter.[113] Not only had Despenser's

---

[109] Rot. Chart., 24. See also the grant of a wardship to Amadeus of Savoy and his resale to the parson of one of the manors (CPR, 1281–1292, 24, 113).

[110] CPR, 1272–1281, 253; CCR, 1302–1307, 123–124; PRO, E.159/51 m. 16; /157 mm. 12, 13; Trabut-Cussac, L'administration anglaise en Gascogne, 181, 382. A number of leases are recorded in the memoranda rolls (e.g., E.159/51 m. 16d; /52 m. 10d; /54 m. 6d).

[111] Bean, "The Percies' Acquisition of Alnwick," 309–319; CPR, 1307–1313, 388, 408, 410; CCR, 1313–1318, 13, 22; CFR, 2:106.

[112] Jocelin of Brakelond, 123. For an example of the rise in value of a private wardship from 40 to 200 marks over two generations, see Dugdale, Monasticon, 5:437.

[113] EB, 28–29; CPR, 1292–1301, 167, 179; CCR, 1288–1296, 517; Catalogue of Ancient Deeds, 4:19, A.6278.

satisfaction been delayed, but his costs had risen. As this example illustrates, it was not unusual, though not common, for wardships to change hands several times. Henry III granted the wardship of the lands and heirs of Stephen de Hampton to Nicholas de Yattingdon, a yeoman of Prince Edward, in 1252. Nicholas granted it to Philip Basset, who granted it to Katherine Lovel, who granted it to Walter de la Poile, who eventually married Stephen's heiress.[114] It is clear that once a wardship left the hands of the initial recipient, it circulated more freely. It is possible in those cases to speak of a market in wardships and marriages in which the price was set by demand. Guardians took advantage of that market, selling or leasing their rights for a clear profit to friends, speculators, or local residents.

Guardians, however, were enmeshed in the same kinds of reciprocal obligations that bound them to the king, so that they had to pass some wardships on to their clients as patronage. Courtiers or ministers in many cases approached the king initially on behalf of someone else who had come to them seeking a wardship or widow's marriage. The king made many grants at the behest of those close to him. He gave wardships to men as diverse as the king of Scotland's merchant, William de Valence's steward, the earl of Norfolk's butler, Joan de Valence's yeoman, or a member of the household of the duke of Brittany.[115] The acquisition of a royal wardship for someone else was one way in which a lord could reciprocate his follower's loyalty and service and advertise his own influence.[116] The same pressures induced guardians to turn wardships over to their men. After Henry III granted his half-brother, Guy de Lusignan, the wardship of the lands and heirs of John le Chamberlain along with the marriage of John's widow in 1256, Guy granted the lands and widow's marriage to his valet, William de Berne, and the heir's marriage to his clerk, Fulcard de Outon. Berne sold his rights for £40.[117] The followers of Prince Edward and Edmund of Lancaster likewise benefited from Henry's grants to their lords.[118] In contrast to wardships that were sold or leased,

---

[114] PRO, E.210/3260; *CIPM*, 1:229, 670; *CPR, 1247–1258*, 134; *Close Rolls*, 7:95.

[115] *CPR, 1247–1258*, 123, 493, 633; *CPR, 1258–1266*, 626; *CIPM*, 3:202.

[116] For examples, see Waugh, "For King, Country, and Patron," 38–39; and idem, "Reluctant Knights and Jurors," 974–979.

[117] *CIPM*, 1:364; *CPR, 1247–1258*, 474, 486, 494; *Close Rolls*, 9:441.

[118] *CPR, 1258–1266*, 156, 238, 265; Cokayne, *Complete Peerage*, 12:1:172; Farrer, "Feudal Baronage," *VCH, Lancashire*, 1:332.

these wardships circulated by favor within a restricted network of social contacts.

Some wardships never left the orbit of the court, but instead passed from one courtier or minister to another. In the decade between 1307 and 1317, for example, Edward II granted the elder Despenser at least twenty-nine wardships of one kind or another. Edward made the majority of these grants to pay off debts of more than £6,700 that had accumulated over the early years of Edward's reign, including £2,544 that Edward's father had owed Hugh for his expenses in Edward I's wars.[119] Hugh's interest in these wardships, therefore, was largely financial, and he sold off at least thirteen of them. Five of those went to ministers in and around the royal household, such as Sandall or Ayrmynne, and one went to Hugh's associate, Ingram de Berenger, who also served as a sheriff and royal commissioner.[120] When Edward I's second queen, Margaret, obtained a large number of wardships at the end of Edward's reign to help pay her debts and expenses, she likewise found a large number of purchasers conveniently located in the household and central administration. Ministers like John de Droxford and Walter de Langeton took advantage of the opportunity to acquire wardships.[121] As might be expected, even the resale of wardships for profit was sometimes bound up with considerations of association and influence that channeled the distribution of those rights in certain directions.

Because the recipients of royal favor often had no particular connection with the ward's family, friends, or community, they were usually willing to grant the custody of lands and heirs back to those who had a more direct interest in them. In this way, royal ministers and family members mediated royal lordship, and acted as a conduit for the transmission of the king's feudal rights from the center back into local communities. In many cases, those most eager to obtain wardships—widows, relatives, friends, or neighbors—did not deal directly with the king or royal institutions, but rather with royal favorites. Those favored by the king were willing to pass their benefits along to others, especially since some, like the elder Despenser, acquired so many.[122]

Widows and kin especially benefited from this secondary distri-

---

[119] For the debts, see *CPR, 1307–1313*, 74, 76, 78, 79, 509, 512; *CPR, 1313–1317*, 7; *CPR, 1317–1321*, 123–124; *CCR, 1307–1313*, 301–302, 534.

[120] *CPR, 1307–1313*, 94–95, 114, 180, 306; *CCR, 1313–1318*, 324.

[121] *CPR, 1301–1307*, 97, 100, 114, 120, 121, 235, 236, 265, 319, 321, 439, 464.

[122] See, for example, Astill, "Pakeman," 18.

bution of feudal rights. Despenser, for instance, sold two wardships to the mothers of the heirs.[123] On the death of Ralph Fitz Nicholas in 1266, Henry III granted the wardship and marriage of his son and heir Nicholas Fitz Ralph to Frederick de Frisco, the count of Lavagna and brother of the papal legate, Ottobuoni. Frederick clearly had no personal interest in the ward, so that a month later he capitalized on the gift by selling the wardship to Ralph's widow, Matilda, for 1,000 marks. Matilda evidently turned custody of the boy over to his uncle, Nicholas Fitz Nicholas, who in turn sold it to William Bluet for 300 marks. Since William married the ward to his daughter, the payment should be regarded as a dowry, arranged by William and Nicholas, rather than as an outright sale.[124] The kin had to pay dearly for the right of marriage. Yet it enabled them to retain control over the ward and to formulate an alliance with another knightly family holding lands in the same region. In cases in which an heir was already betrothed, the guardian, like the king, might give the ward's lands to his or her in-laws, as Robert Walerand did after Henry III gave him the wardship and marriage of Margaret, the ten-year-old daughter and heir of John de Gatesdene in 1262. Margaret was betrothed to John de Camoys, and Walerand regranted the wardship to John's father.[125] Guardians similarly sold the right of wardship to fathers, cousins, and, on occasion, to the ward himself.[126]

Wards and their relatives were eager to buy the right of wardship in order to protect their property from royal grantees whose only interest in the wardship was financial. Just before he died in 1272, Henry III, for instance, granted the wardship and marriage of William, son and heir of William de Say, to a merchant, Poncius de Mora, to help repay Henry's debts to Poncius. Since the heir was nineteen at the time and the custody would be short, there may have been some danger that Poncius would try to recoup his debts by wasting the property. In any case, William purchased his own wardship for 400 marks, and John de Warenne, the earl of

[123] *CPR, 1307–1313*, 94.
[124] *CPR, 1258–1266*, 624, 635, 676; Powicke, *Henry III*, 285 and n. 3; Moor, *Knights*, 1:100–101, 2:53.
[125] *CIPM*, 1:706; *CPR, 1266–1272*, 734; Meekings, introduction to *The 1235 Surrey Eyre*, 197; *HKF*, 3:340.
[126] Father: *CPR, 1258–1266*, 267, 275; *EB*, 45. Cousin: *Patent Rolls*, 2:428; *CChR*, 1:192. Ward: *CPR, 1258–1266*, 495; Altschul, *A Baronial Family*, 146; *CPR, 1266–1272*, 315; *CPR, 1301–1307*, 244; *CCR, 1302–1307*, 377. Half-brother: *CPR, 1292–1301*, 55; *EB*, 101, 117.

Surrey, along with Luke de Poinnings and Richard le Waleys carried out the transaction on William's behalf.[127] It is important to remember, however, that kin did not necessarily know what was best for heirs. Nor did relatives always work together harmoniously. After Prince Edward obtained the wardship of the heirs of the earl of Aumale in 1260, he sold his rights for 3,000 marks to their mother and grandmother, Isabel and Amice, to hold jointly, but the two women did not get along, and the wardship had to be partitioned by royal officials. Amice apparently obtained custody of the eventual heiress, Aveline de Forz, for she sold the girl's marriage to Edmund of Lancaster in 1269 for £1,000, thereby recovering her half of the price of the wardship, and Edmund married the girl.[128]

Mesne lords occasionally benefited from regrants. On the death of James Russell, Edward I granted the wardship and marriage of his heir to Queen Eleanor. Afterward, Eleanor sold the custody of one of the Russell manors in Gloucestershire to the lord of the manor, the bishop of Winchester, for £72.[129] Hugh Despenser, Sr., likewise granted one of the wardships he received from Edward II back to the lord of some of the ward's lands.[130] Yet, as in the case of grants directly from the king, regrants to lords were much less common than those to family.

Many of those who purchased wardships from guardians did so in order to provide marriages for members of their own family. They arranged matches that reinforced the cohesion of local society. Ralph Fitz Nicholas, a steward of the household, was one of those ministers upon whom Henry III showered wealth, receiving over the period of two decades at least eleven wardships and marriages. In 1231 Ralph purchased the wardship and marriage of William, son and heir of Robert de Esseby, for 200 marks. Both families held land in the region of Great Ashby, Northamptonshire, and while it is not known what Ralph actually did with the wardship, it is known that William married Alice, the daughter of William de Camvill, another Northamptonshire landholder.[131] On William's death in 1248, Henry III once again sold Ralph the

---

[127] *CPR, 1266–1272*, 623; *CCR, 1272–1279*, 31; PRO, E.368/46 m. 13; *EB*, 98.
[128] *CPR, 1258–1266*, 97, 161; *CPR, 1266–1272*, 260, 275–276, 281–282, 296, 358; *Close Rolls*, 11:195–196; *EB*, 25, 142–143. The two male heirs died in custody, leaving their sister as sole heir.
[129] *CPR, 1272–1281*, 424; *CCR, 1288–1296*, 24.
[130] *CPR, 1307–1313*, 306; *CIPM*, 5:139; Moor, *Knights*, 1:103–104, 191.
[131] *ERF*, 1:216; *HKF*, 1:169.

wardship and marriage of the minor son and heir, in this case Robert. And as before, Ralph regranted his rights to a Northamptonshire man, this time to Thomas de Estley, who held fees of the same lords as the Esseby family in Crick, Clay Coton, and Lilbourne. Thomas married Robert to his daughter and then sold Robert and his mother the custody of the Esseby lands for 80 marks. It was a typical alliance, providing for the union of two neighboring families, only in this case achieved through the mediation of royal lordship and a royal minister who shared the territorial interests of the two families. Unfortunately, Robert died before coming of age, and the Esseby lands again came into royal custody. After he discovered that Robert's heir was his brother William, Henry III turned custody of the lands and heir back to Estley, who arranged a marriage for the ward with a daughter of Thomas de Elinton.[132] While it is true that Ralph's loyalty and service were directed toward the royal household and administration, it is equally true that his interests and outlook as a landholder were still bound up in county society. His use of wardships bridged the two worlds and brought them closer together. In this way the disposal of wardships and marriages by the recipients of royal favor could work to the advantage of local society.

Viewed solely at the first level of royal grants, the distribution of wardships, marriages, and rights to widows appears to have favored exclusively a small group of administrators and favorites surrounding the king and to have had little regard for the good of landholding society at large. The secondary distribution of feudal rights and the uses to which recipients put those rights proves that the appearance is misleading. Royal wardships were essential to associations, alliances, and cooperation among landholding families. They benefited a wide range of individuals beyond those who occupied the center of power. Guardians, moreover, largely exercised their rights in ways that were consistent with the aspirations and outlook of landholding society. That conformity to social norms meant that royal lordship was less threatening to families in practice than it might have appeared in theory.

Indeed, royal lordship may have subtly influenced the direction

---

[132] *ERF*, 2:39; *CPR, 1247–1258*, 25; *Close Rolls*, 12:201–202; *CIPM*, 1:123, 532; *Book of Fees*, 2:932, 939, 944; PRO, E.368/21 m. 2. On the second occasion, Ralph paid £100 for the Esseby wardship. For another example in Essex involving the Basset, Rivers, and Tany families, see *ERF*, 1:407; *CIPM*, 1:764, 818; *Close Rolls*, 5:51–52; *CChR*, 1:440; *CRR*, 15:435–436 (no. 1717); PRO, CP.25(1)/282/7/120; *EB*, 5; Moor, *Knights*, 5:8–9.

of kinship alliances. Those alliances were not predetermined; parents could usually choose spouses for their children from a variety of acceptable partners who could meet their territorial and dynastic aims. As the examples given above illustrate, blood or affinal relations, status, and landholding powerfully influenced their selection. The factor least visible now is personal taste. Only rarely do personal attitudes, like William de Cantilupe's dislike of marriage or Warenne's vengeance, burst from public records. Those few indications, however, along with the Paston letters at a later date, show that it could be decisive. Families, therefore, chose from an array of marital possibilities in which some matches were more desirable than others but none was preordained. As a result, the configuration of associations or alliances in which families were involved shifted according to the selections that they made. By offering certain opportunities for marriage, royal lordship influenced choice and hence the patterns of association.

The fact that royal wards were alone in the custody of a substitute lord may have made it easier to achieve a specific match. While it is true that the king expected that marriages would be made with the advice of relatives and friends, that advice may have been much less complicated than the negotiations and bargaining that parents usually undertook in arranging marriage contracts for their children.[133] The fortuity of wardship on the one hand allowed some individuals like Roger de Mortimer in the early fourteenth century to carry out marriages that dovetailed with strategies that were already in place and on the other opened new alternatives to someone like William Longspee a century earlier. It permitted others to gain an inheritance and the possibility of establishing a wealthy dynasty. It thus occupied a significant place in the strategies that landholders of the elite class employed to maintain their wealth and to provide for their families.

Two other conclusions can be drawn from this material. It shows in the first place that the king sometimes exercised his lordship to the benefit of tenants-in-chief by protecting their marriage arrangements, granting them the wardships they requested, and watching over widows and wards. These actions were congruent with the respect that the king generally displayed toward the status of baronial and comital wards. The fact that so many of these landholders served the king in government, moreover, may have made it easier for him to reconcile the family interests of the elite with

[133] Palmer, "Contexts of Marriage," 42–67.

his desire to use wardships to reciprocate his servants' loyalty and service.

Therefore, grants of wardships and the way that guardians employed them show, second, that during this period there was no appreciable gulf between court and country. The king drew many of his counselors, ministers, and captains from the higher ranks of landholding society, perpetuating the partnership that had begun at the Conquest. There was no significant difference in social attitudes between those who served the king in influential positions and landholders of knightly status or higher. Indeed, men like Ralph Fitz Nicholas or families like the Bassets, Montagus, or St. Amandos lived in the worlds of both administration and regional society and used their position and influence to the benefit of their associates and neighbors. At most times, landholders like Peter de Montfort did not hesitate to seek royal assistance in arranging marriages for their children. It is of course true that administrators often allied themselves with their colleagues through marriage, landholding, and gifts, much as landholders in a particular region like the Welsh Marches intermarried. Those alliances, however, did not preclude wider attachments or an identification with the interests of tenants-in-chief as a whole. The exercise of royal lordship provided a common ground on which the interests of the king, his favorites, and his important tenants came together. It shows in a very real way how cooperation among those elements functioned.

· 6 ·

INCENTIVE AND DISCIPLINE:
THE POLITICS OF ROYAL LORDSHIP

Although royal lordship usually served the needs of tenants-in-chief, it could nonetheless be abused, posing a threat to their lands and families. The king might authorize unacceptable marriages for wards, guardians could deplete the resources of estates, while an unequal distribution of the king's feudal rights could fracture the elite into competing factions. Furthermore, various aspects of royal lordship, like prerogative wardship and primer seisin, proved to be irritating. The problem confronting the nobility was how to minimize the dangers or annoyances of royal lordship while maintaining its advantages. In the coronation charter of Henry I and Magna Carta, the king "freely" limited his authority by making explicit declarations about the scope of feudal lordship. After Magna Carta, however, baronial opposition largely ceased to demand substantive changes in royal lordship as a means of achieving these goals and instead sought to gain control over the administrative apparatus through which the king exercised his lordship. The change in tactics occurred in response to the institutionalization of royal lordship from the early thirteenth century onward. In this respect, political opposition to the king's feudal rights was part of wider movements to curtail royal activities that threatened baronial interests. Efforts to reform the royal administration were never ends in themselves born of a reforming zeal. They were means to an end, for the barons had learned that the power of the king effectively lay in his institutions and that by controlling those instruments of power, they could prevent the kinds of abuses that had aroused their opposition.

RESISTANCE AND EVASION

It is remarkable that in ordinary circumstances, royal lordship did not provoke the same degree of protest as the king's financial exactions, even though in respect to inheritance and landholding tenants-in-chief were almost as closely supervised as villeins. Between 1200 and 1327 the elite displayed an extraordinary sensitivity toward royal finances. At one time or another with more or less

232

energy they protested shrieval increments, taxes, unpaid military service, and purveyances. They systematically reduced their military obligations to the Crown. They denounced royal patronage that appeared to them wasteful. The barons in 1297 summed up their grievances by declaring that the Crown's demands not only impoverished them but that they also threatened to reduce them to the position of villeins because they were levied at the lord's will. Aside from finances, they protested other intrusions like the quo warranto campaign or governmental interference in the county communities. In comparison, their response to royal lordship was mild.[1] It is indeed striking that on the only occasion on which the danger of being reduced to bondage was voiced politically the barons couched it in terms of finance rather than lordship. Nevertheless, it is clear that tenants-in-chief were uneasy about the power that their lord wielded over them and that they sometimes took informal measures to evade or resist his authority.

Royal lordship produced certain costs to families and mesne lords. It always involved some direct payments: relief, the widow's fine, the expense of getting to the king to perform homage, and so forth. The heir suffered a loss of revenues while the king exercised his right of primer seisin. The loss was all the more annoying when the tenant did not hold in chief of the king. Tenants-in-chief also had to pay for the king's consent to alienations, which was less expensive than the temporary loss of lands and payment of a fine that they suffered if they acted without a license. Minorities could also be costly. The greatest danger lay in waste by royal officials or guardians. The government was aware of the potential for abuse. It ordered escheators to ensure that manorial officials properly maintained the lands and cautioned escheators to exercise care in tallaging unfree tenants or in using woodland and other resources.[2] The countess of Warwick was likewise aware of such dangers and asked Edward II after the death of her husband in 1315 to give her livery of the lands of her inheritance quickly in order to avoid destruction by the escheators.[3] Allegations of waste arose sporadically throughout the thirteenth century.[4] The hundred inquests provide the most comprehensive survey of the problem.

---

[1] Bean, *Decline*, 7, notes the lack of political protest over royal lordship.
[2] BL, Add. MS 32,085, fols. 145v–150.
[3] *CChW*, 420.
[4] Walker, "The Action of Waste," 185–206. For examples, see *Rot. Parl.*, 1:35–36, 79; *Rot. Orig.*, 1:131, 189, 202; *CIM*, 1:436; *CPR, 1292–1301*, 55; *CPR, 1301–1307*, 158, 545; *CCR, 1307–1313*, 4.

They show that it was widespread, at least in the early years of Edward I's reign when royal supervision was lax. Most accusations involved woodland and only small sums, though a few amounted to £10 or more.[5] Waste by guardians or officials, however, was probably no more frequent or costly than that committed by widows or other family members who had possession of lands.[6] Furthermore a wardship usually precluded the possibility of using the income of the estate to pay the deceased's debts. Upon coming of age, therefore, an heir faced the responsibility of paying any outstanding debts to the Crown, performing homage, and replacing any stock that had been sold from the estate. Finally, the king's prerogative right to the custody of all of a ward's lands, along with the right of marriage, seriously diluted the power of mesne lords and deprived them of valuable wardships.

Personal costs are almost impossible to calculate. Being shuffled from mother to escheator to court to guardian to marriage must have caused some resentment, though it is all but undetectable in the official sources. Gross abuses, however, were rare. Individuals and families do not seem to have suffered significant losses during a minority. Widows usually secured their dowers without great difficulty. Heirs, who would not have expected to enjoy the estate while the tenant-in-chief was alive even if they were of age, were usually well cared for, whether at court, in the household of their guardians or in-laws, or by their mothers. Since siblings stood a chance to inherit, they, too, were probably well provided for, though even less is known about their fate. For the most part, arranged marriages were acceptable and sometimes highly beneficial to wards. Most important, the king distributed the benefits of his wardships and marriages to other members of the elite through sales, leases, and gifts. Thus, there were strong reasons for tenants-in-chief to accept the structure of royal lordship.

Nevertheless, tenants-in-chief were understandably troubled about the potential effects of royal lordship on their lands, families, and lordships. They manifested their anxiety in various ways. Some tried to arrange for the wardship and marriage of their lands and heirs during their lifetimes. They sometimes sold the marriages of their children or turned custody of their lands over to a guardian before embarking on a pilgrimage, for instance.[7] But

---

[5] *RH*, 1:17, 58, 116, 131, 155, 159, 162, 164, 172.

[6] See *Rot. Parl.*, 1:309, for a complaint of waste by a father against his son.

[7] *CPR, 1247–1258*, 592–593, cited by Bean, *Decline*, 108; *CRR*, 16:1798. For

if a tenant-in-chief wanted to nominate guardians who would assume their role *after* he died, then he would have to secure a royal license. Such concessions, however, were rare and were usually made in connection with overseas military campaigns or diplomatic missions.[8] In 1253–1254, for example, Henry III granted the right to four men—Amanieu le Bret, Matthew Bezill, Nicholas de Molis, and Peter of Savoy—who served with Henry on his campaign in Gascony that year. Henry had encountered resistance to the enterprise, and the grants may have been made, along with other concessions, to solidify support.[9] Edward I similarly promised some of those serving in the Gascon campaign in 1294 that their executors would have custody of their lands in the event that they died in the king's service.[10] The grants made it clear that these were special favors, which would only go into effect if the individual died leaving a minor heir. In 1235 John Fitz Philip traveled overseas as a royal envoy. Before he left, Henry III promised him that if John died overseas then, first, John's wife would have the wardship and marriage of his heirs and, second, that his brother would have two wardships that Henry had already granted to John. John returned safely, but then died a few years later leaving a minor heir, whose lands and marriage Henry granted to Lady Gwillelma of the queen's chamber for the use of her daughter.[11] Henry did not consider himself bound by his earlier promise. Obviously, the king seldom conceded the power to dispose of the wardship of one's own heirs because it undermined his feudal authority and deprived him of its benefits.

Some tenants-in-chief took matters into their own hands and evaded or resisted royal lordship. It has already been noted, for

---

other examples, see Scott L. Waugh, "From Tenure to Contract: Lordship and Clientage in Thirteenth-Century England," *EHR* 101 (1986): 824–826.

[8] Bean, *Decline*, 26–28; Walker, "Royal Wardship," 203–204.

[9] *CPR, 1247–1258*, 184, 216, 220, 333. All four were present with Henry in Gascony and witnessed his charters (*CPR, 1247–1258*, 241–360, passim). For the politics surrounding the campaign, see Waugh, "Reluctant Knights and Jurors," 945–947. On 4 August 1270, Henry promised William de Valence that his executors or assignees could have the wardship of his heirs, the day before Valence obtained protection to go on Crusade with Prince Edward (*CPR, 1266–1272*, 451; Bruce Beebe, "The English Baronage and the Crusade of 1270," *BIHR* 48 [1975]: 127–148; PRO, E.40/15190). Henry made three other grants, though there were no obvious overseas missions involved (*CPR, 1232–1247*, 487; *CPR, 1258–1266*, 190–191; *CPR, 1266–1272*, 19–20).

[10] Walker, "Royal Wardship," 203–204.

[11] *CPR, 1232–1247*, 120, 121, 423; *ERF*, 1:317, 408; Eyton, *Antiquities*, 5:165–166.

example, that widows occasionally refused to surrender their children to royal officials. Otherwise, evasion basically took three forms. The first was enfeoffment. It was clear that by the mid–thirteenth century, some tenants granted lands during their lifetime in such a way that their lands and heirs would not fall under wardship. As a result, the king and barons in 1267 in the Statute of Marlborough, cap. 6, promulgated measures to protect the lord's rights if it could be proved that a tenant had made a collusive enfeoffment designed to deprive the lord of his rights. The legislation, however, was probably not intended primarily for the king and tenants-in-chief, because the king's rights were theoretically protected by his control over alienations, a control that mesne lords had by that time lost.[12] When tenants-in-chief made collusive enfeoffments, the Crown treated them in the context of unauthorized alienations, not as breaches of the Statute of Marlborough. On the death of John de Derwentwater the Elder in 1317, for example, the king took custody of his lands because John's brother and heir, John Junior, though married, was a minor. John Junior, however, complained that prior to his death, the elder John had granted one manor that he held in chief to a Richard le Brun, who had then jointly enfeoffed the younger John and his wife, that he had granted another manor held in chief to John Junior who then granted it back to his older brother with reversion to himself on John Senior's death, and that John Junior had received a third manor, held of another lord, directly from his brother.[13] Edward II pardoned the younger John's trespass of entering lands held in chief without royal license for a fine of 100s. The motives behind these particular transactions are not clear, but they certainly gave the younger John possession of the lands even though he was a minor. Yet settlements involving minors were rare. The growing number of joint enfeoffments and settlements should not be seen as collusive grants intended primarily to deprive the king of his rights of wardship. Family considerations were probably more compelling.

A second form of evasion was concealment: lying either about the true heir or the heir's age.[14] When Ralph de Grenham died in

---

[12] Bean, *Decline*, 21–25.

[13] *CFR*, 2:327, 338; *CIPM*, 6:81, 441; *CCR, 1313–1318*, 494. For a similar case, see *CIPM*, 4:325; and *CCR, 1302–1307*, 282–283.

[14] *Britton* noted that the government was aware of the possibility of fraud in taking proofs of age and took measures to protect itself (*Britton*, 2:21). For an example

1316, his son and heir Thomas was eighteen years old, and because the Grenhams held some of their lands of the family of Lestrange of Knockin, whose heir was then in custody, Thomas ought to have come into royal wardship.[15] Yet Thomas entered his inheritance illegally. The documents do not make it clear how he was able to do so, but it appears that the escheator failed to take custody of the lands. According to one inquest, Ralph's widow, Joan, sold her son's marriage to Roger de Northborough, the bishop of Coventry and Lichfield and keeper of the wardrobe, who arranged a marriage for the boy. The error was discovered, and on 19 July 1325, Thomas appeared before the council, where he was accused of entering the manor before coming of age and marrying without license. He confessed and was fined 200 marks.[16] Thomas did not let it go at that. With the change of regimes in 1327, he tried to have the fine reduced. He petitioned the new royal council for a remission of the fine, claiming, initially, that Lestrange had never been seised of his ancestors' homage. An inquest proved that false. He tried again, reciting a tale of woe. He argued this time that he had indeed entered under age and had held the lands peacefully until William de Cliff and Hascolf de Wytewell maliciously informed the younger Despenser and Robert Baldock of the wrong. They then ejected him, his mother, his wife, his children, and his brothers and sisters from the house and lands and refused him entry until he paid the fine of 200 marks. His appeal played on the widespread hatred of Despenser and his notorious use of henchmen like Cliff and Baldock to rob widows and children of their lands.[17] The issue went to Parliament, and on 10 October 1327, Edward III, at the request of Northborough, pardoned 100 marks of the fine in consideration of the fact that the lands were worth only £9 15s. 1 1/2d. a year and that his wardship would have lasted only three years.[18] The case exemplifies the kind of tension that could exist between lord and tenant. It shows the lengths to which some tenants would go to avoid the consequences of royal lordship, while Edward II's disproportionate fine demonstrates his determination to discipline resistance and to preserve his feudal authority. Cases like it seem to have been rare, though by the very

---

of deception concerning the true heir, see Fraser, "Four Cumberland Widows," 130–132.
[15] *CIPM*, 5:264, 6:388; *CCR, 1307–1313*, 305.
[16] *CIPM*, 6:388; *CCR, 1323–1327*, 400, 502; *CFR*, 3:369.
[17] N. Fryde, *Tyranny*, 106–118.
[18] *CIPM*, 6:388; *CFR*, 4:66.

nature of the evasion it would be impossible to see successful examples in the royal records.[19]

A final form of evasion was simple disobedience: refusing to comply with the regulations of lordship. The most common acts of disobedience were marrying without license, whether by wards or widows; alienating lands without license; entering an inheritance without permission; and refusing to pay relief. Marrying without license did not necessarily mean a dislike of lordship; it arose more often out of an anxiety that an individual would not obtain the right to marry a particular ward or widow. Before Gilbert le Franceys died in 1278, he had consented to a marriage between his son Richard, a minor, and a daughter of Michael de Harclay. The couple was betrothed but not married when Gilbert died. Michael, perhaps fearing that the king would make some other arrangement for the minor heir, had the couple married without royal permission. The king therefore seized Michael's lands and fined him £300, though he later pardoned half.[20] Eager suitors also abducted desirable wards and widows before the king could grant their marriage to someone else.[21] There was a sense, therefore, that royal wardship did not always work to the advantage of particular individuals. Contemporaries understood that access to the king and the channels of patronage and association radiating outward from the court regulated the distribution of marriages. If one did not stand in favor or could not tap those channels, then it was unlikely that he would be able to secure the marriage he wanted. In some circumstances, it could be better to marry and risk the disciplinary action of the Crown than to wait for a royal favor. As a result, a small number of wards and a significant number of widows married without license over the period as a whole. The difference can be attributed to the fact that widows were of age and much more independent than unmarried wards, who were frequently small children.[22]

The Articles of the Escheators and the escheators' accounts show that there was a constant temptation to enter fees or alienate lands held in chief without first securing a royal license. In doing so, tenants-in-chief risked fines and temporary forfeitures.[23] Some

---

[19] In 1244 Henry III ordered an inquest into concealed escheats and marriages, among other things, but no returns have survived (*Book of Fees*, 2:1142).

[20] *CIPM*, 2:246; *CFR*, 1:97; *CCR, 1272–1279*, 461.

[21] Cokayne, *Complete Peerage*, 5:642 n. c, 9:408.

[22] Walker, "Feudal Constraint and Free Consent," 105–107.

[23] According to the figures compiled by Bean, *Decline*, 72, most felt that it was

also tried to avoid relief. The precise number is not known, but it can be seen from the proceedings in Exchequer that many heirs had to be attached and brought before the barons to answer for their reliefs. Payment was not always automatic, and some apparently hoped to avoid the levy altogether.

Mesne lords acted similarly to protect their feudal lordship from the effects of prerogative wardship. They tried, for instance, to prevent tenants from marrying someone who held in chief of the king or from alienating lands to tenants-in-chief.[24] And they vigorously demanded the custody of lands held of them, guaranteed to them by Magna Carta, when it was discovered that tenants-in-chief held *ut de honore* or by escheat. They, too, were vigilant landlords and wanted to preserve their rights. That desire impelled some to overstep the law. They occupied lands when their tenants died and refused to allow the escheators to take custody even though the king had a right to the wardship.[25] The problem was particularly acute between 1272 and 1274 before Edward I returned from the Crusade. Along with the hundred inquests, Edward ordered special inquisitions into magnates who withheld lands that should have been in royal custody. Both investigations uncovered numerous examples of mesne lords, as well as strangers, who took the opportunity presented by the king's absence to seize lands for themselves.[26] Occasionally, escheator's work could be hazardous, even lethal.[27] One woman erected palisades, defended by followers armed with bows, arrows, and other weapons in order to deny the escheator and sheriff entry into a manor that the king claimed because the lord of the manor was a ward in royal custody.[28] She was convicted, fined, and sent to prison. Prerogative wardship was clearly the most despised aspect of the king's feudal rights. Whatever feudal logic lay at its roots was no longer appar-

---

cheaper to pay for a license than to undergo disciplinary action. For a good example of alienating and entering without license, see Cokayne, *Complete Peerage*, 5:466–467.

[24] Waugh, "Non-Alienation Clauses," 1–14. An explicit statement of a mesne lord's fear of prerogative wardship and his consequent effort to bar an alienation can be seen in PRO, Just.1/1182 m. 7 (*Wake* vs. *Montagu*).

[25] For examples, see *CIPM*, 1:606; and *Close Rolls*, 5:473.

[26] PRO, C.47/1/18, no. 15; *CIPM*, 2:98; *RH*, passim. For the first inquest, see above, Chapter 3, n. 108. The escheators' accounts also provide evidence, though biased, of the problem (PRO, E.136/1/2, 3; E.372/120 mm. 21, 21d; /124 mm. 19, 19d, 20d–21d, 24, 24d, 25).

[27] *CPR, 1301–1307*, 85, escheator's assistants killed performing duties.

[28] PRO, E.13/27 m. 29d.

ent by the thirteenth century, and mesne lords, eager to profit as much as they could from their own feudal lordship, resented the Crown's intrusion. Their resentment surfaced in formal complaints about prerogative wardship in 1258, 1300, and 1327, and regularly manifested itself in private complaints and resistance.

Evasion, disobedience, and the occupation of lands can all be considered acts of political resistance by tenants against their landlord. Like peasant actions against manorial lords, they were sporadic and uncoordinated. Yet they indicate that just beneath the surface of seigniorial relations at the top of English society there simmered an uneasiness about the king's power to interfere in the affairs of his tenants, whether as family men or landlords. For all of the cooperation that those relations engendered, there also existed within them the potential for conflict.

POLITICAL OPPOSITION TO ROYAL LORDSHIP

Royal lordship figured prominently in English politics throughout the thirteenth and early fourteenth centuries, but by itself was seldom the cause of political opposition. Feudal relations oscillated between the poles of discipline and incentive, each of which posed political dangers. At one end, an insensitive enforcement of seigniorial rights would provoke rebellion. Under King John, discipline thus tipped over into tyranny. His exercise of lordship so endangered the lands and families of his tenants that individual grievances coalesced into common opposition. Baronial anger was all the greater because John acted arbitrarily as a lord while his tenants were forced to conduct their seigniorial relations according to legal rules. After that, even though the Crown strengthened its supervisory and disciplinary powers through institutionalization, royal lordship did not spark rebellion. It did, however, become a critical element in quarrels about patronage and finance.

At the opposite pole there lay the dangers that the king would either slight those who expected to share in royal patronage or give too much to too few. Feudal power could be tempered by feudal patronage, but the very incentives that the king used to seal adherence could create dissension if unwisely distributed. It was all a matter of political judgment and perception. There were no rules dictating how or to whom the king should bestow his favor.[29]

[29] Maddicott, *Thomas of Lancaster*, 202–203; Harriss, *King, Parliament and Public Finance*, 166–167.

Much depended on his judgment, for he distributed patronage at his own discretion. Conversely, the fulfillment or frustration of expectations depended on the perception of supplicants. How much was enough? Matthew Paris reported that Richard of Cornwall was upset in 1245 when Henry III granted a wardship that Richard had wanted to Simon de Montfort.[30] Richard's modern biographer takes Richard's position by stating that he received only five wardships in forty years, but that is a lot compared to what other magnates received.[31] The English nobility thus perceived their lord's actions differently according to the particular constellation of politics at any given moment.

Whether justified or not, Richard's disappointment underscores the potential for political conflict that lay in the distribution of patronage. Competition for wardships, marriages, and other rewards could factionalize the court or the elite. Feudal patronage could be especially troublesome because if, as argued here, the safety of landholders' lands and families lay in the smooth circulation of wardships outward from the court and in the arrangement of acceptable marriages, then any misuse of those benefits, whether real or perceived, would be interpreted as jeopardizing that safety. In general, political stability in England did not depend on bribing the higher nobility with an excessive share of feudal patronage. As has been seen, they received a portion of what the king distributed but not so much as royal family members or servants. This pattern of distribution did not by itself create discontent. Protests arose when the elite felt royal gifts to be immoderate or unbalanced. The misapplication of patronage brought to the surface the underlying uneasiness felt by all tenants-in-chief over the issues of minorities and wardship. It gave them cause to oppose openly the king's feudal lordship. Beginning in the thirteenth century, that opposition took the form of a criticism of royal finances.

Henry III's generosity before 1258 led to precisely such a confluence of misgivings and opposition. It has already been noted how Henry gave a disproportionate share of the wardships to a small group of ministers, family members, and favorites who surrounded him at court. Although Henry understood that a judicious allocation of patronage could be an effective political weapon, he largely ignored such considerations in assigning feudal

[30] Paris, *Chronica Majora*, 4:415. Henry sold Simon the wardship and marriage of Gilbert de Umfraville for 10,000 marks (*ERF*, 1:436; *CPR, 1247–1258*, 493; *CIPM*, 1:49; *EB*, 73; Charles Bémont, *Simon de Montfort* [Oxford, 1930], 34, 91 n. 4).

[31] Denholm-Young, *Richard of Cornwall*, 15.

patronage.[32] As a result, he engendered disappointment and jealousy that helped to fracture the court, to distance it from the tenants-in-chief, and to produce political opposition.

In the decade between 1247 and 1258, Henry promised ninety men wardships and marriages to the value of approximately 8,355 marks.[33] This includes only the promises recorded in letters patent; Henry may have made others that did not appear in official enrollments. Furthermore, this does not include promises of cash fees, except in those cases when Henry granted someone an annual fee until he could find him a wardship or marriage of equivalent value. Henry had thus pledged in advance a substantial portion of his feudal resources, and some of the individual undertakings could be quite handsome. For example, William de St. Ermino, a Poitevin, seems to have come into prominence at court in 1253 when Henry granted him a fee of £20 a year until Henry could provide him with wardships or escheats of the same value. After that, Henry steadily escalated his commitments to William: a year later he enlarged his original promise to 40 marks a year, less than five months after that he assigned William the first marriage of a woman that fell in worth £100, then stepped that up in 1256 to a marriage worth £300, and finally promised William 300 marks in wardships valued at less than 50 marks apiece.[34] And Henry followed through on his undertakings to William. Between 1253 and 1258 he granted William the marriages of two widows; £40 worth of land out of the Hastings wardship; custody of the lands of Alina Wake; the wardship of the lands and heirs of Richard de Dover; £20 worth of land out of the Clare wardship; the farm of the royal manor of Havering out of which the king allowed William 120 marks a year as William's fee; the lands of Robert Sauvage who had quitclaimed them to the king for quittance of his debts as sheriff; and the wardship and marriage of the heirs of a Gilbert de Clare, which William sold to Agnes Bauzan, the widow of another royal minister.[35] Altogether, up until 1271, William received nine different wardships from Henry, six of them after 1266. Besides these grants to William, Henry also granted scarlet clothing to William's sister on her marriage.[36]

[32] Bémont, *Simon de Montfort*, 201–203, 202 n. 1.

[33] The grants are those recorded in *CPR, 1247–1258*.

[34] Ibid., 172, 305, 379, 533, 552.

[35] Ibid., 178, 220, 292, 394, 398, 552, 619; *Close Rolls*, 10:74, 200, 254; Waugh, "Reluctant Knights and Jurors," 973 n. 123.

[36] *CPR, 1258–1266*, 596; *CPR, 1266–1272*, 13, 497, 568–569, 611; *CIPM*, 1:716; *Close Rolls*, 10:61.

Yet Henry did not follow through on all of his promises in these years, and there were glaring discrepancies in his distribution of feudal rights. Thus, Henry's promises to his half-brother, William de Valence, of £500 in escheats and 500 marks in wardships of his choice meant that no one else, except Richard of Cornwall, could obtain wards or escheats until Valence had been satisfied.[37] Indeed, only fourteen of the ninety people to whom Henry promised wardships received them during the decade, while eighteen obtained theirs after 1258, and fifty-eight never received any. Because most of them received annual fees, they may not have been acutely disappointed. Nevertheless, they and others would have surely noticed that the Poitevins received all that Henry promised, garnering at least twenty-four wardships. Though the figure represents only a small percentage of the total number of wardships granted out in the decade, it is greater than that received by any other group, with the exception of courtiers including the queen, Prince Edward, Peter of Savoy, Ralph Fitz Nicholas, and John Mansell. In contrast, earls and barons outside of the court received a mere seven wardships over the entire decade, less than 4 percent of all that were granted.[38]

The anger voiced by Matthew Paris, by the barons in 1258, and by the *Song of Lewes* arose from the perception that Henry focused his patronage on an exclusive clique. They denounced the recipients as foreigners, but their foreignness was of less importance in arousing animosity than the perception that they had monopolized royal favor, especially wardships and marriages.[39] Their percep-

[37] *CPR, 1247–1258*, 273; David Carpenter, "What Happened in 1258?" in *War and Government in the Middle Ages: Essays in Honour of J. O. Prestwich* (London, 1984), 118.

[38] Altogether, 164 wards produced 188 separate grants made to 123 individuals. Of the recipients, 16 (13 percent) received 72 (38.3 percent) wardships. They were Bertram de Crioll (3), Edward (9), Philip Lovel (3), Guy de Lusignan (4), John Mansell (4), Henry de la Mare (3), Ebulo de Montibus (3), Ralph Fitz Nicholas (7), Robert Passelewe (3), the queen (11), Elias de Rabayn (3), Guy and Maurice de Rocheford (3), Peter de Savoy (7), William de St. Ermino (3), and William de Valence (6). The barons were William d'Aubigny (1), William de Cantilupe (1), Philip Darcy (1), William de Ferrers (1), Thomas Lascelles (1), Henry de Percy (1), Geoffrey Scales (1), Robert Walerand (2), and Alice Warenne (1). Cantilupe and Walerand were closely connected to the court and served as royal ministers on various occasions. Henry made 50 of the promises while he was in Gascony in 1253–1254, clearly as a reward for service (*CPR, 1247–1258*, 241–360, 378–390). A large number of the recipients were foreign allies, such as Eschivat de Chabbanays, the count of Bigorre, or William de Calviniaco, who probably did not expect to receive *English* wards (*CPR, 1247–1258*, 283, 403).

[39] Paris, *Chronica Majora*, 5:6–7, 205, 328, 410, 514–515, 616, 621, 6:400–405;

tion had some basis in fact, for the distribution of wardships seems to have changed after 1246. Between 1217 and 1246 Henry made just over 12 percent of all of his grants to English earls and barons, but between 1247 and 1257 that percentage dropped below 4 percent while the number of grants to favored ministers and foreigners rose sharply.[40] Contemporaries did not have aggregate figures, but the decline may have been sufficiently steep and abrupt to attract notice, even if it could not be accurately defined. If so, then two factors came together in this decade. The first was resentment outside the court at a reduction in the share of patronage that the baronage had come to expect, and the second was the resentment within the court felt toward the excessive favor displayed to one faction.

Resentment was often expressed in demands for financial reform. If Henry could afford to squander so much on so few, it was argued, why did he have to ask for taxes? On several occasions prior to 1258, the barons demanded that Henry apply his wardships and marriages, along with the income from other sources like ecclesiastical vacancies, to his finances instead of giving them to unworthy favorites as he was accustomed to doing.[41] With their patience exhausted and frustration mounting over Henry's diplomatic schemes in 1258, the barons demanded a resumption of his gifts to the Poitevins.[42]

The barons were also angered because they felt that Henry's misplaced generosity threatened the rights of wards. William de St. Ermino, for example, was among the Poitevins they expelled from England in 1258, claiming that he had abused his power as guardian.[43] They likewise denounced another royal minister, Elias de Rabayn, for exploiting his royal connections to acquire the barony of Thoresway, Lincolnshire, for his wife Maud, one of the two daughters and coheirs of Stephen de Bayeux, and thereby disinheriting her sister. Stephen, at Henry's urging, had granted the

---

The Song of Lewes, ed. Charles L. Kingsford (Oxford, 1890), 10–11, 39 (lines 285–310); Carpenter, "What Happened in 1258?" 112–113, 118–119.

[40] There were 329 grants in 1217–1246, of which 9 went to earls and 51 to barons.

[41] Paris, Chronica Majora, 3:219–220 (1232), 411–412 (1237), 4:181–186 (1242), 372–374 (1244).

[42] Carpenter, "What Happened in 1258?" 118. See also Huw Ridgeway, "The Lord Edward and the Provisions of Oxford (1258): A Study in Faction," in Coss and Lloyd, Thirteenth Century England I (Woodbridge, 1986), 89–99.

[43] Close Rolls, 10:254; CIPM, 1:457; Reginald F. Treharne, The Baronial Plan of Reform, 1258–1263 (1932; reprint, New York, 1971), 78, 125–126.

entire barony to Maud and Elias in free marriage, so that they would hold it jointly of the king in chief. Elias paid Stephen 100 marks and gave him custody of the barony for the rest of his life, for which Stephen paid Elias an annual rent of £30. The date of the agreement is not known, but it must have been shortly before Stephen's death, for in March 1250 Henry promised Elias that if Stephen died before the girls came of age, then he would grant Elias their wardship and marriages. Two months later, Henry fulfilled his promise.[44] Henry may have temporarily placed Maud's sister and coheir in the nunnery of Sixhills, for Robert Grosseteste threatened Henry with excommunication for removing her.[45] When the barons forced Elias into exile in 1258, they denounced him for sending the girl overseas, where she eventually married, and defrauding her of her rightful inheritance. They seized custody of the barony and expelled Rabayn from England. His wife, however, stayed, and Henry later granted her an annual pension of £40.[46] The barons not only considered foreigners like Elias de Rabayn unworthy of such honors, but they feared that such grants would disrupt the customary process of inheritance and descent, especially when guardians abused their position.[47]

Finally, the barons perceived that Henry's devotion to a narrow clique at court had disrupted the opportunities for marriages and alliances that went with the distribution of wardships.[48] His favoritism placed the lands and children of some of the leading families in England in the hands of a few courtiers. Like Elias de Rabayn, they were able to arrange splendid matches for their own families. Henry thus married the heirs of five earldoms who came into royal custody between 1225 and 1258 to foreigners such as the Lusignans and Savoyards. Outsiders were concerned about Henry's marriages and grants not simply because they concentrated so much power in so few hands but also because they blocked the circulation of wealth through the marriage of wards that was such

[44] *CChR*, 2:133 (royal confirmation of the marriage agreement, January 1270, on Elias's return to England); *CPR, 1247–1258*, 62, 65; *ERF*, 2:286; *CIPM*, 1:159, 2:567, 689; *EB*, 88–89. When Stephen inherited from his brother in 1249, he was sixty years old or more.

[45] *CPR, 1247–1258*, 237, 25 July 1253, Henry appoints proctors. Grosseteste died on 9 October (*HBC*, 235), and nothing more is known of the issue.

[46] *ERF*, 2:286; *Close Rolls*, 10:339, 366, 382–383. The order referred to the girls as daughters of John de Bayeux, Stephen's elder brother who died in 1249. For the subsequent story of Maud and her sister, see *Select Cases*, 5:lxxxix–xci.

[47] Paris, *Chronica Majora*, 5:283.

[48] For what follows, see Waugh, "Marriage, Class, and Royal Lordship," 181–207.

an essential part of their strategies of landholding and descent. Taken together, this patronage threatened to upset the patterns of alliance, association, and marriage that the barons had so carefully cultivated, and it deepened their resentment to the clique at court. It was one factor that helped solidify baronial opposition to Henry in 1258.

It is a remarkable testament to the strength of cooperation between the king and tenants-in-chief that after the period of baronial reform royal lordship did not constitute a major source of irritation. Nor was it the primary focus of any of the subsequent opposition movements before 1327. Edward I, for example, did not give his barons a greater share of his feudal patronage than Henry had. Yet his use of royal lordship was not so overtly political as his father's had been. On the contrary, it was far more politic than Henry's, for in the early part of his reign Edward applied his patronage more evenly than his father had. It conformed more closely to the expectations and aspirations of landed families. He used marriages and feudal patronage to reward service and to weave a tight social endogamy in and around the court. It brought together royal kin, ministers, and tenants-in-chief instead of driving them apart as the Poitevins had done. While Edward's marriage arrangements did not by themselves secure the participation of nobles and gentry in his enterprises, they did foster a sense of partnership and cooperation. The St. Amandos, Montagus, and Montforts, for example, loyally served Edward, served together in some instances, and even remained attached to the Crown into Edward II's reign. This balance of interests seems to have been upset only after 1296, when the financial strains on the Crown demanded that Edward use his feudal resources largely for income instead of patronage. To win support for military ambitions that went beyond the interests of most tenants-in-chief, Edward probably should have been more generous.[49]

Edward's treatment of three minor earls exemplifies his seigniorial policies. The first was John de Warenne, whose father William died in 1286 (though John's grandfather, the elder John de Warenne, earl of Surrey, was still living). Edward had promised the wardship of William's lands to William's in-laws, Robert de Vere and his wife, and there is no record of any grant of wardship or marriage. After the earl of Surrey died in 1304, Edward married

[49] Prestwich, *War, Politics and Finance*, 245–246.

the ward to Edward's granddaughter, Joan of Bar.[50] The heir to the earldom of Gloucester, Gilbert de Clare, was also a minor on his father's death in 1295. Edward granted his marriage to Queen Margaret, but she failed to arrange a match, so that Edward II granted him the right to marry whomever he pleased in 1308.[51] Finally, when Edmund Fitz Alan, the heir to the earldom of Arundel, fell into wardship on his father's death in 1302, Edward granted custody of his lands to Amadeus of Savoy as partial fulfillment of Edward's promise to the count of 10,000 marks in wardships, and gave Edmund's marriage to the elder John de Warenne. He arranged a match between Edmund and his granddaughter Alice, sister of the younger Warenne.[52] Edward's provisions for these and other wards contrast with his father's. Edward distributed his favor widely, while Henry subordinated the interests of royal wards to his policies and limited the benefits of lordship to a small faction.[53]

As K. B. McFarlane forcefully argued, not all of Edward's actions were evenhanded.[54] The Ferrers family certainly suffered at his hands, and Edward exploited the financial weakness of other families to acquire land.[55] His single-minded dedication to creating landed endowments for his own family may have at times jeopardized relations between himself and the nobility.[56] Yet other factors were at work besides royal conniving. Take, for example, the marriage arranged between Thomas of Lancaster and Alice de Lacy between 1292 and 1294. McFarlane saw the marriage settlement as an instance in which collateral heirs "were cut off from their legitimate expectations" and asked why Alice's parents, Henry de Lacy and Margaret Longspee, would have submitted to such an apparently unfair bargain. The answer lies as much in their experience of what William Marshal's biographer called "gluttonous death" as

[50] *CPR, 1281–1292*, 173; Cokayne, *Complete Peerage*, 12:1:507.

[51] Cokayne, *Complete Peerage*, 5:712, 714 and n. c; *CPR, 1292–1301*, 592; *CPR, 1301–1307*, 257; *CPR, 1307–1313*, 50.

[52] *CPR, 1301–1307*, 46, 113, 308; Cokayne, *Complete Peerage*, 1:242; *EB*, 71.

[53] Waugh, "Marriage, Class, and Royal Lordship," 199–201.

[54] McFarlane, "Had Edward I a 'Policy' towards the Earls?" See also Thomas F. Tout, "The Earldoms under Edward I," *TRHS*, n.s. 8 (1894): 129–155.

[55] For example, Peche (Cokayne, *Complete Peerage*, 10:335–336; Parsons, *CHEC*, 88 n. 126; Edward Miller, *The Abbey and Bishopric of Ely: The Social History of an Ecclesiastical Estate from the Tenth Century to the Early Fourteenth Century* [Cambridge, 1951], 177); Fitz Reginald (Cokayne, *Complete Peerage*, 5:466–467; *EB*, 9; *CIPM*, 5:205); and Fitz John (*EB*, 42; *CIPM*, 5:213; *CCR, 1307–1313*, 510).

[56] Prestwich, *War, Politics and Finance*, 243–246.

in Edward's plotting.[57] What near collateral heirs were there in 1292? Henry and Margaret had already lost two sons. Henry's brother and sister died young, while his father, Edmund de Lacy, had been an only son. The situation was not much more hopeful on the Longspee side. Margaret was the only daughter of William, who died in 1257. Her aunt Ela had had at least five sons, but in 1292 only two of them survived, and the heir of the eldest was a mere four years old. Only by going back another generation to that of Margaret's grandfather could they have found many collateral relatives.[58] Henry and Margaret knew firsthand the terrible precariousness of family survival. Their hopes for continuing their blood lines and keeping their estate intact rested with their only daughter. It was a situation which families must have dreaded and in which many found themselves. Henry and Margaret turned to their lord for help, and he offered them an honorable marriage. The settlement ensured that their lands would stay intact but within the *husband's* family. Under the circumstances, it must have seemed a reasonable gamble.

If Edward II reawakened baronial fears about royal lordship, it was not because he recklessly disposed of wardships. Early in his reign, Bartholomew de Badlesmere and Roger d'Amory were the only courtiers to garner more than five wardships. Gilbert de Clare did better. He received six wardships in 1310–1311, five of which were granted by the Ordainers in the fall of 1311 to make up 3,500 marks out of 5,000 marks that Edward owed Clare for his expenses in the king's service.[59] Neither Gaveston nor the younger Despenser, moreover, cornered the inordinate share of wardships and marriages that the Poitevins had under Henry III: Gaveston received three and Despenser four. The twenty-nine wardships given to the elder Despenser were intended to repay the Crown's debts to Hugh, which Edward had inherited from his father.[60] It is another example of the way in which the fiscal troubles at the end of Edward I's reign continued to haunt Edward II after he came to the throne. When the Ordainers demanded a resumption of royal gifts in 1311, they included wardships, therefore, not because they were a leading cause of discontent but rather because

---

[57] McFarlane, "Had Edward I a 'Policy' towards the Earls?" 263; *L'histoire de Guillaume le Maréchal*, 3:208–209.

[58] Cokayne, *Complete Peerage*, 1:336–340, 346–348, 7:676–688, 11:382–385, appendix F, 126–132.

[59] *CPR, 1307–1313*, 409–410.

[60] PRO, E.159/86 mm. 73, 89–89d, for an account of the debts and grants.

the barons, like their predecessors in 1258, wanted to put them to sound fiscal use. Finance, not feudal lordship, was uppermost in the minds of the king's opponents.

The importance of royal lordship in assembling alliances and the reaction it could cause emerge clearly in the collapse of political order between 1315 and 1318.[61] Two important tests of royal lordship occurred in these years: the minority of the earl of Warwick and the partitioning of the Clare estate. Both raised delicate issues, and Edward proceeded cautiously until the end of 1316. After the young earl of Gloucester died childless at Bannockburn in 1314, Edward allowed the widow to put forth her claim that she was pregnant. He probably hoped that it was true for two reasons. First, a child would have meant that the estate would not have to be divided, while second, it would have given the king a long wardship. Edward even held back the younger Despenser, who was champing at the bit, eager to lay his hands on his wife's share of the estate. He was married to Eleanor, one of the earl's three sisters and eventual coheirs.[62] Similarly, when Warwick died in 1315, Edward delivered the custody of his lands to his executors as he had promised, and he punctiliously observed the terms of his promise.[63] Edward's restraint in both cases can perhaps be attributed to Lancaster's presence on the council in these years, though it also shows that Edward was not necessarily out of step with baronial interests.

Only after relations between Lancaster and Edward soured at the end of 1316 did Edward use his lordship to bolster a court party. He let the Clare partition go ahead in December. The following spring he married the two remaining heiresses, Margaret and Elizabeth, to two other courtiers, Hugh d'Audeley the Younger and Roger d'Amory. This placed them at the forefront of the nobility. At the same time, he married one of the daughters and coheirs of Theobald de Verdun to the son of another courtier, William de Montagu. The year before he had given the wardship of the Verdun lands to d'Amory.[64] The grant annoyed Lancaster, who later seized custody of some of Verdun's lands and would not

[61] For the political background, see Maddicott, *Thomas of Lancaster*, 190–239; and John R. S. Phillips, "The 'Middle Party' and Negotiating the Treaty of Leake, August 1318: A Reinterpretation," *BIHR* 46 (1973): 11–27.

[62] *CIPM*, 5:538; *Rot. Parl.*, 1:355; Altschul, *A Baronial Family*, 165–174.

[63] *CFR*, 2:255, 265; *CChW*, 425, 432.

[64] Cokayne, *Complete Peerage*, 4:43–44, 12:2:177–178, 250–251; *CFR*, 2:294, 316.

surrender them to the escheator.[65] Edward channeled most wardships into the hands of a small faction around the court: d'Amory
received four, Montagu three, while the younger Despenser and
Audeley each received one. Their associates and other ministers
likewise obtained wardships: Edmund Bacon one, John de Foxley
two, Adam Lymbergh one, Walter de Norwich three, and John de
Sandall one.[66] Some of the guardians used those rights to arrange
marriages. The Greystoke heir married the sister of the younger
d'Audeley, the Ufford heir married Walter de Norwich's daughter, and Richard de Cogan married one of William de Montagu's
daughters. Then, in June Edward took back custody of the Warwick lands and turned them over to the elder Despenser.[67]

In a different political context, Edward's grants and marriage
arrangements might have been acceptable. His actions in many re-
spects resembled his father's: using marriages and wardships to
solidify his household and to forge relations with landed families.
Montagu, for example, had participated in Edward I's schemes.
But in the strained atmosphere of 1317, Edward II's efforts were
merely provocative. To add to the tension, in May Warenne abducted Lancaster's wife, Alice de Lacy. Lancaster obviously felt
threatened. He was affronted by Edward's disposal of the lands of
Verdun and Warwick, both of whom had been his close allies. In
fact, Lancaster was the godfather of Thomas, the young earl of
Warwick.[68] Lancaster displayed his anger by seizing the chief castle
of the Verdun estate and refusing to surrender it to royal officials.
Probably as a result of Lancaster's influence, the article against the
Despensers in 1321 singled out Edward's recision of his grant of
the Warwick wardship to the executors.[69] The terms of the article
are interesting. It stresses that Parliament ratified both the promise
and the subsequent grant. There is in fact no evidence that Parlia-

[65] *CFR*, 2:346–347; *CCR, 1313–1318*, 575; Maddicott, *Thomas of Lancaster*, 196, 207.

[66] *CPR, 1313–1317*, 535, 620, 622, 631, 640, 649; *CPR, 1317–1321*, 14, 38, 125, 187, 379; *CFR*, 2:290, 293, 294, 295, 297, 306, 316–317, 322, 331, 337, 385; Co-kayne, *Complete Peerage*, 6:190 n. f.

[67] Cokayne, *Complete Peerage*, 3:358, 6:190 n. f, 9:82 n. f, 12:1:151, 12:2:429–432; *CFR*, 2:245, 331, 336; *CPR, 1313–1317*, 620. Edward gave some of the Warwick lands to others (*CFR*, 2:267, 300, 304, 332, 336), so that Despenser received only a portion of the estate, which he held at farm for the assessed value plus an incre-ment of £80.

[68] Maddicott, *Thomas of Lancaster*, 196.

[69] *Statutes of the Realm*, 1:183.

ment played any role.[70] Whether they were telling the truth or not, the barons had to put their case in those terms because there was no reason that Edward could not have rescinded a grant of a wardship. Indeed, the resumptions called for by the Ordinances rested on the assumption that he could. The point is that Lancaster and his allies, much like the barons in 1258, were not opposed to the essence of royal lordship but to its use. Circumstances could make all the difference. For example, Edward's arrangement in 1308 of a marriage between Gaveston and Margaret de Clare, Edward's own niece, did not elicit anywhere near the same reaction as his later decisions. It helped Gaveston rise to social heights that the English baronage resented, but the marriage itself, according to chroniclers, improved Gaveston's reputation and may have helped save his life at the time of his banishment.[71] At that time, political uneasiness had not yet degenerated into factionalization. The marriage was therefore not perceived to be so threatening as Edward's actions in 1317, which only fueled an already volatile situation.

Edward's most irresponsible exercise of feudal lordship, with the most serious political repercussions, came later. In 1321 he seized the honor of Gower in south Wales on the pretext that it had been alienated without license. As several historians have explained, William de Braose's intention, as early as 1315, to dispose of Gower had attracted the interest of several Marcher lords including Humphrey de Bohun (the earl of Hereford), Roger de Mortimer, and John de Mowbray.[72] It also attracted the younger Despenser, a newcomer who had gained a foothold in the region through his marriage to one of the Clare heiresses. Despenser had been harassing and intimidating the other coheirs as well as neighboring landholders in an effort to enlarge his holdings. With such powerful competition, however, Despenser had no hope of acquiring Gower legitimately. His efforts rested on his influence with Edward and more specifically on the enforcement of the king's right of consent to alienations by tenants-in-chief.

[70] Edward made his promise on 18 July 1315, Warwick died by 16 August, and Edward granted the wardship on 1 December (*CFR*, 2:255, 265; *CIPM*, 5:615). The enrollments do not mention Parliament. Parliament met at Westminster from 20 January 1315 to 9 March, again at Lincoln from 27 January 1316 to 20 February, and finally at Westminster between April and May (*HBC*, 515).

[71] *Vita*, 2; *Gesta Edwardi de Carnarvan Auctore Canonico Bridlingtoniensi*, in *Chronicles of the Reigns of Edward I and Edward II* (London, 1882–1883), 2:34.

[72] J. C. Davies, "The Despenser War," 32–42; Maddicott, *Thomas of Lancaster*, 260–261; R. R. Davies, *Lordship and Society*, 287–288; Bean, *Decline*, 98–101.

Although some claimed that the king's right of consent did not extend to the Welsh Marches, the issue of Marcher liberties was insignificant compared to Edward's rash violation of English custom when, at Despenser's instigation, he declared Gower forfeit in 1321.[73] Up to that point, the king's procedure in the matter had been ominous but legitimate. In July 1319 Edward ordered an investigation into past alienations in Gower by Braose and his ancestors. Although such inquests were routine, this one was headed by Despenser's agent in south Wales, John Inge.[74] The exact sequence of events after that is somewhat unclear. According to one account, Hereford had obtained royal consent for his contract with Braose, but Despenser used his influence with the king to upset that consent.[75] In any case, on 26 October 1320, because Mowbray had entered Gower without the king's license, Edward ordered his escheator to take the honor into royal custody and to keep it until further orders and then assigned a custodian for the lands. The process itself was not out of the ordinary, for the king customarily seized lands that had been alienated without license, though, as before, the order was carried out by a Despenser agent.[76] What was novel, and intolerable, was that Edward treated the honor as forfeit and granted it to Despenser, which may have been his intention all along. In the *Vita*'s report of the affair, Despenser himself put forth the argument that lands alienated without license should be returned to the royal fisc, instead of being redeemed by a fine and a royal pardon as had been the usual practice until then.[77] Edward heeded his favorite and gave him the honor. That

[73] Bean, *Decline*, 98–101. The issue of Marcher liberties is not clear. The *Vita* clearly states that the custom of the March did not recognize the king's right of consent, as did petitions after the affair (*Vita*, 108–109; *Calendar of Ancient Petitions*, 292–293).

[74] *CFR*, 3:2–3; PRO, C.145/83, no. 12. Similar inquests can be found in E.153/1957, no. 17 (26 Edward I); E.143/4/6, no. 8; and elsewhere.

[75] *Annales Paulini*, in *Chronicles of Edward I and Edward II*, 1:292–293. See also *Johannis de Trokelowe*, in *Chronica Monasterii Sancti Albani*, ed. Henry T. Riley (London, 1866), 3:107.

[76] *CCR, 1318–1323*, 268; *CFR*, 3:40–41, 43; *CPR, 1317–1321*, 547, 551; PRO, E.372/167 m. 2d; Waugh, "For King, Country, and Patron," 31. Examples of the seizure and farming of lands alienated without license can be found in PRO, E.159/83 m. 7; /86 m. 3d; /88 mm. 3d, 4 (farmed "quamdiu placuit").

[77] *Vita*, 108: "ut nullus sine licentia regis ingressum haberet in feodum quod de rege teneretur in capite; et, si contrarium a quocumque foret attemptatum, feodum sic occupatum redigeretur in fiscum." The first clause echoes Henry III's declaration in 1256, but the second is entirely novel. For the "fisc," see Harriss, *King, Parliament and Public Finance*, 131.

was too much for the barons. If allowed to stand, the forfeiture threatened the holdings of tenants-in-chief throughout England, and Lancaster astutely used that threat to rally support in the summer of 1321. The bill drawn up at Sherburn thus demanded a remedy for the novelties incited by the king's ministers against the *proceres*. Purchasers of lands and tenements held in chief of the Crown had been driven away from them, had forfeited their own lands, and had been judged and disinherited without the assent of their peers and against the laws of the land. The issue touched all tenants-in-chief and potential purchasers, and the phrasing of the petition reveals the legal issues that Edward's actions had raised. The confederates hammered at the issue of disinheritance throughout the summer.[78] In fact, as soon as the Despensers had been exiled in August 1321, Edward pardoned Mowbray for the acquisition and restored Gower to him, though he forfeited it yet again in the rebellion that followed.[79]

Baronial Remedies to the Abuses of Lordship

On occasion between 1200 and 1327, therefore, royal lordship along with other issues produced sufficient friction to ignite political action. The problem facing the king's opponents was how to translate their grievances into concrete measures that would rectify or eliminate the abuses that they perceived.

In 1215 the barons extracted a promise from John to observe specific limitations on his feudal lordship. They were stated as customary principles that he freely recognized. Even under those circumstances, however, the barons stopped short of a complete evisceration of royal lordship. They acknowledged that wardship and marriage were essential aspects of their own authority and of the galaxy of social relations in which they lived. They were not prepared to forgo those benefits or to turn control of wards over to the care of relatives. They were clearly ambivalent about royal lordship but they would not exchange those misgivings for the greater uncertainties of unregulated family relations. Nor were they willing to cut off the patronage that royal wardship offered them.[80]

There were, however, difficulties with this approach. The limi-

---

[78] *Gesta Edwardi de Carnarvan*, 2:63; Maddicott, *Thomas of Lancaster*, 277, 300–301; George L. Haskins, "The Doncaster Petition, 1321," *EHR* 53 (1938): 483–484.

[79] *CPR, 1321–1324*, 21; *CFR*, 3:98.

[80] Holt, *Magna Carta*, 212–216.

tations of Magna Carta and the fact that contemporaries were aware of them emerge clearly in Matthew Paris's account of a confrontation between the countess of Arundel and Henry III in 1252 over the right to a wardship.[81] Thomas de Ingoldesthorp held lands of several lords including a knight's fee of the honor of Haughley, which was in the king's hands as an escheat. When Thomas died in 1252 leaving a minor heir, Henry took custody of *all* of Thomas's lands, including a quarter of a knight's fee held of the earl of Arundel that had been assigned to the earl's widow, Isabel.[82] According to Paris, Isabel approached Henry and asked for her share of the wardship. Henry refused, whereupon Isabel denounced him for failing to provide justice. In response, Henry sneered and asked if the nobles had given her a charter to speak on their behalf. Paris gives Isabel a set speech in reply, playing on the term *charter*. Henry, not the barons, she stated, had given her the charter in Magna Carta. The theme of the speech is the weakness of Henry's promises, and hence, the frailty of political settlements based on liberties "freely" granted by the king. As Isabel laments, "Where are the liberties of England, so often recorded, so often granted, and so often ransomed?"[83] She then threatened Henry with divine judgment. Her appeal to Magna Carta was sound, for Henry violated it by exercising prerogative wardship over lands held in chief *ut de escaeta*. It should be noted that, as in other cases, Paris, through Isabel, did not challenge the right of royal lordship nor enunciate a competing ideology. He accepts the king's authority but wants that authority exercised according to the rules laid out in Magna Carta. He pictured Isabel withdrawing from court without permission and empty-handed, but in fact a little over a year later Henry surrendered her part of the wardship.[84]

---

[81] Paris, *Chronica Majora*, 5:336–337. The incident was probably related to Paris by the countess herself. See Richard Vaughan, *Matthew Paris* (Cambridge, 1958), 13.

[82] *Book of Fees*, 2:906, 909, 1465; *EB*, 120–121; *CIPM*, 1:238; *HKF*, 3:145–146, 426–427; Tout, *Chapters*, 6:25. Henry sold the wardship to Peter Chaceporc who granted it back to the ward's mother (*ERF*, 2:126; *Close Rolls*, 9:348, 10:87–88, 493–494).

[83] Paris, *Chronica Majora*, 5:337: "Ubi libertates Angliae totiens in scripta redactae, totiens concessae, totiensque redemptae?" The translation is based on *Matthew Paris's English History, from the Year 1235 to 1273* (London, 1853), 2:529.

[84] *Close Rolls*, 7:357; C.60/51 (pardon of fine in plea concerning wardship against Chaceporc); Carpenter, "King, Magnates, and Society," 44; Waugh, "Marriage, Class, and Royal Lordship," 181–182.

Through this speech, Paris pointed out the critical problem in baronial opposition: how to make the king adhere to his promises. The framers of Magna Carta had recognized that shortcoming and had instituted a body much like a feudal court to control royal actions. Yet it arose again and again.[85] The stress placed by the reformers on the participation of the barons in the royal council during the century after Magna Carta was, at least in part, a practical attempt to overcome this weakness. They also concentrated on royal offices and officials, hoping to restrain royal lordship by imposing controls on the administrative machinery of lordship and placing it under the supervision of a council. In other words, they shifted tactics from a direct adjustment of royal prerogatives themselves to a manipulation of the institutions through which the king exercised those rights.

The shift is apparent in the baronial reform movement of 1258. In their petition of grievances, the barons addressed themselves to two general issues. On the one hand they complained about prerogative wardship and asked, as a "common right," that in the future the king take only the marriage of the ward and allow the lords of other lands held by the tenant-in-chief to have custody of those tenements. On the other, they asked that the notion of disparagement be widened to cover anyone who was not considered a "true-born" Englishman.[86] In fact, no lasting legislation came out of these requests, and the reformers did not attempt any substantive changes in the king's rights of lordship. Instead, they instituted measures designed to limit the king's discretion in the disposal of those rights. According to the Provisions of Oxford, for example, the chancellor had to swear in his oath of office that he would not seal any grant of a greater wardship or escheat without the consent of the council. In the Provisions of Westminster, the reformers appointed a committee composed of the justiciar, the treasurer, the chancellor of the Exchequer, and two justices to sell wardships and to formulate policy concerning wardships and escheats, which henceforth would be sold by two good men.[87] The fiscal consequences of Henry's unbridled generosity had engendered some of the loudest complaints, and the reformers tried to correct them and to check royal patronage by monitoring the channels through which it was dispensed.

[85] Holt, *Magna Carta*, 48–49, 239–240; Palmer, "Origins," 394–395.
[86] *DBMRR*, 79 (no. 3), 81 (no. 6).
[87] Ibid., 103 (no. 7), 151–153 (nos. 8, 14, 17).

The council immediately put the proposals into effect. The Chancery did not issue any grants of wardship after June. Once grants resumed early in 1259, they were usually authorized by the justiciar or council of magnates. Conciliar authorization continued until 1261, when Henry reasserted his control over the government.[88] In the debate that followed, Henry bitterly deplored the council's restriction of his power to grant wardships. He made it clear that he regarded that power as essential to the maintenance of his authority in general and that he used it in particular to reward faithful service. The council replied that they had imposed the measures so that wardships and marriages could be used to pay the king's debts and to maintain his household. For their part, they deplored Henry's gifts, which they saw as squandering the Crown's resources on unworthy individuals.[89] The council had indeed introduced changes in the exercise of royal lordship. For one thing, the council kept closer tabs on the escheators. Their accounts were promptly audited in the Exchequer, and the inquest of 1258 tried to ascertain whether escheators had misappropriated revenues.[90] In addition, escheators seem to have kept the lands of minors in custody longer, and the number of payments they made to the wardrobe seems to have declined. A greater proportion of their revenue may therefore have flowed through the Exchequer, though because the escheators' accounts are incomplete, a precise comparison is impossible.[91] Furthermore, fines for wardships jumped from an average of about 86 marks a year in 1256–1258

[88] *ERF*, 2:296, 309, 334; *CPR, 1258–1266*, 12, 37, 82, 95, 97, 127, 128. The last conciliar authorization that I have found is dated 17 November 1260. For the politics of the period, see *DBMRR*, 33–40; and Powicke, *Henry III*, 411–428.

[89] *DBMRR*, 218–219, 220–221 (no. 1), 226–229 (no. 12), 260–265 (nos. 8, 12), 270–271 (no. 2), 276–277 (no. 7).

[90] Ernest F. Jacob, *Studies in the Period of Baronial Reform and Rebellion, 1258–1267* (Oxford, 1925), 32–33. Some of the escheators' accounts are enrolled on the pipe rolls: PRO, E.372/105 m. 21 (pipe roll, 44–45 Henry III; and escheator's account, 34–36 Henry III); E.372/122 m. 28d (pipe roll, 5–6 Edward I; and escheator's account, Somerset, 34–39 Henry III); E.372/105 mm. 20d–21 (escheators' accounts, north and south of the Trent, 43–46 Henry III); E.372/106 mm. 21–21d (pipe roll, 45–46 Henry III; and escheator's account, south of the Trent, 45–47 Henry III).

[91] John Evan Davis, "The Wardrobe of Henry III of England, 1234–1272" (Ph.D. diss., Mississippi State University, 1970), 100–104. The author shows that, according to the liberate rolls, payments to the wardrobe reached their peak around 1263, which seems consistent with the evidence of the wardrobe accounts (PRO, C.47/3/5 [ca. 41–42 Henry III]; C.47/35/1 [ca. 47 Henry III]). For a general assessment of the financial reforms in this period, see Treharne, *The Baronial Plan of Reform*, 369–373.

to 2,425 marks a year in 1259–1261. In one of the sales, moreover, the council made the buyer swear that he would not ask the king or council for any allocation or pardon of the debt and that he would pay the fine in full.[92]

The council, however, did not tamper with the traditional distribution of wardships to ministers and others close to the king. Councilors such as James d'Audcley, John de Balliol, and Hugh Bigod each received wardships, as did prominent ministers like Ebulo de Montibus, Roger de Thurkelby, and Henry de Wingham. The council also granted several to the queen as well as to her sons Edward and Edmund.[93] Otherwise, most of the wardships went to various knights and royal servants. The reformers, in other words, seem to have stuck to their word. They tried to increase the financial benefits from royal lordship without undertaking a radical redistribution of the king's feudal resources. It was enough, however, to anger Henry.

Between 1263 and 1266, in the turmoil that followed the initial period of baronial opposition, reform fell behind the struggle for political survival. Neither the king nor his opponents attempted any additional changes in royal lordship, and politics dictated the distribution of wardships. According to one chronicler, Henry thus used his resources in 1263 to seduce adherents away from Simon de Montfort.[94] Henry, in fact, gave the most valuable wardships that fell in that year, such as the lands and heirs of the baronial families of Beauchamp, Cressy, Lenham, and Mowbray, to some of his most faithful followers: James d'Audeley, Philip Basset, William de Valence, Ebulo de Montibus, and Richard of Cornwall. Such other royal supporters as Adam de Gesemuth, John de Grey, and Robert Walerand also received wardships and marriages.[95] These were all outright gifts; Henry did not demand fines.

Once Simon de Montfort took command of the government after the battle of Lewes on 14 May 1264, he, too, used patronage to solidify his position. He rewarded allies like Humphrey de Bo-

[92] Three fines of 3,000 marks, 1,200 marks, and 1,000 marks charged to the justiciar, Hugh Bigod, William Latimer, and a widow constituted 71 percent of the total in the latter period (*ERF*, 2:308, 317, 318 [condition on payment]).

[93] *CPR, 1258–1266*, 15, 29, 87, 92, 97, 127, 139, 141, 153, 156; *ERF*, 2:296, 306, 318.

[94] Bémont, *Simon de Montfort*, 201–202, and 202 n. 1.

[95] *CPR, 1258–1266*, 243, 267, 268, 275, 291, 292, 295, 297, 304, 317; *Close Rolls*, 12:200–201; *EB*, 10–11, 16, 45, 51, 146. Simon's supporters are identified in Treharne, *The Baronial Plan of Reform*, 335.

hun, Hugh Despenser, John Fitz John, and Thomas Fitz Thomas with wardships.[96] Yet, Simon also charged them a total of 1,200 marks in fines. He also seized the wardship of the lands of Stephen de Cressy from William de Valence and granted them to Isabel, wife of Maurice de Berkeley, who had fought with Simon at Lewes.[97] Simon's regime, however, did not grant out all of the wardships that came into custody. Robert de Vipont, for example, died shortly after the battle of Lewes, leaving two minor daughters and coheirs. Simon committed the younger daughter to the custody of John Fitz John who turned her over to Bertha de Furnivall, but there was no mention of any grant of wardship or marriage. There is likewise no record of any grants while Simon held power of the wardships of the lands and heirs of Ralph de Immworth, Richard Pikard, or Fulk Fitz Warin, all of whom were killed at Lewes. Furthermore, the baronial council authorized the grant of a wardship to Henry de Montfort specifically to defray the expenses of stocking Dover Castle.[98] Simon thus made some effort to reestablish the fiscal guidelines that the barons laid out in 1258 for the disposal of royal wardships. His determination to enforce the Provisions of Oxford, however, had to be tempered by the realities of politics. He raised some income from wardships, but used them primarily for patronage.[99]

With Henry's victory at Evesham on 4 August 1265, these reforms were once again overturned. Along with their lands, Montfort's followers forfeited whatever wardships they held, which Henry redistributed among his own allies. Henry resumed complete command of the institutions of royal lordship, which he likewise employed for the benefit of his supporters.[100] Four days after the battle, for example, Henry granted the Vipont coheirs to two

[96] *CPR, 1258–1266*, 316, 341, 349, 351–352, 353; Moor, *Knights*, 2:42–43; G. A. Williams, *Medieval London*, 216–217, 221–225.

[97] *Close Rolls*, 12:353–355; Moor, *Knights*, 1:83; *EB*, 13, 16. For a similar case, see *Close Rolls*, 12:359–360.

[98] *CPR, 1258–1266*, 322, 341, 435, 450, 465, 555; Meekings, introduction to *The 1235 Surrey Eyre*, 210; Eyton, *Antiquities*, 11:38; Treharne, *The Baronial Plan of Reform*, 326 n. 2, 335.

[99] For Simon's policies in these years, see John R. Maddicott, "The Mise of Lewes, 1264," *EHR* 98 (1983): 588–603; and David A. Carpenter, "Simon de Montfort and the Mise of Lewes," *BIHR* 58 (1985): 1–11.

[100] *DBMRR*, 328–329, Dictum of Kenilworth, cap 16. For the disposition of mesne wardships, see cap. 15; and Clive H. Knowles, "Provision for the Families of the Montfortians Disinherited after the Battle of Evesham," in Coss and Lloyd, *Thirteenth Century England I*, 126.

of Prince Edward's most loyal followers: Roger de Clifford, who married his ward to his son and heir, and Roger de Leyburn, who married her sister to his younger son, Roger. Vipont had been one of Simon's leading supporters, and the marriages of his heirs into the families of leading royalists helped Henry and Edward break up the baronial coalition and achieve a significant realignment of power in the north. Leyburn was also supposed to have saved Henry's life at Evesham.[101] The same day, Henry granted the Fitz Warin wardship to Robert Walerand, the Tony wardship forfeited by Humphrey de Bohun to Richard de Brus, and the wardship of the lands and heirs of William de Keynes to Hamo Lestrange. Henry also granted the lands and heirs of Ralph de Immworth to the lord of some of Immworth's lands, John de Gatesdene. The lord and his tenant had been tangled in a legal dispute that the special eyre of 1258 settled in Immworth's favor.[102] Following his earlier practice, moreover, Henry did not charge his followers for their rewards. In 1266 and 1267 he levied only 405 marks in fines for wardships and marriages, and none in 1265. For the time being, Henry repudiated the dictates of the Provisions of Oxford, determined to use his feudal authority for his political needs.

Nevertheless, the reforms of 1258 were not completely forgotten. In the last years of his reign, Henry used the income from the sale of wardships and marriages to pay various debts and expenses. In 1266, for example, he promised the duke of Brittany that in order to repay 4,000 marks that he owed the duke, he would assign him all of the profits of escheats, wardships, marriages, and vacancies that fell in until the debt was satisfied.[103] Finally, as part of Henry's preparations for a Crusade after a serious illness in 1271, he and his council initiated a strict financial regime in which he declared that the receipts from all escheats, wardships, marriages, reliefs, and other sources would be used solely to pay his household expenses and to settle his debts. He permitted himself a meager £120 for gifts to his household knights and servants.[104] It was a belated attempt to impose some discipline on Henry's generosity.

Edward, too, seems to have adopted at least part of the spirit of

---

[101] *CPR, 1258–1266*, 435; *EB*, 103–104; Moor, *Knights*, 1:212–213, 3:35–37; Cokayne, *Complete Peerage*, 7:633, 642–643; Treharne, *The Baronial Plan of Reform*, 335; Powicke, *Henry III*, 504 n. 2; Prestwich, "Royal Patronage," 42.

[102] Meekings, introduction to *The 1235 Surrey Eyre*, 210.

[103] *CPR, 1258–1266*, 668. For others, see *CPR, 1266–1272*, 324, 622.

[104] *CPR, 1266–1272*, 531, 622; Powicke, *Henry III*, 582–583.

reform in exercising royal lordship. As has been seen, he attempted to extract greater profits from wardships and marriages and to apply those profits to the costs of government as well as to the repayment of royal debts.[105] He displayed greater restraint than his father had in rewarding servants and avoided giving too much, in terms of feudal rewards, to too few. The influence of the baronial reforms of 1258 that aimed at practical changes in the exercise of royal lordship, therefore, outlived the reform movement itself and lasted through the reign of Edward II.

The harmonious lord-tenant relations that Edward I established once he came to the throne survived largely intact throughout his reign. Indeed, it is notable that during the political troubles between 1296 and 1300, the barons suggested only modest reforms in the administration of royal lordship. This in spite of the fact that at precisely the same time the government was stepping up its enforcement of alienations by tenants-in-chief and was seeking to extract as much revenue as possible from feudal sources. The enormous burden of taxation and purveyance had pushed seigniorial issues off to the side, but those issues were not particularly troublesome to most tenants-in-chief at that time.

Nevertheless, in 1300 the *Articuli super Cartas* revealed two complaints about the machinery of lordship. The first was the recurrent problem of waste: the barons complained about damage caused by escheators and their assistants. Edward granted that anyone suffering such waste should have a Chancery writ against the official involved to recover damages according to the provisions of the Statute of Gloucester of 1278.[106] The second issue related to the seizure of lands by escheators or sheriffs when the king had no right to them, as in the case of primer seisin when a landholder held nothing in chief of the king. It had been the government's practice to take custody of all lands over which it had any potential claim and to surrender custody only after a claimant had shown that the government did not have a right to them. A landholder or a mesne lord had to petition the king and perhaps wait for a second inquest before he could recover possession. In the meantime, he lost the issues of the lands. It was a cumbersome procedure that benefited the Crown alone. It also occurred fairly regularly; the close rolls record thirty-one instances in the decade between 1290 and 1300.[107]

[105] Cf. Harriss, *King, Parliament and Public Finance*, 141.
[106] *Statutes of the Realm*, 1:140 (no. 18).
[107] Ibid., no. 19; *CCR, 1288–1296*, 170, 177, 214, 217, 234, 300, 304, 347, 371,

The complaint produced the statute of the escheators, which simplified the recovery of lands in such cases. The king and council agreed that henceforth if the inquisition post mortem or other inquest revealed that a landholder held nothing in chief, then as soon as the inquest was returned to Chancery, the chancellor would issue a writ ordering the official to remove his hands from the property and to deliver the issues he had collected to the person entitled to them. Once again, however, it could not be presumed that any single inquest or precedent overruled prerogative wardship. The king reserved the right to review such cases in Chancery if it were subsequently discovered that the king had some claim to the wardship. In that case, the mesne lord would be summoned to Chancery to present his own evidence to support his own claim.[108] Chancery practice changed accordingly. After 1300 new writs appeared on the fine rolls, ordering an escheator, "pursuant to inquisitions made by him," to restore to the proper individuals lands that he had taken into custody along with any issues.[109] The process of protest and correction reveals the maturity of political relations between the king and the elite at the end of the thirteenth century. The barons did not attack royal lordship outright. Instead, they identified particular problems in the administrative machinery and asked for appropriate remedies. The king and council responded by making simple adjustments in Chancery procedure.

Edward II encountered greater resistance. Having inherited substantial debts from his father, Edward exacerbated his financial problems in the early years of his reign by continuing the high level of taxation and purveyance, failing to achieve any military success in Scotland, and displaying immoderate favoritism toward

---

414, 433, 468, 478, 487 (2); *CCR, 1296–1302*, 9, 14, 18, 22, 38, 45, 142, 151–152, 235, 241, 256, 280, 332, 349, 363. The procedure had been the subject of investigation earlier in the hundred inquests (Cam, *The Hundred*, 254, no. 38). See also Ehrlich, *Proceedings against the Crown*, 62–64.

[108] *Statutes of the Realm*, 1:142–143; and enrolled in *CCR, 1296–1302*, 484–485. As written, the provision would apply equally to cases of wardship and alienation without license.

[109] *CFR*, 1:437, 438, 443 (2), 448 (2), 455. Such writs probably appear on the fine rolls to provide a warrant for the payment of the issues, which would be charged against the escheator at the Exchequer. The number of lands taken into custody and restored because the tenant held nothing in chief did not change significantly; the close rolls record thirty-seven cases between 1300 and 1310 (*CCR, 1296–1302*, 417, 423, 458, 465, 472, 543, 548; *CCR, 1302–1307*, 20, 21, 131, 137, 151, 160, 166, 237, 238, 256, 276, 289, 292, 297, 368, 390, 415, 478; *CCR, 1307–1313*, 1, 32, 84, 92, 93, 111, 177, 179, 188, 189, 201, 219, 275).

Gaveston.[110] Royal lordship was not a central issue. Edward preferred as patronage grants of royal demesne lands, escheated honors, and forfeited estates. Gaveston received a remarkable number of baronial lands, but only a few wardships. The grievances that barons presented to Edward in 1310, therefore, did not mention the misuse of royal lordship. They concentrated instead on the bad counsel that had led him to waste his resources, on his failures in Scotland, and on the way in which tax revenues had been spent without any military success or alleviation of prises and purveyances. These were the kinds of issues that had been troubling the barons since 1294.[111] The Ordinances of 1311 aimed at correcting financial abuses through a tighter control over financial institutions and personnel as well as over policy making. The Ordainers relied on the same mechanisms employed by the reformers of 1258: removal of royal officers, control of appointments, swearing of oaths, and overall supervision of the administration vested in a council. Since wardships, marriages, and escheats were valuable resources that could be applied to the king's finances, the Ordainers lumped them together with other assets and proclaimed that those assets could not be granted without the Ordainers' permission, that they should be applied to the reduction of the king's debts, and that those which had been granted out should be resumed into the king's hands.[112]

For the first time, therefore, the Ordinances provided for the systematic resumption of royal gifts including wardships and marriages.[113] It was the most ambitious effort to restrict the exercise of royal lordship and patronage that the barons devised during the thirteenth and early fourteenth centuries. The reform barons had seized some lands and rights held by the Poitevins when they sent them into exile in 1258, but they did not attempt a general resumption of Henry's gifts. The Ordainers limited their attention to grants made by Edward after the election of the Ordainers on 16 March 1310. A list of the lands and wardships to be resumed had probably been drawn up from the patent rolls and was ready

---

[110] Maddicott, *Thomas of Lancaster*, 67–120.

[111] *Annales Londonienses*, in *Chronicles of Edward I and Edward II*, 1:168–169, cited by Maddicott, *Thomas of Lancaster*, 110–111; and Prestwich, *War, Politics and Finance*, 221, 272–277.

[112] *Statutes of the Realm*, 1:157–168, esp. caps. 3 and 7. For a general summary of the Ordinances and their precedents, see J. C. Davies, *Baronial Opposition*, 343–393; and Harriss, *King, Parliament and Public Finance*, 160–178.

[113] Wolffe, *The Royal Demesne*, 72–75.

when the Ordinances were published on 10 October 1311, for a schedule of such assets was delivered the following day to the two escheators north and south of the Trent.[114] The writ directed the escheators to seize such lands and keep them until further orders. The escheators had custody only a short time before the king ordered them to restore the lands to the former guardians or to turn them over to new ones. The government did not retain the lands indefinitely to raise revenue.

The process of resumption can be seen clearly in the fate of the lands of John Wake, baron of Bourne, Liddel Strength, and Cottingham, which came under Edward's control in 1309.[115] Edward used the lands to reward a variety of friends and pay some debts. He farmed manors, at their extended value, to John de Wigeton, a northern knight; John de Hotham, one of Gaveston's stewards and later bishop of Ely and treasurer; and to Henry de Lacy, the earl of Lincoln.[116] Edward ordered Lacy to pay the farm to Guy Ferre, in order to repay Edward's debts to Guy, but Lacy died in 1311. Edward then granted the lands to his queen, Isabella, under the same conditions. Isabella had already received custody of other Wake lands.[117] William Trente received the wardship of some lands for a term of four years to repay Edward's debt of £400 to Trente. Edward also granted lands to Henry de Percy, John de Segrave, and Henry de Appleby. Percy granted his rights in the manor of Kirkby Moreshead to a group of merchants from Lucca to repay his debts to them.[118] On the whole, Edward's use of the wardship had not been irresponsible. Indeed, as the Ordainers demanded, it had been directed toward the reduction of some of Edward's debts. Nevertheless, all but one of these grants were annulled by the Ordinances, and the wardships were taken back into the king's hands. The exception was the grant to Wigeton that had been made in December 1309, before the election of the Ordainers. Within a few months, Edward restored most of the others to

[114] CChRV, 98–102; PRO, E.163/3/11 (schedule for north of the Trent); J. C. Davies, Baronial Opposition, 386–387.

[115] Wake died in 1300 but was jointly enfeoffed of his lands with his wife who survived to 1309 (CCR, 1296–1302, 295, 353, 401; CIPM, 3:597; CFR, 2:50; Cokayne, Complete Peerage, 12:2:302–304; Moor, Knights, 5:134–135; EB, 37, 107–108, 129).

[116] CFR, 2:53–54, 55, 56, 64, 76.

[117] CPR, 1307–1313, 235, 330, 349, 395; CCR, 1307–1313, 270, 300, 307–308, 391–392; CCR, 1313–1318, 299–300; CFR, 2:107.

[118] CPR, 1307–1313, 218–219, 224, 277, 287, 388; CFR, 2:61.

the previous recipients.[119] The lands formerly held by Hotham went to the queen instead, while her lands went to William Inge, who enjoyed them only until the following March, when Edward turned them over to Thomas Wake, even though he was not yet of age. The wardship of the manor of Kirkby took a more tortuous path but eventually returned to the possession of the merchants of Lucca. The marriage of the heir, which Edward had originally given to Gaveston so that he could arrange a marriage for his daughter, was likewise resumed and likewise restored in March 1312, after the Ordinances had been revoked.[120]

The resumptions caused an upheaval in the possession of wardships but did not result in permanent losses for most guardians. The Ordainers ordered the resumption of twenty-nine wardships. In at least one case, they were overly zealous. Robert de Wateville had received the wardship and marriage of the lands and heirs of Robert de Wassingley from Edward on 7 October 1309. On 7 August 1310, within the period specified by the Ordinances, Edward enlarged the original grant to include the right to successive heirs if the first heir died while a minor. Presumably, the Ordainers ordered the resumption on the basis of that amplification. On the other hand, they left untouched at least ten grants of wardships that Edward made within the specified term. The royal council had authorized one of the grants, but most were issued under privy seal.[121] It is not known why these were overlooked. The Ordainers did not betray any special preference in ordering the resumptions, for they included one of their members, Gilbert de Clare, as well as the hated Henry de Beaumont and others. Some of these wardships, especially those forfeited by Beaumont, were granted to others.[122]

The resumptions fulfilled the fiscal goals of the Ordinances primarily through the imposition of fines. The lands themselves produced only modest gains for the Crown. They were in custody only a short time, and Edward often gave the guardians the issues when he restored the lands. The escheator north of the Trent thus ac-

[119] PRO, E.372/160 m. 48 (account of the escheator north of the Trent, 5 Edward II); *CCR, 1307–1313*, 390, 391–392; *CPR, 1307–1313*, 407.

[120] *CPR, 1307–1313*, 219, 408, 410, 434, 452; *CCR, 1307–1313*, 428–429, 442; *CCR, 1313–1318*, 13, 22; *CFR*, 2:53; Maddicott, *Thomas of Lancaster*, 121–123, for the revocation of the Ordinances.

[121] *CPR, 1307–1313*, 319, 338, 339, 349, 357, 379, 407; *CFR*, 2:82, 102.

[122] *CPR, 1307–1313*, 412, 414, 416; *CFR*, 2:151, 376; *CCR, 1307–1313*, 394, 396; PRO, E.372/160 m. 48.

counted for receipts of just over £24 10s. from resumed wardships.[123] The real benefits came from fines. In the three years between 1308 and 1311, Edward had levied a total of 224 marks in fines for wardships. As in the case of the Wake lands, some guardians paid rents for their wardships, but on the whole, Edward did not extract as much as he could have from his grants. In contrast, fines totaled 16,829 marks between 1311 and 1315, or an average of about 3,366 marks a year. Many of those were levied when wardships were restored after having been resumed, such as the 6,000 marks charged to Ralph de Monthermer for the restoration of the wardship of the barony of Beverstone.[124] Finally, aside from resuming old wardships, the Ordainers authorized only four new grants of wardships after October, and all four went to one of their number, Gilbert de Clare, to help pay the king's debts to him.[125]

Although the Ordainers ruled only a short time before Edward reasserted his authority, the idea of restricting and resuming royal gifts was not forgotten. It formed the central element of the earl of Lancaster's program when he gained sufficient strength to impose his views on the government in 1314–1316 and again, briefly, in 1318. Lancaster pushed for the revival of the Ordinances in Parliament in the autumn of 1314, and Edward complied the following spring, ordering resumptions on 5 March 1315.[126] In 1318 the politics were more delicate, and Lancaster encountered tenacious opposition from the courtiers over his proposal for a sweeping revocation of royal gifts. After prolonged negotiations between April and June, Lancaster finally prevailed, and on 9 June Edward ordered lands, wardships, and other assets resumed.[127]

In each case, the administrative process followed the pattern laid out in 1311. The king sent the order for resumption to the Exchequer, which then drew up a schedule of items granted after 16 March 1310 that were to be taken into custody and delivered it to

---

[123] PRO, E.372/160 m. 48.

[124] CPR, 1307–1313, 352, 393, 408; CFR, 2:109, 121; CCR, 1307–1313, 390; PRO, SC.1/45/165; EB, 14–15; J. C. Davies, Baronial Opposition, 387. Edward attempted to sell the wardship to Despenser for 2,500 marks after it had been resumed, but the Ordainers prevented him from doing so. Edward pardoned 3,000 marks of Ralph's fine in consideration of Ralph's expenses in the king's service in Scotland.

[125] CPR, 1307–1313, 409–410.

[126] J. C. Davies, Baronial Opposition, 400–405; Maddicott, Thomas of Lancaster, 160–189, esp. 178–180.

[127] Maddicott, Thomas of Lancaster, 216, 218–219, 221–226, 237–239, 337; Auctore Bridlingtoniensi, in Chronicles of Edward I and Edward II, 2:54–55; Vita, 85–87.

the escheators to be executed.[128] The escheators then seized the lands and wards and kept them until further orders. In most cases, the king quickly authorized a restoration of the items to the former recipient though under new terms, such as for a fine or rent. Edward learned in 1316 that the lands, wardships, castles, and so forth seized the year before had not only been insufficiently cared for but also been leased for less than their true value, and he ordered the leases revoked and the assets relet at new rates.[129] The order of 1318 was the most thorough of all, calling for a resumption of the receipts from lands given away as well as the lands themselves, whether they had been sold in the meantime or not.[130]

The intention of these resumptions was to increase the king's revenues and to strengthen his finances, but the results were disappointing. The government raised some income from rents and increased fines, but officials encountered problems that hindered their efforts, as an account of the escheator north of the Trent for 1315–1316 makes clear.[131] Of twelve tenements and wardships that the escheator had taken into custody in the months after the order of March 1315, one had been granted to the queen, one had been rented out, five had been restored, and five produced no income because they were located in the Marches of Scotland and had been devastated by the Scots. Those which had been in the escheator's custody were retained for only a few months at most. Even when fines were levied, they did not always produce the intended revenue. After the wardship and marriage of Roger, son and heir of William de Huntingfeld, had been resumed into royal custody in 1315, for example, Edward sold them back to Hugh Despenser the Younger for £950: £650 for the lands (£50 a year for thirteen years) and £300 for the marriage.[132] Yet shortly after the sale, Edward pardoned Despenser the £950, ostensibly for expenses that Despenser had incurred on Edward's service in Scotland.[133] The total income received from the resumptions was therefore slight. The proceeds from the resumptions of 1318, in spite of their scope, were likewise meager, this time because Ed-

---

[128] *CFR*, 2:240–244 (1315); PRO, E.372/162 m. 40 (escheator's account, 1315); E.372/164 m. 37 (1318). The first account refers to a schedule and the second to a roll.

[129] PRO, E.159/89 m. 34, 25 April 1316.

[130] Maddicott, *Thomas of Lancaster*, 337.

[131] PRO, E.136/3/18.

[132] *CFR*, 2:242, 278.

[133] PRO, E.159/89 m. 39.

ward successfully bought off Lancaster in the parliament at York in the fall and was able to curtail the resumptions.[134] The escheator north of the Trent accounted for less than £25 from the issues of the lands that had been resumed into custody. He noted that most had been restored to the former guardians "ex assensu prelatorum, comitum, baronum, et procerum regni in parliamento apud Eborum."[135]

The restriction of the king's freedom to distribute patronage attacked a crucial instrument of feudal monarchy and infuriated Edward. Not surprisingly, when his power revived in 1316–1317, he used his command of these resources to build up a party at court that he hoped would protect him from his baronial opponents. This political favoritism in turn angered Lancaster and explains the vehemence of his attack on the courtiers as well as the scope of the resumptions that he called for in 1318. In the factionalized politics of those years, both sides perceived that control of the mechanisms for the distribution of royal patronage was essential to the maintenance of political advantage. In this way, what had originated largely as a device to improve royal finances and ease the king's fiscal demands on tenants-in-chief and subjects became politicized. There had, of course, always been a political dimension to the measures, but after 1316, grants and resumptions were more thoroughly subordinated to short-term political goals. This stands out clearly in Lancaster's attack on the courtiers in 1318 and in their consequent apprehension about the effects of the resumptions: "All the others hated the earl because he wanted to uphold the Ordinances. For they, according to the Ordinances, were to be removed from the king's court and would likewise lose the lands they had received from the king. They therefore intrigued against the earl as best they could."[136]

In 1321 Lancaster seized on the issue of disinheritance raised by Edward's seizure of Gower to mobilize yet another assault on the court in hopes of putting his reform program into place. Although the issue was of general concern to tenants-in-chief, neither the rebellion nor Lancaster himself was popular. As a result, only the Marcher lords supported it enthusiastically, and the Contrariants, as they were called, had difficulty raising support. They resorted to coercion in some cases, which probably made their cause all the

[134] Maddicott, *Thomas of Lancaster*, 229–239.
[135] PRO, E.372/164 m. 37.
[136] *Vita*, 87; Maddicott, *Thomas of Lancaster*, 190–213.

more unpopular.[137] In any case, Edward defeated the rebels at Boroughbridge in March 1322.

Edward's victory eliminated the threat of further baronial interference and left Edward free to exercise his lordship as he pleased. In the last years of his reign, the names of the Despensers and their associates, such as Bacon, Baldock, Camoys, Cliff, and Constantine de Mortimer, stand out prominently among those who received gifts of wardships and marriages.[138] If the Despensers received less than might have been expected, it was due to the fact that they received a substantial share of the lands forfeited by the Contrariants in 1321 and then augmented those lands by terrorizing other landholders.[139]

The thoroughness of Edward's victory meant that politics receded somewhat and were overtaken by financial concerns. Pulled by greed, Despenser's as well as his own, and pushed by financial necessity when he was unable to raise taxes after 1323, Edward turned to the exploitation of his traditional sources of revenue, including royal lordship.[140] In the four years between 1322 and 1325, for instance, he charged a total of 6,591 marks in fines for wardships and marriages, or about 1,648 marks a year. At the same time, he levied at least 2,000 marks a year in rent on twenty-five wardships. He also persisted in seizing lands alienated without license and levying fines for the trespass, as he did on widows and others who married without license. As a result, receipts from the escheators rose. The government reorganized the escheatries in 1322, dividing the country into eight districts, each managed by a separate escheator. The intention was probably to improve the efficiency of the escheators, who had become overburdened with work from the later years of Edward I onward. If so, the experiment was successful, for the income from feudal sources increased significantly.[141] The Exchequer reforms of 1326 also called for a tightening of procedures regarding the collection of reliefs, the payment of fines or farms by widows, and the accounting of ward-

[137] Scott L. Waugh, "The Profits of Violence: The Minor Gentry in the Rebellion of 1321–1322 in Gloucestershire and Herefordshire," *Speculum* 52 (1977): 849–850.
[138] *CPR, 1321–1324*, 301, 416; *CPR, 1324–1327*, 95, 261–262; *CFR*, 3:206–207, 275, 312, 349, 358, 365, 375.
[139] N. Fryde, *Tyranny*, 69–86, 106–118.
[140] Ibid., 87–105; Mark Buck, "The Reform of the Exchequer, 1316–1326," *EHR* 98 (1983): 241–260; idem, *Politics, Finance and the Church*, 163–196.
[141] Stevenson, "The Escheator," 119–120; S. T. Gibson, "The Escheatries, 1327–1341," *EHR* 36 (1921): 218–219; Buck, "Reform of the Exchequer," 257 n. 5.

ships.¹⁴² Ironically, therefore, Edward in the last years of his reign put into practice some of the principles called for in 1258 and again in 1311 and made better fiscal use of his rights of wardship and marriage than either his father or grandfather.

Edward's wealth, however, did not save him, and his regime fell with remarkable ease when Isabella and Mortimer invaded in 1326. Edward's deposition and the accession to the throne of a boy under the tutelage of his mother and her accomplice weakened the monarchy. Royal lordship was momentarily vulnerable to baronial attack. In the first parliament of the new reign, the "communalte" of the realm presented a series of petitions calling for certain modifications in the governance of the realm, including the exercise of royal lordship.¹⁴³ They did not call for an enforcement of the Ordinances and did not seek wide-ranging reforms. Instead they asked for changes in practices that affected their interests. The only echo of the financial provisions of the Ordinances could be heard in their request that escheats be used to support the royal family rather than raising money from the king's subjects, which the council accepted.¹⁴⁴

A group of five petitions related to the exercise of royal lordship.¹⁴⁵ The self-interest of the petitioners was made evident in their request that the king levy the debts of deceased tenants-in-chief from the executors or from the heirs when they came of age instead of from the guardians of the lands, who lost the profits of their wardship when that happened.¹⁴⁶ Two other petitions took up the issue raised by the forfeiture of Gower and asked, first, that lands alienated without license no longer be seized and treated as forfeit and, second, that lands held in chief *ut de honore* or by escheat or purchase not be seized when alienated without license, since the king only exercised the rights of other lords over such lands.¹⁴⁷ The petition asserted that in the former case only a fine

¹⁴² *Red Book*, 3:952–955, cited by Buck, "Reform of the Exchequer," 255.

¹⁴³ *Rotuli Parliamentorum Anglie Hactenus Inediti, MCCLXXIX–MCCCLXXIII*, ed. H. G. Richardson and George Sayles (London, 1935), 100–103, 116–126; *Rot. Parl.*, 2:7–11. According to Richardson and Sayles, their petitions (100–103, 116–126) represent an earlier stage of the proceedings than those in *Rot. Parl.* In what follows, references to the earlier petitions are in brackets. The council's replies are printed in *Rot. Parl.*, 2:11–12.

¹⁴⁴ *Rot. Parl.*, 2:7–11: 23, 24 [24, 25].

¹⁴⁵ Ibid.: 27, 28, 30, 34, 35 [29–33]. It is clear from the earlier stage that the petitions were considered as a unit.

¹⁴⁶ Ibid.: 28 [30].

¹⁴⁷ Ibid.: 27, 30 [29, 31].

should be levied. The latter had been the subject of a petition in 1325, which complained that after the forfeitures of 1322 escheators had acted on the assumption that forfeited lordships were held *ut de corona* and had been seizing lands that tenants of those lordships alienated without license contrary to Magna Carta. The king and council agreed that Magna Carta limited his rights with respect to lands held *ut de honore*.[148]

Two petitions in 1327 related to prerogative wardship. One claimed that in cases in which a tenant-in-chief held some lands in socage and other lands in chief of the king by military service, the wardship of the socage lands belonged to the nearest friend, not to the king who had taken custody of such lands contrary to custom.[149] The other asked for a more radical change in the king's rights: that when a tenant-in-chief died holding of other lords besides the king, the king take the wardship of only those lands held of him as well as the marriage, leaving other lands to the custody of their proper lords.[150] This request recalled that made in the Petition of the Barons in 1258. Prerogative wardship was the least popular aspect of royal lordship, and since the late twelfth century, at least, mesne lords had been trying to cut it back.

Although the king was in a vulnerable position, he did not give the commonalty all that they requested, as is evident in the replies to the petitions and in the statute that resulted from them. The council straightforwardly rejected the request for the abandonment of prerogative wardship and in the case of socage tenures stated that since the Crown had been seised of that right and the king was underage, judgment would have to wait until he came of age.[151] The council referred the request about debts to the Exchequer. The two issues concerning alienation found their way into the statute. In reference to the alienation of lands held *ut de honore*, it enacted that the king could not seize such lands.[152] The enactment concerning alienations of other lands was somewhat less significant than has been asserted.[153] The petition stated that in such cases lands should not be seized and regarded as forfeit. The council was surely correct, though somewhat disingenuous, when it re-

---

[148] Ibid., 1:430.
[149] Ibid., 2:7–11: 34 [32].
[150] Ibid.: 35 [33].
[151] Ibid., 2:12.
[152] *Statutes of the Realm*, 1:256 (no. 13).
[153] Bean, *Decline*, 101.

plied that alienated lands had never been forfeit.[154] The forfeiture of Gower had been an aberration, but it was a dangerous precedent, and the barons wanted to ensure that it would not be repeated. Had the statute followed through with the petition as it was presented and had it in fact prohibited the king from *seizing* such lands, then it would have seriously eroded the king's authority. Such seizures were like distraints, intended to encourage the purchaser to pay the fine, and were, in that sense, part of the due process that the petition sought. The statute thus stated that henceforth alienated lands would not be forfeit and that there would be a reasonable fine levied in Chancery by due process.[155] The escheators' accounts, in fact, make it clear that during the early years of Edward III's reign they continued to take custody of alienated lands held *ut de corona* while explicitly obeying the statute by not seizing lands held *ut de honore*.[156] In as weak a position as he was in 1327, Edward III did not concede any of the essential elements of his lordship. Mortimer, who dominated the government, was no Montfort, nor even a Lancaster. He did not seek any fundamental reforms. As a political opportunist he was not about to hobble royal lordship just at the point that he was able to manipulate it for his profit.

Like the period of baronial reform in the thirteenth century, Edward II's reign witnessed a series of political convulsions in which the exercise of royal lordship was subordinated to the immediate political needs of the contestants. Factionalization brought about by perceived abuses in the distribution of the king's wealth, including but not primarily his feudal wealth, polarized the political community. Those opposing the king sought, as before, to control that distribution in order to alleviate the king's fiscal demands on the community of the realm and to secure the share of patronage to which they felt they were entitled.

The political treatment of royal lordship between 1217 and 1326, therefore, reflects the attitude of tenants-in-chief toward their lord. Relations between the king and his tenants were conditioned by the seigniorial framework in which they flourished. They had achieved a high degree of cooperation because the exercise of royal lordship had been beneficial to both lord and tenants. The distribution of rights and the arrangement of marriages con-

---

[154] *Rot. Parl.*, 2:12. For the seizure of alienated lands after 1327, see PRO, E.136/2/1, and E.357/2.

[155] *Statutes of the Realm*, 1:256 (no. 12).

[156] PRO, E.136/2/1; E.357/2 m. 29d.

formed, for the most part, to the expectations of the families of the landholding community, and most of the wealth that came into the king's hands was recirculated through the ranks of the land-holders via patronage. There is no evidence of gross abuse of the king's rights over wards and widows. The only one of the king's rights that consistently rankled was prerogative wardship, because it undercut the profits that lords could enjoy from some of their military tenants. Tenants therefore came to expect that royal lord-ship would not weigh heavily on them, that it would be exercised reasonably, and that they would enjoy some of its benefits. They also regarded feudal incidents as assets that should be applied to royal expenses, in place of making extra demands on them. The most significant difference in outlook, therefore, arose over the issue of patronage. It was an important issue because it brought together all of these expectations and attitudes: that tenants would share their lord's wealth when it consisted of their own property, that government would be inexpensive and nonintrusive, that a lord should not make undue demands on free tenants, and that the tenants could restrain the actions of their lord if they perceived those actions to be harmful to their interests. The principle aim of the barons whenever they opposed the king during that century was to restrict the king's absolute freedom to distribute his feudal incidents. To legitimize their efforts, they declared that feudal re-sources should be put to responsible fiscal use.

CONCLUSION

Until the early fourteenth century, the feudal authority of the king of England was neither anachronistic nor inconsequential. Thomas Bisson has stated that the "problem of feudal monarchy is to explain how the rulers of the later feudal age adapted vassalic and feudal principles to their residual structures of higher authority, to analyze the mix of feudal and regalian resources in those critical generations when the precedents for effective royal power were hardening into law."[1] In England, sovereignty and suzereinty reinforced one another. Strong lordship was an impetus behind bureaucratic development, while the increasing sophistication of institutions, routines, and record keeping held English tenants more closely to their feudal obligations. Lordship and its adjuncts from law to feudal incidents retained a prominent place at the center of political relations throughout the era of bureaucratic kingship. From Magna Carta onward, Crown and tenants worked within a cooperative framework of agreed rules and routines that endured through the Middle Ages into the Tudor era. Yet it must also be noted that Magna Carta marked an important change in emphasis in feudal relations. It can be characterized as a shift from discipline to incentive: away from the harsh enforcement of tenurial duties to the inducement of loyalty through the distribution of feudal patronage. That change and its consequences are evident in three areas: the politics of royal lordship, institutionalization, and family and property.

The Crown's seigniorial authority was based on customs and ceremonies that had developed in the brutal political landscape of Normandy and the early Norman kingdom in England, when the survival of the duke-king depended on the rigorous enforcement of tenurial obligations. As part of the discipline he imposed on his tenants-in-chief, the royal overlord demanded standards of conduct for the exercise of their lordship over subtenants. The king wanted to ensure that honorable men would be honorably treated. This use of law was not exceptional. Everywhere in Europe, kings relied on justice and law to gain recognition that they occupied a superior place within the community of the realm. What was special about the English case was the *form* that that justice took. Henry II and his judges formulated a deceptively simple set of

[1] Thomas N. Bisson, "The Problem of Feudal Monarchy: Aragon, Catalonia, and France," *Speculum* 53 (1978): 460–478, quote at 477.

273

rules and procedures for protecting a tenancy from seigniorial ca-
priciousness. The reform had far-reaching consequences. It demanded that landlords exercise their feudal authority according to
certain rules. Tenants-in-chief learned the lesson all too well, for
they imposed it on their own lord in Magna Carta. In that sense,
Magna Carta marks the end of customary lordship in England. It
also ended the era of arbitrary discipline, so that in ruling his tenants the king henceforth had to emphasize the other aspect of feudal relations—patronage.

Rewards were an important aspect of a polity marked by the mutual dependence of Crown and baronage. The mix of regalian and
feudal authority in England depended heavily on a mix of baronial
and royal responsibility. Outside of the household, the king could
not govern without the nobility and the knightly class in every
county. He depended on them for military assistance, for extraordinary monetary support, and for governance itself. They looked
to the Crown to settle disputes, protect property, ensure smooth
succession, and promote themselves and their kin. Gifts served the
obvious economic function of distributing wealth and compensat-
ing work. They played an equally important role in reifying the
ideal of reciprocal exchange upon which the success of this interdependence rested. The act of offering and accepting rewards fulfilled the obligation created by the offer of service and loyalty. It
simultaneously established a hierarchy of honor and differentiated
lord and servant, or superior and inferior. Gifts of feudal incidents
enhanced this differentiation since the gifts derived from the
king's power as a landlord and involved his tenants' families and
resources. They, too, raised the issue of reciprocity: the landlord's
responsibility toward his tenant, which was mirrored in the king's
Christian obligation to protect widows and orphans. From beginning to end, the exchange encapsulated the values of feudal society shared by the Crown, nobility, and administration.

There were, however, limits to this cooperation. Royal lordship
not only set the Crown apart from tenants-in-chief but contained
potential dangers for them. The misuse of feudal authority could
upset the arrangements they made for the protection of their
lands and families. A more constant danger was the misuse of patronage. Those closest to the throne were tempted to skew the distribution of rewards in their favor, just as the king was tempted to
lavish gifts on his friends. An immoderate distribution of rewards
or the unjust exercise of lordship alike threatened the rapport between the king and elite as well as the harmony within the elite

itself. Either could result in unsuitable marriages, wasting of property, and factionalization.

It was the weakness of the feudal system of governance, however, that once a king or lord was set on a particular practice or policy, only a demonstration of power—of the cohesion and determination of the elite—could force him to act contrary to his wishes. The relationship between the king and his tenants-in-chief was punctuated by bouts of distrust that sometimes led to outright conflict. When it did occur in the thirteenth and early fourteenth centuries, political conflict served in part to define the limits of the king's seigniorial authority. Magna Carta did not eviscerate royal lordship, nor did it regulate all aspects of lordship. It set out a few explicit markers that outlined the general territory within which the king was supposed to exercise his power. Between those markers, there were numerous points at which conduct was unspecified: primer seisin, consent to marriage, alienation of lands, disposal of wardships, and so on. It was precisely at those points that Henry III and most especially Edward I asserted their authority. And it was there that controversy sometimes arose. In the absence of any explicit restrictions, the Crown always proceeded on the assumption that it could exercise its lordship as it pleased or that it was entitled to whatever it sought. It likewise assumed that it could distribute feudal gifts as it pleased. For the most part, patronage and lordship were not objectionable, but when they were, the nobility acted to correct behavior that appeared to threaten its dearest interests. That was the function of conflict: a kind of discipline imposed by tenants on their lord.

The nature of the baronial challenge to royal lordship also changed after Magna Carta. It can be summarized as a shift from principles to technicalities. Instead of trying to formulate broad, customary principles, baronial reformers tried to control the exercise of lordship through administration and law. Yet the control of patronage in particular proved to be a complex issue. It was divisive because the barons did not all view it the same way. It was not amenable to statements of principle because the barons recognized that it was the lord's right to give away what he had and because, out of self-interest, they did not want to restrict too closely his powers of gift giving. That statement assumes that they thought of the issue as an absolute choice between restricted and unrestricted lordship, which they probably did not. Their reaction to royal patronage was more likely based on their immediate perception of how it affected their own interests. If it was deemed harmful, the harm had to be stopped. That could be achieved most effectively in the short term by regulating the flow of favors rather than by stating unchanging principles. Officials' oaths, committees, baronial councils, and finally resumptions made up the stock of devices they employed to control feudal patronage. The only principle that they enunciated was vague: a sense that the king should not dispense gifts when his finances would not bear it. These are the seeds of the notion that he should "live on his own," which in this case included his feudal resources. More and more over the thirteenth century, the questioning of the king's exercise of lordship thus took a financial form: complaints about the cost of government and the proper role of feudal resources in royal finances. Though financial in form, it was in substance a question of how the king wielded his power. Financial remedies restricted his exercise of lordship and curtailed his ability to reward allies, one of the basic tools of a feudal monarch. They also aimed at protecting the elite as a whole from the dangers of a faction.

Opposition to royal lordship was thus largely conducted in the language of fiscal reform. To oppose the immoderate distribution of wardships or the effects of royal lordship on families and property, the barons had to argue that they were acting for the common good, in contrast to the narrow self-interest of the king or his courtiers. As defenders of the common good, they could not be seen to put forth their own interests. Fiscal language afforded them the means of making what was essentially a private (lord-tenant) dispute a public issue. For they were able to focus on the public consequences of royal lordship rather than on its fundamental attributes. Those attributes were, moreover, difficult to attack after Magna Carta. The Charter was of course beneficial to tenants-in-chief because it fixed many of their seigniorial obligations to their lord. Yet it was also helpful to the king. It was, after all, a written recognition of the feudal status quo. In limiting the king's lordship, it acknowledged the king's position as a feudal lord and solidified the lord-tenant relationship between him and the landed elite. Thus it would have been difficult to argue for modifying that relationship without fundamentally changing the provisions of the Charter. It was more efficacious to attack the effects of royal lordship. Reformers sought substantive change only in prerogative wardship, which Magna Carta did not mention and which had a clear financial impact on mesne lordship.

Baronial attitudes and tactics are especially evident in the petitions submitted in 1327. The violent change in regimes offered an opportunity to wring concessions. Yet the barons aimed only for narrow legal adjustments in royal lordship. The only request of broad scope called for the dismantling of prerogative wardship. The petitions illustrate the degree to which tenants-in-chief accepted the basic principles of lordship and the framework of the royal administration. They were not constitutional theorists. They were hardheaded pragmatists with an acute appreciation of their material interests. And they sought administrative protection for those interests. They did not question lordship, rather its exercise. Compared to denunciations of the Court of Wards in the sixteenth and seventeenth centuries, their criticism of royal lordship was feeble. The difference lay in the fact that lordship was still an essential aspect of social relations in the early fourteenth century.

Their pragmatism was, in part, a product of the growing institutionalization of government, law, and lordship over the preceding century. The process is striking in the realm of royal lordship because of the contrast with feudal military service, where the Crown lacked the will to force its tenants-in-chief to provide their full, customary services. Otherwise, the change was not exceptional. The thirteenth century has long been known as the era of bureaucratic kingship. What is less widely appreciated is the degree to which the tenants of English kings were swept up into this process. The establishment of the escheators, the enforcement of primer seisin, controls on widows, restrictions on alienation, and the use of the council or Chancery as a tribunal for the adjudication of disputes affected all tenants-in-chief. The Crown steadily improved the administration of feudal incidents to the point that it supervised every step in the life cycle of its tenants-in-chief. Only villeins were watched more closely. It affected others beyond that circle, for the king's officials always acted on the presumption that a seller of land, a deceased landholder, or a widow held some lands in chief. If they did not, or if they felt their rights had been infringed, they had to go through the procedure of petition, inquest, and hearing to recover their lands. Every landholding family of substance went through that process at one time or another. The institutions of lordship gave the king considerable leverage over his tenements. Indeed, the effectiveness of institutionalized lordship troubled tenants-in-chief and made them wary of royal government. That effectiveness lay behind two recurring complaints about royal lordship: prerogative wardship and waste. It must have been much harder for mesne lords in the thirteenth century to avoid the consequences of tenants' somehow coming to hold lands of the Crown. And the Crown pushed its rights to a fine point. Similarly, estates came into royal custody more frequently, so that there was all the more danger of mischief by royal officials.

While institutionalization produced some tension, it also worked for social stability. It ensured the smooth descent of lands to proper heirs and reduced the opportunities for family quarrels. It provided disinterested procedures for assigning dowers and shares in inheritances. Those routines, moreover, flattened out irregularities in the exercise of power and reduced the unpredictability of customary lordship. Institutionalization, moreover, did not entail a novel centralization of power. Lordship was already centralized; there was only one lord, after all. It is clear that the institutions of the thirteenth century did not mark a radical departure from past practice. They were simple, based on the triad of Chancery, Exchequer, and escheators knit together through writs and inquests. The system may have been irritating at times, but it was orderly and contained remedies for petty abuses. Thus a model of institutionalization that sees the growth of a bureaucratic kingship taking place solely at the expense of other elements of the community fails to account for the many ways in which feudal cooperation survived down through the thirteenth century and beyond. The Crown's development of its feudal rights and institutional procedures in the thirteenth century created a remarkably stable system that functioned effectively for more than two centuries after it came into being.

Nor did it deprive the king of his discretion over tenants. This simplicity allowed the king to keep a close watch on the system and to intervene personally in cases of major tenants, whether to discipline or assist them, or to distribute patronage. The exercise of lordship was entirely in his hands. That is one reason that patronage became such a volatile issue. In general, royal lordship functioned routinely and justly. Patronage, however, was still dispensed at the king's will. Hence, it was still arbitrary, still unpredictable. The imposition of institutional checks was the barons' attempt to rationalize or tame the process of gift giving and bring it under some kind of bureaucratic discipline.

That discipline was important because of the part played by royal lordship in family strategies for descent and inheritance. In those areas, arbitrary actions were especially dangerous. It has been stressed throughout this study that wardship was an imperfect solution to the problem of a minority. It would be seen now as imperfect because it meant trusting a landlord with the welfare of one's children. But medieval men and women would not have seen the issue as a clear-cut choice between two alternatives: family or lordship. What family was there to care for orphaned children? Widows were an obvious choice, but they tended to remarry, and stepfathers had an unsavory reputation. Legal sources show that uncles and other male kin who had the possibility of inheriting were likewise not looked upon as completely trustworthy.

How, then, was kinship instrumental in this society? Clear throughout has been a preoccupation among the elite with inheritance, descent, and alliance. Hope lay with one's children, one's direct lineage, but safety lay in wider ties. That is, the nuclear family was the basic unit for transmitting property and status. Medieval Englishmen in the elite conceived of the family first and foremost as the parents and children and immediate in-laws. This conception is made clear in accounts of deathbed scenes. William Marshal in 1219 and Saher de Quincy the same year in the Holy Land supposedly summoned their children, and Henry de Lacy his son-in-law in 1311, to be by their sides as they died.[2] In the few wills that have survived, men and women bestowed gifts on their sons, made provisions for the marriage of their daughters, and occasionally reached out to nephews and nieces, but did not acknowledge more distant kin.[3] In a fictional setting, when Havelock set about to reclaim his inheritance, he relied on his foster brothers and his friends but did not seek out collateral kin to help him.

Beyond the nuclear group, kin, marriage, and in-laws were instrumental in two ways. In the first place, they represented a safety device for descent, in case the paternal line failed. Above all, it was the precariousness of the nuclear unit in the face of grave demographic uncertainties that made all of these ties necessary. Cousins and other kin were useful in marriage strategies and as a last resort in preserving an inheritance. They provided a means of counteracting some of the effects of diverging devolution. Second, they were important in terms of alliance and exchange. The family was not an independent, autonomous unit. It was woven into a series of relations and bonds that overlapped and crisscrossed one another. It could not act on its own. If men and women were to defend their property, marry their children, guarantee their acts, or participate in public life, then they needed kin, neighbors, clients,

---

[2] *Annales de Waverleia*, in *Annales Monastici*, 2:292; and *Trokelowe*, 3:72.

[3] See, for example, the thirteenth- and early-fourteenth-century wills summarized in *Testamenta Vetusta, Being Illustrations from Wills of Manners, Customs, etc.*, ed. Nicholas Harris Nicholas (London, 1826), 1:47–59; and M. S. Giuseppi, "On the Testament of Sir Hugh Nevill Written at Acre, 1267," *Archaeologia*, 2d ser., 56 (1899): 351–370; Sheehan, *The Will*, 263–265.

and in-laws. Landholders helped one another acquire wardships and arrange marriages. Marriage pacts, wills, contracts, and deeds were witnessed by a range of in-laws, clients, and some kin. This outer circle of relations could also be a source of political support. But that was not its prime purpose, and it is a mistake to conceive of power and the role of kinship solely in the narrow terms of high politics. The class cohesion that arose out of the multiplicity of ties that families formed with one another was crucial in maintaining the elite's authority over its sources of livelihood and profit: land and labor. The process of marriage, alliance, and filiation were fundamental to this cohesion because they were based on a perception of shared interest in the exchange of children and lands and in the descent of property through inheritance.

Families were therefore constantly seeking ways to make more secure provisions for their property. In that regard they also turned to royal lordship, but through the royal courts. As Robert C. Palmer has argued, they trusted the legal system, and the enduring structure of the courts to provide a continuity or stability over time that could not be ensured biologically. Their gradual adoption of jointures and entails in the late thirteenth century can be attributed to the unsatisfactory nature of marital strategies in general rather than to specific grievances with feudal lordship. Indeed, the king often aided them. The ultimate step, taken much later, was the creation of uses, which nicely summarize the argument presented here. They expressed with legal precision the network of relations upon which landholders had long relied for the protection of their property and families. They also posed a threat to royal lordship. At that point, the aims of tenants and of their landlord diverged radically.

In the thirteenth century, the divergence was barely perceptible and not yet harmful. Royal lordship performed the invaluable functions of providing marriage opportunities and distributing wealth within the elite. It was an essential force in maintaining the network of relations and interests that bound the elite into such a cohesive society. It was equally essential in demonstrating the honor and prestige of the monarchy. Royal lordship, therefore, brought landlord and tenants together in a network of patronage, rules, and personal ceremonies that strengthened the cooperation between the monarch and his leading subjects and made it possible for them to work together in developing the mechanisms of sovereignty.

APPENDIX:
RECEIPTS OF THE ESCHEATORS

It is difficult to calculate the total income from feudal sources because it was composed of several different kinds of revenue that were received by different officials. There was no centralized receipt for fines, leases, or amercements. Fines for wardships and marriages, for example, were paid either to the escheator in the case of minor wardships, to the sheriff, or directly to the Exchequer, wardrobe, or chamber. The government likewise received income from leases and amercements in a variety of ways at a variety of locations. Information about feudal income is thus dispersed through household records, receipt rolls, memoranda rolls, pipe rolls, and the escheators' accounts.

Under these circumstances, the receipts of the escheators provide the best single indication, aside from fines, of changes in the king's feudal revenue, though the information they contain needs to be handled with caution. The escheators accounted for a wide variety of items. The most important were the receipts from lands in their custody whether because of wardship, primer seisin, alienation or marriage without license, forfeiture, or an ecclesiastical vacancy. The exact proportion of those elements changed from year to year, and, in the case of forfeitures and vacancies, they did not represent the full income because other officials often had custody of such lands. Escheators sometimes accounted for the sales and farms of minor wardships. In a few cases they also collected reliefs, though in that respect their duties were more often confined simply to taking security that the relief would be paid. Some items were charged fictitiously. The government, for example, initially held the escheator responsible for the income from lands, based on the value contained in the inquisitions post mortem, that were eventually turned over to Hugh le Despenser, Sr., as repayment of the king's debts to him. Those amounts were then allowed to him in his expenses. The gross receipts, therefore, can be misleading, though they give a sense of the scale of revenues available to the Crown.

In addition, the format of the accounts changed in several ways over the thirteenth and early fourteenth centuries. During the reign of Henry III, the accounts of the two chief escheators were essentially compilations of the accounts of the subescheators in each county and were organized by county. The escheator thus accounted to the Crown for the receipts of his subescheators along with miscellaneous items such as reliefs, the sale of goods, and the sale of wards.[1] In a sense, therefore, the chief escheator acted as the supervisor for the subescheator. This accounting practice may

[1] PRO, E.136/1/2, account of the escheator south of the Trent for 50–52 Henry III; E.372/115 m. 11d; E.372/120 mm. 24–24d and /124 mm. 19–22 (south of the Trent, 54 Henry III–2 Edward I); E.136/1/3, 4, 5, 6, 7 (particulars by county).

281

explain the reforms introduced with the stewards, for the stewards simply acted in the same capacity as the chief escheators and supervised the work of the sheriffs instead of the subescheators in each county. The stewards, however, did not render a composite account, and the sheriffs accounted separately to the Exchequer for the receipts from feudal sources.[2] In the 1280s the accounts changed. Receipts were grouped by tenant rather than by county and were informally divided into two groups: old and new. The account opened with a list of those lands which the escheator had retained in custody from the previous year and followed with those taken into custody during the year of account. The reorganization implies an elaboration of the office of the chief escheator because he now had to organize the information he received from the subescheators into the format of his account at the Exchequer.[3] He did not simply gather information from his subordinates to present to his superiors; he had greater responsibility over the entire process. This division of receipts was formalized in the reign of Edward II, when accounts were explicitly divided into new and old escheats. Under old escheats, the lands were grouped by county, while under the new escheats they were grouped by landholder.[4] Finally, at the beginning of Edward III's reign, the account reverted to the earlier format; it was divided by county, and each county was subdivided into old and new escheats.[5]

The survival of the escheators' accounts has been uneven. There are few for the reign of Henry III, and complete series for both north and south of the Trent survive continuously only from the later years of Edward I. Most of the original accounts (E.136) for this period have been lost, and the table is compiled largely from the enrollments of the escheators' accounts in the section of foreign accounts on the pipe rolls (E.372). Separate enrollments of escheators' accounts survive from the later years of Edward II onward (E.357). The accounts for the period of the experiment with stewards, 1275–1282/1283, are fragmentary. As explained above, each sheriff accounted separately for the escheats and wardships in his county, and only a few of those county accounts survive either as original accounts or as enrollments on the pipe rolls.

The quality of the information thus changes over time so that the receipts are not strictly comparable. The earlier totals probably underestimate the true amount received. Furthermore, the income fluctuated according to the kinds of lands taken into custody and the length of time they were held in custody. For example, the sudden jump in income from north of the Trent in 3–4 Edward II can be attributed to the fact that the lands of Johanna Wake came into custody and produced £585 9s. 7 3/4d.,

---

[2] E.372/125 m. 2; /127 mm. 2, 2d; /128 m. 32; /134 m. 2; E.136/1/10 (Somerset and Dorset).

[3] For example, PRO, E.372/141 mm. 23–24d.

[4] PRO, E.372/166 m. 3; /167 mm. 1–2d.

[5] PRO, E.357/2 mm. 1–4d, 65–66.

or more than two-thirds of the total receipts for those two years. Nevertheless, the overall trend toward higher receipts in the reign of Edward I is undoubtedly an accurate reflection of his effort to raise as much money as possible from his resources. The receipts from the escheatorships after Edward II's reorganization in 1322 likewise reflect his emphasis on increasing his revenues and the improved efficiency of the system.

The figures in the table are primarily gross receipts. They include income from whatever ecclesiastical vacancies the escheator controlled as well as from other feudal sources. All figures have been rounded to the nearest penny. In a few cases, the accounts give totals for multiple years only, and no attempt has been made to average them out.

RECEIPTS OF THE ESCHEATORS (in £)

	South	North	Total
43–46 Henry III	—	398 17s. 10d.	—
43–47 Henry III	206 13s. 3d.	—	—
46–50 Henry III	—	617 19s. 4d.	—
49–50 Henry III	143 6s. 7d.	—	—
50–52 Henry III	360 4s. 5d.	—	—
53–54 Henry III	158 17s.	—	—
52–54 Henry III	—	143 19s. 9d.	—
54 Henry III–2 Edward I	1,571 8s. 7d.	—	—
55 Henry III–2 Edward I	—	496 15s. 7d.	—
2–3 Edward I	—	1,174 3d.	—
2–4 Edward I	2,313 1s. 10d.	—	—
9 Edward I	—	130 15s. 3d.	—
10 Edward I	—	1,065 16d.	—
11 Edward I	—	146 18s. 3d.	—
12 Edward I	—	32 8s. 6d.	—
13 Edward I	—	235 18s. 1d.	—
11–13 Edward I	1,534 18s. 5d.	(416 8s. 11d.)	1,951 7s. 3d.
14 Edward I	1,057 12s. 8d.	153 3s. 3d.	1,210 15s. 11d.
15 Edward I	449 7s. 3d.	111 14s. 4d.	561 1s. 7d.
16 Edward I	749 17s. 11d.	197 11s. 11d.	947 9s. 10d.
17 Edward I	434 8s. 9d.	187 1s. 10d.	621 10s. 7d.
18 Edward I	—	139 6s. 7d.	—
19 Edward I	1,510 16s. 6d.	103 14s.	1,614 10s. 6d.
20 Edward I	—	141 7s. 1d.	—
21 Edward I	—	186 9s. 8d.	—
22 Edward I	—	189 14s. 2d.	—
23 Edward I	—	—	—
24 Edward I	—	573 1s. 5d.	—
25 Edward I	—	512 17s. 9d.	—
26 Edward I	—	312 3s. 4d.	—
27 Edward I	—	215 15s. 3d.	—
26–27 Edward I	2,707 11s. 1d.	(527 18s. 7d.)	3,235 9s. 8d.
28 Edward I	714 9s. 9d.	239 2s. 3d.	953 13s.
29 Edward I	926 15s. 5d.	257 12s. 4d.	1,184 7s. 9d.
30 Edward I	2,317 13s. 1d.	348 14s. 7d.	2,666 7s. 8d.
31 Edward I	1,046 15s. 7d.	295 17s. 3d.	1,342 12s. 10d.
32 Edward I	4,960 11s. 8d.	253 19s. 1d.	5,214 10s. 9d.
33 Edward I	2,097 14s. 10d.	515 2s.	2,612 16s. 10d.
34 Edward I	2,537 19s. 6d.	318 19s.	2,856 18s. 6d.
35 Edward I	1,457 12s. 4d.	114 16s. 2d.	1,572 8s. 6d.
1 Edward II	1,250 5s. 3d.	117 6s. 2d.	1,367 11s. 5d.
2 Edward II	1,866 11s. 5d.	99 12s. 7d.	1,966 4s.

RECEIPTS OF THE ESCHEATORS (in £) (*cont'd*)

	South	North	Total
3 Edward II	1,294 19s. 11d.	387 10s. 11d.	1,682 10s. 10d.
4 Edward II	578 15s. 9d.	473 16s.	1,052 11s. 9d.
5 Edward II	633 5s.	128 17s. 11d.	762 2s. 11d.
6 Edward II	491 4s. 11d.	61 8s. 10d.	552 13s. 9d.
7 Edward II	448 2s. 6d.	65 6s. 9d.	513 9s. 3d.
8 Edward II	993 15s. 9d.	167 10s. 3d.	1,161 6s.
9 Edward II	645 5s.	212 11s. 6d.	857 16s. 6d.
10 Edward II	448 17s. 7d.	96 7s. 3d.	545 4s. 10d.
11 Edward II	233 14s.	104 10s. 10d.	338 4s. 10d.
12 Edward II	207 10s. 4d.	88 4s. 4d.	295 14s. 8d.
13 Edward II	206 14s.	75 8s. 7d.	282 2s. 7d.
14 Edward II	193 12s. 2d.	98 9d.	291 12s. 11d.
15 Edward II	501 11d.	227 13s. 5d.	728 14s. 4d.
16 Edward II	898 15s. 8d.	179 3d.	1,077 15s. 11d.
17 Edward II	—	—	2,248 17s. 2d.
18 Edward II	—	—	2,409 8s. 1d.
19 Edward II	—	—	1,733 10s. 4d.
20 Edward II	—	—	220 15s. 5d.
1 Edward III	670 7s. 7d.	74 1s. 3d.	744 8s. 10d.

SOURCES (chronologically)—*South of Trent*: E.372/105 m. 21; 106 m. 21; /112 m. 2; E.136/1/2; E.372/115 m. 11d; /120 mm. 24–24d; /124 mm. 19–22; /122 m. 7; /133 mm. 31–31d; /141 m. 23–24d; /136 m. 26d; /149 mm. 28–38; /155B mm. 9–11; /158 mm. 33–36d; /161 mm. 45–51; /162 mm. 39–41d; /167 mm. 1–4d, 37–41d; E.352/111 mm. 26–27d; /117 mm. 39–41d; E.357/1; /2 mm. 1–4d.

North of Trent: E.372/105 m. 20d; /112 m. 2; /114 m. 19; /117 m 7; /127 m. 2; /119 m. 21; /128 mm. 34–34d; /133 m. 30d; /136m. 25; /141 m. 26–26d; /147 mm. 32–32d; /150 mm. 41–43d; /153 mm. 33–35; /154 m. 53; /155B mm. 25–25d; /156 m. 50; /160 mm. 48–50d; /162 mm. 34–34d; /164 mm. 37–37d; /166 mm. 31–31d; /177 mm. 37d–38d; /168 mm. 42–45; E.357/1; /2 mm. 65–66.

NOTE: Figures in parentheses are total amounts for the preceding years corresponding to the years in the other escheatorship, when the receipts are recorded for several years.

BIBLIOGRAPHY

Manuscript Sources

Public Record Office

C.47	Chancery Miscellany
C.60	Fine Rolls
C.132	Inquisitions Post Mortem, Henry III
C.133	Inquisitions Post Mortem, Edward I
C.134	Inquisitions Post Mortem, Edward II
C.145	Miscellaneous Inquisitions
C.148	Ancient Deeds, Series CS
C.245	Writs *Scire Facias*
C.257	Writs *Certiorari*
C.270	Marriage and Divorce
CP.25(1)	Feet of Fines
CP.40	Common Pleas
DL.27	Duchy of Lancaster Ancient Deeds
E.13	Exchequer Plea Rolls
E.40	Exchequer Ancient Deeds, Series A
E.101	Exchequer Accounts, Various
E.136	Escheators' Accounts
E.143	Extents and Inquisitions
E.152	Enrolled Escheators' Inquisitions
E.153	Escheators' Files
E.159	Exchequer Memoranda Rolls, King's Remembrancer (KR)
E.163	Exchequer Miscellany
E.202	Exchequer Writs
E.210	Exchequer Ancient Deeds, Series D
E.326	Exchequer Ancient Deeds, Series B
E.352	Chancellor's Rolls
E.368	Exchequer Memoranda Rolls, Lord Treasurer's Remembrancer (LTR)
E.371	Originalia Rolls
E.372	Pipe Rolls
E.401	Exchequer Receipt Rolls
Just.1	Justices Itinerant
KB.26	Curia Regis Rolls
KB.27	Plea Rolls of the King's Bench
SC.1	Ancient Correspondence
SC.6	Ministers' Accounts
SC.8	Ancient Petitions
SC.12	Rentals and Surveys

British Library

Add. MS 32,085, Statute Book
Egerton MS 3724, Mohun Cartulary
Harleian MS 1240, Mortimer Cartulary

Huntington Library

HM. 19,920, Statute Book

PRINTED SOURCES

Chronicles and Narratives

Annales de Waverleia. In vol. 2 of *Annales Monastici*, q.v.
Annales Monastici. Edited by Henry R. Luard. 5 vols. Rolls Series 36. London, 1864–1869.
Annales Prioratus de Dunstaplia, AD 33 to 1297. In vol. 3 of *Annales Monastici*, q.v.
Chronica Monasterii Sancti Albani. Edited by Henry T. Riley 7 vols. Rolls Series 28. London, 1865.
The Chronicle of Bury St. Edmunds, 1212–1301. Edited and translated by Antonia Gransden. London: Thomas Nelson and Sons, 1964.
The Chronicle of Jocelin of Brakelond. Edited and translated by Harold E. Butler. London: Thomas Nelson and Sons, 1949.
The Chronicle of Richard of Devizes. Edited and translated by John T. Appleby. London: Thomas Nelson and Sons, 1963.
The Chronicle of Walter of Guisborough. Edited by Harry Rothwell. Camden Society Publications, 3d ser. 89. London, 1956.
Chronicles of the Reigns of Edward I and Edward II. Edited by William Stubbs. 2 vols. Rolls Series 76. London, 1882–1883.
De Antiquis Legibus Liber: Chronica Majorum et Vicecomitum Londoniarum, 1188–1274. Edited by Thomas Stapleton. Camden Society Publications, o.s. 34. London, 1846.
Gesta Regis Henrici Secundi Benedicti Abbatis. Edited by William Stubbs. 2 vols. Rolls Series 49. London, 1867.
L'histoire de Guillaume le Maréchal, comte de Striguil et de Pembroke, régent d'Angleterre de 1216 à 1219. Edited by Paul Meyer. 3 vols. Paris: Société de l'histoire de France, 1891–1901.
Johannis de Trokelowe. In vol. 3 of *Chronica Monasterii Sancti Albani*, q. v.
Le Lai d'Haveloc and Gaimar's Haveloc Episode. Edited by Alexander Bell. Manchester: Manchester University Press, 1925.
The Lay of Havelock the Dane. Edited by Walter W. Skeat. 2d ed. edited by K. Sisam. Oxford: Oxford University Press, 1915.

Paris, Matthew. *Chronica Majora*. Edited by Henry R. Luard. 7 vols. Rolls Series 57. London, 1872–1883.
————. *Matthew Paris's English History, from the Year 1235 to 1273*. Translated by John A. Giles. 3 vols. London: Henry G. Bohn, 1853.
Roger of Hoveden. *Chronica Rogeri de Houedene*. Edited by William Stubbs. 4 vols. Rolls Series 51. London, 1868–1871.
Trivet, Nicholas. *Nicolai Triveti Annalium Continuatio*. Edited by Anthony Hall. Oxford: Theatro Sheldoniano, 1722.
Vita Edwardi Secundi. Edited and translated by Noël Denholm-Young. London: Thomas Nelson and Sons, 1957.
Vitalis, Orderic. *The Ecclesiastical History of Orderic Vitalis*. Edited by and translated by Marjorie Chibnall. Vol. 6. Oxford: Oxford University Press, 1978.
Willelmi Rishanger, quondam monachi S. Albani, Chronica et Annales. In vol. 2 of *Chronica Monasterii Sancti Albani*, q. v.
William of Newburgh. *Historia Rerum Anglicarum*. In *Chronicles of the Reigns of Stephen, Henry II, and Richard I*. edited by Richard Howlett. 4 vols. Rolls Series 82. London, 1884–1889.

Published and Calendared Documents

Ancient Petitions Relating to Northumberland, edited by Constance M. Fraser. Surtees Society Publications 176. London, 1966.
The Beauchamp Cartulary Charters, 1100–1268, edited by Emma Mason. Pipe Roll Society Publications, n.s. 43. London, 1980 for 1971–1973.
Bracton, Henry de. *De Legibus et Consuetudinibus Angliae*, edited by George E. Woodbine; edited and translated by Samuel E. Thorne. 4 vols. Cambridge: Harvard University Press, Belknap Press; London: Selden Society, 1968–1977.
————. *Bracton's Notebook*, edited by Frederic W. Maitland. 3 vols. London: C. J. Clay for Cambridge University Press, 1887.
Britton, edited and translated by Francis M. Nichols. 2 vols. Oxford: Clarendon Press, 1865.
Calendar of Ancient Petitions Relating to Wales, edited by William Rees. Board of Celtic Studies, History and Law Series 28. Cardiff, 1975.
Calendar of Chancery Rolls, Various, 1277–1326. London: HMSO, 1912.
Calendar of Chancery Warrants (Privy Seals), 1244–1326. London: HMSO, 1927.
Calendar of Entries in the Papal Registers Relating to Great Britain and Ireland: Papal Letters, edited by William H. Bliss and Jesse A. Twemlow. 14 vols. London: HMSO, 1893–1960.
Calendar of Inquisitions Miscellaneous (Chancery), Henry III–Henry V. 7 vols. London: HMSO, 1916–1968.
Calendar of Inquisitions Post Mortem, Henry III–7 Richard II. 15 vols. London: HMSO, 1904–1970.

Calendar of Liberate Rolls, 1226–1272. 6 vols. London: HMSO, 1917–1964.
Calendar of Memoranda Rolls (Exchequer), Michaelmas 1326–Michaelmas 1327. London: HMSO, 1968.
Calendar of the Charter Rolls, 1226–1516. 6 vols. London: HMSO, 1903–1927.
Calendar of the Close Rolls (1272–1485). 45 vols. London: HMSO, 1892–1954.
Calendar of the Fine Rolls. 22 vols. London: HMSO, 1911–1962.
Calendar of the Gormanston Register, edited by James Mills and M. J. Mc-Enery. Royal Society of Antiquaries of Ireland, supplement. Dublin, 1916.
Calendar of the Patent Rolls (1232–1509). 52 vols. London: HMSO, 1891–1916.
Calendar of the Plea Rolls of the Exchequer of the Jews. 4 vols. Vol. 3, edited by Hillary Jenkinson. Jewish Historical Society, London, 1929.
Cartularium Monastarii de Ramesia. edited by William H. Hart and Ponsonby A. Lyons. 3 vols. Rolls Series 79. London, 1884–1893.
Catalogue of Ancient Deeds in the Public Record Office. 6 vols. London: HMSO, 1890–1915.
Close Rolls of the Reign of Henry III (1227–1272). 14 vols. London: HMSO, 1902–1938.
Crown Pleas of the Wiltshire Eyre, 1249, edited by Cecil A. F. Meekings. Wiltshire Archaeological and Natural History Society, Records Branch 16. Devizes, 1961.
Curia Regis Rolls. 16 vols. to date. London: HMSO, 1922–1984.
Documents of the Baronial Movement of Reform and Rebellion, 1258–1267, edited by Ivor J. Sanders and Reginald F. Treharne. Oxford Medieval Texts. Oxford: Oxford University Press, 1973.
Dugdale, William. *Monasticon Anglicanum,* edited by John Caley, Henry Ellis, and Bulkeley Bandinel. 6 vols. in 8. London: James Bohn, 1846.
Early Yorkshire Charters, edited by Charles T. Clay. Yorkshire Archaeological Association Record Series, extra series, The Percy Fee. Wakefield, (1963).
Excerpta e Rotulis Finium, edited by Charles Roberts. 2 vols. London: Record Commission, 1835–1836.
Fitz Nigel, Richard. *Dialogus de Scaccario,* edited and translated by Charles Johnson; corrected by F.E.L. Carter and D. E. Greenway. Oxford: Oxford University Press, 1983.
Fleta, edited and translated by Henry G. Richardson and George O. Sayles. 4 vols. Vols. 2, 3. Selden Society Publications 72, 79. London, 1955, 1972.
Foedera, Conventiones, Litterae, et Cujuscunque Generis Acta Publica, etc., edited by Thomas Rymer; new ed. by John Caley, Adam Clarke, and Frederic Holbrooke. 4 vols. in 7. London: Record Commission, 1816–1869.

Fourth Report of the Royal Commission on Historical Manuscripts. 1 vol. in 2. London: HMSO, 1874.

The Great Roll of the Pipe, 5 Henry II–3 Henry III, A.D. 1158–1219. 56 vols. London: Pipe Roll Society Publications, 1884–1976.

The Great Roll of the Pipe for the First Year of the Reign of King Richard the First, A.D. 1189–1190, edited by Joseph Hunter. London: Record Commission, 1844.

The Great Roll of the Pipe for the Fourteenth Year of the Reign of Henry III, Michaelmas 1230, edited by H. L. Cannon. New Haven: Yale University Press, 1918.

The Great Roll of the Pipe for the Second, Third, and Fourth Years of the Reign of King Henry the Second, A.D. 1156–1158, edited by Joseph Hunter. London: Record Commission, 1844.

Leges Henrici Primi, edited and translated by L. J. Downer. Oxford: Oxford University Press, 1972.

Liber Feodorum: The Book of Fees Commonly Called Testa de Nevill (1198–1293). 2 vols. in 3. London: HMSO, 1920–1931.

Liber Quotidianus Contrarotuloris Garderobae. London: Society of Antiquaries, 1787.

The Memoranda Roll for the Michaelmas Term of the First Year of the Reign of King John, 1199–1200, edited by H. G. Richardson. Pipe Roll Society Publications, n.s. 21. London, 1943.

The Memoranda Roll for the Michaelmas Term of the Tenth Year of the Reign of King John, 1207–1208, edited by R. Allen Brown. Pipe Roll Society Publications, n.s. 31. London, 1957.

The Memoranda Roll of the King's Remembrancer for Michaelmas 1230–Trinity 1231, edited by Chalfant Robinson. Pipe Roll Society Publications, n.s. 11. London, 1933.

Novae Narrationes, edited by Elsie Shanks; completed by S.F.C. Milsom. Selden Society Publications 80. London, 1963.

Parliamentary Writs and Writs of Military Summons, edited by Francis Palgrave. 2 vols. in 4. London: Record Commission, 1827–1834.

Paston Letters and Papers of the Fifteenth Century, edited by Norman Davis. 2 vols. Oxford: Oxford University Press, 1971.

Patent Rolls of the Reign of Henry III (1216–1232). 2 vols. London: HMSO, 1901–1903.

Percy Chartulary, edited by M. T. Martin. Surtees Society Publications 117. London, 1911.

Placita de Quo Warranto Temporibus Edw. I, II, et III. London: Record Commission, 1818.

Placitorum in Domo Capitulari Westmonasterii Asservatorum Abbreviatio. London: Record Commission, 1811.

Pleas before the King or His Justices, 1198–1212, edited by Doris Mary Stenton. 4 vols. Selden Society Publications, 67, 68, 83, 84. London: 1952, 1953, 1967.

Prerogativa Regis: Tertia Lectura Roberti Constable de Lyncolnis Inne Anno 11 H. 7, edited by Samuel E. Thorne. New Haven: Yale University Press, 1949.

Records of the Parliament Holden at Westminster on the Twenty-eighth Day of February, in the Thirty-third Year of the Reign of King Edward the First (A.D. 1305), edited by Frederic W. Maitland. Rolls Series 98. London, 1893.

Records of the Wardrobe and Household, 1285–1286, edited by Benjamin F. Byerly and Catherine Ridder Byerly. London: HMSO, 1977.

The Red Book of the Exchequer, edited by Hubert Hall. 3 vols. Rolls Series 99. London, 1896.

Regesta Regum Anglo-Normannorum. 3 vols. Vol. 2, edited by Charles Johnson and H. A. Cronne. Oxford: Oxford University Press, 1956.

Reports from the Lords Committees Touching the Dignity of a Peer of the Realm (Reports 1–5). 5 vols. London: HMSO, 1820–1829.

Roll of Divers Accounts for the Early Years of the Reign of Henry III, edited by Fred A. Cazel. Pipe Roll Society Publications, n.s. 44. London, 1982.

Rolls of the Justices in Eyre, Being the Rolls of Pleas and Assizes for Gloucester-shire, Warwickshire and Staffordshire, 1221–1222, edited by Doris Mary Stenton. Selden Society Publications 59. London, 1940.

Rotuli Chartarum, 1199–1216, edited by Thomas D. Hardy. London: Record Commission, 1837.

Rotuli de Dominabus et Pueris et Puellis de Donatione Regis in XII Comitatibus, 31 Henry II, 1185, edited by John Horace Round. Pipe Roll Society Publications 35. London, 1913.

Rotuli de Oblatis et Finibus, edited by Thomas D. Hardy. London: Record Commission, 1835.

Rotuli Hundredorum. 2 vols. London: Record Commission, 1812–1818.

Rotuli Litterarum Clausarum, 1204–1227, edited by Thomas D. Hardy. 2 vols. London: Record Commission, 1833–1844.

Rotuli Parliamentorum, ut et Petitiones, et Placita in Parliamento. 6 vols. London: Record Commission, 1832.

Rotuli Parliamentorum Anglie Hactenus Inediti, MCCLXXIX–MCCCLXXIII, edited by Henry G. Richardson and George O. Sayles. Camden Society Publications, 3d ser., 51. London, 1935.

Rotulorum Originalium in Curia Scaccarii Abbreviatio, edited by John Caley and H. Playford. 2 vols. London: Record Commission, 1805–1810.

Rotulorum Patentium et Clausarum Cancellariae Hiberniae Calendarium. Dublin: Irish Record Commission, 1928.

Select Cases in the Court of King's Bench, Edward I–Edward III, edited by George O. Sayles. 5 vols. Selden Society Publications 55, 57, 58, 74, 76. London, 1936, 1938, 1939, 1955, 1958.

Select Charters and Other Illustrations of English Constitutional History, edited by William Stubbs. 9th ed. edited by Henry W. C. Davis. 1870. Reprint. Oxford: Clarendon Press, 1966.

The Song of Lewes, edited and translated by Charles L. Kingsford. Oxford: Oxford University Press, 1890.

State Trials of the Reign of Edward I (1289–1293), edited by Thomas F. Tout and Hilda Johnstone. Camden Society Publications, 3d ser., 9. London, 1906.

Statutes of the Realm, 1101–1713, edited by Alexander Luders, Thomas E. Tomlins, John Raithby et al. 11 vols. London: Record Commission, 1810–1828.

Testa de Nevill, edited by John Caley and William Illingworth. London: Record Commission, 1807.

Testamenta Vetusta, Being Illustrations from Wills of Manners, Customs, etc., edited by Nicholas Harris Nicolas. 2 vols. London: Nichols and Son, 1826.

The Treatise on the Laws and Customs of the Realm of England Commonly Called Glanvill, edited and translated by George D. G. Hall. London: Nelson, in association with the Selden Society, 1965.

Walter of Henley and Other Treatises on Estate Management and Accounting, edited by Dorothea Oschinsky. Oxford: Oxford University Press, 1971.

Wrottesley, George, ed. "The Chetwynd Chartulary." *William Salt Society* 12 (1891): 242–336.

Year Books of Edward II. Vol. 1, *1 and 2 Edward II*, edited by Frederic W. Maitland. Selden Society Publications 17. London, 1903.

Secondary Sources

Allmand, Christopher T. *Lancastrian Normandy, 1415–1450: The History of a Medieval Occupation*. Oxford: Oxford University Press, 1983.

Altschul, Michael. *A Baronial Family in Medieval England: The Clares, 1217–1314*. Baltimore: Johns Hopkins University Press, 1965.

Astill, G. G. "Social Advancement through Seigneurial Service? The Case of Simon Pakeman." *Transactions of the Leicestershire Archaeological and Historical Society* 54 (1978-1979): 14–25.

Aylmer, G. E. *The King's Servants: The Civil Service of Charles I, 1625–1642*. Rev. ed. London: Routledge and Kegan Paul, 1974.

Baker, John H., ed. *Legal Records and the Historian*. London: Royal Historical Society, 1978.

Baldwin, John W. *Masters, Princes, and Merchants: The Social Views of Peter de Chanter and His Circle*. 2 vols. Princeton: Princeton University Press, 1970.

Batten, John. "The Barony of Beauchamp of Somerset." *SANHS* 36 (1891): 20–59.

Bean, John M. W. *The Decline of English Feudalism, 1215–1540*. Manchester: Manchester University Press, 1968.

———. "The Percies' Acquisition of Alnwick." *Archaeologia Aeliana*, 4th ser., 32 (1954): 309–319.

Beebe, Bruce. "The English Baronage and the Crusade of 1270." *BIHR* 48 (1975): 127–148.

Bell, Henry E. *An Introduction to the History and Records of the Court of Wards and Liveries*. Cambridge Studies in English Legal History. Cambridge: Cambridge University Press, 1953.

Bémont, Charles. *Simon de Montfort*, edited and translated by Ernest F. Jacob. Oxford: Oxford University Press, 1930.

Bennett, Michael J. *Community, Class and Careerism: Cheshire and Lancashire Society in the Age of Sir Gawain and the Green Knight*. Cambridge: Cambridge University Press, 1983.

―――. "A County Community: Social Cohesion amongst the Cheshire Gentry, 1400–1425." *Northern History* 8 (1973): 24–43.

Benton, John F. "Clio and Venus: An Historical View of Medieval Love." In *The Meaning of Courtly Love*, edited by F. X. Newman. Albany: State University of New York Press, 1967.

Bisson, Thomas N. "The Problem of Feudal Monarchy: Aragon, Catalonia, and France." *Speculum* 53 (1978): 460–478.

Bourdieu, Pierre. *Outline of a Theory of Practice*. Cambridge Studies in Social Anthropology. Cambridge: Cambridge University Press, 1977.

Brand, Paul A. "Control of Mortmain Alienation in England, 1200–1300." In Baker, *Legal Records and the Historian*, q. v.

Bridgeman, George T. O. "Some Account of the Families of Beysin, Morehall, and Clopton, Lords of Billingsley, Co. Salop." *Transactions of the Shropshire Archaeological and Natural History Society* 1 (1878): 281–309.

Buck, Mark. *Politics, Finance and the Church in the Reign of Edward II: Walter de Stapeldon Treasurer of England*. Cambridge: Cambridge University Press, 1983.

―――. "The Reform of the Exchequer, 1316–1326." *EHR* 98 (1983): 241–260.

Cam, Helen M. *The Hundred and the Hundred Rolls: An Outline of Local Government in Medieval England*. 1930. Reprint. London: Merlin, 1963.

Carpenter, David A. "The Decline of the Curial Sheriff in England, 1194–1258." *EHR* 91 (1976): 1–32.

―――. "The Gold Treasure of King Henry III." In Coss and Lloyd, *Thirteenth Century England I*, q. v.

―――. "King, Magnates, and Society: The Personal Rule of King Henry III, 1234–1258." *Speculum* 60 (1985): 39–70.

―――. "Simon de Montfort and the Mise of Lewes." *BIHR* 58 (1985): 1–11.

―――. "Was There a Crisis of the Knightly Class in the Thirteenth Century? The Oxfordshire Evidence." *EHR* 95 (1980): 721–752.

―――. "What Happened in 1258?" In *War and Government in the Middle Ages: Essays in Honour of J. O. Prestwich*, edited by John Gillingham and James C. Holt. London: Boydell and Brewer, 1984.

Chambers, C. G., and George Herbert Fowler. "The Beauchamps, Barons of Bedford." *Bedfordshire Historical Record Society* 1 (1913): 1–24.

Clanchy, Michael T. "Did Henry III Have a Policy?" *History* 53 (1968): 203–216.

———. *From Memory to Written Record: England, 1066–1307.* Cambridge: Harvard University Press, 1979.

Clay, Charles. "The Family of Longvillers." *YAJ* 42 (1967): 41–51.

Cokayne, George E. *The Complete Peerage of England,* edited by Vicary Gibbs, Herbert A. Doubleday, Duncan Warrand, Geoffrey White et al. 12 vols. in 13. London: St. Catherine's Press, 1910–1959.

Conway, A. E. "The Owners of Allington Castle, Maidstone (1086–1279)." *Archaeologia Cantiana* 29 (1911): 16–20.

Cooke, William H. *Collections towards the History and Antiquities of the County of Hereford, in Continuation of Duncumb's History.* 3 vols. London: John Murray, 1882.

Cooper, J. P. "Patterns of Inheritance and Settlement by Great Landowners from the Fifteenth to the Eighteenth Centuries." In Goody et al., *Family and Inheritance,* q. v.

Coss, Peter R. "Sir Geoffrey de Langeley and the Crisis of the Knightly Class in Thirteenth-Century England." *PP* 68 (1975): 3–37.

———, and Simon D. Lloyd, eds. *Thirteenth Century England I: Proceedings of the Newcastle upon Tyne Conference, 1985.* Woodbridge, Suffolk: Boydell Press, 1986.

Cox, Eugene L. *The Eagles of Savoy: The House of Savoy in Thirteenth-Century Europe.* Princeton: Princeton University Press, 1974.

Critchley, John S. "Summonses to Military Service Early in the Reign of Henry III." *EHR* 86 (1971): 79–95.

Crook, David. "The Later Eyres." *EHR* 97 (1982): 241–268.

Davies, James C. *The Baronial Opposition to Edward II, Its Character and Policy: A Study in Administrative History.* Cambridge: Cambridge University Press, 1918.

———. "The Despenser War in Glamorgan." *TRHS,* 3d ser., 9 (1915): 21–64.

Davies, R. Rees. "Kings, Lords and Liberties in the March of Wales, 1066–1272." *TRHS,* 5th ser., 29 (1979): 41–61.

———. *Lordship and Society in the March of Wales, 1282–1400.* Oxford: Oxford University Press, 1978.

Davis, John Evan. "The Wardrobe of Henry III of England, 1234–1272." Ph.D. diss. Mississippi State University, 1970.

Davis, Ralph H. C. "What Happened in Stephen's Reign." *History* 40 (1964): 1–12.

DéAragon, RaGena. "The Growth of Secure Inheritance in Anglo-Norman England." *Journal of Medieval History* 8 (1982): 381–91.

Denholm-Young, Noël. "The Authorship of the Vita Edwardi Secundi." *EHR* 71 (1956): 189–211.

———. "Feudal Society in the Thirteenth Century: The Knights." *History* 29 (1944): 107–119.

Denholm-Young, Noël. *Richard of Cornwall.* Oxford: Oxford University Press, 1947.

DuBoulay, F.R.H. *The Lordship of Canterbury: An Essay on Medieval Society.* London: Nelson, 1966.

Duby, Georges. "Lignage, noblesse et chevalerie au XIIe siècle dans la région mâconnaise: Une révision." *Annales ESC* 27 (1972): 802–823. Reprinted in idem, *Hommes et structures du Moyen Age.* Paris: Mouton, 1973.

————. *Medieval Marriage: Two Models from Twelfth-Century France,* translated by Elborg Forster. Baltimore: Johns Hopkins University Press, 1978.

Dumont, Louis. "The Marriage Alliance." In *Kinship: Selected Readings,* edited by Jack Goody. Penguin Modern Sociology Readings. Harmondsworth: Penguin Books, 1971.

Ehrlich, Ludwik. *Proceedings against the Crown, 1216–1377.* Oxford Studies in Social and Legal History, edited by Paul Vinogradoff. No. 12. Oxford: Oxford University Press, 1921.

Elton, Geoffrey R. *The Tudor Revolution in Government: Administrative Changes in the Reign of Henry VIII.* Paperback ed. Cambridge: Cambridge University Press, 1966.

Eyton, Robert W. *Antiquities of Shropshire.* 12 vols. London: John Russell Smith, 1853–1860.

————. "Pedigree of the Baronial Houses of Mauduit." *Herald and Genealogist* 7 (1873): 385–394.

Fairbank, F. Royston. "The Last Earl of Warenne and Surrey, and the Distribution of His Possessions." *YAJ* 19 (1907): 193–264.

Farrer, William. "The Feudal Baronage." In *VCH, Lancashire,* vol. 1, q. v.

————. *Honors and Knights' Fees.* 3 vols. Manchester: Manchester University Press, 1923–1925.

————. "The Honour of Old Wardon," introduction by James Tait. *Bedfordshire Historical Record Society* 11 (1927): 1–46.

Foss, Edward. *The Judges of England: With Sketches of Their Lives.* 9 vols. London: Longman, Brown, Green, and Longmans, 1848–1864.

Fowler, George Herbert. "Calendars of Inquisitions Post Mortem II, 1272–1286: Notes." *Bedfordshire Historical Record Society* 19 (1937): 142–170.

Fox, Robin. *Kinship and Marriage: An Anthropological Perspective.* Paperback ed. with new preface. Cambridge: Cambridge University Press, 1983.

Franklin, Peter. "Peasant Widows, 'Liberation' and Remarriage before the Black Death." *Economic History Review,* 2d ser., 39 (1986): 186–204.

Fraser, Constance M. "Edward I and the Regalian Franchise of Durham." *Speculum* 31 (1956): 329–342.

————. "Four Cumberland Widows in the Fourteenth Century." *Transactions of the Cumberland and Westmoreland Antiquarian and Archaeological Society,* n.s. 64 (1964): 130–137.

————. "Prerogative and the Bishops of Durham." *EHR* 74 (1959): 467–476.

Fryde, Edmund B., and Frederick M. Powicke, eds. *Handbook of British Chronology.* 2d ed. London: Royal Historical Society, 1961.

Fryde, Natalie. *The Tyranny and Fall of Edward II, 1321–1326.* Cambridge: Cambridge University Press, 1979.

Gibson, S. T. "The Escheatries, 1327–1341." *EHR* 36 (1921): 218–225.

Giesey, Ralph E. "Rules of Inheritance and Strategies of Mobility in Pre-revolutionary France." *American Historical Review* 82 (1977): 271–289.

Giuseppi, M. S. "On the Testament of Sir Hugh Nevill Written at Acre, 1267." *Archaeologia*, 2d ser., 56 (1899): 351–370.

Goody, Jack. *The Development of the Family and Marriage in Europe.* Past and Present Publications. Cambridge: Cambridge University Press, 1983.

————. "Inheritance, Property and Women: Some Comparative Considerations." In Goody et al., *Family and Inheritance*, q. v.

————. *Production and Reproduction: A Comparative Study of the Domestic Domain.* Cambridge Papers in Social Anthropology 17. Cambridge: Cambridge University Press, 1976.

————, and S. J. Tambiah. *Bridewealth and Dowry.* Cambridge Papers in Social Anthropology 7. Cambridge: Cambridge University Press, 1973.

————, Joan Thirsk and Edward P. Thompson, eds. *Family and Inheritance: Rural Society in Western Europe, 1200–1800.* Past and Present Publications. Cambridge: Cambridge University Press, 1976.

Grassi, J. L. "Royal Clerks from the Archdiocese of York in the Fourteenth Century." *Northern History* 5 (1970): 12–33.

Greenfield, B. W. "Meriet of Meriet and of Hestercombe." *SANHS* 28 (1883): 99–216.

Hallam, Elizabeth M. *Capetian France, 987–1328.* London: Longmans, 1980.

Harriss, Gerald L. *King, Parliament and Public Finance in Medieval England to 1369.* Oxford: Oxford University Press, 1975.

Harvey, Paul D. A. "The English Inflation of 1180–1220." *PP* 61 (1973): 3–30.

Haskins, George L. "Charter Witness Lists in the Reign of King John." *Speculum* 13 (1938): 319–325.

————. "The Doncaster Petition, 1321." *EHR* 53 (1938): 478–485.

Helmholz, Richard H. "Bastardy Litigation in Medieval England." *American Journal of Legal History* 13 (1969): 360–383.

————. *Marriage Litigation in Medieval England.* Cambridge Studies in English Legal History. Cambridge: Cambridge University Press, 1974.

Héritier, Françoise. *L'exercice de la parenté.* Paris: Gallimard, 1981.

Hilton, Rodney H. *A Medieval Society: The West Midlands at the End of the Thirteenth Century.* London: Weidenfield and Nicolson, 1966.

Holdsworth, Christopher J. Introduction to *Rufford Charters*, edited by

Christopher J. Holdsworth. 2 vols. Thoroton Society, Record Series 29. Nottingham, 1972.

Holmes, George A. *The Estates of the Higher Nobility in Fourteenth-Century England.* Cambridge: Cambridge University Press, 1957.

Holt, James C. "Feudal Society and the Family in Early Medieval England: I. The Revolution of 1066." *TRHS,* 5th ser., 32 (1982): 193–212.

———. "Feudal Society and the Family in Early Medieval England: II. Notions of Patrimony." *TRHS,* 5th ser., 33 (1983): 193–220.

———. "Feudal Society and the Family in Early Medieval England: III. Patronage and Politics." *TRHS,* 5th ser., 34 (1984): 1–25.

———. "Feudal Society and the Family in Early Medieval England: IV. The Heiress and the Alien." *TRHS,* 5th ser., 35 (1985): 1–28.

———. *Magna Carta.* Cambridge: Cambridge University Press, 1965.

———. *The Northerners: A Study in the Reign of King John.* Oxford: Oxford University Press, 1961.

———. "Politics and Property in Early Medieval England." *PP* 57 (1972): 3–52.

Howell, Margaret. *Regalian Right in Medieval England.* London: University of London Press, 1962.

Hoyt, Robert S. *The Royal Demesne in English Constitutional History, 1066–1272.* Ithaca: Cornell University Press, 1950.

Hurstfield, Joel. "The Profits of Fiscal Feudalism, 1541–1602." *Economic History Review,* 2d ser., 8 (1955–1956): 53–61.

———. *The Queen's Wards: Wardship and Marriage under Elizabeth I.* London: Longmans, 1958.

Hyams, Paul. *King, Lords and Peasants in Medieval England: The Common Law of Villeinage in the Twelfth and Thirteenth Centuries.* Oxford: Oxford University Press, 1980.

Jacob, Ernest F. *Studies in the Period of Baronial Reform and Rebellion, 1258–1267.* Oxford Studies in Social and Legal History, edited by Paul Vinogradoff. No. 8. Oxford: Oxford University Press, 1925.

Jefferies, Peggy. "The Medieval Use as Family Law and Custom: The Berkshire Gentry in the Fourteenth and Fifteenth Centuries." *Southern History* 1 (1979): 45–69.

Johnson, John H. "The King's Wardrobe and Household." In W. A. Morris, *The English Government at Work, 1327–1336,* q. v.

Johnstone, Hilda. *Edward of Carnarvon, 1284–1307.* Manchester: Manchester University Press, 1947.

Jolliffe, J.E.A. *Angevin Kingship.* 2d ed. London: Adam and Charles Black, 1963.

———. *The Constitutional History of Medieval England: From the English Settlement to 1485.* 4th ed., paperback. New York: Norton, 1967.

Kelly, Henry Ansgar. *Love and Marriage in the Age of Chaucer.* Ithaca: Cornell University Press, 1975.

Kimball, Elisabeth G. *Serjeanty Tenure in Medieval England.* New Haven: Yale University Press, 1936.

King, Edmund. "Large and Small Landholders in Thirteenth-Century England." *PP* 47 (1970): 26–52.

Kingsford, Charles L. "Sir Otho de Grandison, 1238?–1328." *TRHS*, 3d ser., 3 (1909): 125–195.

Knowles, Clive H. "Provision for the Families of the Montfortians Disinherited after the Battle of Evesham." In Coss and Lloyd, *Thirteenth Century England I*, q. v.

———. "The Resettlement of England after the Barons' War, 1264–67." *TRHS*, 5th ser., 32 (1982): 25–41.

Lally, John E. "Secular Patronage at the Court of King Henry II." *BIHR* 49 (1976): 159–184.

List of Sheriffs for England and Wales, to 1831. PRO Lists and Indexes 9. London: HMSO, 1898.

Lyon, Bryce. *A Constitutional and Legal History of Medieval England.* 2d ed. New York: Norton, 1980.

Lyte, H. C. Maxwell. "Burci, Falaise and Martin." *SANHS* 65 (1920): 1–27.

———. *A History of Dunster and of the Families of Mohun and Luttrell.* 2 vols. London: St. Catherine's Press, 1909.

McFarlane, Kenneth B. "The English Nobility in the Later Middle Ages." In *XIIe Congrès International des Sciences Historiques*, vol. 1, *Grands thèmes* (1965). Reprinted in idem, *The Nobility of Later Medieval England*, q. v.

———. "Had Edward I a 'Policy' towards the Earls?" *History* 50 (1965): 145–159. Reprinted in idem, *The Nobility of Later Medieval England*, q. v.

———. *The Nobility of Later Medieval England.* Oxford: Oxford University Press, 1973.

McKechnie, William S. *Magna Carta: A Commentary on the Great Charter of King John.* 2d ed. Glasgow: J. Maclehose and Sons, 1919.

MacLean, John. *Historical and Genealogical Memoir of the Family of Poyntz; or, Eight Centuries of an English House.* 2 vols. Exeter: William Pollard, 1886.

Maddicott, John R. "Magna Carta and the Local Community, 1215–1259." *PP* 102 (1984): 25–65.

———. "The Mise of Lewes, 1264." *EHR* 98 (1983): 588–603.

———. *Thomas of Lancaster, 1307–1322: A Study in the Reign of Edward II.* Oxford: Oxford University Press, 1970.

Madox, Thomas. *The History and Antiquities of the Exchequer of the Kings of England.* 2d. ed. 2 vols. London: William Owen and Benjamin White, 1769.

Maitland, Frederic W. "The 'Praerogativa Regis.'" *EHR* 6 (1891): 366–370. Reprinted in *The Collected Papers of Frederic William Maitland*, edited by H.A.L. Fisher. 3 vols. Cambridge: Cambridge University Press, 1911.

Mason, Emma. "*Maritagium* and the Changing Law." *BIHR* 49 (1976): 286–289.

Mason, Emma. "The Resources of the Earldom of Warwick in the Thirteenth Century." *Midland History* 3 (1975): 67–75.

May, Theresa. "The Cobham Family in the Administration of England, 1200–1400." *Archaeologia Cantiana* 82 (1967): 1–31.

———. "The Estates of the Cobham Family in the Later Thirteenth Century." *Archaeologia Cantiana* 84 (1969): 211–229.

Meekings, Cecil A. F. Introduction to *CRR*, vol 15, q. v.

———. Introduction to *The 1235 Surrey Eyre*, edited by Cecil A. F. Meekings. 2 vols. Vol 1, Surrey Record Society 31. Guildford, 1979.

Miller, Edward. *The Abbey and Bishopric of Ely: The Social History of an Ecclesiastical Estate from the Tenth Century to the Early Fourteenth Century.* Cambridge: Cambridge University Press, 1951.

Mills, Mabel H. "Exchequer Agenda and Estimate of Revenue, Easter Term 1284." *EHR* 40 (1925): 229–234.

Milsom, S.F.C. *Historical Foundations of the Common Law.* London: Butterworths, 1969.

———. "Inheritance by Women in the Twelfth and Early Thirteenth Centuries." In *On the Laws and Customs of England: Essays in Honor of Samuel Thorne*, edited by Morris S. Arnold et al. Chapel Hill: University of North Carolina Press, 1981.

———. *The Legal Framework of English Feudalism.* Cambridge Studies in English Legal History. Cambridge: Cambridge University Press, 1976.

———. "Legal Introduction." In *Novae Narrationes*, q. v.

Moor, Charles. *Knights of Edward I.* 5 vols. Harleian Society Publications 80–84. London, 1929–1932.

Morris, John E. *The Welsh Wars of Edward I.* 1901. Reprint. Oxford: Oxford University Press, 1968.

Morris, William A., ed. *The English Government at Work, 1327–1336.* 2 vols. Vol. 1, *Central and Prerogative Administration.* Cambridge: Mediaeval Academy of America, 1940.

———. and Joseph R. Strayer, eds. *The English Government at Work, 1327–1336.* 2 vols. Vol. 2, *Fiscal Administration.* Cambridge: Mediaeval Academy of America, 1947.

Norgate, Kate. *The Minority of Henry the Third.* London: Macmillan and Company, 1912.

Northumberland County Historical Committee. *A History of Northumberland.* 15 vols. Newcastle upon Tyne: Andrew Reid, 1893–1940.

Ormerod, George. *The History of the County Palatine and City of Chester*, edited by Thomas Helsby. 2d ed. 3 vols. London: George Routledge and Sons, 1875–1882.

Otway-Ruthven, Annette J. "The Constitutional Position of the Great Lordships of South Wales." *TRHS*, 5th ser., 8 (1958): 1–20.

———. "The Medieval County of Kildare." *Irish Historical Studies* 11 (1959): 181–199.

Painter, Sidney. "The Family and the Feudal System in England." *Specu-*

lum 35 (1960): 1–16. Reprinted in *Feudalism and Liberty*, edited by Fred A. Cazel. Baltimore: Johns Hopkins University Press, 1961.

Palmer, Robert C. "Contexts of Marriage in Medieval England: Evidence from the King's Court circa 1300." *Speculum* 59 (1984): 42–67.

———. "The Origins of Property in England." *Law and History Review* 3 (1985): 1–50.

———. *The Whilton Dispute, 1264–1380: A Social-Legal Study of Dispute Settlement in Medieval England.* Princeton: Princeton University Press, 1984.

Parsons, John Carmi, ed. *The Court and Household of Eleanor of Castile in 1290: An Edition of British Library Additional Manuscript 35294 with Introduction and Notes.* Studies and Texts 37. Toronto: Pontifical Institute of Mediaeval Studies, 1977.

Phillips, John R. S. *Aymer de Valence, Earl of Pembroke, 1307–1324: Baronial Politics in the Reign of Edward II.* Oxford: Oxford University Press, 1972.

———. "The 'Middle Party' and Negotiating the Treaty of Leake, August 1318: A Reinterpretation." *BIHR* 46 (1973): 11–27.

Plucknett, Theodore F. T. *Legislation of Edward I.* 1949. Reprint. Oxford: Oxford University Press, 1962.

Pollock, Frederick, and Frederic W. Maitland. *The History of English Law before the Time of Edward I.* 2d ed; reissued with a new introduction by S.F.C. Milsom. 2 vols. Cambridge: Cambridge University Press, 1968.

Post, J. B. "Another Demographic Use of Inquisitions Post Mortem." *Journal of the Society of Archivists* 5 (1974–1977): 110–114.

Powell, J. Enoch, and Keith Wallis. *The House of Lords in the Middle Ages: A History of the English House of Lords to 1540.* London: Weidenfeld and Nicolson, 1968.

Powicke, Frederick M. *King Henry III and the Lord Edward: The Community of the Realm in the Thirteenth Century.* 2 vols. in 1. Oxford: Oxford University Press, 1966.

———. "Loretta, Countess of Leicester." In *Historical Essays in Honour of James Tait*, edited by John G. Edwards, Vivian H. Galbraith, and Ernest F. Jacob. Manchester: Manchester University Press, 1933.

———. *Thirteenth Century.* 2d ed. Oxford History of England. Oxford: Oxford University Press, 1962.

Powley, Edward B. *The House of de la Pomerai.* London: Hodder and Stoughton, 1944.

Poynton, E. M. "The Fee of Creon." *The Genealogist*, n.s. 18 (1902): 162–166, 219–225.

Prestwich, Michael. "Exchequer and Wardrobe in the Later Years of Edward I." *BIHR* 46 (1973): 1–10.

———. "Royal Patronage under Edward I." In Coss and Lloyd, *Thirteenth Century England I*, q. v.

———. *The Three Edwards: War and State in England, 1272–1377.* New York: St. Martin's, 1980.

Prestwich, Michael. *War, Politics and Finance under Edward I*. London: Faber and Faber, 1972.

Raban, Sandra. *Mortmain Legislation and the English Church, 1279–1500*. Cambridge: Cambridge University Press, 1982.

Raftis, J. A. *Tenure and Mobility: Studies in the Social History of the Mediaeval English Village*. Studies and Texts 8. Toronto: Pontifical Institute of Mediaeval Studies, 1964.

Ridgeway, Huw. "The Lord Edward and the Provisions of Oxford (1258): A Study in Faction." In Coss and Lloyd, *Thirteenth Century England I*, q. v.

Rosenthal, Joel T. "Aristocratic Marriage and the English Peerage: Social Institution and Personal Bond." *Journal of Medieval History* 10 (1984): 181–194.

Round, John Horace. "The Fitz-Walter Pedigree." *TEAS*, n.s. 7 (1901): 329–330.

———. "Gaynes in Upminster." *TEAS*, n.s. 11 (1909): 98–100.

———. "The Honour of Ongar." *TEAS*, n.s. 7 (1901): 142–152.

———. "The Manor of Colne Engaine," *TEAS*, n.s. 8 (1900): 192–198.

Russell, Josiah Cox. "Attestation of Charters in the Reign of John." *Speculum* 15 (1940): 480–498.

———. *British Medieval Population*. Albuquerque: University of New Mexico Press, 1948.

———. "Social Status at the Court of King John." *Speculum* 12 (1937): 319–329.

Sanders, Ivor J. *English Baronies: A Study of Their Origin and Descent, 1086–1327*. Oxford: Oxford University Press, 1960.

———. *Feudal Military Service in England: A Study of the Constitutional and Military Powers of the Barones in Medieval England*. Oxford: Oxford University Press, 1956.

Saul, Nigel. "The Despensers and the Downfall of Edward II." *EHR* 99 (1984), 1–33.

———. *Knights and Esquires: The Gloucestershire Gentry in the Fourteenth Century*. Oxford: Oxford University Press, 1981.

Searle, Eleanor. "The Abbey of the Conquerors: Defensive Enfeoffment and Economic Development in Anglo-Norman England." In *Proceedings of the Battle Conference on Anglo-Norman England II*, edited by Reginald Allen Brown. Woodbridge, 1979.

———. "Fact and Pattern in Heroic History: Dudo of St.-Quentin." *Viator* 15 (1984): 119–137.

———. "Women and the Legitimisation of Succession at the Norman Conquest." In *Proceedings of the Battle Conference on Anglo-Norman England III*, edited by Reginald Allen Brown. Woodbridge, 1980.

———. "Family Reconstruction and the Construction of a Polity: The Ducal Lineage of Early Normandy." Paper presented at the California Institute of Technology–Weingart Humanities Conference on Family and Property in Traditional Europe. Pasadena, 30 March–3 April 1981.

―――. "Kinship to State: Normandy in the Eleventh Century." Paper presented at the California Institute of Technology–Weingart Conference on the Political Economy of Pre-Industrial Society. Pasadena, 5–7 May 1983.

―――. *Lordship and Community: Battle Abbey and Its Banlieu, 1066–1538.* Studies and Texts 26. Toronto: Pontifical Institute of Mediaeval Studies, 1974.

―――. "Seigneurial Control of Women's Marriage: The Antecedents and Function of Merchet in England." *PP* 82 (1979): 3–43.

Segalen, Martine, and Philippe, Richard. "Marrying Kinsmen in Pays Bigouden Sud, Brittany." *Journal of Family History* 11 (1986): 109–130.

Segrave, Charles W. *The Segrave Family, 1066 to 1935.* London: Novello, 1936.

Shaw, William A. *The Knights of England.* 2 vols. London: Sherratt and Hughes, 1906.

Sheehan, Michael M. "Choice of Marriage Partner in the Middle Ages: Development and Mode of Application of a Theory of Marriage." *Studies in Medieval and Renaissance History*, n.s. 1 (1978): 3–33.

―――. "The Formation and Stability of Marriage in Fourteenth-Century England: Evidence of an Ely Register." *Mediaeval Studies* 33 (1971): 228–263.

―――. *The Will in Medieval England: From the Conversion of the Anglo-Saxons to the End of the Thirteenth Century.* Studies and Texts 6. Toronto: Pontifical Institute of Mediaeval Studies, 1963.

Smyth, John. *The Berkeley Manuscripts.* 3 vols. Vol 1, *The Lives of the Berkeleys*, edited by John Maclean. Gloucester: Bristol and Gloucestershire Archaeological Society, 1883.

Snellgrove, Harold S. *The Lusignans in England, 1247–1258.* University of New Mexico Publications in History 2. Albuquerque: University of New Mexico Press, 1950.

Stapleton, Thomas. "Brief Summary of the Wardrobe Accounts of the Tenth, Eleventh, and Fourteenth Years of King Edward the Second." *Archaeologia* 26 (1836): 318–345.

Stenton, Frank M. *The First Century of English Feudalism, 1066–1166.* 2d ed. Oxford: Oxford University Press, 1961.

Stevenson, E. R. "The Escheator." In W. A. Morris and Strayer, *The English Government at Work, 1327–1336*, q. v.

Stewart-Brown, Ronald. "The End of the Norman Earldom of Chester." *EHR* 35 (1920): 26–54.

Stone, Lawrence. *The Crisis of the Aristocracy.* Abr. ed. Oxford: Oxford University Press, 1967.

Strayer, Joseph R. Introduction to W. A. Morris and Strayer, *The English Government at Work*, q. v.

Sutherland, Donald W. "Peytevin v. La Lynde: A Case in the Medieval Land Law." *Law Quarterly Review* 83 (1967): 527–546.

———. *Quo Warranto Proceedings in the Reign of Edward I, 1278–1294.* Oxford: Oxford University Press, 1963.

Thorne, Samuel. "English Feudalism and Estates in Land." *Cambridge Law Journal* 23 (1959): 193–209.

Thrupp, Sylvia L. *The Merchant Class of Medieval London, 1300–1500.* Paperback ed. Ann Arbor: University of Michigan Press, 1962.

Titow, Jan Z. "Some Differences between Manors and the Effects òn the Conditions of the Peasants in the Thirteenth Century." *Agricultural History Review* 10 (1962), 1–13.

Tout, Thomas F. *Chapters in the Administrative History of Medieval England: The Wardrobe, the Chamber and the Small Seals.* 6 vols. Manchester: Manchester University Press, 1920–1933.

———. "The Earldoms under Edward I." *TRHS*, n.s. 8 (1894): 129–155.

———. "The English Civil Service in the Fourteenth Century." *Bulletin of John Rylands Library* 3 (1916-1917). Reprinted in *The Collected Papers of Thomas Frederick Tout with a Memoir and Bibliography.* 3 vols. Manchester: Manchester University Press, 1934.

———. *The Place of the Reign of Edward II in English History.* Manchester: Manchester University Press, 1914.

Trabut-Cussac, J. P. *L'administration anglaise en Gascogne sous Henry III et Edouard I de 1254 à 1307.* Geneva: Librairie Droz, 1972.

Treharne, Reginald F. *The Baronial Plan of Reform, 1258–1263.* Reprint ed. Manchester: Manchester University Press; New York: Barnes and Noble, 1971.

Trueman, John H. "The Personnel of Medieval Reform: The English Lords Ordainers of 1311." *Mediaeval Studies* 21 (1959): 247–271.

Tuck, Anthony. *Crown and Nobility, 1272–1461.* Fontana History of England, edited by Geoffrey R. Elton. Paperback ed. London: Fontana Press, 1985.

Vaughan, Richard. *Matthew Paris.* Paperback ed. Cambridge: Cambridge University Press, 1958.

Victoria History of the Counties of England, edited by Herbert A. Doubleday, William Page, Louis Salzman, and Ralph B. Pugh. 169 vols. to date. London: Oxford University Press, 1900–.

Walker, Sue Sheridan. "The Action of Waste in the Early Common Law." In *Legal Records and the Historian,* edited by John H. Baker. London: Royal Historical Society, 1978.

———. "Feudal Constraint and Free Consent in the Making of Marriages in Medieval England: Widows in the King's Gift." *Historical Papers* (Canadian Historical Association) (1979): 97–110.

———. "Free Consent and Marriage of Feudal Wards in Medieval England." *Journal of Medieval History* 8 (1982): 123–134.

————. "The Marrying of Feudal Wards in Medieval England." *Studies in Medieval Culture and Society* 4 (1974): 209–224.

————. "Proof of Age of Feudal Heirs in Medieval England." *Mediaeval Studies* 35 (1973): 306–323.

————. "Royal Wardship in Medieval England." Ph.D. diss., University of Chicago, 1966.

————. "Violence and the Exercise of Feudal Guardianship: The Action of 'Ejectio Custodia.' " *American Journal of Legal History* 16 (1972): 320–333.

————. "Widow and Ward: The Feudal Law of Child Custody in Medieval England." In *Women in Medieval Society*, edited by Susan M. Stuard. Philadelphia: University of Pennsylvania Press, 1976.

Warren, Wilfred L. *Henry II*. London: Eyre Methuen, 1973.

————. *King John*. Paperback ed. Berkeley and Los Angeles: University of California Press, 1978.

Watson, C. Ernest. "The Minchampton Customal and Its Place in the History of the Manor." *Transactions of the Bristol and Gloucestershire Archaeological Society* 54 (1932): 203–384.

Watson, G. W. "Alice de la Marche, Countess of Gloucester and Hereford." *Genealogist*, n.s. 38 (1922): 169–172.

————. "The Families of Lacy, Geneva, Joinville and La Marche." *Genealogist*, n.s. 21 (1905): 1–16, 73–82, 163–172, 234–243.

————. "Marriage Settlements." *Genealogist*, n.s. 33, 34, 35, 36 (1917–1920).

Waugh, Scott L. "The Confiscated Lands of the Contrariants in Gloucestershire and Herefordshire, in 1322: An Economic and Social Study." Ph.D. thesis, University of London, 1975.

————. "The Fiscal Uses of Royal Wardships in the Reign of Edward I." In Coss and Lloyd, *Thirteenth Century England I*, q. v.

————. "For King, Country, and Patron: The Despensers and Local Administration, 1321–1322." *Journal of British Studies* 22 (1983): 23–58.

————. "From Tenure to Contract: Lordship and Clientage in Thirteenth-Century England." *EHR* 101 (1986): 811–839.

————. "Marriage, Class, and Royal Lordship in England under Henry III." *Viator* 16 (1985): 181–207.

————. "Non-Alienation Clauses in Thirteenth-Century English Charters." *Albion* 17 (1985): 1–14.

————. "The Profits of Violence: The Minor Gentry in the Rebellion of 1321–1322 in Gloucestershire and Herefordshire." *Speculum* 52 (1977): 843–869.

————. "Reluctant Knights and Jurors: Respites, Exemptions, and Public Obligations in the Reign of Henry III." *Speculum* 58 (1983): 937–986.

White, Albert B. *Self Government by the King's Command*. Minneapolis: University of Minnesota Press, 1933.

Wilkinson, Bertie. "The Chancery." In W. A. Morris, *The English Government at Work, 1327–1336*, q. v.

Williams, Gwyn A. Medieval London: From Commune to Capital. London: University of London, Athlone Press, 1970.

Williams, Penry. *The Tudor Regime.* Oxford: Oxford University Press, 1979.

Wolffe, Bertram P. *The Royal Demesne in English History: The Crown Estate in the Governance of the Realm from the Conquest to 1509.* London: George Allen and Unwin, 1971.

Young, Charles R. *Hubert Walter, Lord of Canterbury and Lord of England.* Durham: University of North Carolina Press, 1968.

INDEX

abduction, 78n, 153, 218–220, 238, 250. *See also* rape

Acre, Joan of, 81n, 90, 218

Adam, Thomas ap, 30

adoption, 28–29

advowsons, 149, 151, 152

affinity, 36, 47

alienation, to evade lordship, 236

alienation by tenants-in-chief: confirmation of, 92, 93–94, 96, 103; fines for, 97, 270–271; inquests into, 93; king's control of, 9, 92–97, 103, 233, 236, 251–253, 260, 269; opposition to and limits on king's control of, 12, 102; *se dimisit*, 103n; by substitution, 98, 103; without license, 136, 270–271

Alnwick, 224

Amory, Roger d': marriage of, 207, 249; wardships granted to, 186, 248, 250; Elizabeth wife of, *see* Clare, Elizabeth de

Anesty, Denise de, 203, 204

Anesty, Nicholas de (d. 1225), 203

Anjou, Charles of, 190; Beatrice wife of, *see* Raymond-Berenger

Annandale, 47

Appleby, Henry de, 263

Aragon, king of, 190

Articles of the Barons (1215), 160

Articles of the Escheator, 92, 95, 111, 116, 154, 238

Articles of the Eyre, 115

Articuli Super Cartas (1300), 260

Arundel, countess of. *See* Warenne, Isabel de

Arundel, earls of. *See* Aubigny, Fitz Alan

Arundel, John de, 58

assessments, feudal, 171–173, 176

Aston, Northamptonshire, 136

Aubigny, Ascelina d', 209

Aubigny, William d' (d. 1193), earl of Arundel, 160

Aubigny, William d' (d. 1221), earl of Arundel, 55n, 243n

Aubigny family, 208

Audeham, Baldwin de (d. 1291), 150–151

Audeham, Francis de (d. 1327), 150–151, 153

Audeham, Isabel de, 153

Audeley, Hugh d', 210

Audeley, Hugh d', Jr. (d. 1347), 249, 250; Margaret wife of, *see* Clare, Margaret de

Audeley, James d', 257

Audeley, Thomas d', 121

Aumale, earls of. *See* Béthune, Forz, Gros

Aumale, Hawise, 86

Ayrmynne, William de, 226

Bacon, Edmund, 250, 268

Badlesmere, Bartholomew de, 248

Badlesmere, Margery de, 23n

Badmondisfield, Suffolk, 34

Baldock, Robert, 237, 268

Balliol, Alexander de, 123

Balliol, Eustace de (d. 1274), 74n

Balliol, Hugh de, 198; Agnes wife of, *see* Valence, Agnes de

Balliol, John de, 257

Ballon family, 31

Bamburgh, Gunhilda of, 33; Emma daughter of, 33–34; Christina granddaughter of, 34; Simon great-grandson of, 34

Bamburgh, Odard of, 33

bankers and merchants: royal indebtedness to, 175; grants to, 189; Italian, 224; of Lucca, 190, 263–264

bannerets, 184

Bannockburn, battle of (1314), 249

Bar, Henry count of, 175

Bar, Joan of, 217, 219–220, 247

Bard, William, 170

Bardolf, Hugh, escheator, 106

Bardolf, Thomas, 91

baronies named: Aldington, 18n; Beckley, 30n; Berkhampstead, 30n; Beverstone, 31, 265; Bourne, 145, 263;

311

entails, 61–62, 101–102

escheat, 18, 97

escheator: office of, 13; origins, 105–106

escheators: abuses by, 80, 137, 142; accounts of, 100, 117–118, 132, 256, 281–282; careers of, 111–112; dangers to, 239; lands held in custody by, 167–168; payments by to support minors, 109, 174; receipts of, 166–167, 268, 281–285; responsibilities and work of, 107, 142–143; ex officio, 110–111, 120, 252; sales of wardships by, 164, 172, 281; seizure of lands by, 252; subofficials of, 111–112, 167; supervision of widows by, 116–117; wardships granted to, 187

escheatorships: reorganization of, 169, 268, 282, 283. *See also* stewards

escheats, 92

Esseby, Robert son of William de, 228–229

Esseby, William son of Ralph de, 228; Alice wife of, *see* Camvill, Alice de

Esseby, William son of William de, 229

Estley, Thomas de, 229

Evesham, battle of (1265), 20, 258

Ewell, Richard de, 186

Exchequer: adjudication of disputes in, 124, 125, 126, 131; estimate of revenue (1284), 100; feudal receipts in, 118, 155; marriage offers in, 217; practices of, 70; reform of, 106, 255, 268–269; responsibilities of, 117–118; searches of records in, 123, 126, 127, 128; supervision of wards and widows by, 108, 116

executors. *See* wardship

eyres, 93, 115–116, 159, 171

Falaise, Sibyl de la, 34

families, baronial, 210

family: attachment between mothers and minors, 108–109; attitudes of toward minorities and lordship, 7, 108, 195, 278–279; conception of, 279; grants within, 15–16, 26, 32–33, 103; as guardians, 279; provisions for in wills, 279

Faucomberg, John de, 54n; Eve wife of, *see* Bulmer, Eve de

Faucomberg, Walter de, 54

Faucomberg, Walter de, Jr., 54n; Isabel wife of, *see* Ros, Isabel de; Alice wife of, *see* Killingham, Alice de

fee farms, 85

fees, promised, 242; wardships in place of, 151, 155, 173n, 183

felons, 77

Ferandi, Bernard de, 207

Ferre, Guy, 213, 263

Ferrers, Agatha, 40, 75n

Ferrers, Idonia de, 32

Ferrers, Isabel de, 49, 50, 51

Ferrers, Joan de, 50, 51

Ferrers, Robert de, 32

Ferrers, William de (d. 1254), 21, 32, 40, 50, 51; Margaret wife of, *see* Quincy, Margaret de; Sibyl wife of, *see* Marshal, Sibyl

Ferrers, William de (d. 1279), 27, 32, 243n

Ferrers family, 247

feudal incidents, 273; definition of, 4, 65; fiscal use of, 10–11, 92, 144, 156, 165, 170, 272; impact of, 15, 63; management of, 106; as patronage, 7n, 144, 180, 186–187, 188; preservation of, 106; valuation of, 171. *See also* feudal marriage, prerogative wardship, primer seisin, relief, seigniorial consent, wardship

feudal marriage: disputes over, 71; marriages arranged through, 207–215; nature and scope of, 4, 9, 75–76, 99; refusal of, 90–91, 216. *See also* disparagement, Magna Carta

feudal revenues: assignment of, 173–174; composition and size of, 169; during baronial reform, 256–257; receipt of, 118, 281–283; royal policy regarding, 156–180, 268

Fiennes, Giles de, 178nn

Fiennes, Margaret daughter of William de, 192, 215n

Fiennes, Maud daughter of Engerraud de, 192

Fiennes family, 191

Filiol, Baldwin, 128

Filiol, John, 127, 129, 214

fines: for evasion of wardship, 237; for
marriages of heiresses or widows,
70–71, 157–161, 176, 203, 216, 218;
for marrying without consent, 238;
pardons of, 171; payment of, 155–
156, 171; for unlicensed alienations,
236; for wardships, 157–158, 161–
164, 197, 256–257, 258, 259, 264–
265, 266, 281. *See also* dower, wardship, widows
Fitz Alan, Edmund (d. 1326), earl of
Arundel, 247; Alice wife of, *see*
Warenne, Alice de
Fitz Alan, John (d. 1267), 40; Maud
wife of, *see* Butler, Maud
Fitz Alan, John (d. 1272), 40, 131; Isa-
bel wife of, *see* Mortimer, Isabel de
Fitz Alan, Richard de (d. 1302), earl of
Arundel, 191n, 247; Alasia wife of,
see Saluzzo, Alasia
Fitz Alan of Wolverton family, 178n
Fitz Geoffrey, Joan daughter of John,
40, 48, 49
Fitz Geoffrey, John, 40, 44, 48, 49,
210; Isabel wife of, *see* Bigod, Isabel
Fitz Geoffrey, Matilda daughter of
John, 44, 48
Fitz John, John (d. 1275), 150, 205,
258
Fitz John, Robert, household steward,
148, 184, 186, 214
Fitz Nicholas, Margaret widow of
Ralph, 227
Fitz Nicholas, Nicholas, 227
Fitz Nicholas, Ralph, 186, 227, 228–
229, 243
Fitz Nigel, Ralph, 76n
Fitz Otto, Beatrice, 213
Fitz Otto, Hugh, 213
Fitz Otto, Joan, 213
Fitz Otto, Matilda, 213
Fitz Otto, Otto, minority of, 213
Fitz Otto family, 178n
Fitz Pons, Bertha daughter of Richard,
43
Fitz Pons, Richard (d. 1138), 43; Maud
wife of, *see* Gloucester, Maud daugh-
ter of Walter of
Fitz Ralph, Nicholas, 227, 243
Fitz Richard, Walter (d. 1190), 43

Fitz Robert, Walter (d. 1258), 212; Ida
wife of, *see* Longspee, Ida
Fitz Thomas, Thomas, mayor of Lon-
don, 150, 189, 258
Fitz Warin, Fulk (d. 1264), 258, 259
Fitz Warin, William, daughter of, 128
Fleming, Alard le, 201
Fleming, Joan le, 201
Fleta, 69n
foreigners, denounced, 243–244
forfeiture, 27–28, 95, 262
Forz, Aveline de, 228
Forz, William de (d. 1195), 86
Forz, William de (d. 1260), earl of Au-
male, 228; Isabel wife of, *see* Reviers,
Isabel de
Foxley, John de, 250
France, English territory in. *See* Gas-
cony
Franceys, Gilbert le (d. 1278), 238
Franceys, Richard le, 238
Frederick II, 190
Freschville, Anker de, 172; Amice
widow of, 172
Frethorne, John, 151
friends, assistance of in marriage and
wardship, 57–58, 81n, 82n, 202–203,
230, 279–280
Frisco, Frederick de, count of Lavagna,
227
Furnivall, Bertha de, 258
Furnivall, Thomas de (d. 1332), 209,
216; Elizabeth wife of, *see* Montfort,
Elizabeth de; Joan wife of, *see* Des-
penser, Joan le
Furnivall, Thomas de (d. 1339), 209;
Joan wife of, *see* Verdun, Joan de

gard per cause de gard. *See* wardship
Gascony, royal policy toward, 71, 178–
179
Gatesdene, John de, 227, 259
Gatesdene, Margaret de, 227
Gaveston, Piers: death of, 199; estate
of, 30; favor shown to, 261–262; in-
fluence of, 147; marriage of, 207,
251; wardships granted to, 109, 184,
248, 264; Margaret wife of, *see* Clare,
Margaret de; steward of, *see*
Hotham, John de

Henry I (*cont.*)
232; fines for wardship and consent,
157–158; wardships granted by, 34
Henry II, 88; fines for wardship and
consent, 157–158; inquests of, 113;
legal reforms of, 28, 30, 65–66, 81,
92, 97, 273–274; management of
wardships and marriage, 106, 160;
marriages arranged by, 191; treatment of widows, 158–160; wardships
granted by, 32, 196
Henry III: on alienations, 92–93, 96;
children of, 109; creation of escheatorships, 83, 106, 108; death of, 135;
defends self and attacks reformers,
254, 256–257; exercise of royal lordship by, 91–92, 118, 122, 128, 133,
275; exercise of seigniorial consent
by, 38, 71n, 89, 200, 201; homage
taken by, 206n; inquests of, 113–
114; military campaigns of, 109n,
131, 133, 198, 235; patronage of,
241–246, 255; policy of toward
wardships, 167–169, 171, 259; right
to arrange wardship granted by, 235;
treatment of widows, 68–69, 86–87,
132, 161; wardships and marriages
arranged by, 81n, 202; on women's
inheritance and custody of coheiresses, 97–98, 196, 198, 223
    wardships granted and sold by, 51, 78,
149–150, 151, 154, 162, 165, 176n,
183, 203, 225, 227; to family, 30, 177–
178, 184, 191, 203–204, 225, 241; to
foreigners and favorites; 175, 218; to
officials, 186, 228; to ward's kin and
widows, 198, 218, 223; to pay debts,
174–175; for political support, 179,
190–191; wardships promised by,
208n, 242–243. *See also* Barons' War
Henry VII, 95
Hereford, bishop of. *See* Orleton,
Adam de
Hereford, earls of. *See* Bohun
Hodonet, Odo de (d. 1284), 203
Hodonet, Odo son of Odo de, 203
Holebroke, Richard de, steward,
139nn, 140n
Holt, James C., 81, 81n, 87n
homage, 9, 67, 73n, 79, 97, 130

Hotham, John de, bishop of Ely, es-
cheator, and Gaveston's steward,
111, 185n, 263, 264
Houel, Hubert, 153; Ada wife of, *see*
Hastings, Ada de
household: knights of, 184, 213–214;
stewards of, wardships granted to,
175, 185, 205. *See also* Fitz John,
Robert
Household Ordinance (1279), 175
Household Ordinance (1318), 110
Howell, Geoffrey de, 142
Hugham, Beatrice wife of Robert (d.
1259), 123n
Hugham, Benedicta de, 123n
Hugham, Helen de, 123n
Hugham, Robert de (d. 1233), 122
Hugham, Robert de (d. 1259), 123n
Hugham, Robert de (d. 1301), 123
Hugham, Robert de (d. 1317), 123n
Hugham, Waresius de, 123n
Huntingfeld, Roger son of William de,
266
Huntingfeld, Sarah de, 47
Huntingfeld, William de, 47, 127, 128,
266
husbands, remarriage of, 46, 52–53
Huscote, William de, 39n
Huse, Henry, 201
Huse, Matthew, marriage of son and
daughter, 201
Huse, Roger, 185

idiots, king's guardianship of, 77, 98–99
Immworth, Ralph de, 258, 259
Inge, John, 252
Inge, William, 264
Ingoldesthorp, Thomas de, 254
inheritance: entering without license,
238–239; failure of male heirs, 18–
20, 248; half blood, 46, 49, 53, 215–
216. *See also* women's inheritance
inheritance and descent, 8, 28–29, 204
inquest system, 113, 116; impact of,
116–117
inquests: *ad quod damnun*, 110; into
alienations, 93, 113; hundred (1274),
94, 100–101, 114, 116, 136–137,
239; proof of age, 136; purpose and
usefulness of, 113, 114, 116, 141; for

also Holebroke, Richard de; Sandwich, Ralph de; Normanville, Thomas de
stock. *See* land
Stoke, Peter de, 55n
Strenie, Robert de, 217
subenfeoffment, 95
subtenants, alienations by, 92
Sutton, Robert de (d. 1273), 136
Sutton, Stephen de, 136n
suzereinty, 3

tallage, during wardship, 152, 166
Tateshal, Robert de, 200n
Tateshal, Walter de (d. 1199), 23n; Isolda wife of, *see* Pantolf, Isolda
taxation, 169, 233, 260, 261
tenant, acceptance of by lord, 67–68
tenants-in-chief: defined, 3; disobedience of, 135–136; estates of, 12; homage of, 67; obligations and tenure of, 130, 160; *ut de corona*, 84, 107, 119; *ut de honore, ut de escaeta, ut de baronia*, 84–85, 119, 239, 254, 269–270, 271
Thurkelby, Walter de, 151, 257
Tibetot, Robert de (d. 1298), 148, 200n, 210
Tonbridge, honor of, 90
Tony, Alice de, 44, 46, 103, 233
Tony, Ralph de (d. 1295), 103
Tony, Robert de (d. 1309), 46
Tony family, 45, 259
Traneys, Idonia wife of John de, 122
Traneys, John de (d. 1311), 121–122
Traynes, Thomas de, 121
treasurer: influence of, 147; rewards given to, 184–185, 186; work of, 108, 112, 119, 123, 139–140, 176, 217. *See also* Exchequer
Trente, William, 263
Tres Ancien Coutoumier, 108, 110, 196
trespass. *See* seigniorial consent
Triple, John de, 190
Trussebut, Hillary de, 34
Tudors, 6, 7, 179

Ufford, Robert de, 205n
Umfraville, Gilbert de, 241n
Urtiaco family, 131

uses. *See* landholding, legal controls over

Valence, Agnes de, marriage of, 198
Valence, Aymer de (d. 1324), earl of Pembroke, 204, 215n
Valence, Isabel de, 210
Valence, William de (d. 1296), earl of Pembroke: arrangement of wardship by, 235n; influence of, 148; marriage of, 203, 204, 207; seeks wardship, 203–204; wardships and marriages granted to, 83, 198, 224, 243, 243n, 257, 258; Joan wife of, *see* Mountchesney, Joan
Vaux, John de, 131, 212, 216
Vaux, Oliver de, 212, 216; Pernell wife of, *see* Craon, Pernell de
Vaux, Pernell daughter of John de, 131
Vavassour, Richard le, 222
Verdun, Joan de, 209
Verdun, John de, 48; Margery wife of, *see* Lacy, Margery de
Verdun, Rohese de, 40
Verdun, Theobald de (d. 1309), 40
Verdun, Theobald de (d. 1316), 40, 41, 219, 249, 250; Elizabeth wife of, *see* Clare, Elizabeth de; Maud wife of, *see* Mortimer, Maud de
Verdun, Thomas de (d. 1199), 158, 211, 212, 216; Eustachia wife of, *see* Basset, Eustachia
Vere, Aubrey de (d. 1194), earl of Oxford, 39; Isabel wife of, *see* Bolbec, Isabel de
Vere, Aubrey de (d. 1214), earl of Oxford, 39
Vere, Hugh de (d. 1301), 123, 204; Denise wife of, *see* Mountchesney, Denise de
Vere, Robert de (d. 1221), earl of Oxford, 39
Vere, Robert de (d. 1296), earl of Oxford, 134n
Vescy, Eustace de, 160, 213
Vescy, William de, 212, 213, 223; Isabel wife of, *see* Longspee, Isabel
Vescy family, 131, 192